Readings for

American Government

Third Edition

Readings for

American Government Freedom and Power

Third Edition

THEODORE J. LOWI
Cornell University

BENJAMIN GINSBERG
Johns Hopkins University

and

ALICE HEARST
Smith College

W.W. NORTON & COMPANY
NEW YORK LONDON

Printed in the United States of America

Composition and manufacturing by The Haddon Craftsmen, Inc.

ISBN 0-393-96492-2

W. W. Norton & Company, Inc., 500 Fifth Avenue, New York, N.Y. 10110
W. W. Norton & Company Ltd., 10 Coptic Street, London WC1A 1PU

2 3 4 5 6 7 8 9 0

Contents

Preface

The readings contained in this volume are intended to enrich students' comprehension of the structure and operation of American government by providing a number of materials—articles, essays, and court cases—that illustrate the key concepts presented in the parallel chapter of the textbook. A headnote introducing each reading explains its significance and its precise relationship to the major concept presented in the core text.

The readings include classic pieces such as selections from major Federalist and Antifederalist writings and de Tocqueville's *Democracy in America,* contemporary essays from important newspapers and magazines, excerpts from major Supreme Court cases and selected federal statutes. By reprinting classic works in American government, we hope to acquaint students with some of the most profound thinking and writing on politics—thereby reinforcing the theoretical issues raised in the text. The contemporary essays are designed to provide students with lively and current illustrations of the phenomena and institutions discussed in the text; the court cases are selected for their importance in establishing the legal and institutional framework of American government. In every instance, we strongly urge students to read the headnote introducing each reading to gain an understanding of the significance of each piece and its relationship to the text, and to use the questions following each set of readings as an aid in studying the materials in both the reader and the text.

New to this edition are the "Debating the Issues: Opposing Views" essays appearing in each chapter. The essays center on the topics introduced in the "Debating the Issues" boxes in the corresponding chapter in the text. Offering opposing views, the essays will help students think critically about important issues in American politics.

In preparing the second edition of this reader, we benefitted from the comments of a number of reviewers: Lydia Andrade, San Jose State University; Peri Arnold, University of Notre Dame; Cal Jillson, University of Colorado; Wayne MacIntosh, University of Maryland; Evan MacKenzie, Albright Coilege; and Mark Silverstein, Boston University. Their insights helped guide us in selecting updated materials and making the reader more responsive to the needs of students using it.

We encourage students to review and ponder the readings and cases in conjunction with the text, and utilize them as a learning tool. We are confident that these materials will assist students in learning more about issues of freedom and power in American government.

Theodore Lowi
Benjamin Ginsberg
Alice Hearst

July 1993

Readings

CHAPTER 1

Freedom and Power

Debating the Issues: Opposing Views

FREEDOM AND POWER: THE ENDURING DEBATE

See text pp. 6–7

As the text notes, all governments must have, at the very least, the power to enforce public order and to collect public revenues. In the debates preceding the ratification of the United States Constitution, which creates the framework for the operation of the national government, the scope of these powers was directly at issue as the Federalists and Antifederalists battled over whether to create a strong central government or retain the confederated structure under which the country had operated since the Revolution. The arguments were advanced against the backdrop of state sovereignty: under the Articles of Confederation, states maintained their own militias and controlled the means by which revenues were generated for public purposes. Alexander Hamilton, a leading Federalist, argued that this structure left the federal government "in a kind of tutelage to the State governments," sapped of the energy and creativity required to sustain a union.

The following excerpts present the Federalist and Antifederalist positions on the potential gains and problems that would result from the emergence of a strong national government. The two Federalist papers authored by Hamilton argue in favor of creating a strong central government with power to raise an army and the revenues necessary to perform public functions.

The author of the third selection is not known for certain: the Antifederalist writer styled himself "Brutus" and was responding to Hamilton's arguments in Federalist No. 23. *The Antifederalist writer warns against the aggregation of power in the national government that is certain to result from the delegation of such authority from the states to the national government.*

The principle argument is over which level *of government, state or national, should exercise military and fiscal power. Antifederalists warned that the remoteness of the national government would lead to abuses of power, and the only way to prevent this was to keep power with the states and close to the people who had consented to be governed.*

Alexander Hamilton
*The Federalist No. 23**

The necessity of a Constitution, at least equally energetic with the one proposed, to the preservation of the Union is the point at the examination of which we are now arrived.

This inquiry will naturally divide itself into three branches—the objects to be provided for by a federal government, the quantity of power necessary to the accomplishment of those objects, the persons upon whom that power ought to operate. Its distribution and organization will more properly claim our attention under the succeeding head.

The principal purposes to be answered by union are these—the common defense of the members; the preservation of the public peace, as well against internal convulsions as external attacks; the regulation of commerce with other nations and between the States; the superintendence of our intercourse, political and commercial, with foreign countries.

The authorities essential to the common defense are these: to raise armies; to build and equip fleets; to prescribe rules for the government of both; to direct their operations; to provide for their support. These powers ought to exist without limitation, *because it is impossible to foresee or to define the extent and variety of national exigencies, and the correspondent extent and variety of the means which may be necessary to satisfy them.* The circumstances that endanger the safety of nations are infinite, and for this reason no constitutional shackles can wisely be imposed on the power to which the care of it is committed. This power ought to be coextensive with all the possible combinations of such circumstances; and ought to be under the direction of the same councils which are appointed to preside over the common defense. . . .

Whether there ought to be a federal government intrusted with the care of the common defense is a question in the first instance open to discussion; but the moment it is decided in the affirmative, it will follow that that government ought to be clothed with all the powers requisite to complete execution of its trust. And unless it can be shown that the circumstances which may affect the public safety are reducible within certain determinate limits; unless the contrary of this position can be fairly and rationally disputed, it must be admitted as a necessary consequence that there can be no limitation of that authority which is to provide for the defense and protection of the community in any matter essential to its efficacy—that is, in any matter essential to the *formation, direction,* or *support* of the NATIONAL FORCES.

Defective as the present Confederation has been proved to be, this principle appears to have been fully recognized by the framers of it; though they have not made proper or adequate provision for its exercise. Congress have an unlimited discretion to make requisitions of men and money; to

*Alexander Hamilton, *The Federalist No. 23,* ed. Clinton Rossiter (New York: NAL, 1961).

govern the army and navy; to direct their operations. As their requisitions are made constitutionally binding upon the States, who are in fact under the most solemn obligations to furnish the supplies required of them, the intention evidently was that the United States should command whatever resources were by them judged requisite to the "common defense and general welfare." It was presumed that a sense of their true interests, and a regard to the dictates of good faith, would be found sufficient pledges for the punctual performance of the duty of the members to the federal head.

The experiment has, however, demonstrated that this expectation was ill-founded and illusory; and the observations made under the last head will, I imagine, have sufficed to convince the impartial and discerning that there is an absolute necessity for an entire change in the first principles of the system; that if we are in earnest about giving the Union energy and duration we must abandon the vain project of legislating upon the States in their collective capacities; we must extend the laws of the federal government to the individual citizens of America; we must discard the fallacious scheme of quotas and requisitions as equally impracticable and unjust. The result from all this is that the Union ought to be invested with full power to levy troops; to build and equip fleets; and to raise the revenues which will be required for the formation and support of an army and navy in the customary and ordinary modes practiced in other governments.

If the circumstances of our country are such as to demand a compound instead of a simple, a confederate instead of a sole, government, the essential point which will remain to be adjusted will be to discriminate the OBJECTS, as far as it can be done, which shall appertain to the different provinces or departments of power; allowing to each the most ample authority for fulfilling the objects committed to its charge. Shall the Union be constituted the guardian of the common safety? Are fleets and armies and revenues necessary to this purpose? The government of the Union must be empowered to pass all laws, and to make all regulations which have relation to them. The same must be the case in respect to commerce, and to every other matter to which its jurisdiction is permitted to extend. Is the administration of justice between the citizens of the same State the proper department of the local governments? These must possess all the authorities which are connected with this object, and with every other that may be allotted to their particular cognizance and direction. Not to confer in each case a degree of power commensurate to the end would be to violate the most obvious rules of prudence and propriety, and improvidently to trust the great interests of the nation to hands which are disabled from managing them with vigor and success.

Who so likely to make suitable provisions for the public defense as that body to which the guardianship of the public safety is confided; which, as the center of information, will best understand the extent and urgency of the dangers that threaten; as the representative of the WHOLE, will feel itself most deeply interested in the preservation of every part; which, from the responsibility implied in the duty assigned to it, will be most sensibly impressed with the necessity of proper exertions; and which, by the extension of its authority throughout the States, can alone establish uniformity and concert in the plans and measures by which the common safety is to be secured? Is there not a manifest inconsistency in devolving upon the federal government the care of the general defense and leaving in the State governments the *effective* powers by which it is to be provided for? Is not a want of co-operation the infallible consequence of such a system? And will not weakness, disorder, an undue distribution of the burdens and calamities of war, an unnecessary and intolerable increase of expense, be its natural and inevitable concomitants? Have we not had unequivocal experience of its effects in the course of the revolution which we have just achieved?

Every view we may take of the subject, as candid inquirers after truth, will serve to convince us that it is both unwise and dangerous to deny the federal government an unconfined authority in respect to all those objects which are intrusted to its management. It will indeed deserve the most vigilant and careful attention of the people to see that it be modeled in such a manner as to admit of its being safely vested with the requisite powers. If any plan which has been, or may be, offered to our consideration should not, upon a dispassionate inspection, be found to answer this description, it ought to be rejected. A government, the constitution of which renders it unfit to be trusted with all the powers which a free people *ought to delegate to any government*, would be an unsafe and improper depository of the NATIONAL INTERESTS. Wherever THESE can with propriety be confided, the coincident powers may safely accompany them. This is the true result of all just reasoning upon the subject. And the adversaries of the plan promulgated by the convention would have given a better impression of their candor if they had confined themselves to showing that the internal structure of the proposed government was such as to render it unworthy of the confidence of the people. They ought not to have wandered into inflammatory declamations and unmeaning cavils about the extent of the powers. The POWERS are not too extensive for the OBJECTS of federal administration, or, in other words, for the management of our NATIONAL INTERESTS; nor can any satisfactory argument be framed to show that they are chargeable with such an excess. If it be true, as has been insinuated by some of the writers on the other side, that the difficulty arises from the nature of the thing, and that the extent of the country will not permit us to form a government in which such ample powers can safely be reposed, it would prove that we ought to contract our views, and resort to the expedient of separate confederacies, which will move within more practicable spheres. For the absurdity must continually stare us in the face of confiding to a government the direction of the most essential national interests, without daring to trust to it the authorities which are indispensable to their proper and efficient management. Let us not attempt to reconcile contradictions, but firmly embrace a rational alternative. . . . I trust, however, that the impracticability of one general system cannot be shown. I am greatly mistaken if anything of weight has yet been advanced of this tendency; and I flatter myself that the observations which have been made in the course of these papers have served to place the reverse of that position in as clear a light as any matter still in the womb of time and experience is susceptible of. This, at all events, must be evident, that the very difficulty itself, drawn from the extent of the country, is the strongest argument in favor of an energetic government; for any other can certainly never preserve the Union of so large an empire. If we embrace the tenets of those who oppose the adoption of the proposed Constitution as the standard of our political creed we cannot fail to verify the gloomy doctrines which predict the impracticability of a national system pervading the entire limits of the present Confederacy.

PUBLIUS

Alexander Hamilton
*The Federalist No. 30**

It has been already observed that the federal government ought to possess the power of providing for the support of the national forces; in which proposition was intended to be included the expense of raising troops, of building and equipping fleets, and all other expenses in any wise connected with military arrangements and operations. But these are not the only objects to which the jurisdiction of the Union in respect to revenue must necessarily be empowered to extend. It must embrace a provision for the support of the national civil list; for the payment of the national debts contracted, or that may be contracted; and, in general, for all those matters which will call for disbursements out of the national treasury. The conclusion is that there must be interwoven in the frame of the government a general power of taxation, in one shape or another.

Money is, with propriety, considered as the vital principle of the body politic; as that which sustains its life and motion and enables it to perform its most essential functions. A complete power, therefore, to procure a regular and adequate supply of revenue, as far as the resources of the community will permit, may be regarded as an indispensable ingredient in every constitution. From a deficiency in this particular, one of two evils must ensue: either the people must be subjected to continual plunder, as a substitute for a more eligible mode of supplying the public wants, or the government must sink into a fatal atrophy, and, in a short course of time, perish. . . .

The present Confederation, feeble as it is, intended to repose in the United States an unlimited power of providing for the pecuniary wants of the Union. But proceeding upon an erroneous principle, it has been done in such a manner as entirely to have frustrated the intention. Congress, by the articles which compose that compact (as has already been stated), are

*Alexander Hamilton, *The Federalist No. 30,* ed. Clinton Rossiter (New York: NAL, 1961).

authorized to ascertain and call for any sums of money necessary in their judgment to the service of the United States; and their requisitions, if conformable to the rule of apportionment, are in every constitutional sense obligatory upon the States. These have no right to question the propriety of the demand; no discretion beyond that of devising the ways and means of furnishing the sums demanded. But though this be strictly and truly the case; though the assumption of such a right would be an infringement of the articles of Union; though it may seldom or never have been avowedly claimed, yet in practice it has been constantly exercised and would continue to be so, as long as the revenues of the Confederacy should remain dependent on the intermediate agency of its members. What the consequences of this system have been is within the knowledge of every man the least conversant in our public affairs, and has been abundantly unfolded in different parts of these inquiries. It is this which affords ample cause of mortification to ourselves, and of triumph to our enemies.

What remedy can there be for this situation, but in a change of the system which has produced it—in a change of the fallacious and delusive system of quotas and requisitions? What substitute can there be imagined for this *ignis fatuus* in finance, but that of permitting the national government to raise its own revenues by the ordinary methods of taxation authorized in every well-ordered constitution of civil government? Ingenious men may declaim with plausibility on any subject; but no human ingenuity can point out any other expedient to rescue us from the inconveniences and embarrassments naturally resulting from defective supplies of the public treasury.

The more intelligent adversaries of the new Constitution admit the force of this reasoning; but they qualify their admission by a distinction between what they call *internal* and *external* taxation. The former they would reserve to the State governments; the latter, which they explain into commercial imposts, or rather duties on imported articles, they declare themselves willing to concede to the federal head. This distinction, however, would violate that fundamental maxim of good sense and sound policy, which dictates that every POWER ought to be proportionate to its OBJECT; and would still leave the general government in a kind of tutelage to the State governments, inconsistent with every idea of vigor or efficiency. Who can pretend that commercial imposts are, or would be, alone equal to the present and future exigencies of the Union? Taking into the account the existing debt, foreign and domestic, upon any plan of extinguishment which a man moderately impressed with the importance of public justice and public credit could approve, in addition to the establishments which all parties will acknowledge to be necessary, we could not reasonably flatter ourselves that this resource alone, upon the most improved scale, would even suffice for its present necessities. Its future necessities admit not of calculation or limitation; and upon the principle more than once averted to the power of making provision for them as they arise ought to be equally unconfined. I believe it may be regarded as a position warranted by the history of mankind that, *in the usual progress of things, the necessities of a nation, in every stage of its existence, will be found at least equal to its resources.*

To say that deficiencies may be provided for by requisitions upon the States is on the one hand to acknowledge that this system cannot be depended upon, and on the other hand to depend upon it for every thing beyond a certain limit. Those who have carefully attended to its vices and deformities as they have been exhibited by experience or delineated in the course of these papers must feel an invincible repugnancy to trusting the national interests in any degree to its operation. Its inevitable tendency, whenever it is brought into activity, must be to enfeeble the Union, and sow the seeds of discord and contention between the federal head and its members, and between the members themselves. Can it be expected that the deficiencies would be better supplied in this mode than the total wants of the Union have heretofore been supplied in the same mode? It ought to be recollected that if less will be required from the States, they will have proportionably less means to answer the demand. If the opinions of those who contend for the distinction which has been mentioned were to be received as evidence of truth, one would be led to conclude that there was some known point in the economy of national affairs at which it would be safe to stop and to say: Thus far the ends of public happiness will be promoted by supplying the wants of government, and all beyond this is unworthy of our care or anxiety. How is it possible that a government half supplied and always necessitous can fulfil the purposes of its institution, can provide for the security, advance the prosperity, or support the reputation of the commonwealth? How can it ever possess either energy or stability, dignity or credit, confidence at home or respectability abroad? How can its administration be anything else than a succession of expedients temporizing, impotent, disgraceful? How will it be able to avoid a frequent sacrifice of its engagements to immediate necessity? How can it undertake or execute any liberal or enlarged plans of public good?

Let us attend to what would be the effects of this situation in the very first war in which we should happen to be engaged. We will presume, for argument's sake, that the revenue arising from the impose duties answers the purposes of a provision for the public debt and of a peace establishment for the Union. Thus circumstanced, a war breaks out. What would be the probable conduct of the government in such an emergency? Taught by experience that proper dependence could not be placed on the success of requisitions, unable by its own authority to lay hold of fresh resources, and urged by considerations of national danger, would it not be driven to the expedient of diverting the funds already appropriated from their proper objects to the defense of the State? It is not easy to see how a step of this kind could be avoided; and if it should be taken, it is evident that it would prove the destruction of public credit at the very moment that it was becoming essential to the public safety. To imagine that at such a crisis credit might be dispensed with would be the extreme of infatuation. In the modern system of war, nations the most wealthy are obliged to have recourse to large loans. A country so little opulent as ours must feel this necessity in a much stronger degree. But who would lend to a government that prefaced its overtures for borrowing by an act which demonstrated that no reliance could be placed on the steadiness of its measures for paying? The loans it might be able to procure would be as limited in their extent as burdensome in their conditions. They would be made upon the same principles that usurers commonly lend to bankrupt and fraudulent debtors—with a sparing hand and at enormous premiums. . . .

It may perhaps be imagined that from the scantiness of the resources of the country the necessity of diverting the established funds in the case supposed would exist, though the national government should possess an unrestrained power of taxation. But two considerations will serve to quiet all apprehension on this head: one is that we are sure the resources of the community, in their full extent, will be brought into activity for the benefit of the Union; the other is that whatever deficiencies there may be can without difficulty be supplied by loans.

The power of creating new funds upon new objects of taxation by its own authority would enable the national government to borrow as far as its necessities might require. Foreigners, as well as the citizens of America, could then reasonably repose confidence in its engagements; but to depend upon a government that must itself depend upon thirteen other governments for the means of fulfilling its contracts, when once its situation is clearly understood, would require a degree of credulity not often to be met with in the pecuniary transactions of mankind, and little reconcilable with the usual sharp-sightedness of avarice.

Reflections of this kind may have trifling weight with men who hope to see realized in America the halcyon scenes of the poetic or fabulous age; but to those who believe we are likely to experience a common portion of the vicissitudes and calamities which have fallen to the lot of other nations, they must appear entitled to serious attention. Such men must behold the actual situation of their country with painful solicitude, and deprecate the evils which ambition or revenge might, with too much facility, inflict upon it.

PUBLIUS

The Antifederalist: Brutus

In a confederated government, where the powers are divided between the general and the state government, it is essential . . . that the revenues of the country, without which no government can exist, should be divided between them, and so apportioned to each, as to answer their respective exigencies, as far as human wisdom can effect such a division and apportionment. . . .

No such allotment is made in this constitution, but every source of revenue is under the control of Congress; it therefore follows, that if this system is intended to be a complex and not a simple, a confederate and not an entire consolidated government, it contains in it the sure seeds of its own dissolution. One of two things must happen. Either the new constitution will become a mere *nudum pactum,* and all the authority of the rulers under it be cried down, as has happened to the present confederacy. Or the authority of the individual states will be totally supplanted, and they will retain the mere form without any of the powers of government. To one or the other of these issues, I think, this new government, if it is adopted, will advance with great celerity.

It is said, I know, that such a separation of the sources of revenue, cannot be made without endangering the public safety—"unless (says a writer) it can be shown that the circumstances which may affect the public safety are reducible within certain determinate limits; unless the contrary of this position can be fairly and rationally disputed, it must be admitted, as a necessary consequence, that there can be no limitation of that authority which is to provide for the defense and protection of the community, etc."[1]

The pretended demonstration of this writer will instantly vanish, when it is considered, that the *protection and defense* of the community is not intended to be entrusted *solely* into the hands of the general government, and by his own confession it ought not to be. It is true this system commits to the general government the protection and defense of the community against foreign force and invasion, against piracies and felonies on the high seas, and against insurrection among ourselves. They are also authorized to provide for the administration of justice in certain matters of a general concern, and in some that I think are not so. But it ought to be left to the state governments to provide for the protection and defense of the citizen against the hand of private violence, and the wrongs done or attempted by individuals to each other. Protection and defense against the murderer, the robber, the thief, the cheat, and the unjust person, is to be derived from the respective state governments. The just way of reasoning therefore on this subject is this, the general government is to provide for the protection and defense of the community against foreign attacks, etc. They therefore ought to have authority sufficient to effect this, so far as is consistent with the providing for our internal protection and defense. The state governments are entrusted with the care of administering justice among its citizens, and the management of other internal concerns; they ought therefore to retain power adequate to that end. The preservation of internal peace and good order, and the due administration of law and justice, ought to be the first care of every government. The happiness of a people depends infinitely more on this than it does upon all that glory and respect which nations acquire by the most brilliant martial achievements. And I believe history will furnish but few examples of nations who have duly attended to these, who have been subdued by foreign invaders. If a proper respect and submission to the laws prevailed over all orders of men in our country; and if a spirit of public and private justice, economy, and industry influenced the people, we need not be under any apprehensions but what they would be ready to repel any invasion that might be made on the country. And more than this, I

[1]Federalist, No. 23.

would not wish from them. A defensive war is the only one I think justifiable. I do not make these observations to prove, that a government ought not to be authorised to provide for the protection and defense of a country against external enemies, but to show that this is not the most important, much less the only object of their care.

The European governments are almost all of them framed, and administered with a view to arms, and war, as that in which their chief glory consists. They mistake the end of government. It was designed to save men's lives, not to destroy them. We ought to furnish the world with an example of a great people, who in their civil institutions hold chiefly in view, the attainment of virtue, and happiness among ourselves. . . . The most important end of government then, is the proper direction of its internal police, and economy; this is the province of the state governments, and it is evident, and is indeed admitted, that these ought to be under their control. Is it not then preposterous, and in the highest degree absurd, when the state governments are vested with powers so essential to the peace and good order of society, to take from them the means of their own preservation?

The idea that the powers of congress in respect to revenue ought to be unlimited, because 'the circumstances which may affect the public safety are not reducible to certain determinate limits' is novel, as it relates to the government of the United States. The inconveniences which resulted from the feebleness of the present confederation was discerned, and felt soon after its adoption. It was soon discovered, that a power to require money, without either the authority or means to enforce a collection of it, could not be relied upon either to provide for the common defense, discharge the national debt, or for support of government. Congress therefore, as early as February 1781, recommended to the states to invest them with a power to levy an impost of five per cent ad valorem, on all imported goods, as a fund to be appropriated to discharge the debts already contracted, or which should hereafter be contracted for the support of the war, to be continued until the debts should be fully and finally discharged. There is not the most distant idea held out in this act, that an unlimited power to collect taxes, duties and excises was necessary to be vested in the United States, and yet this was a time of the most pressing danger and distress. The idea then was, that if certain definite funds were assigned to the union, which were certain in their natures, productive, and easy of collection, it would enable them to answer their engagements, and provide for their defense, and the impost of five per cent was fixed upon for the purpose.

This same subject was revived in the winter and spring of 1783, and after a long consideration of the subject, many schemes were proposed. The result was, a recommendation of the revenue system of April 1783; this system does not suggest an idea that it was necessary to grant the United States unlimited authority in matters of revenue. A variety of amendments were proposed to this system, some of which are upon the journals of Congress, but it does not appear that any of them proposed to invest the general government with discretionary power to raise money. On the contrary, all of them limit them to certain definite objects, and fix the bounds over which they could not pass. This recommendation was passed at the conclusion of the war, and was founded on an estimate of the whole national debt. It was computed, that one million and an half of dollars, in addition to the impost, was a sufficient sum to pay the annual interest of the debt, and gradually to abolish the principal. Events have proved that their estimate was sufficiently liberal, as the domestic debt appears upon its being adjusted to be less than it was computed; and since this period a considerable portion of the principal of the domestic debt has been discharged by the sale of the western lands. It has been constantly urged by Congress, and by individuals, ever since, until lately, that had this revenue been appropriated by the states, as it was recommended, it would have been adequate to every exigency of the union. Now indeed it is insisted, that all the treasures of the country are to be under the control of that body, whom we are to appoint to provide for our protection and defense against foreign enemies. The debts of the several states, and the support of the governments of them are to trust to fortune and accident. If the union should not have occasion for all the money they can raise, they will leave a portion for the state, but this must be a matter of mere grace and favor. Doctrines like these would not have been listened to by any state in the union, at a time when we were pressed on every side by a powerful enemy, and were called upon to make greater exertions than we have any reason to expect we shall ever be again. . . .

I may be asked to point out the sources, from which the general government could derive a sufficient revenue, to answer the demands of the union. . . . There is one source of revenue, which it is agreed, the general government ought to have the sole control of. This is an impost upon all goods imported from foreign countries. This would, of itself, be very productive, and would be collected with ease and certainty. It will be a fund too, constantly increasing, for our commerce will grow with the productions of the country. And these, together with our consumption of foreign goods, will increase with our population. It is said, that the impost will not produce a sufficient sum to satisfy the demands of the general government; perhaps it would not. . . . My own opinion is, that the objects from which the general government should have authority to raise a revenue, should be of such a nature, that the tax should be raised by simple laws, with few officers, with certainty and expedition, and with the least interference with the internal police of the states. Of this nature is the impost on imported goods. And it appears to me that a duty on exports, would also be of this nature. Therefore, for ought I can discover, this would be the best source of revenue to grant the general government. I know neither the Congress nor the state legislatures will have authority under the new constitution to raise a revenue in this way. But I cannot perceive the reason of the restriction. It appears to me evident, that a tax on articles exported, would be as nearly equal as any that we can expect to lay, and it certainly would be collected with more ease and less expense than any direct tax. I do not however, contend for this mode; it may be liable to well founded objections that have not occurred to me. But this I do contend for, that some mode is practicable, and that limits must be marked between the general government, and the states on this head, or if they be not, either the Congress in the exercise of this power, will deprive the state legislatures of the means of their existence, or the states by resisting the constitutional authority of the general government, will render it nugatory. . . .

The next powers vested by this Constitution in the general government, which we shall consider, are those which authorize them to "borrow money on the credit of the United States, and to raise and support armies." I take these two together and connect them with the power to lay and collect taxes, duties, imposts and excises, because their extent, and the danger that will arise from the exercise of these powers, cannot be fully understood, unless they are viewed in relation to each other.

The power to borrow money is general and unlimited, and the clause so often before referred to, authorizes the passing [of] any laws proper and necessary to carry this into execution. Under this authority, Congress may mortgage any or all the revenues of the union, as a fund to loan money upon; and it is probable, in this way, they may borrow of foreign nations, a principal sum, the interest of which will be equal to the annual revenues of the country. By this means, they may create a national debt, so large, as to exceed the ability of the country ever to sink. I can scarcely contemplate a greater calamity that could befall this country, than to be loaded with a debt exceeding their ability ever to discharge. If this be a just remark, it is unwise and improvident to vest in the general government a power to borrow at discretion, without any limitation or restriction.

It may possibly happen that the safety and welfare of the country may require, that money be borrowed, and it is proper when such a necessity arises that the power should be exercised by the general government. But it certainly ought never to be exercised, but on the most urgent occasions, and then we should not borrow of foreigners if we could possibly avoid it.

The constitution should therefore have so restricted the exercise of this power as to have rendered it very difficult for the government to practice it. The present confederation requires the assent of nine states to exercise this, and a number of other important powers of the confederacy. It would certainly have been a wise provision in this constitution, to have made it necessary that two thirds of the members should assent to borrowing money. When the necessity was indispensable, this assent would always be given, and in no other cause ought it to be.

The power to raise armies is indefinite and unlimited, and authorises the raising [of] forces, as well in peace as in war. Whether the clause which impowers the Congress to pass all laws which are proper and necessary, to carry this into execution, will not authorise them to impress men for the army, is a question well worthy [of] consideration. If the general legislature deem it for the general welfare to raise a body of troops, and they cannot be procured by voluntary enlistments, it seems evident, that it will be proper and necessary to effect it, that men be impressed from the militia to make up the deficiency.

These powers taken in connection, amount to this: that the general government have unlimited authority and control over all the wealth and all the force of the union. The advocates for this scheme, would favor the world with a new discovery, if they would show, what kind of freedom or independency is left to the state governments, when they cannot command any part of the property or of the force of the country, but at the will of the Congress. It seems to me as absurd, as it would be to say, that I was free and independent, when I had conveyed all my property to another, and was tenant to him, and had beside, given an indenture of myself to serve him during life. . . .

BRUTUS

See text p. 11

In 1989 a series of political upheavals resulted in the end of the Cold War between the United States and the countries of Eastern Europe. Major democratic reforms were introduced in the Soviet Union, and East and West Germany moved to reunification, leading some observers to remark that the United States had "won" the Cold War.

The attempts to move toward increasingly democratic systems have not been easy. Ethnic conflicts in former Eastern Bloc countries have led to bloody and intractable clashes such as in Bosnia–Herzegovina. Even in Germany, where reunification proceeded relatively smoothly, tensions continue to grow as prosperous West Germany copes with the problems of East Germany's faltering economy and the influx of immigrants from the former Soviet Union and communist bloc.

Western countries must think carefully about what the advent of a new democratic era actually means for global politics and human rights. In the following article Raymond Gastil argues that a truly democratic system must guarantee both political and civil rights. Movement toward a political democracy means little, according to Gastil, without movement toward civil rights at the same time.

Raymond D. Gastil
"What Kind of Democracy?"*

As we congratulate ourselves on a world becoming increasingly democratic, we should recall that several times before in the past century it seemed that democracy had won universal acceptance, but the acceptance was much less trustworthy than had been imagined. In 1900–1901 leading newspapers announced the good news that the twentieth century was to be the century of democracy; in 1920 a prominent authority on political systems could write that democracy no longer had any challengers.

A society is generally said to be a full democracy if it has a political system that guarantees both the civil and political liberties of its people. In other words, a democracy must not only allow its people to choose freely who will govern them but also guarantee the freedoms of expression and organi-

*Raymond D. Gastil, "What Kind of Democracy?" in *The Atlantic Monthly* (June 1990). Reprinted with permission.

zation, which make possible effective oppositions that can compete for, and eventually attain, office. Unfortunately, in most historical treatments of the growth of democracy the emphasis tends to be on the existence of electoral or legislative mechanisms that allow for choice, with less attention paid to those civil liberties that make that choice effectively free.

It is easy, and probably fundamentally wrong, to assume that the most important characteristics of democracy are the political rights that the word "democracy" most clearly implies. Let me use personal experience to explain this. Annually from 1973 until last year I produced the Comparative Survey of Freedom, which placed countries on a continuum of freedom. I tried to balance aspects of democracy by using a rating system that included both political rights and civil liberties in the final score. During the first few years of the survey I considered that when the final scores of two countries tied, I would give the rating for political freedom—that is, for the extent to which there were free elections and those elected gained power—the greater weight. Perhaps I made this choice because it was much easier to get information on elections and legislators than on the state of civil liberties in a country. However, as time went on and experience accumulated, I dropped this largely theoretical distinction in weighting. In the past few years I have come to believe that if one thinks of freedom, or in this case democracy, in time periods longer than a year, civil liberties will be seen as the more important of the two kinds of democratic freedom. I came to realize that political rights without civil freedoms would offer few of the values that I cherish in democratic societies, while civil freedoms without political rights (insofar as this is conceivable) would offer the major values that I understand democracy to promote. The primacy of civil freedoms becomes even more apparent in societies whose governments appear to respond to the popular will as expressed by the communications media, demonstrations, and other informal channels with more alacrity than they do to the often indeterminate results at the polling station.

Democracy as we know it has two quite different roots. The first is the universal desire of people to manage their own affairs, or at least to have a say in who manages their affairs. In the primitive band all adults, or sometimes all heads of families, tended to have a say in the affairs of the band. This tribal or village democracy can be traced down through all of history. The democracy of ancient Athens is no doubt the most famous example of a community ruling itself—a community of relatively large scale. Of course, women, slaves, and other outsiders were excluded. But a substantial part of the population took an active role in the decisions of the society; when "the people," thus defined, changed their minds, society moved in the direction of the change. When we speak of the democracy of the medieval Swiss cantons, or of the units of the Iroquois confederacy, this is also the democracy we have in mind. The democracy of the New England towns of the seventeenth century and the democracy of the Swiss communities of Rousseau's day, including his native Geneva, were essentially successive expressions of the tribal or community democracy of primitive society. Though for limited purposes these might form together in larger "leagues," they were little more than alliances among independent units whose interrelationships might be no more democratic than those in nondemocratic leagues.

The second root of modern democracy is liberalism, defined as that set of social and political beliefs, attitudes, and values which assumes the universal and equal application of the law and the existence of basic human rights superior to those of state or community. As used here, the term "liberal" is not meant to suggest any particular economic doctrine, or doctrine regarding the state's economic role; nor is it meant to be an antonym of "conservative." It does imply that the state's interests cannot override those of the citizenry. Derived from a variety of secular and religious tenets, liberalism affirms the basic worth of individuals, their thoughts, and their desires. In the liberal canon no one, whether king or majority, has the right to tell people how to think, or even act (except in instances of imminent threat to social well-being). Although it has ancient foundations, liberalism is primarily the outgrowth of the efforts of political and social philosophers since the seventeenth century to free humanity from the fetters of unchecked state power and imposed religious dogma. Before the eighteenth century, liberal democracy's role in history was much less important than tribal democracy's.

It was liberal democracy that abolished political censorship, that eventually found it impossible to justify slavery of any kind, or torture for any reason, or the unequal position of women and minority races and ethnic groups. It is liberal democracy that is always teetering on the edge of denying that the individual has any substantial duty to sacrifice himself for the community if he chooses not to. It was liberal democracy that fascism and similar ideologies sought to destroy utterly. It was liberal democracy that the Marxist-Leninist regimes now dissolving in Eastern Europe found so repugnant in its individualism and inherent tendency to sacrifice group interests to individual interests.

The international human-rights movement is based on the tenets of liberal democracy, and is a natural product of this political system. Everywhere, these rights have become the hope of the oppressed, and the societies that support these rights become the natural allies of all peoples.

When the current democratic revolution is discussed, we should remember that we are referring to changes that represent the legacy of both these traditions, the tribal democratic and the liberal democratic. We must remember that their conjunction in modern democracies is the result of a long historical process, and far from automatic. Historically, democracies have tended to be more tribal than liberal. Regardless of the Constitution and the Bill of Rights and the values of the Founding Fathers, acceptance of liberal democracy came slowly to the American public. Even in recent years the United States has had periods in which tribal democracy rode roughshod over liberal democracy, as in the expulsion of the Japanese from the West Coast in the Second World War. Public-opinion polls continue to show that the tenets of liberal democracy may not be as thoroughly accepted in the United States and other democracies as we would like.

The slow pace of the liberalization of democracy, even in recent years, explains why as we go further back in history, the association of democracy and peace becomes more and more tenuous. Although the political systems of Athens and Sparta were far apart, both states were warlike; indeed, Athens became a specialist in imperial wars. The democratic Swiss cantons produced the mercenaries of Europe for several centuries. At the same time that democracy was being perfected in the West, its military forces conquered most of the world. Yet gradually the record has improved, as democracies have become more liberal. War became unfashionable in the democratic West after the First World War. Colonies became unfashionable after the Second World War. But if there is to be a "peace dividend" from the democratic revolution, it will occur only to the extent that tribal democracy has been overcome by liberal democratic attitudes that respect the rights of all peoples.

Today, as we contemplate a democratizing world, we must ask ourselves how strong the tribal and liberal elements actually are in the new democratic movements. We should recall that fascism in Italy, Japan, and Germany grew to maturity in democratizing societies, societies that provided the tools for free discussion and mobilization of small groups. Those groups were then able to use these privileges to overthrow the democratic system by capturing the attention and perhaps the majority support of peoples in whom the assumptions of liberal democracy were only weakly rooted.

Outside the West democracy is beset with the problem of incorporating basically illiberal peoples and movements into the democratic framework. In the recent Indian election the third most powerful party was a Hindu party dedicated to advancing the cause of the Hindu majority at the expense of both the rights of Muslims and the concept of the secular state. In some parts of India many Sikhs and Muslims and members of other groups are equally intolerant of those whose beliefs or backgrounds are different from their own. Pakistan's emergence as a democracy has been repeatedly delayed by the claims of Muslim movements against the rights of others, and these claims may again cause the collapse of democracy in Pakistan.

The clash of tribal democracy and liberal democracy has been particularly acute in the Middle East. It is either the case or feared to be the case that a really open electoral process in most Middle Eastern states would result in the establishment of an oppressive Muslim fundamentalism in place of the less oppressive current regimes. Sudan's most recent attempt at democracy was ultimately torn apart by tribalism, which made democracy as we know it impossible. We should note that Iran, under Islamic guidance, has had several contested elections with fair voting procedures since 1980. From the political-rights viewpoint it can be argued that Iran is now ruled by an elected democratic government, a government more democratic than most in the Third World. But its oppression of individuals or groups that lie beyond the boundaries of tribal morality or acceptance has been persistent. Its initial unwillingness, for example, to allow the Bahais any place in Iranian society, and its equally vicious destruction of the radical left, represented tribalisms that an elected parliament could overwhelmingly endorse. Despite the panoply of Western political institutions in Iran, it remains outside the democratic world that requires a commitment to civil liberties as well as political rights.

From one perspective, the demand for self-determination is a demand for freedom. From another, it is a demand for independence unrelated to the maintenance of those freedoms basic to liberal democracy. Too often the demand for self-determination is a tribalist demand that ends by narrowing rather than broadening the sphere of human rights. It is the demand that has torn Sri Lanka apart, destroying what was a functioning democratic system. It is the demand that came very close on several occasions to arresting the development of democracy in our own South. In itself, self-determination is a legitimate right, and should be recognized insofar as it does not threaten other rights. But this right should not be confused with those basic civil rights fundamental to liberal democracy, nor is it as important as they are.

It is with this consciousness that we must consider the prospects for democracy in those areas of the world that remain nondemocratic but may soon institute full political democracies if current trends continue. We must ask particularly what values we hold most dear. Do we want the establishment of democratic regimes that will soon come to deny those liberal, humanistic values we see as essential to a full human life? Do we want, for example, a politically more democratic but also more fundamentalist Egypt? Would we really want a "free Afghanistan" whose political system put women back in the Middle Ages? Would we still endorse the democracy of an India that ended up exacerbating religious or ethnic tensions to the point of new and endemic slaughter?

If we are lucky, we may be able to avoid facing such questions. But if the development of democracy in the Soviet Union, for example, proceeds as it has, with an increasing emphasis on self-determination at the popular level, will we not find larger and larger sections of the population developing independent political systems in which the desires and opinions and interests of the majority allow for the suppression of all those who disagree, or all those who belong to other "tribes"? Some years ago I regarded descriptions of the danger of the highly nationalistic Pamyat movement in the USSR as little more than the scare-mongering of scholars or anti-Soviets. Today I wonder if "pamyats" might not break out all over the Soviet world, fueled by the frustrations of failure in other sectors of life, much as fascism was fueled between the wars.

What do we bring away from this discussion? Certainly we should not conclude that because democratic movements are often less than thoroughly imbued with modern liberal ideals, we should stop pushing for the democratization of the world. We should continue the effort for several reasons. First, people do have democratic rights to self-determination, even if we do not like what they do with these rights. Second, the continued rolling of the democratic bandwagon may bring us closer to our overall goals. Third, nondemocratic regimes are often as illiberal as democratic ones. Fourth, since democratic systems are often initially more tribal than liberal, by denying the right of tribal democracy we may end up denying the right of a people to any democracy at all.

But the discussion suggests some dangers, and perhaps some changes in direction, in the pursuit of the millennium. It suggests that the campaign for liberal democracy, represented in part by the human-rights movement, should be continued and enhanced even as states become democratic in form. Also, we should develop educational programs that teach liberal values to broader and broader segments of the population in new democracies or states that have not yet become politically democratic. To avoid the arrest of this educational process we should in particular instances and for particular countries avoid pressing for the establishment of political democracy so long as the system in power takes an active role in developing and teaching the concepts of a liberal society.

I suspect that one reason for the collapse of communist systems in the Soviet sphere is that they appeared increasingly estranged from the world culture that has penetrated nearly everywhere since the Second World War. This culture simply no longer accepts the controls on movement and thought that characterized most of the world until recently. It no longer accepts discrimination for reasons of ideology, religion, gender, or ethnicity. It no longer accepts rulers that are not freely elected by their peoples. This culture has come upon the world rapidly, and may ultimately be destructive of essential values. But for now it advances the cause of the assumptions basic to liberal democracy, and therefore becomes an important aspect of the struggle for the extension of democracy.

In promoting democracy, governments and private organizations should place at least as much stress on the liberal underpinnings of modern democracy as on the forms of political democracy. The emphasis should be on the absolute value of the individual and the universal applicability of basic rights. We should support movements that undercut tribal thinking. We should refrain from insisting on rapid transitions to the political forms of democracy when establishing these forms appears likely to threaten the eventual attainment of the freedoms due every individual, and not just every group. We should be careful not to confuse the demand for self-determination with the demand for democracy. Thus the campaign for democracy, the campaign for human rights, and the campaign against war and armaments must become ever more closely identified with one another as we press on, both publicly and privately, toward a world of peace and freedom.

FROM COERCION TO CONSENT

See text p. 13

In the United States, as in most other democratic regimes, governmental efforts to create a base of support are continuous, albeit not outwardly coercive. One of the most obvious arenas within which national unity may be fostered is that of the public school system, as the text discusses in greater detail in succeeding chapters. Public schools have always been understood to have an obligation to teach civic virtues and cultivate responsible citizens.

Requiring children to salute the American flag every morning has been widely understood to be a means of teaching children to respect the public order. The following Supreme Court case discusses limits upon that method of generating feelings of national loyalty, although the language reaches far beyond the simple question of saluting the flag.

In 1940 the United States Supreme Court considered a challenge to a Pennsylvania statute requiring public school children to pledge allegiance to the U.S. flag every morning. The suit was brought on behalf of two children whose religious beliefs prohibited them from claiming loyalty to the United States. In Minersville v. Gobitis *the Court assumed that the state had the authority to enlist public support even when that declaration of support conflicted with an individual's religious beliefs. In an unprecedented move, however, the Supreme Court reversed itself three years later in* Board of Education v. Barnette, *holding that compelling a flag salute violated an individual's First Amendment rights, including the freedom to dissent "as to things that touch the heart of the existing order."*

Minersville School District v. *Gobitis* (1940)*

JUSTICE FRANKFURTER delivered the opinion of the Court.

A grave responsibility confronts this Court whenever in course of litigation it must reconcile the conflicting claims of liberty and authority. But when the liberty invoked is liberty of conscience, and the authority is authority to safeguard the nation's fellowship, judicial conscience is put to its severest test. Of such a nature is the present controversy.

Lillian Gobitis, aged twelve, and her brother William, aged ten, were expelled from the public schools of Minersville, Pennsylvania, for refusing to salute the national flag as part of a daily school exercise. . . . The Gobitis family are affiliated with "Jehovah's Witnesses," for whom the Bible as the Word of God is the supreme authority. The children had been brought up conscientiously to believe that such a gesture of respect for the flag was forbidden by command of Scripture.

The Gobitis children were of an age for which Pennsylvania makes school attendance compulsory. Thus they were denied a free education, and their parents had to put them into private schools. To be relieved of the financial burden thereby entailed, their father, on behalf of the children and in his own behalf, brought this suit. . . .

Certainly the affirmative pursuit of one's convictions about the ultimate mystery of the universe and man's relation to it is placed beyond the reach of law. Government may not interfere with organized or individual expression of belief or disbelief. Propagation of belief—or even of disbelief—in the supernatural is protected, whether in church or chapel, mosque or synagogue, tabernacle or meeting-house. Likewise the Constitution assures generous immunity to the individual from imposition of penalties for of-

*Minersville School District v. Gobitis, 310 U.S. 586, 1940.

fending, in the course of his own religious activities, the religious views of others, be they a minority or those who are dominant in government.

But the manifold character of man's relations may bring his conception of religious duty into conflict with the secular interests of his fellowmen. When does the constitutional guarantee compel exemption from doing what society thinks necessary for the promotion of some great common end, or from a penalty for conduct which appears dangerous to the general good? . . .

Our present task, then, as so often the case with courts, is to reconcile two rights in order to prevent either from destroying the other. But, because in safeguarding conscience we are dealing with interests so subtle and so dear, every possible leeway should be given to the claims of religious faith.

In the judicial enforcement of religious freedom we are concerned with a historic concept.

[But in determining the authority of the state to take measures to maintain an orderly, tranquil, and free society, we] are dealing with an interest inferior to none in the hierarchy of legal values. National unity is the basis of national security. . . .

Situations like the present are phases of the profoundest problem confronting a democracy—the problem which Lincoln cast in memorable dilemma: "Must a government of necessity be too *strong* for the liberties of its people, or too *weak* to maintain its own existence?" No mere textual reading or logical talisman can solve the dilemma. And when the issue demands judicial determination, it is not the personal notion of judges of what wise adjustment requires which must prevail.

Unlike the instances we have cited, the case before us is not concerned with an exertion of legislative power for the promotion of some specific need or interest of secular society—the protection of the family, the promotion of health, the common defense, the raising of public revenues to defray the cost of government. But all these specific activities of government presuppose the existence of an organized political society. The ultimate foundation of a free society is the binding tie of cohesive sentiment. Such a sentiment is fostered by all those agencies of the mind and spirit which may serve to gather up the traditions of a people, transmit them from generation to generation, and thereby create that continuity of a treasured common life which constitutes a civilization. "We live by symbols." The flag is the symbol of our national unity, transcending all internal differences, however large, within the framework of the Constitution. This Court has had occasion to say that ". . . the flag is the symbol of the Nation's power, the emblem of freedom in its truest, best sense . . . it signifies government resting on the consent of the governed; liberty regulated by law; the protection of the weak against the strong; security against the exercise of arbitrary power; and absolute safety for free institutions against foreign aggression."

The case before us must be viewed as though the legislature of Pennsylvania had itself formally directed the flag-salute for the children of Minersville; had made no exemption for children whose parents were possessed of conscientious scruples like those of the Gobitis family; and had indicated its belief in the desirable ends to be secured by having its public school children share a common experience at those periods of development when their minds are supposedly receptive to its assimilation, by an exercise appropriate in time and place and setting, and one designed to evoke in them appreciation of the nation's hopes and dreams, its sufferings and sacrifices. The precise issue, then, for us to decide is whether the legislatures of the various states and the authorities in a thousand counties and school districts of this country are barred from determining the appropriateness of various means to evoke that unifying sentiment without which there can ultimately be no liberties, civil or religious. To stigmatize legislative judgment in providing for this universal gesture of respect for the symbol of our national life in the setting of the common school as a lawless inroad on that freedom of conscience which the Constitution protects, would amount to no less than the pronouncement of pedagogical and psychological dogma in a field where courts possess no marked and certainly no controlling competence. The influences which help toward a common feeling for the common country are manifold. Some may seem harsh and others no doubt are foolish. Surely, however, the end is legitimate. And the effective means for its attainment are still so uncertain and so unauthenticated by science as to preclude us from putting the widely prevalent belief in flag-saluting beyond the pale of legislative power. It mocks reason and denies our whole history to find in the allowance of a requirement to salute our flag on fitting occasions the seeds of sanction for obeisance to a leader.

The wisdom of training children in patriotic impulses by those compulsions which necessarily pervade so much of the educational process is not for our independent judgment. Even were we convinced of the folly of such a measure, such belief would be no proof of its unconstitutionality. For ourselves, we might be tempted to say that the deepest patriotism is best engendered by giving unfettered scope to the most crochety beliefs. Perhaps it is best, even from the standpoint of those interests which ordinances like the one under review seek to promote, to give to the least popular sect leave from conformities like those here in issue. But the courtroom is not the arena for debating issues of educational policy. It is not our province to choose among competing considerations in the subtle process of securing effective loyalty to the traditional ideals of democracy, while respecting at the same time individual idiosyncracies among a people so diversified in racial origins and religious allegiances. So to hold would in effect make us the school board for the country. That authority has not been given to this Court, nor should we assume it.

We are dealing here with the formative period in the development of citizenship. Great diversity of psychological and ethical opinion exists among us concerning the best way to train children for their place in society. Because of these differences and because of reluctance to permit a single, iron-cast system of education to be imposed upon a nation compounded of so many strains, we have held that, even though public education is one of our most cherished democratic institutions, the Bill of Rights bars a state from compelling all children to attend the public schools. But it is a very different thing for this Court to exercise censorship over the conviction of legislatures that a particular program or exercise will best promote in the minds of children who attend the common schools an attachment to the institutions of their country.

What the school authorities are really asserting is the right to awaken in the child's mind considerations as to the significance of the flag contrary to those implanted by the parent. In such an attempt the state is normally at a disadvantage in competing with the parent's authority, so long—and this is the vital aspect of religious toleration—as parents are unmolested in their right to counteract by their own persuasiveness the wisdom and rightness of those loyalties which the state's educational system is seeking to promote. Except where the transgression of constitutional liberty is too plain for argument, personal freedom is best maintained—so long as the remedial channels of the democratic process remain open and unobstructed—when it is ingrained in a people's habits and not enforced against popular policy by the coercion of adjudicated law. That the flag-salute is an allowable portion of a school program for those who do not invoke conscientious scruples is surely not debatable. But for us to insist that, though the ceremony may be required, exceptional immunity must be given to dissidents, is to maintain that there is no basis for a legislative judgment that such an exemption might introduce elements of difficulty into the school discipline, might cast doubts in the minds of the other children which would themselves weaken the effect of the exercise.

The preciousness of the family relation, the authority and independence which give dignity to parenthood, indeed the enjoyment of all freedom, presuppose the kind of ordered society which is summarized by our flag. A society which is dedicated to the preservation of these ultimate values of civilization may in self-protection utilize the educational process for inculcating those almost unconscious feelings which bind men together in a comprehending loyalty, whatever may be their lesser differences and difficulties. That is to say, the process may be utilized so long as men's right to believe as they please, to win others to their way of belief, and their right to assemble in their chosen places of worship for the devotional ceremonies of their faith, are all fully respected.

Reversed.

QUESTIONS

1. What reasons does Hamilton advance in *The Federalist No. 23* to support his assertion that the federal government ought to have "unconfined authority in respect to all those objects which are intrusted to its management"?
2. Does Brutus believe that *no* government should have expansive powers over the sword and the purse, or simply that it is a mistake to vest those

powers in the *national* government? Why would it be permissable to entrust unlimited powers to state governments rather than the national government?

3. Raymond Gastil expresses concern that democratization unaccompanied by the expansion of political and civil rights will not result in respect for the value of the individual. What is he referring to when he speaks of the "liberal underpinnings" of a democratic system?
4. In the *Minersville* case the United States Supreme Court held that "a society . . . dedicated to the preservation of the ultimate values of civilization may in self-protection utilize the educational process for inculcating those almost unconscious feelings which bind men together in a comprehending loyalty." In the subsequent case, *Barnett v. Board of Education,* the Court held that a school could not compell students to salute the American flag. Does this decision repudiate the basic assertion of *Gobitis*?

CHAPTER 2

Constructing a Government: The Founding and the Constitution

THE FIRST FOUNDING: INTERESTS AND CONFLICTS

See text p. 27

Edmund Burke, a British statesman, is best known as the author of a political treatise entitled Reflections on the Revolution in France, *published in 1790. Burke was appalled by the bloodshed and chaos he observed during the French Revolution, which he attributed to the misguided attempts of the French revolutionaries to introduce an entirely new social order, without respect for traditional rights and liberties.* Reflections on the Revolution in France *is a classic in conservative political philosophy.*

Burke did not oppose the American Revolution, which took place while he was a member of British Parliament, with the vehemence he later exhibited during the French Revolution. Indeed, he suggested that the colonists' complaints had merit because the British government had disregarded their natural rights. In a speech before the House of Commons in 1770, Burke urged fellow members of Parliament to grant greater powers of self-government to the colonies. He pointed out that attempts to control the colonies from across the Atlantic, without any real understanding of the conditions under which the colonies operated, was doomed to failure. Every act of Parliament in governing the colonies was poorly thought out, with the result that the British government itself had to take the blame for the unrest that had resulted. He asserted: ". . . Your acts have not been listened to. . . . You have neither military nor civil power from the senseless manner in which you exercised them. A government without wisdom never will be without woe. All is shaken to the foundation by the entire absence of common sense."

By 1775, matters had gone from bad to worse. In the following excerpt from another speech given at that time, Burke urges the British government to attempt conciliation, restating his position that the situation called for "prudent management" rather than force of arms. In making out his case, he gives a detailed explanation of the American character—and the need to accommodate it—to convince his listeners that no other course of action would be likely to succeed.

Edmund Burke
"On Conciliation" (March 22, 1775)*

The proposition is peace. Not peace through the medium of war; not peace to be hunted through the labyrinth of intricate and endless negotiations; not peace to arise out of universal discord fomented from principle in all parts

*From Elliott Robert Barkan, ed., *Edmund Burke on the American Revolution* (Gloucester, MA: Peter Smith Publisher, Inc., 1972). Reprinted with permission.

of the empire; not peace to depend on the juridical determination of perplexing questions or the precise marking the shadowy boundaries of a complex government. It is simple peace, sought in its natural course, and in its ordinary haunts—it is peace sought in the spirit of peace, and laid in principles purely pacific. I propose, by removing the ground of the difference, and by restoring the *former unsuspecting confidence of the colonies in the mother country,* to give permanent satisfaction to your people; and (far from a scheme of ruling by discord) to reconcile them to each other in the same act, and by the bond of the very same interest which reconciles them to British government. . . .

[Burke explains in detail the economic advantages that had accrued to the British through trade with the colonies in North America; two-thirds of all British export trade alone was conducted with the North American and West Indian colonies.]

. . . America, gentlemen say, is a noble object. It is an object well worth fighting for. Certainly it is, if fighting a people be the best way of gaining them. Gentlemen in this respect will be led to their choice of means by their complexions and their habits. Those who understand the military art will of course have some predilection for it. Those who wield the thunder of the state may have more confidence in the efficacy of arms. But I confess, possibly for want of this knowledge, my opinion is much more in favour of prudent management than of force, considering force not as an odious, but a feeble instrument for preserving a people so numerous, so active, so growing, so spirited as this in a profitable and subordinate connection with us. . . .

[Burke argues that force is not a desirable alternative since its effect is temporary and Britain has no great experience with using force as its sole means of governance.]

. . . But there is still behind a third consideration concerning this object, which serves to determine my opinion on the sort of policy which ought to be pursued in the management of America, even more than its population and its commerce—I mean its *temper and character.*

In this character of the Americans, a love of freedom is the predominating feature which marks and distinguishes the whole; and as an ardent is always a jealous affection, your colonies become suspicious, restive, and untractable whenever they see the least attempt to wrest from them by force or shuffle from them by chicane what they think the only advantage worth living for. The fierce spirit of liberty is stronger in the English colonies probably than in any other people of the earth; and this from a great variety of powerful causes, which, to understand the true temper of their minds and the direction which this spirit takes, it will not be amiss to lay open somewhat more largely.

First, the people of the colonies are descendants of Englishmen. England, Sir, is a nation which still I hope respects, and formerly adored, her freedom. The colonists emigrated from you when this part of your character was most predominant, and they took this bias and direction the moment they parted from your hands. They are therefore not only devoted to liberty, but to liberty according to English ideas and on English principles. Abstract liberty, like other mere abstractions, is not to be found. Liberty inheres in some sensible object; and every nation has formed to itself some favourite point, which by way of eminence becomes the criterion of their happiness. It happened you know, Sir, that the great contests for freedom in this country were from the earliest times chiefly upon the question of taxing. . . . On this point of taxes the ablest pens and most eloquent tongues have been exercised; the greatest spirits have acted and suffered. . . .

[The British themselves have made it most clear that the people must have power over their own money.] The colonies draw from you, as with their life-blood, these ideas and principles. Their love of liberty, as with you, fixed and attached on this specific point of taxing. Liberty might be safe or might be endangered in twenty other particulars, without their being much pleased or alarmed. Here they felt its pulse, and as they found that beat they thought themselves sick or sound. . . . The fact is, that they did thus apply those general arguments; and your mode of governing them, whether through lenity or indolence, through wisdom or mistake, confirmed them in the imagination that they, as well as you, had an interest in these common principles.

They were further confirmed in this pleasing error by the form of their provincial legislative assemblies. Their governments are popular in a high degree, some are merely popular, in all the popular representative is the most weighty, and this share of the people in their ordinary government never fails to inspire them with lofty sentiments and with a strong aversion from whatever tends to deprive them of their chief importance.

If anything were wanting to this necessary operation of the form of government, religion would have given it a complete effect. Religion, always a principle of energy, in this new people is no way worn out or impaired, and their mode of professing it is also one main cause of this free spirit. The people are Protestants, and of that kind which is the most adverse to all implicit submission of mind and opinion. This is a persuasion not only favourable to liberty, but built upon it. . . . All Protestantism, even the most cold and passive, is a sort of dissent. But the religion most prevalent in our northern colonies is a refinement on the principle of resistance; it is the dissidence of dissent and the Protestantism of the Protestant religion. . . . The colonists left England when this spirit was high, and in the emigrants was the highest of all; and even that stream of foreigners, which has been constantly flowing into these colonies, has, for the greatest part, been composed of dissenters from the establishments of their several countries, and have brought with them a temper and character far from alien to that of the people with whom they mixed.

. . . It is [true] that in Virginia and the Carolinas they have a vast multitude of slaves. Where this is the case in any part of the world, those who are free are by far the most proud and jealous of their freedom. Freedom is to them not only an enjoyment, but a kind of rank and privilege. Not seeing there that freedom, as in countries where it is a common blessing and as broad and general as the air, may be united with much abject toil, with great misery, with all the exterior of servitude liberty looks amongst them like something that is more noble and liberal. I do not mean, Sir, to commend the superior morality of this sentiment, which has at least as much pride as virtue in it; but I cannot alter the nature of man. . . . In such a people, the haughtiness of domination combines with the spirit of freedom, fortifies it, and renders it invincible.

Permit me, Sir, to add another circumstance in our colonies, which contributes no mean part towards the growth and effect of this untractable spirit. I mean their education. In no country perhaps in the world is the law so general a study. The profession itself is numerous and powerful, and in most provinces it takes the lead. . . . [But] when great honours and great emoluments do not win over this knowledge [of law] to the service of the state, it is a formidable adversary to government. If the spirit be not tamed and broken by these happy methods, it is stubborn and litigious. *Abeunt studia in mores.*[1] This study renders men acute, inquisitive, dexterous, prompt in attack, ready in defence, full of resources. . . .

The last cause of this disobedient spirit in the colonies is hardly less powerful than the rest, as it is not merely moral, but laid deep in the natural constitution of things. Three thousand miles of ocean lie between you and them. No contrivance can prevent the effect of this distance in weakening government. Seas roll, and months pass, between the order and the execution, and the want of a speedy explanation of a single point is enough to defeat a whole system. . . . The Sultan gets such obedience as he can. He governs with a loose rein that he may govern at all. . . . This is the immutable condition, the eternal law, of extensive and detached empire.

Then, Sir, from these six capital sources: of descent, of form of government, of religion in the northern provinces, of manners in the southern, of education, of the remoteness of situation from the first mover of government—from all these causes a fierce spirit of liberty has grown up. It has grown with the growth of the people in your colonies, and increased with the increase of their wealth; a spirit that unhappily meeting with an exercise of power in England which, however lawful, is not reconcilable to any ideas of liberty, much less with theirs, has kindled this flame that is ready to consume us.

I do not mean to commend either the spirit in this excess or the moral causes which produce it. Perhaps a more smooth and accommodating spirit of freedom in them would be more acceptable to us. Perhaps ideas of liberty might be desired more reconcilable with an arbitrary and boundless authority. Perhaps we might wish the colonists to be persuaded that their liberty is more secure when held in trust for them by us (as their guardians during a perpetual minority) than with any part of it in their own hands. The question is, not whether their spirit deserves praise or blame, but—what, in the name of God, shall we do with it? . . . We are called upon to fix some rule and line for our future conduct which may give a little stability to our politics and

[1]"Pursuits influence character."

prevent the return of such unhappy deliberations as the present. . . . Until very lately, all authority in America seemed to be nothing but an emanation from yours. Even the popular part of the colony constitution derived all its activity, and its first vital movement, from the pleasure of the crown. We thought, Sir, that the utmost which the discontented colonists could do was to disturb authority; we never dreamt they could of themselves supply it, knowing in general what an operose business it is to establish a government absolutely new. . . . They have formed a government, sufficient for its purposes, without the bustle of a revolution or the troublesome formality of an election. Evident necessity and tacit consent have done the business in an instant. . . . The evil arising from hence is this: that the colonists, having once found the possibility of enjoying the advantages of order in the midst of a struggle for liberty, such struggles will not henceforward seem so terrible to the settled and sober part of mankind as they had appeared before the trial.

. . . In order to prove that the Americans have no right to their liberties, we are every day endeavouring to subvert the maxims which preserve the whole spirit of our own. To prove that the Americans ought not to be free, we are obliged to depreciate the value of freedom itself. . . .

. . . There are but three ways of proceeding relative to this stubborn spirit which prevails in your colonies and disturbs your government. These are: to change that spirit, as inconvenient, by removing the causes; to prosecute it as criminal; or, to comply with it as necessary. . . . [The first two ideas are unworkable in practice.]

The temper and character which prevail in our colonies are, I am afraid, unalterable by any human art. We cannot, I fear, falsify the pedigree of this fierce people, and persuade them that they are not sprung from a nation in whose veins the blood of freedom circulates. The language in which they would hear you tell them this tale would detect the imposition—your speech would betray you. An Englishman is the unfittest person on earth to argue another Englishman into slavery.

I think it is nearly as little in our power to change their republican religion as their free descent, or to substitute the Roman Catholic as a penalty, or the Church of England as an improvement. . . . The education of the Americans is also on the same unalterable bottom with their religion. You cannot persuade them to burn their books of curious science, to banish their lawyers from their courts of laws, or to quench the lights of their assemblies by refusing to choose those persons who are best read in their privileges. . . .

With regard to the high aristocratic spirit of Virginia and the southern colonies, it has been proposed, I know, to reduce it by declaring a general enfranchisement of their slaves. . . .

Slaves as these unfortunate black people are, and dull as all men are from slavery, must they not a little suspect the offer of freedom from that very nation which has sold them to their present masters?—from that nation, one of whose causes of quarrel with those masters is their refusal to deal any more in that inhuman traffic? An offer of freedom from England would come rather oddly, shipped to them in an African vessel, which is refused an entry into the ports of Virginia or Carolina, with a cargo of three hundred Angola negroes. . . .

If then the removal of the causes of this spirit of American liberty be, for the greater part, or rather entirely, impracticable; if the ideas of criminal process be inapplicable, or, if applicable, are in the highest degree inexpedient—what way yet remains? No way is open, but the third and last—to comply with the American spirit as necessary, or, if you please, to submit to it as a necessary evil.

THE SECOND FOUNDING: FROM COMPROMISE TO CONSTITUTION

See text p. 33

If the debates over the structure of the American federal system seem to be of historical interest only, even a brief consideration of changes in the world political system should convince us otherwise. As a number of Western European nations moved toward joining the integrated market of the European Economic Community in 1992, the critical importance of the nature of a union between states came into focus. The following article from the British magazine The Economist *invites readers to consider the implications of a federal system uniting Western Europe with specific comparisons to the conditions under which the American colonies created a union. Given* The Economist's *traditional endorsement of free-market economies, it is not surprising that the article cautions against any arrangement that might limit the ability of nations to leave the Community at will. The article was written just prior to the advent of the European Economic Community; the success of the venture remains to be seen.*

The Economist
"If You Sincerely Want to Be a United States"*

Imagine a hot summer in Paris. By grace of a kindly time-warp, a group of European eminences have assembled for a conference. Charles de Gaulle is their chairman. Among those attending are John Maynard Keynes (who has a continent-wide reputation, though he is still only 29) and Albert Einstein. Bertrand Russell is not there—he is holidaying on Cape Cod—but he barrages the proceedings by fax. Russell is kept abreast of things by young King Juan Carlos of Spain, who, with Keynes, provides the driving force of the conference.

Impossible, except in one of those rosy early-morning dreams. Now remember the men who gathered at Philadelphia in the summer of 1787. George Washington was the chairman. Alexander Hamilton, whose short

*"If You Sincerely Want to be a United States," *The Economist* (March 23, 1991).

life never knew a dull moment, was there, as was James Madison, a pragmatic man of principle who would later become president. Together, they directed the conference. Benjamin Franklin was there too, though somewhat in his dotage. Thomas Jefferson (compared with whom Bertrand Russell was a startlingly narrow fellow) was not there, but kept an eye on things from Paris.

It is no offence to Jacques Delors and his friends to say that the people now charged with trying to create a political union in Europe do not inspire such awe. Yet the job of the two intergovernmental conferences the European Community has assembled this year is not different in kind from that which faced America's constitutional convention 204 years ago. Constitution-writing is also in vogue in the Soviet Union, as that country's central government and its 15 surly republics struggle to redefine their relations with each other; though that is a matter of trying to stop a bad union falling apart, not creating a good new one. Might the most mature and successful constitutional settlement in the world have some lessons for these European parvenus?

They Were One, and They Knew It

Start with two great differences between America then and Europe now. The America that declared its independence from Britain in 1776 was, except for its black slaves, an extraordinarily homogeneous society.

Think of those huge distances, and those primitive communications, and wonder at the early Americans' sense of cohesion. Although North and South already showed the difference that had to be bridged by war in 1861–65, Americans shared some essential attributes. A few German and Dutch dissenters apart, their stock was solidly British. Their intellectual heroes (a nod to Montesquieu notwithstanding) were from the British tradition: Hobbes and Locke, Smith and Hume. Their language was English; their law was English law; their God an English God.

Wherever on the coast they settled, they had originally had to win the land by back breaking struggle (even in the Carolinas, whose plantations were far bigger than New England farms). Three thousand perilous miles from England, they had all learnt the same self-sufficiency. Most of them, or their fathers, had fought Indians.

And those who did not leave for Canada after the break with Britain had a second thing in common: they had all won their independence from an external power, by force of arms. Their successful war of liberation made them feel more clearly "American" than ever before.

Yet that war had been prosecuted by 13 states, not one; and it did not forge anything that, to modern eyes, looks like a nation-state. Indeed, this absence of unity was made explicit by the articles of confederation, which the 13 states signed in 1781. Article 2 said that the states retained their "sovereignty, freedom and independence." They merely (article 3) entered into a "firm league of friendship with each other."

After only six years, the articles of 1781 were deemed unsatisfactory enough to warrant revision. The result—today's constitution—provided a system of government that was federal in form, but with a much stronger central government than had existed before. So, if Europe wants to learn from America, it had better start with a look at the supposed defects of those articles.

In broad terms, critics of the confederation argued that it was unstable, an awkward half-way house between a collection of independent states and a truly single country. Their criticisms concentrated on two things: economics, in particular the internal market of the 13 states; and foreign policy, the ability of the states to fend off foreign dangers.

Take economics first. The monetary and fiscal policy of the America that had just chucked out the British was chaotic. Congress (the body of delegates that had, so far as possible, directed the war against Britain, and whose position was formalised by the articles) could not pay off its creditors. It had no taxing power, and could only issue "requisitions" (in effect, requests for money) to the states. Some paid; some did not. Some states took over the responsibility for the part of the national debt that was owed to their own citizens, and then paid this in securities they issued themselves. There was a shortage of sound money (coin). Some states issued paper money themselves; much of it soon lost its face value. The currency of one state was not normally legal tender in another.

Tariff policy was a particular bugbear. States with small towns and few ports, such as New Jersey and Connecticut, were at the mercy of big states like Pennsylvania and New York, through whose ports America's imports flowed. Tariffs levied by New York would be paid by consumers in (say) Connecticut; but Connecticut's treasury derived no benefit from these tariffs. In short, the internal barriers to trade were big.

Abroad, the 13 states faced a ring of dangers. Britain still held Canada and a string of forts to the west of the United States. If it wished, it could have encircled the 13 states; its troops burnt Washington in 1812. Spain controlled Florida and—worse—it presided over navigation on the Mississippi.

Americans with a sense of where history was taking them (meaning most Americans of the time) well knew that, in Europe, loose confederations were vulnerable to their enemies. Some members of Congress compared that body to the Polish parliament, whose every member had a veto. The comparison hurt: at that time, Poland was being divided three ways by its enemies. The German confederation, or Holy Roman Empire, was notoriously feeble. It was characterised, said Madison, by "the licentiousness of the strong and the oppression of the weak"—a "nerveless" body "agitated with unceasing fermentation in its bowels."

The Americans decided they wanted calmer bowels and a better circulation. In the Federalist Papers—the collection of essays written by Hamilton, Madison and John Jay after the convention of 1787—Hamilton was to weave together the economic and political arguments. Trade wars between the states, he suggested, would sooner or later turn into shooting wars. Given the lack of unity of the American states, European powers (with their "pernicious labyrinths of politics and wars") would divide and rule. The destiny to which God had pointed America would vanish in the ensuing strife.

That was putting it a bit high. Many historians today argue that, far from being on the edge of economic collapse, the America of 1780s was happy and rich. Peter Aranson of Emory University in Georgia says that, although there was little immigration, the new country's population grew as fast in that decade as at almost any time in American history. No sign of hardship there. Trade wars were ending as the states found ways to reduce or remove the tariffs on goods passing through their territory to another state. Had each state's currency been legal tender elsewhere, good money might sooner or later have driven out bad.

The Three Big Things of 1787

For all that, Hamilton and the others who wanted a stronger central government won the day in Philadelphia. The convention's report was adopted by the states, though not without a few close shaves. And America got the constitution it still has. How has it lasted so long? For three main reasons that should interest today's Europeans.

The first was that the constitution created an executive—the president—where none had existed before. The president embodied a response to those external threats. He was to be the commander-in-chief of the armed forces. Although Congress had the power to declare war (and jealously preserves it), the president, with the advice and consent of the Senate, could conclude treaties and appoint ambassadors. He was to be the instrument of a unified foreign policy. This was made explicit by the constitution's first article, which prohibited any of the states from entering into any treaty, alliance or confederation, and from keeping troops, and from engaging in war unless it was invaded or was in imminent danger.

Second, the constitution was a document of limited powers. It gave to the central government (or so went the theory) only those powers specifically allocated to it. The tenth amendment made plain what Hamilton and Madison though implicit: "The powers not delegated to the United States by the Constitution," it says, "nor prohibited to it by the states, are reserved to the states respectively, or to the people."

Third, the constitution recognised a "judicial power," and established a Supreme Court. The court, among other things, was to have jurisdiction over all cases arising "under the constitution" (and the constitution itself was declared to be "the supreme law of the land"). It also had jurisdiction over disputes between any one of the states and the United States, and between two or more states themselves. Members of the Supreme Court had no date of retirement. In other words, the Supreme Court was to be charged with deciding whether the practice of government conformed with the theory as laid down in the constitution.

How might modern Europeans use the American experience? Those who believe that the European Community is destined to be more than a collection of nation-states—an argument heard since the days of Monnet and Schuman—concentrate on the supposed instability of the original American confederation. Look at the Soviet Union, on the other hand, and you may conclude that that argument cuts the other way. It is the tight union of Stalin and Brezhnev that is unstable; it will survive, if it survives at all, only if it is converted into a much looser confederation.

Western Europe's federalists have a reply. In two respects, they argue, the Community has already learnt the lesson of the American constitution's success. Since the late 1950s the European Court of Justice has arrogated to itself the power to declare acts of member states or of Community institutions to have no effect if they contravene the Treaty of Rome, the EC's founding charter. And the notion of subsidiarity—that decisions in the Community should be taken at the lowest governmental level possible—is a rough-and-ready approximation to the American constitution's commitment to limited powers. Subsidiarity is not, or not yet, a matter of general Community law, but the idea is treated with growing respect.

Moreover, late 20th-century Europeans share the 18th-century American desire to create a single market and remove barriers to internal trade. Here the Americas found it necessary to make the states cede some sovereignty, and to grant the union some powers it had not previously possessed. The states were forbidden to levy their own external tariffs. In the so-called "commerce clause" of the constitution, the federal government was given the exclusive power to "regulate commerce with foreign nations, and among the several states."

In much the same way, Project 1992 is designed to realise the Community's dream of a single market, free of all internal impediments. European federalists would argue that the goal of monetary union is all of a piece with this. If a single trading block has 12 national currencies, the transactions costs of trade will always be higher than if there was but one. Americans at the 1787 convention would have recognised the force of this; the constitution they wrote forbids states to coin their own money. (Still, it was not until 1913 that America established a stable system for guiding national monetary policy.)

But that is not the whole of the American lesson. Those Europeans who doubt whether the American experience of federalism can be applied to Europe will find Americans ready to argue their case for them. One argument of America's own anti-federalists (still around, two centuries later) strikes a particular chord.

America's anti-federalists say the combination of a broad commerce clause and a powerful Supreme Court has been disastrous. It is a simple matter to show that almost anything is a matter of "inter-state commerce." Even if a company does almost all its business within one state, for instance, it may still use the federal postal service. Once interstate commerce has been proved, the central government can easily decide that such commerce is within its regulatory competence. As Mr. Aranson has pointed out, as early as 1870 the Supreme Court held that Congress could insist on the inspection of steamships travelling entirely within the waters of one state, if other vessels on those waters carried goods bound for other states.

According to the anti-federalists, the breadth of the commerce clause means that an activist Supreme Court, given an inch, takes a mile. The power of states to regulate their own affairs has been diminished, and the power of the central government has been allowed to increase excessively.

Non-Americans living in America, wrapped in the red tape of federalism (try working out where to get your car exhaust tested each year if you bought the car in Virginia, live in Maryland and work in the District of Columbia), may think the argument over-done; they usually pray for less power for the individual states, no more. But many Americans still worry about excessive centralisation. So do people on the other side of the Atlantic.

Europeans fearful of being turned into "identikit Europeans," the Margaret Thatcher's phrase, therefore have American allies. Such Europeans will note Mr. Aranson's warning that America's commerce clause "sustains national cartels that cross state boundaries and empower states, often with federal assistance, to cartelise markets." These Europeans suspect that a Community "social charter" will mean all European states sooner or later being required to have the same laws on health and welfare.

The Right to Opt Out

Europe's anti-federalists can draw further succour from America. The part of a future Europe that most Europeans find it hardest to picture clearly is the idea of Europe acting towards the outside world with a united mind, a single will.

Different Europeans, faced with a challenge abroad, can behave in radically different ways. This partly because Europe is still far from being the homogeneous society that America was from the start. Europe is still a place of separate nationalisms, to an extent that America never was; those nationalisms have grown milder in the past half-century, but they have not vanished. Although almost all of Europe suffered the same frightful war 50 years ago, the various Europeans have very different memories of it. And this past year they have displayed very different feelings about such things as standing up to Saddam Hussein, and rebuking Mikhail Gorbachev for reembracing his country's old guard.

This has a direct constitutional implication. Recall how important foreign policy, the threat abroad, was to Madison and Hamilton. They would have considered a union without a single foreign and defence policy to be a nonsense on stilts. So they created a powerful executive, independent of the states, to take control of that policy. Even those Europeans who want a single foreign policy shy away from a European equivalent of the American presidency. Yet without a president, embodying within his person a common will towards the world outside, it is hard to see how Europeans can create what Americans would regard as a federal Europe.

The non-homogeneity, and the hesitation about a European president as powerful as America's, will not necessarily remain as influential as they are today. But one awkward lesson from America is permanent. This is the fact that America did not take its final political shape in 1787; three-quarters of a century later, the founding fathers' structure blew up.

Most non-Americans do not realise how large the civil war of 1861–65 looms in America's collective memory. It killed more than 600,000 people, foreshadowing the efficient slaughter that Europe did not experience until Verdun and the Somme 50 years later. In its last year when the North's armies under Grant and Sherman marched into the South's heartland, it became unbearably brutal. If you are going to have a constitution linking several states that cherish their sovereignty, it is worth making sure in advance that it does not lead to the kind of war America's constitution led to.

Unfair! yell Northern historians, for whom it is an article of faith that the civil war was fought not over a constitutional principle (the right of states to secede from the union) but over a social injustice (slavery). The Northerners have a case, even though—as Southerners never tire of pointing out—the abolition of slavery was not formally an original aim of the war: the fact is that, without slavery, the Southerners would not have wanted to secede. Since Europe's federalists would argue that nothing divides European countries from each other as passionately as slavery divided North and South, they may feel justified in ignoring the terrible warning of the civil war.

They would be wrong. Nobody knows what explosive arguments the future of Europe will bring. Some countries may see relations with Russia as the right centrepiece for Europe's foreign policy; others may put relations with America in that place; still others will focus on the Arab world to Europe's south. Some Europeans may want far more restrictive immigration policies than others, which could lead to some sharp intra-European border tensions. Country X will favour fewer controls on arms sales abroad than Country Y. Europe's capacity to speak and act as one is still almost entirely theoretical. If Europeans are genuinely interested in learning from the American experience, this lesson should be taken to heart: make it clear in advance that, whatever union is to be forged, states can leave it, unhindered, at will.

THE CONSTITUTION

See text p. 42

In The Federalist No. 10, *reprinted as an appendix to the text, James Madison observed that the strength of the new union—the division of its powers between state and federal governments and among different branches at the same level of government—lay in its ability to limit the power of factions, which, he observed, arise naturally where any collection of human beings occurs. The elaborate limiting of powers means, at the same time, that government tends to be fairly cumbersome and exasperatingly slow.*

The two-hundredth anniversary of the Constitution was in 1987. As Americans pondered the meaning of that anniversary, they also thought about whether it was time to overhaul the system; after all, Thomas Jefferson once suggested that a constitution ought to be revised approximately once every twenty years. In the following article from a special issue of the Los Angeles Times *celebrating the Constitution's birthday, com-*

mentator David Lauter reviews some of the arguments that have been made for and against an overhaul of the Constitution.

David Lauter
"We the People: The American Constitution After 200 Years: Celebrating the Nation's Charter as Problem and Solution"*

The traveler wandered the rutted roads from New England south to the Carolinas and rode the mule-drawn canal barges west through the mountains toward the Mississippi, all the while taking notes on the strange young country spread out before him.

When he returned to France, Alexis de Tocqueville wrote in 1835, "I have never been more struck by the good sense and the practical judgment of the Americans than in the manner in which they elude the numberless difficulties resulting from their federal Constitution."

A century-and-a-half later, the nation de Tocqueville viewed in adolescence has grown to adulthood. The Constitution, signed by its framers in Philadelphia on Sept. 17, 1787, is now the oldest written national charter of government in effect anywhere in the world. And Americans are still demonstrating a pragmatic genius for overcoming what de Tocqueville took to be the Constitution's "numberless difficulties."

Americans themselves complain ceaselessly about the inefficiencies and frustrations it entails, from the Fifth Amendment's protection of criminals to the seemingly archaic checks and balances that almost paralyze modern government. Critics of the Constitution yearn for the more streamlined decision making of parliamentary systems in which prime ministers have extraordinary freedom of action and are quickly replaced if they lose popular support.

Why, then, with all the manifest burdens it imposes, has the Constitution been so widely admired and so little changed in 200 years? Why did British Prime Minister William Gladstone declare, in 1878, that "the American Constitution is the most wonderful work ever struck off at a given time by the brain and purpose of man"?

The answer appears to be that the mechanisms designed by the Founding Fathers, while maddeningly slow and cumbersome, have proven remarkably effective at enabling the people of a huge and heterogeneous nation to preserve the pattern of "conflict within consensus" that historians identify as the unique feature of America's politics.

With one terrible exception, the Civil War, the constitutional process has enabled Americans to pass through periods of profound change, to

*David Lauter, "We the People: The American Constitution After 200 Years: Celebrating the Nation's Charter as Problem and Solution," *Los Angeles Times* (September 13, 1987). Reprinted with permission.

disagree, struggle ferociously and sometimes violently over policies, yet ultimately reach decisions that most can support and almost all accept—without plunging into the abyss of fanaticism that has torn and destroyed so many societies.

'Intense Disagreements'

A constitution should "allow very intense disagreements to be handled without violence and without loss of legitimacy" of the nation's institutions, said UC Berkeley political scientist Raymond Wolfinger. By that measure, the Constitution has been a resounding success.

Unlike Marx and other more theoretical political thinkers, the framers of the Constitution started with human nature, which they saw as severely flawed and limited, then tried to design a government that would guarantee "the blessings of liberty" to the maximum extent possible within those limitations. After all, Madison wrote in the Federalist papers, "If men were angels, no government would be necessary. If angels were to govern men, neither external nor internal controls on government would be necessary."

Reinforcing such pragmatism, a tradition of almost-religious veneration has grown up around the Constitution. One 19th-Century President called it the "ark of the people's covenant" and said it must be "shield(ed) . . . from impious hands." Advocates of sundry causes claim the Constitution's support, and tourists line up in droves to see its first and last pages encased in bulletproof glass at the National Archives.

The American lexicon contains few political epithets more powerful than "unconstitutional."

Bending the System

To be sure, this veneration has not eliminated the frustrations inherent in the system. Nor has it always been strong enough to prevent abuses of the rights and values embodied in the Constitution and the Bill of Rights. In race relations particularly, as well as in periods of national crisis and in circumstances when public passions ran out of control, events have occurred that dishonored the Constitution's high ideals.

The importance of those ideals has become so ingrained in the nation's consciousness, however, that the system has shown a remarkable tendency to right itself and return to its intended course.

"Though written constitutions may be violated in moments of passion or delusion, yet they furnish a text to which those who are watchful may again rally and recall the people," Jefferson wrote to a friend in 1802, "they fix too for the people the principles of their political creed."

Within the framework of the Constitution, strong national leaders have tried to bend the system to their will—including Jefferson himself, who entered the White House with a restrictive view of presidential power but pushed his authority to the limit when the opportunity arose in 1803 to make the Louisiana Purchase and double the size of the nation.

Abraham Lincoln suspended portions of the Constitution during the Civil War. Theodore Roosevelt complained that the Constitution "permit(s) one set of people to hoist sails for their own amusement, and another set of people to put down anchors for their own purposes."

"The result from the standpoint of progress has not been happy," he said.

In contemporary times, writers, political scientists and practicing politicians all have advocated overhauls of the Constitution, arguing that the intricate system of checks and balances designed under 18th-Century theory will not do for the practice of the 21st.

Revision of Old Charter

Said political scientist Robert A. Dahl: "I'm increasingly doubtful that the Constitution is functioning really well. . . . I find it hard to engage in this year of celebrating the Constitution as if it were somehow a perfect document."

Indeed, over recent years, 32 states have called for a new Constitutional Convention to revise the old charter, mostly responding to popular frustration with the federal deficit. Two more states joining the call would suffice to bring a convention into being for the first time since the one that ended 200 years ago this week. While no such conventions have been held since the first one, the Constitution has been amended 26 times. The 10 amendments constituting the Bill of Rights were added in 1791, and later amendments introduced such far-reaching changes as ending slavery, creating national guarantees of due process and individual rights, granting women the vote and providing for direct popular election of senators.

Important as such changes have been and wracking as was the history that produced them, all can be seen as extending and intensifying the nation's commitment to the values and ideas underlying the original Constitution and, before it, the Declaration of Independence.

Many factors—including economic, regional and cultural differences—led to the cataclysm of the Civil War, for example. But one of the things that ultimately made a confrontation unavoidable was the inherent contradiction between the institution of slavery and the ideas of equality and fairness implicit in the Constitution.

Though the Founding Fathers had made clear their intention to create a national government superior to the states, they had sidestepped and compromised on what Madison called the "powder keg" of slavery—which many delegates even then saw in starkly moral terms.

In the end, more than 500,000 Americans died—more than in World War I and World War II combined—to meet the issue head-on. Henceforth, no state would have the right to abridge freedoms guaranteed to individuals by the national Constitution, and no institution or practice could stand permanently unchallenged if it contradicted the nation's fundamental values.

What accounts for the relative stability of the American system during two centuries in which the governments of so many other countries were ripped apart and radically changed not once but several times? Scholars point to several factors:

- A nation that seems always in the midst of rapid change in its social rules and economic relationships has been correspondingly conservative in changing the political framework within which those changes occur.
- A people who concentrate in overwhelming numbers on the pragmatic and immediate problems of their private lives have been highly resistant to the fanatical approaches to politics and religion that have shattered other societies. "The great middle-of-road-consensus impulse of Americans," one historian called it.

Indeed, American politics has tended to become most turbulent when large numbers of people believed that their personal lives—and hopes for the future—were threatened.

- A society that lacked an established church, a native aristocracy and a universal culture has clung to the Constitution as a symbol of unity.

"The Constitution has been to us what a king has often been to other nationalities," Harvard President A. Lawrence Lowell said in 1886.

The Constitution, of course, can neither be credited with all that has gone well in American history nor blamed for all failures. "There are other things in society" that help determine the fates of government and that can overwhelm even the most flexible of constitutions, as shown by the experience of numerous Latin American nations, political scientist Wolfinger pointed out.

Isolated Country

America has been both wealthy and physically isolated. The nation's wealth—natural resources, abundant land and salubrious climate—tended to reduce social conflict by holding out the hope of improving standards of living for most citizens most of the time. Politics in America has most often—though not always—been fought out on a relatively narrow middle ground of shared assumptions, values and symbols, lacking the intense, class-based politics that in France, for example, have caused three revolutions and nine different systems in the last 200 years.

U.S. institutions also have been free to develop without the distortions caused by fear of external enemies.

The importance of such natural advantages cannot be underestimated: Even with them, World War I, which brought widespread jailing of socialists and pacifists, World War II, with its internment of Japanese-Americans, and the McCarthy-era assaults on civil liberties in the 1950s all hinted at how fragile constitutional liberties can be when war or other threats convulse a nation.

At the same time, the nation's wealth and size have posed unusual problems for the constitutional system. When the Constitution was written, many doubted that a republic could survive except in a geographically small unit.

In devising a system for a nation of continental proportions, "what's at stake is the difference between trying to turn the Queen Mary around and trying to turn a rowboat," UC Berkeley political scientist Nelson W. Polsby said.

The image of the Queen Mary is exactly what most of the Constitution's current critics seize on. Just like an ocean liner, they claim, the constitutional system is simply too slow to respond to the accelerating pace of life in the age of instant global communications, instant food and instant nuclear annihilation.

The system has been strained still further, many political scientists say, by the decline of effective political parties, which helped for many years to knit Presidents and Congress together and thereby counterbalance the system's tendency toward fractionation.

For all those reasons, "the fragmentation of power institutionalized in the system of checks and balances poses very severe questions for the constitutional system," political scientist James McGregor Burns said.

Source of Stability

But the separation of powers, the inefficiency that so often makes government cumbersome, may, in fact, have been the greatest source of the Constitution's stability.

"Most of the founders believed the idea that, given power, men would abuse it," Degler said. Because of that belief, the governmental structure was built for distance, not for speed. To the Founding Fathers, a government that could handle day-to-day problems easily was less important than a government that could assure freedom and stability to generation after generation.

"Democratical states must always feel before they can see," George Washington wrote in 1785 to his Revolutionary War aide, the Marquis de Lafayette. "It is this that makes their governments slow, but the people will be right at last."

"The heterogeneity of the nation demands that we pay attention to the opinions of others," Polsby said. "It's a strength of our Constitution that a consensus is necessary to do large things."

The relationship between the Constitution and periods of national crisis has illustrated that point from the beginning.

While some states ratified the new charter quickly, in others the debates were long and arduous.

New Consensus

The unusual aspect of the debate, however, is that once it ended, so did serious opposition to the Constitution. Through the process of debate, a new consensus had been formed, and even those who had so strongly opposed the Constitution decided to accept it.

A more drawn-out, sometimes brutal process of consensus building centered on the nation's attempts, beginning in the late 19th Century, to strengthen the rights and protect the welfare of individuals by bridling the powers of massive corporations and their owners—"the malefactors of great wealth," as President Theodore Roosevelt called them.

As the Industrial Revolution transformed a country of villages, farms and small businesses into a nation of cities and giant factories, wrenching struggles took place—marked by political radicalism, riots, bloody confrontations, even anarchists' bombs.

Yet the period illustrates the way the system works for long-term stability, even at the price of near-term upheaval.

Over time, Congress and Presidents responded to the rising demand for economic and social reform; new laws were passed providing for collective bargaining of labor contracts, regulations of wages and hours, restrictions on child labor and similar reforms.

The establishment of an oversight role for the federal government in the realm of economics and commerce represented a dramatic change. Few nations have so fundamentally changed their economic systems except in a revolution or the aftermath of a war.

Universal Problems

"The underlying problems faced by human communities everywhere have to do with the intractable primordial differences that people have over race, religion and language," Berkeley's Polsby said.

"Religion was something they (the authors of the Constitution) solved right at the beginning," language has never yet become the serious social division for the United States that it is, for example, in Canada, and, he said, "we're on the road to doing something meaningful about race."

The Constitution no doubt will face challenges in the next 200 years, but having handled those three "primordial differences," perhaps it will continue to justify the boast of 19th-Century orator Sen. Henry Clay of Kentucky: "The Constitution of the United States was made not merely for the generation that then existed, but for posterity—unlimited, undefined, endless, perpetual posterity."

Debating the Issues: Opposing Views

THE CONSTITUTION: PROPERTY VERSUS PRAGMATISM

See text p. 36–37

Despite the deference accorded to it today, the instrument drafted at the Constitutional Convention of 1787 did not command instant respect. The fight for ratification was bitter; as discussed later in the text, many were suspicious of the powers being vested in a national government.

The Federalist Papers, *several of which are reprinted throughout these readings, are the most valuable exposition of the political theory of the Constitution available today. Written by Alexander Hamilton, James Madison, and John Jay, they contain a detailed exposition of the arguments used to justify the new Constitution. They do not represent, however, a necessarily balanced view of the various arguments for and against the Constitution; they were written as political propaganda to convince readers to support the new system. In* The Federalist No. 15, *reprinted below, Alexander Hamilton is at his best arguing for the necessity of a stronger central government than that established under the Articles of Confederation, pointing out the practical impossibility of engaging in concerted action when each of the thirteen states retains virtual sovereignty.*

Opposed to the Federalists were such well-known patriots as Patrick Henry, whose speech to the Virginia ratifying convention is reprinted below. Henry warned that the new Constitution was being pushed too quickly on the people, and that it was destined to "ruin and oppress" them. The part of his speech excerpted here outlines his concerns that there would be no effective checks on the power of federal officers and institutions.

Alexander Hamilton
*The Federalist No. 15**

In the course of the preceding papers I have endeavored, my fellow-citizens, to place before you in a clear and convincing light the importance of Union to your political safety and happiness. . . . [T]he point next in order to be examined is the "insufficiency of the present Confederation to the preservation of the Union." . . . There are material imperfections in our national system and . . . something is necessary to be done to rescue us from impending anarchy. The facts that support this opinion are no longer objects of speculation. They have forced themselves upon the sensibility of the people at large, and have at length extorted . . . a reluctant confession of the reality of those defects in the scheme of our federal government which have been long pointed out and regretted by the intelligent friends of the Union. . . .

We may indeed with propriety be said to have reached almost the last

*Alexander Hamilton, *The Federalist No. 15*, ed. Clinton Rossiter (New York: NAL, 1961).

stage of national humiliation. There is scarcely anything that can wound the pride or degrade the character of an independent nation which we do not experience. Are there engagements to the performance of which we are held by every tie respectable among men? These are the subjects of constant and unblushing violation. Do we owe debts to foreigners and to our own citizens contracted in a time of imminent peril for the preservation of our political existence? These remain without any proper or satisfactory provision for their discharge. . . . Are we in a condition to resent or to repel the aggression? We have neither troops, nor treasury, nor government. . . . Is public credit an indispensable resource in time of public danger? We seem to have abandoned its cause as desperate and irretrievable. Is commerce of importance to national wealth? Ours is at the lowest point of declension. Is respectability in the eyes of foreign powers a safeguard against foreign encroachments? The imbecility of our government even forbids them to treat with us. . . . Is private credit the friend and patron of industry? That most useful kind which relates to borrowing and lending is reduced within the narrowest limits, and this still more from an opinion of insecurity than from a scarcity of money. . . .

This is the melancholy situation to which we have been brought by those very maxims and counsels which would now deter us from adopting the proposed Constitution; and which, not content with having conducted us to the brink of a precipice, seem resolved to plunge us into the abyss that awaits us below. Here, my countrymen, impelled by every motive that ought to influence an enlightened people, let us make a firm stand for our safety, our tranquillity, our dignity, our reputation. Let us at last break the fatal charm which has too long seduced us from the paths of felicity and prosperity.

. . . While [opponents of the Constitution] admit that the government of the United States is destitute of energy, they contend against conferring upon it those powers which are requisite to supply that energy. . . . This renders a full display of the principal defects of the Confederation necessary in order to show that the evils we experience do not proceed from minute or partial imperfections, but from fundamental errors in the structure of the building, which cannot be amended otherwise than by an alteration in the first principles and main pillars of the fabric.

The great and radical vice in the construction of the existing Confederation is in the principle of LEGISLATION for STATES or GOVERNMENTS, in their CORPORATE or COLLECTIVE CAPACITIES, and as contradistinguished from the INDIVIDUALS of whom they consist. Though this principle does not run through all the powers delegated to the Union, yet it pervades and governs those on which the efficacy of the rest depends. Except as to the rule of apportionment, the United States have an indefinite discretion to make requisitions for men and money; but they have no authority to raise either by regulations extending to the individual citizens of America. The consequence of this is that though in theory their resolutions concerning those objects are laws constitutionally binding on the members of the Union, yet in practice they are mere recommendations which the States observe or disregard at their option. . . .

There is nothing absurd or impracticable in the idea of a league or alliance between independent nations for certain defined purposes precisely stated in a treaty regulating all the details of time, place, circumstance, and quantity, leaving nothing to future discretion, and depending for its execution on the good faith of the parties. . . .

If the particular States in this country are disposed to stand in a similar relation to each other, and to drop the project of a general DISCRETIONARY SUPERINTENDENCE, the scheme would indeed be pernicious and would entail upon us all the mischiefs which have been enumerated under the first head; but it would have the merit of being, at least, consistent and practicable. Abandoning all views towards a confederate government, this would bring us to a simple alliance offensive and defensive; and would place us in a situation to be alternate friends and enemies of each other, as our mutual jealousies and rivalships, nourished by the intrigues of foreign nations, should prescribe to us.

But if we are unwilling to be placed in this perilous situation; if we still will adhere to the design of a national government, or, which is the same thing, of a superintending power under the direction of a common council, we must resolve to incorporate into our plan those ingredients which may be considered as forming the characteristic difference between a league and a government; we must extend the authority of the Union to the persons of the citizens—the only proper objects of government.

Government implies the power of making laws. It is essential to the idea of a law that it be attended with a sanction; or, in other words, a penalty or punishment for disobedience. If there be no penalty annexed to disobedience, the resolutions or commands which pretend to be laws will, in fact, amount to nothing more than advice or recommendation. This penalty, whatever it may be, can only be inflicted in two ways: by the agency of the courts and ministers of justice, or by military force; by the COERCION of the magistracy, or by the COERCION of arms. The first kind can evidently apply only to men; the last kind must of necessity be employed against bodies politic, or communities, or States. . . . In an association where the general authority is confined to the collective bodies of the communities that compose it, every breach of the laws must involve a state of war; and military execution must become the only instrument of civil obedience. Such a state of things can certainly not deserve the name of government, nor would any prudent man choose to commit his happiness to it.

There was a time when we were told that breaches by the States of the regulations of the federal authority were not to be expected; that a sense of common interest would preside over the conduct of the respective members, and would beget a full compliance with all the constitutional requisitions of the Union. This language, at the present day, would appear as wild as a great part of what we now hear from the same quarter will be thought, when we shall have received further lessons from that best oracle of wisdom, experience. It at all times betrayed an ignorance of the true springs by which human conduct is actuated, and belied the original inducements to the establishment of civil power. Why has government been instituted at all?

Because the passions of men will not conform to the dictates of reason and justice without constraint. . . .

In addition to all this . . . it happens that in every political association which is formed upon the principle of uniting in a common interest a number of lesser sovereignties, there will be found a kind of eccentric tendency in the subordinate or inferior orbs by the operation of which there will be a perpetual effort in each to fly off from the common center. This tendency is not difficult to be accounted for. It has its origin in the love of power. Power controlled or abridged is almost always the rival and enemy of that power by which it is controlled or abridged. This simple proposition will teach us how little reason there is to expect that the persons intrusted with the administration of the affairs of the particular members of a confederacy will at all times be ready with perfect good humor and an unbiased regard to the public weal to execute the resolutions or decrees of the general authority. . . .

If, therefore, the measures of the Confederacy cannot be executed without the intervention of the particular administrations, there will be little prospect of their being executed at all. . . . [Each state will evaluate every federal measure in light of its own interests] and in a spirit of interested and suspicious scrutiny, without that knowledge of national circumstances and reasons of state, which is essential to a right judgment, and with that strong predilection in favor of local objects, which can hardly fail to mislead the decision. The same process must be repeated in every member of which the body is constituted; and the execution of the plans, framed by the councils of the whole, will always fluctuate on the discretion of the ill-informed and prejudiced opinion of every part. . . .

In our case the concurrence of thirteen distinct sovereign wills is requisite under the Confederation to the complete execution of every important measure that proceeds from the Union. It has happened as was to have been foreseen. The measures of the Union have not been executed; and the delinquencies of the States have step by step matured themselves to an extreme, which has, at length, arrested all the wheels of the national government and brought them to an awful stand. Congress at this time scarcely possess the means of keeping up the forms of administration, till the States can have time to agree upon a more substantial substitute for the present shadow of a federal government. . . . Each State yielding to the persuasive voice of immediate interest or convenience has successively withdrawn its support, till the frail and tottering edifice seems ready to fall upon our heads and to crush us beneath its ruins.

PUBLIUS

Patrick Henry
Speech at Virginia Ratifying Convention (June 9, 1788)*

. . . A number of characters of the greatest eminence in this country, object to this Government, for its consolidating tendency. This is not imaginary. It is a formidable reality. If consolidation proves to be as mischievous to this country, as it has been to other countries, what will the poor inhabitants of this country do? This Government will operate like an ambuscade. It will destroy the State Governments, and swallow the liberties of the people, without giving them previous notice. . . . Sir, I ask you, and every other Gentleman who hears me, if he can retain his indignation, at a system, which takes from the State Legislatures the care and preservation of the interests of the people; 180 Representatives, the choice of the people of Virginia cannot be trusted with their interests. . . . So degrading an indignity—so flagrant an out-rage to the States—so vile a suspicion is humiliating to my mind, and many others.

Will the adoption of this new plan pay our debts? This, Sir, is a plain question. It is inferred, that our grievances are to be redressed, and the evils of the existing system to be removed by the new Constitution. Let me inform the Honorable Gentleman, that no nation ever paid its debts by a change of Government, without the aid of industry. You never will pay your debts but by a radical change of domestic economy. At present you buy too much, and make too little to pay. Will this new system promote manufactures, industry and frugality? If instead of this, your hopes and designs will be disappointed; you relinquish a great deal, and hazard infinitely more, for nothing. Will it enhance the value of your lands? Will it lessen your burthens? Will your looms and wheels go to work by the act of adoption? If it will in its consequence produce these things, it will consequently produce a reform, and enable you to pay your debts. . . . I am a sceptic—an infidel on this point. . . . The evils that attend us, lie in extravagance and want of industry, and can only be removed by assiduity and economy. Perhaps we shall be told by Gentlemen, that these things will happen, because the administration is to be taken from us, and placed in the hands of the luminous few, who will pay different attention, and be more studiously careful than we can be supposed to be. . . .

[W]e can live happily without changing our present despised Government. Cannot people be as happy under a mild, as under an energetic Government? Cannot content and felicity be enjoyed in a republic, as well as in a monarchy, because there are whips, chains and scourges used in the latter? If I am not as rich as my neighbour, if I give my mite—my all—

*Patrick Henry, "Speech at Virginia Ratifying Convention," in *The Anti-Federalist,* Herbert Storing, ed., an abridgement by Murray Dry (Chicago: Chicago University Press, 1985).

republican forbearance will say, that it is sufficient. . . . For better will it be for us to continue as we are, than go under that tight energetic Government.—I am persuaded of what the Honorable Gentleman says, that separate confederacies will ruin us. In my judgment, they are evils never to be thought of till a people are driven by necessity.—When he asks my opinion of consolidation—of one power to reign over America, with a strong hand; I will tell him, I am persuaded, of the rectitude of my honorable friend's opinion (Mr. *Mason*) that one Government cannot reign over so extensive a country as this is, without absolute despotism. Compared to such a consolidation, small Confederacies are little evils; though they ought to be recurred to, but in case of necessity. . . .

When we come to the spirit of domestic peace—The humble genius of Virginia has formed a Government, suitable to the genius of her people. I believe the hands that formed the American Constitution triumph in the experiment. . . . After all your reforms in Government, unless you consult the genius of the inhabitants, you will never succeed—your system can have no duration. . . . On this awful occasion [of the Revolution] did you want a Federal Government? Did federal ideas possess your minds? Did federal ideas lead you to the most splendid victories? I must again repeat the favorite idea, that the genius of Virginia did, and will again lead us to happiness. To obtain the most splendid prize, you did not consolidate. You accomplished the most glorious ends, by the assistance of the genius of your country. Men were then taught by that genius, that they were fighting for what was most dear to them. . . . Among all our troubles we have paid almost to the last shilling, for the sake of justice. We have paid as well as any State: I will not say better. To support the General Government, our own Legislature, to pay the interest of the public debts, and defray contingencies, we have been heavily taxed. To add to these things, the distresses produced by paper money, and by tobacco contracts, were sufficient to render any people discontented. These, Sir, were great temptations; but in the most severe conflict of misfortunes, this code of laws—this genius of Virginia, call it what you will, triumphed over every thing.

Some here speak of the difficulty in forming a new code of laws. Young as we were, it was not wonderful if there was a difficulty in forming and assimilating one system of laws. . . . My worthy friend said, that a republican form of Government would not suit a very extensive country; but that if a Government were judiciously organized and limits prescribed to it; an attention to these principles might render it possible for it to exist in an extensive territory. Whoever will be bold to say, that a Continent can be governed by that system, contradicts all the experience of the world. It is a work too great for human wisdom. Let me call for an example. Experience has been called the best teacher. I call for an example of a great extent of country, governed by one Government, or Congress, call it what you will. I tell him, that a Government may be trimmed up according to Gentlemen's fancy, but it never can operate—it will be but very short-lived. . . . I beseech Gentlemen to consider, whether they can say, when trusting power, that a mere patriotic profession will be equally operative and efficatious, as the check of self-love.

In considering the experience of ages, is it not seen, that fair disinterested patriotism, and professed attachment to rectitude have never been solely trusted to by an enlightened free people?—If you depend on your President's and Senators patriotism, you are gone. . . . A good President, or Senator, or Representative, will have a natural weakness.—Virtue will slumber. The wicked will be continually watching: Consequently you will be undone. . . . In this system, there are only ideal balances. Till I am convinced that there are actual efficient checks, I will not give my assent to its establishment. The President and Senators have nothing to lose. . . . What powerful check is there here to prevent the most extravagant and profligate squandering of the public money? What security have we in money matters? Enquiry is precluded by this Constitution. I never wish to see Congress supplicate the States. But it is more abhorent to my mind to give them an unlimited and unbounded command over our souls—our lives—our purses, without any check or restraint. How are you to keep enquiry alive? How discover their conduct? We are told by that paper, that a regular statement and account of the receipts and expenditures of all public money, shall be published from time to time. Here is a beautiful check! What time? Here is the utmost latitude left. If those who are in Congress please to put that construction upon it, the words of the Constitution will be satisfied by publishing those accounts once in 100 years. They may publish or not as they please. Is this like the present despised system, whereby the accounts are to be published monthly?

The power of direct taxation was called by the Honorable Gentlemen the soul of the Government: Another Gentleman, called it the lungs of the Government. We all agree, that it is the most important part of the body politic. If the power of raising money be necessary for the General Government, it is no less so for the States. If money be the vitals of Congress, is it not precious for those individuals from whom it is to be taken? Must I give my soul—my lungs, to Congress? Congress must have our souls. The State must have our souls. This is dishonorable and disgraceful. These two coordinate, interferring unlimited powers of harassing the community, is unexampled: It is unprecedented in history: They are the visionary projects of modern politicians: Tell me not of imaginary means, but of reality; This political solecism will never tend to the benefit of the community. It will be as oppressive in practice as it is absurd in theory. . . . I tell you, they shall not have the soul of Virginia. They tell us, that one collector may collect the Federal and State taxes. The General Government being paramount to the State Legislatures; if the Sheriff is to collect for both; his right hand for the Congress, his left for the State; his right hand being paramount over the left, his collections will go to Congress. We will have the rest. Deficiencies in collections will always operate against the States. Congress being the paramount supreme power, must not be disappointed. Thus Congress will have an unlimited, unbounded command over the soul of this Commonwealth. After satisfying their uncontrolled demands, what can be left for the States? Not a sufficiency even to defray the expense of their internal administration. They must therefore glide imperceptibly and gradually out of existence.

This, Sir, must naturally terminate in a consolidation. If this will do for other people, it never will do for me.

. . . I shall be told in this place, that those who are to tax us are our Representatives. To this I answer, that there is no real check to prevent their ruining us. There is no actual responsibility. The only semblance of a check is the negative power of not re-electing them. This, Sir, is but a feeble barrier when their personal interest, their ambition and avarice come to be put in contrast with the happiness of the people. All checks founded on any thing but self-love, will not avail. This constitution reflects in the most degrading and mortifying manner on the virtue, integrity, and wisdom of the State Legislatures: It presupposes that the chosen few who go to Congress will have more upright hearts, and more enlightened minds, than those who are members of the individual Legislatures. To suppose that ten Gentlemen shall have more real substantial merit, than 170 [members of the Virginia legislature] is humiliating to the last degree. . . .

Congress by the power of taxation—by that of raising an army, and by their control over the militia, have the sword in one hand, and the purse in the other. Shall we be safe without either? Congress have an unlimited power over both: They are entirely given up by us. Let him candidly tell me, where and when did freedom exist, when the sword and purse were given up from the people? Unless a miracle in human affairs interposed, no nation ever retained its liberty after the loss of the sword and purse. Can you prove by any argumentative deduction, that it is possible to be safe without retaining one of these? If you give them up you are gone.

QUESTIONS

1. Edmund Burke suggests that British policy toward the colonies should be guided by an understanding of the "temper and character" of America. How does he characterize that character and temperament?
2. The article from *The Economist* suggests that the federal system created in the colonies cannot be transplanted wholesale into Europe to facilitate the creation of an integrated economic community. What lessons does the article suggest that European Antifederalists might learn from examining American history?
3. What does David Lauter mean when he argues that the American constitutional system has allowed "the people of a huge and heterogenous nation to preserve [a unique] pattern of 'conflict within consensus' "?
4. For what reasons does Alexander Hamilton assert that the confederation of states is insufficient to preserve the union? What obstacles to cooperation does he claim are built into the framework of the confederation?
5. What is the value of the confederation of states, according to Patrick Henry? What dangers does he see in erecting a centralized national government?

CHAPTER 3

The Constitutional Framework: Federalism and the Separation of Powers

THE FEDERAL FRAMEWORK

See text p. 61

The federal structure of the American government has become increasingly difficult to discern as the powers of the national government have expanded in the last half century. Nonetheless, as the text points out, the concept of federalism lies at the heart of the American political system. The degree to which the states retained sovereign authority over matters affecting the welfare of their own citizens was, in fact, the key issue in the debates over the ratification of the Constitution.

In The Federalist No. 39, *James Madison conceded that the new Union would not be wholly federal in character, but would be a mixed system. In some respects, the new government would be national, exercising its powers directly on people in their individual capacities, while in other—and more important—respects its operation would be federal, since it was a government of limited authority, leaving "a residuary and inviolable sovereignty over all other objects" to the states. Madison argued that this combination of operations and functions would create the strength and flexibility required in the new government.*

But the very specter of national powers disturbed many who feared encroachment on state sovereignty. In The Federalist No. 46, *reprinted here, Madison went to great lengths to reassure the states that they would continue to wield a high degree of power, arguing that "the first and most natural attachment of the people will be to the governments of their respective states." While recognizing the potential for conflicts between state and federal governments, Madison concluded that the large measure of power retained by the states would be sufficient to overcome any efforts to usurp that power by the newly established national government.*

James Madison
*The Federalist No. 46**

I proceed to inquire whether the federal government or the State governments will have the advantage with regard to the predilection and support of the people. Notwithstanding the different modes in which they are appointed, we must consider both of them as substantially dependent on the

*James Madison, *The Federalist No. 46,* ed. Clinton Rossiter (New York: NAL, 1961).

great body of the citizens of the United States. . . . The federal and State governments are in fact but different agents and trustees of the people, constituted with different powers and designed for different purposes. The adversaries of the Constitution seem to have lost sight of the people altogether in their reasonings on this subject; and to have viewed these different establishments not only as mutual rivals and enemies, but as uncontrolled by any common superior in their efforts to usurp the authorities of each other. These gentlemen must here be reminded of their error. They must be told that the ultimate authority, wherever the derivative may be found, resides in the people alone, and that it will not depend merely on the comparative ambition or address of the different governments whether either, or which of them, will be able to enlarge its sphere of jurisdiction at the expense of the other. Truth, no less than decency, requires that the event in every case should be supposed to depend on the sentiments and sanction of their common constituents.

Many considerations . . . seem to place it beyond doubt that the first and most natural attachment of the people will be to the governments of their respective States. Into the administration of these a greater number of individuals will expect to rise. From the gift of these a greater number of offices and emoluments will flow. By the superintending care of these, all the more domestic and personal interests of the people will be regulated and provided for. With the affairs of these, the people will be more familiarly and minutely conversant. And with the members of these will a greater proportion of the people have the ties of personal acquaintance and friendship, and of family and party attachments; on the side of these, therefore, the popular bias may well be expected most strongly to incline.

The remaining points on which I propose to compare the federal and State governments are the disposition and the faculty they may respectively possess to resist and frustrate the measures of each other.

It has been already proved that the members of the federal will be more dependent on the members of the State governments than the latter will be on the former. It has appeared also that the prepossessions of the people, on whom both will depend, will be more on the side of the State governments than of the federal government. So far as the disposition of each towards the other may be influenced by these causes, the State governments must clearly have the advantage. But in a distinct and very important point of view, the advantage will lie on the same side. The prepossessions, which the members themselves will carry into the federal government, will generally be favorable to the States; whilst it will rarely happen that the members of the State governments will carry into the public councils a bias in favor of the general government. A local spirit will infallibly prevail much more in the members of Congress than a national spirit will prevail in the legislatures of the particular States.

. . . What is the spirit that has in general characterized the proceedings of Congress? A perusal of their journals, as well as the candid acknowledgments of such as have had a seat in that assembly, will inform us that the members have but too frequently displayed the character rather of partisans of their respective States than of impartial guardians of a common interest; that where on one occasion improper sacrifices have been made of local considerations to the aggrandizement of the federal government, the great interests of the nation have suffered on a hundred from an undue attention to the local prejudices, interests, and views of the particular States. I mean not by these reflections to insinuate that the new federal government will not embrace a more enlarged plan of policy than the existing government may have pursued; much less that its views will be as confined as those of the State legislatures; but only that it will partake sufficiently of the spirit of both to be disinclined to invade the rights of the individual States, or the prerogatives of their governments.

Were it admitted, however, that the federal government may feel an equal disposition with the State governments to extend its power beyond the due limits, the latter would still have the advantage in the means of defeating such encroachments. If an act of a particular State, though unfriendly to the national government, be generally popular in that State, and should not too grossly violate the oaths of the State officers, it is executed immediately and, of course, by means on the spot and depending on the State alone. The opposition of the federal government, or the interposition of federal officers, would but inflame the zeal of all parties on the side of the State, and the evil could not be prevented or repaired, if at all, without the employment of means which must always be resorted to with reluctance and difficulty. On the other hand, should an unwarrantable measure of the federal government be unpopular in particular States, which would seldom fail to be the case, or even a warrantable measure be so, which may sometimes be the case, the means of opposition to it are powerful and at hand. The disquietude of the people; their repugnance and, perhaps, refusal to co-operate with the officers of the Union; the frowns of the executive magistracy of the State; the embarrassments created by legislative devices, which would often be added on such occasions, would oppose, in any State, difficulties not to be despised; would form, in a large State, very serious impediments; and where the sentiments of several adjoining States happened to be in unison, would present obstructions which the federal government would hardly be willing to encounter.

But ambitious encroachments of the federal government on the authority of the State governments would not excite the opposition of a single State, or of a few States only. They would be signals of general alarm. Every government would espouse the common cause. A correspondence would be opened. Plans of resistance would be concerted. One spirit would animate and conduct the whole. The same combinations, in short, would result from an apprehension of the federal, as was produced by the dread of a foreign, yoke; and unless the projected innovations should be voluntarily renounced, the same appeal to a trial of force would be made in the one case as was made in the other.

The only refuge left for those who prophesy the downfall of the State governments is the visionary supposition that the federal government may previously accumulate a military force for the projects of ambition. The reasonings contained in these papers must have been employed to little purpose indeed, if it could be necessary now to disprove the reality of this danger. That the people and the States should, for a sufficient period of time, elect an uninterrupted succession of men ready to betray both; that the traitors should, throughout this period, uniformly and systematically pursue some fixed plan for the extension of the military establishment; that the governments and the people of the States should silently and patiently behold the gathering storm and continue to supply the materials until it should be prepared to burst on their own heads must appear to everyone more like the incoherent dreams of a delirious jealousy, or the misjudged exaggerations of a counterfeit zeal, than like the sober apprehensions of genuine patriotism. Extravagant as the supposition is, let it, however, be made. Let a regular army, fully equal to the resources of the country, be formed; and let it be entirely at the devotion of the federal government: still it would not be going too far to say that the State governments with the people on their side would be able to repel the danger.

Besides the advantage of being armed, which the Americans possess over the people of almost every other nation, the existence of subordinate governments, to which the people are attached and by which the militia officers are appointed, forms a barrier against the enterprises of ambition, more insurmountable than any which a simple government of any form can admit of.

Let us not insult the free and gallant citizens of America with the suspicion that they would be less able to defend the rights of which they would be in actual possession than the debased subjects of arbitrary power would be to rescue theirs from the hands of their oppressors. Let us rather no longer insult them with the supposition that they can ever reduce themselves to the necessity of making the experiment by a blind and tame submission to the long train of insidious measures which must precede and produce it.

The argument under the present head may be put into a very concise form, which appears altogether conclusive. Either the mode in which the federal government is to be constructed will render it sufficiently dependent on the people, or it will not. On the first supposition, it will be restrained by that dependence from forming schemes obnoxious to their constituents. On the other supposition, it will not possess the confidence of the people, and its schemes of usurpation will be easily defeated by the State governments, who will be supported by the people.

On summing up the considerations stated in this and the last paper, they seem to amount to the most convincing evidence that the powers proposed to be lodged in the federal government are as little formidable to those reserved to the individual States as they are indispensably necessary to accomplish the purposes of the Union; and that all those alarms which have been sounded of a meditated and consequential annihilation of the State governments must, on the most favorable interpretation, be ascribed to the chimerical fears of the authors of them.

PUBLIUS

See text p. 67

As the text points out, early in the nation's history, the United States Supreme Court interpreted the powers of the national government expansively. The first Supreme Court case to directly address the scope of federal authority under the Constitution was McCulloch v. Maryland *(1819). The facts, recited in the text, were straightforward: Congress created the Bank of the United States—to the dismay of many states who viewed the creation of a national bank as a threat to the operation of banks within their own state borders. As a result, when a branch of the Bank of the United States was opened in Maryland, that state attempted to limit the bank's ability to do business under a law that imposed taxes on all banks not chartered by the state.*

In an opinion authored by Chief Justice Marshall, the Court considered two questions: whether Congress had the authority to create a national bank; and whether Maryland could in turn tax it. Marshall's answer to these two questions defends an expansive theory of implied powers for the national government and propounds the principle of national supremacy with an eloquence rarely found in judicial decisions.

McCulloch v. *Maryland* (1819)*

CHIEF JUSTICE JOHN MARSHALL delivered the opinion of the Court.

The first question made in the cause is, has Congress power to incorporate a bank? The power now contested was exercised by the first Congress elected under the present constitution. The bill for incorporating the Bank of the United States did not steal upon an unsuspecting legislature, and pass unobserved. Its principle was completely understood, and was opposed with equal zeal and ability. . . . In discussing this question, the counsel for the state of Maryland have deemed it of some importance, in the construction of the constitution, to consider that instrument not as emanating from the people, but as the act of sovereign and independent states. The powers of the general government, it has been said, are delegated by the states, who alone are truly sovereign; and must be exercised in subordination to the states, who alone possess supreme dominion. . . . No political dreamer was ever wild enough to think of breaking down the lines which separate the states, and of compounding the American people into one common mass. Of consequence, when they act, they act in their states. But the measures they adopt do not, on that account, cease to be the measures of the people themselves, or become the measures of the state governments.

From these conventions the constitution derives its whole authority. The government proceeds directly from the people; is "ordained and established" in the name of the people; and is declared to be ordained, "in order to form a more perfect union, establish justice, insure domestic tranquility, and secure the blessings of liberty to themselves and to their posterity." The assent of the states, in their sovereign capacity, is implied in calling a

*McCulloch v. Maryland, 17 U.S. 316, 1819.

convention, and thus submitting that instrument to the people. But the people were at perfect liberty to accept or reject it; and their act was final. It required not the affirmance, and could not be negatived, by the state governments. The constitution, when thus adopted, was of complete obligation, and bound the state sovereignties.

The government of the Union, then (whatever may be the influence of this fact on the case), is, emphatically, and truly, a government of the people. In form and in substance it emanates from them. Its powers are granted by them, and are to be exercised directly on them, and for their benefit.

This government is acknowledged by all to be one of enumerated powers. The principle, that it can exercise only the powers granted to it, is now universally admitted. But the question respecting the extent of the powers actually granted, is perpetually arising, and will probably continue to arise, as long as our system shall exist. The government of the United States though limited in its powers, is supreme; and its laws, when made in pursuance of the constitution, form the supreme law of the land, "anything in the constitution or laws of any state to the contrary notwithstanding." . . .

A constitution, to contain an accurate detail of all the subdivisions of which its great powers will admit, and of all the means by which they may be carried into execution, would partake of the prolixity of a legal code, and could scarcely be embraced by the human mind. It would probably never be understood by the public. Its nature, therefore, requires, that only its great outlines should be marked, its important objects designated, and the minor ingredients which compose those objects be deduced from the nature of the objects themselves. . . . in considering this question, then, we must never forget, that it is a constitution we are expounding.

Although, among the enumerated powers of government, we do not find the word "bank" or "incorporation," we find the great powers to lay and collect taxes; to borrow money; to regulate commerce; to declare and conduct a war; and to raise and support armies and navies. The sword and the purse, all the external relations, and no inconsiderable portion of the industry of the nation, are entrusted to its government. . . . [I]t may with great reason be contended, that a government, entrusted with such ample powers, on the due execution of which the happiness and prosperity of the nation so vitally depends, must also be entrusted with ample means for their execution. The power being given, it is the interest of the nation to facilitate its execution. It can never be their interest, and cannot be presumed to have been their intention, to clog and embarrass its execution by withholding the most appropriate means. . . . It is, then, the subject of fair inquiry, how far such means may be employed.

The government which has a right to do an act, and has imposed on it the duty of performing that act, must, according to the dictates of reason, be allowed to select the means. . . .

But the constitution of the United States has not left the right of Congress to employ the necessary means, for the execution of the powers conferred on the government, to general reasoning. To its enumeration of powers is added that of making "all laws which shall be necessary and proper, for carrying into execution the foregoing powers, and all other powers vested by this constitution, in the government of the United States, or in any department [or officer] thereof."

The counsel for the state of Maryland have urged various arguments, to prove that this clause . . . is really restrictive of the general right, which might otherwise be implied, of selecting means for executing the enumerated powers.

. . . [Maryland argues that] Congress is not empowered by it to make all laws, which may have relation to the powers conferred on the government, but such only as may be "necessary and proper" for carrying them into execution. The word "necessary" is considered as controlling the whole sentence, and as limiting the right to pass laws for the execution of the granted powers, to such as are indispensable, and without which the power would be nugatory. That it excludes the choice of means, and leaves to Congress, in each case, that only which is most direct and simple.

Is it true, that this is the sense in which the word "necessary" is always used? . . . We think it does not. If reference be had to its use, in the common affairs of the world, or in approved authors, we find that it frequently imports no more than that one thing is convenient, or useful, or essential to another. To employ the means necessary to an end, is generally understood as employing any means calculated to produce the end, and not as being confined to those single means, without which the end would be entirely unattainable.

Let this be done in the case under consideration. The subject is the execution of those great powers on which the welfare of a nation essentially depends. It must have been the intention of those who gave these powers, to insure, as far as human prudence could insure, their beneficial execution. This could not be done by confiding the choice of means to such narrow limits as not to leave it in the power of Congress to adopt any which might be appropriate, and which were conducive to the end. This provision is made in a constitution intended to endure for ages to come, and consequently, to be adapted to the various crises of human affairs. To have prescribed the means by which government should, in all future time, execute its powers, would have been to change, entirely, the character of the instrument, and give it the properties of a legal code. It would have been an unwise attempt to provide, by immutable rules, for exigencies which, if foreseen at all, must have been seen dimly, and which can be best provided for as they occur. To have declared that the best means shall not be used, but those alone without which the power given would be nugatory, would have been to deprive the legislature of the capacity to avail itself of experience, to exercise its reason, and to accommodate its legislation to circumstances. If we apply this principle of construction to any of the powers of the government, we shall find it so pernicious in its operation that we shall be compelled to discard it. . . .

We admit, as all must admit, that the powers of the government are limited, and that its limits are not to be transcended. But we think the sound construction of the constitution must allow to the national legislature that discretion, with respect to the means by which the powers it confers are to be carried into execution, which will enable that body to perform the high duties assigned to it, in the manner most beneficial to the people. Let the end be legitimate, let it be within the scope of the constitution, and all means which are appropriate, which are plainly adapted to that end, which are not prohibited, but consist with the letter and spirit of the constitution, are constitutional. . . .

It being the opinion of the court that the act incorporating the bank is constitutional, and that the power of establishing a branch in the state of Maryland might be properly exercised by the bank itself, we proceed to inquire: Whether the state of Maryland may, without violating the constitution, tax that branch?

That the power of taxation is one of vital importance; that it is retained by the states; that it is not abridged by the grant of a similar power to the government of the Union; that it is to be concurrently exercised by the two governments; are truths which have never been denied. But, such is the paramount character of the constitution that its capacity to withdraw any subject from the action of even this power, is admitted. . . . [T]he paramount character [of the Constitution] would seem to restrain, as it certainly may restrain, a state from such other exercise of this power as is in its nature incompatible with, and repugnant to, the constitutional laws of the Union. A law, absolutely repugnant to another, as entirely repeals that other as if express terms of repeal were used. . . .

This great principle is, that the constitution and the laws made in pursuance thereof are supreme; that they control the constitution and laws of the respective states, and cannot be controlled by them. From this, which may be almost termed an axiom, other propositions are adduced as corollaries, on the truth or error of which, and on their application to this case, the cause has been supposed to depend. These are, 1st. That a power to create implies a power to preserve. 2d. That a power to destroy, if wielded by a different hand, is hostile to, and incompatible with, these powers to create and to preserve. 3d. That where this repugnance exists, that authority which is supreme must control, not yield to that over which it is supreme.

. . . [T]axation is said to be an absolute power, which acknowledges no other limits than those expressly prescribed in the constitution, and like sovereign powers of every other description, is trusted to the discretion of those who use it. But the very terms of this argument admit that the sovereignty of the state, in the article of taxation itself, is subordinate to, and may be controlled by the constitution of the United States. How far it has been controlled by that instrument must be a question of construction. In making this construction, no principle not declared can be admissible, which would defeat the legitimate operations of a supreme government. . . .

All subjects over which the sovereign power of a state extends, are objects of taxation; but those over which it does not extend, are, upon the soundest principles, exempt from taxation. . . . The sovereignty of a state extends to everything which exists by its own authority, or is introduced by its permission; but does it extend to those means which are employed by

Congress to carry into execution—powers conferred on that body by the people of the United States? We think it demonstrable that it does not. Those powers are not given by the people of a single state. They are given by the people of the United States, to a government whose laws, made in pursuance of the constitution, are declared to be supreme. Consequently, the people of a single state cannot confer a sovereignty which will extend over them.

If we apply the principle for which the state of Maryland contends, to the constitution generally, we shall find it capable of changing totally the character of that instrument. We shall find it capable of arresting all the measures of the government, and of prostrating it at the foot of the states. The American people have declared their constitution, and the laws made in pursuance thereof, to be supreme; but this principle would transfer the supremacy, in fact, to the states. If the controlling power of the states be established; if their supremacy as to taxation be acknowledged; what is to restrain their exercising this control in any shape they may please to give it? Their sovereignty is not confined to taxation. That is not the only mode in which it might be displayed. The question is, in truth, a question of supremacy; and if the right of the states to tax the means employed by the general government be conceded, the declaration that the constitution, and the laws made in pursuance thereof, shall be the supreme law of the land, is empty and unmeaning declamation. . . .

We are unanimously of opinion, that the law passed by the legislature of Maryland, imposing a tax on the Bank of the United States, is unconstitutional and void. This opinion does not deprive the states of any resources which they originally possessed. It does not extend to a tax paid by the real property of the bank, in common with other real property within the state, nor to a tax imposed on the interest which the citizens of Maryland may hold in this institution, in common with other property of the same description throughout the state. But this is a tax on the operations of the bank, and is, consequently, a tax on the operation of an instrument employed by the government of the Union to carry its powers into execution. Such a tax must be unconstitutional.

Reversed.

FEDERALISM

See text p. 67

McCulloch v. Maryland *provided the framework around which American federalism developed. As the text points out, however, a strict division of responsibilities has become blurred over time. In the following piece, written prior to her appointment as Clinton's Deputy Budget Director, Alice Rivlin discusses the need to revamp traditional ideas about federalism. She argues that increasing global interdependence, increasingly complex domestic issues, fiscal stress, and general dissatisfaction with the current govern-*

mental structure have created a need to re-examine the current structure. A revitalized federalist structure would entail three primary changes: the federal government would provide broader basic social insurance programs (like health care); states would assume more responsibility for education, job training, and public infrastructure; and a new tax system would equalize revenues among states.

Alice M. Rivlin
"A New Vision of American Federalism"*

Why Worry About Federalism Right Now?

One might well question whether federal/state relations deserve a place on the current list of high-priority public concerns. After all, there is so much else to worry about. The United States is trying to find its role in an increasingly complicated world where power is diffused, and just about everything is interdependent. The American economy is stagnating and inequality is growing. The list of policies needed to revitalize the economy is long and difficult—improve education, modernize infrastructure, control health costs, etc. The federal government is running a massive budget deficit, which ten years of budget agreements have not dented, and state and local finances are in crisis as well. People do not trust government anymore. Both politics and politicians are held in low esteem. With all these problems to agonize about, why reopen old arguments about the relationship between the states and the federal government?

My point is precisely that addressing these urgent concerns requires new thinking about the roles of federal and state governments. A cleaner distinction between the responsibilities of different levels of government, and a new approach to financing the states could contribute to solving a broad range of apparently diverse problems both economic and political.

Four Arguments for Addressing Federalism

There are at least four reasons for taking a new look at the division of responsibilities between state and federal government. The first is that rapidly increasing global interdependence is making new demands, not just on our economic system, but on our political system as well.

*Alice M. Rivlin, "A New Vision of American Federalism," *Public Administration Review* (July/August, 1992). Reprinted with permission.

Global Interdependence

Rapid advances in the technology of transportation, communications, and weaponry have shrunk distances dramatically and intertwined the United States with the rest of the world intimately and irreversibly. Increasingly, goods and services, capital, and people are flowing across oceans and borders. So are economic, political, and environmental problems. The United States has a growing stake in expanding global trade and in stabilizing world-wide financial markets and institutions. It also has an increasing need to strengthen international economic and political systems so that they are able to prevent famine, mass migrations, damage to the global environment, and outbreaks of high-tech destruction.

Global interdependence inevitably requires increasing international cooperation to solve mutual problems and some delegation of sovereignty to supra-national authorities. The BCCI scandal illustrates that individual countries can no longer adequately regulate banks and other financial institutions all by themselves. The Iraq war and recent revelations about growing nuclear capacity in developing nations leave no doubt that stronger international controls are needed on sophisticated weapons. The rapidly thinning ozone layer shows that all have a stake in controlling damaging atmospheric emissions.

Eventually, a global federal structure may be in order, but, for the foreseeable future, it will be far more effective to deal with specific problems that require international cooperation on an *ad hoc* basis. This will require U.S. involvement in an overlapping network of international partnerships focused on everything from chemical weapons to acid rain to enforcing patents and copyrights. The complexities of these partnerships are already demanding increasing attention from both the executive and legislative branches of the federal government.

Global interdependence creates a paradox for the U.S. government, which is already affecting national politics. On the one hand, both the legislative and executive branches of the federal government will be spending escalating amounts of time and energy on international affairs. Domestic policy will inevitably get less attention in Washington; it already is. At the same time, global interdependence makes what used to be called domestic policy more important than ever. The United States needs rising productivity, a skilled labor force, and modern physical capital, both public and private, if it is to compete in world markets and generate the improving standard of living we need, not only for domestic well-being, but also to command respect on the international scene. With the federal government necessarily preoccupied with the rest of the world, states must take responsibility for part of the domestic agenda.

Top-Down or Bottom-Up Reform

The second reason for rethinking federalism is that major policy changes are needed to revitalize the American economy, and responsibility for carrying them out ought to be assigned to the level of government most likely to do a good job. Some require top-down national action and some require bottom-up community solutions.

The agenda of needed policy changes is actually remarkably uncontroversial. A great many voices are singing the same tune: save and invest more; invest in basic and applied science, in education and labor force skills, and in infrastructure; and improve health care availability and control the costs. The controversies are over who should be in charge of what—and who should pay.

What should the federal government do? Besides inherently national functions like national defense and foreign affairs, there are two kinds of domestic government functions for which the federal government is well suited. These are activities whose benefits clearly spill over state lines in a major way (support of scientific research, air-traffic control, prevention of acid rain) and those for which national uniformity is highly desirable (Social Security).

Social Security is the federal government's biggest domestic success. It is an immensely popular and well-supported program. People apparently do not mind paying the taxes, because they know exactly what the money goes for and expect to benefit themselves. Because it involves tracking people over a lifetime, it could not easily be handled by the states; too many people would move in and out of state systems and end up with conflicting and overlapping coverage.

There are other activities, however, for which national uniformity is a liability. They are likely to succeed only if they are well adapted to local conditions, have strong local support and community participation, and are managed by accountable officials who can be voted out if things go badly. With respect to these programs, top-down reform by means of a federal program with rigid nation-wide rules is likely to do more harm than good.

Improving education is a challenge that cannot be met at the national level. Presidential speeches and photo opportunities, national testing programs, and federally funded experimental schools, even significant new money (if any were available) spent in accordance with federal guidelines, can make only marginal contributions to fixing the schools. Education in America will not be much better until states and communities decide they want it to be. Improving education will require parents who care, committed teachers, community support, and accountable school officials. It is an open question whether an "education president" does sufficient good by focusing media attention on the problem to offset the harm of diluting state and local responsibility by implying that there is something Washington can actually do to help.

The dilution of responsibility is real. For example, the federal government made a major contribution by demonstrating that preschool education helps children from poor families in some marginal but apparently lasting ways. The negative legacy of Headstart, however, is that states and communities across the country have come to believe that the responsibility for improving preschool education lies with Washington, not with them. Improvement would come more rapidly if concerned citizens, parents, and educators got to work on their own preschools without waiting for Washington to allocate more funds for Headstart.

Street crime, drug use, and teenage pregnancy are all examples of problems that the federal government can deplore but cannot fix. A resurgence of community concern and effort is needed. Federal programs may help a little, but at the price of confusing the issue of who needs to take charge. Social services, housing, community development, and most infrastructure are also activities that must be carefully adapted to the needs of particular places, for which the national government has no special aptitude and which it has no demonstrated ability to carry out effectively.

On the other hand, the problem of rapidly rising health costs (combined with lack of health insurance for millions of people) probably can *only* be solved by the federal government. The U.S. health care system is the most expensive in the world, now consuming about 13 percent of the gross national product (GNP), but it does not provide commensurate benefits. Millions are left out or inadequately insured. Sentiment is growing for shifting to some kind of national health insurance system that would provide universal coverage for basic health services and control costs by setting reimbursement rates for doctors, hospitals, and other medical providers. State efforts to solve the problem of medical cost and coverage on their own are likely to fail because both taxpayers and providers cross borders. A nationally organized single-payer system will be necessary.

Another important role that the federal government is uniquely positioned to play at the moment is increasing national saving. The federal government's big success program, Social Security, is currently running surpluses, as indeed it should. The surpluses should be adding to national saving; they should be channelled into productive investment that will generate higher incomes in the future out of which to pay the retirement claims of future retirees. At present, however, the growing Social Security reserves are simply being lent to the Treasury to finance its ongoing expenses.

If the federal government is to use the Social Security surpluses to enhance future productivity, it must bring the rest of the federal budget into balance and use the Social Security surpluses to retire some of the federal debt held by the public. This brings me to the third reason for worrying about federalism right now: the perilous state of public finances at both the federal and state levels.

Fiscal Stress at All Levels

The federal budget deficit is the biggest single impediment to revitalizing the American economy and is the third reason for taking a new look at federalism. It diverts a large portion of America's inadequate supply of saving into financing the on-going expenses of the government, rather than productivity-enhancing investment. It keeps real interest rates high and requires that a substantial share of federal tax revenues be devoted to debt service. It has paralyzed the federal government's ability to address new problems, at home and abroad, and weakened fiscal policy as a tool for achieving economic stabilization.

The federal deficit is definitely not withering away. To be sure, the recession and the savings and loan bailout are inflating the deficit to higher than normal levels at present. Even when these temporary factors recede, however, the deficit is projected by the Congressional Budget Office to remain in the range of $200 billion in 1996 and to rise significantly by the beginning of the next century if policies are not changed. Why should the deficit rise? A big part of the answer is that medical costs are projected to keep going up faster than revenues, if nothing is done to control them.

Even with expected declines in defense spending, more revenue will be needed to bring the federal budget into balance, even more to get it to surplus, and still more if the federal government is to take on new responsibilities for education, health insurance, infrastructure, or whatever. The only option for eliminating the deficit without significant revenue increase would be to count on the states for these new activities and devolve big chunks of current federal responsibilities to the states as well. This would move the financing crisis from the federal to the state level.

Increasing the responsibilities of state and local governments is a dubious proposition because they are also in deep fiscal trouble at present. At first glance, however, their fiscal distress seems more temporary than that of the federal government. State and local governments generally suffer serious fiscal stress in recessions. Their revenues fall off as sales, income, and property values stop growing or decline, while claims on their services continue to increase. As soon as their reserves are exhausted, which does not take long, they are forced to raise taxes and cut payrolls and services.

Coping with recession, however, has historically put state and local governments in good shape for the ensuing boom. With higher tax rates and a leaner work force, they are likely to run surpluses when the economy begins growing again. In 1984 and 1985, state and local governments in the aggregate were running significant surpluses. One might hope that recovery from the 1991 recession would have a similar effect.

There are reasons for greater pessimism, however, as one looks at the prospects for state and local finance in the 1990s, even if the economy returns to moderate growth. The operating surpluses of state and local governments in the aggregate actually declined in the second half of the 1980s as a percent of GNP, reflecting rising pressures for spending that were generally out-running even fairly healthy revenue increases. The fiscal stress, especially in cities, reflected the increase in crime, drug addiction, AIDS, homelessness, and the proportion of low-income people, all of which continued to increase through the long recovery from the recession of the early 80s. Moreover, a major villain of the federal budget drama appears again on the state and local scene. Rising medical care costs and increasing federal mandates, especially for medicaid, have put enormous pressure on state and local budgets—pressure which seems unlikely to abate. Hence, stress in state and local budgets seems likely to continue, even when the economy improves.

The bottom line is that all levels of government will likely continue to face considerable fiscal stress. The policy agenda for improving the economy—increase public investment, get the federal budget surplus, solve the problem of health costs and access—looks impossible unless more revenue comes from somewhere. The public, however, seems angry and dissatisfied with government at all levels and unwilling to increase its support.

Dissatisfaction with Government

This brings me to my fourth reason for rethinking federalism in the 1990s, the general dissatisfaction with politics and politicians. In recent years, many Americans have tuned out political debate and stopped participating in political life. Voter participation has dropped Polls reveal declining confidence in government institutions, rising skepticism that politicians care about the views of ordinary people, disgust at political campaigns, and cynicism about the democratic process.

Dissatisfaction with government and politics doubtless has multiple causes, including the need to blame someone for the stress of adjusting to slower economic growth, the crass role of big money in campaigns, the negative tone of campaign advertising, the dominance of extreme ideologies in both major party platforms, and the insensitivity of public officials to the impact on their collective image of bouncing checks, getting parking tickets fixed, and other peccadillos.

A significant contribution to disillusionment with government may also be rising confusion over who is supposed to be in charge of what. The explosion of federal activities from the 1930s to the late 1970s, blurred all the neat distinctions between federal and state responsibilities. When the federal money ran out in the 1980s, however, candidates for federal office (even those who favored less government) continued to tell voters that if they were elected all the problems of the country would get better, including those that the federal government can barely influence at all.

Americans are concerned about crime and drugs, improving schools and child care, and making communities work better. They may, however, correctly perceive that Washington is too remote from these problems to make a difference. Schools will not improve because someone in Washington says they should. Streets will not be safer because a federal drug czar is appointed. The problems that concern average citizens most immediately demand bottom-up not top-down solutions. Candidates for federal office only contribute to cynicism about politics by implying they can solve these problems.

The pattern of recent revenue increases offers some clues to citizen sentiment. State and local revenues have risen appreciably in recent years (as a percent of GNP) while federal revenues have not. One might infer that voters are less resistent to paying for services closer to home, where they have more evidence of what they are buying. Perhaps, more important, the only federal tax to increase over recent decades has been the payroll tax for Social Security and medicare. Perhaps the rule for raising revenue to fund the consensus agenda is: raise it close to home or for clearly identifiable benefits. . . .

Federalism Scenarios for the Future

What might happen to the division of responsibilities between state and federal government (and to public financing) in the 1990s? Let me offer three scenarios for the sake of argument.

The first I call, "The 1980s Continued." Under this scenario, the federal government makes little or no progress on reducing its deficit. Congress and the President keep tinkering with the tax system, but revenue losers (capital gains reductions and savings incentives) outweigh the gainers (surcharge on millionaires or another nickel for gasoline). Congress and the President also tinker with discretionary spending; defense comes down while a variety of modest new initiatives are undertaken (some education, some child care, some low-income housing, some aid to the former Soviet empire, etc.). The division of responsibilities remains muddy. Medicare and Medicaid continue to escalate because nothing serious has been done about controlling rises in medical cost. Meanwhile, the states keep struggling with rising expenditures, especially for health care. They raise taxes and fees as much as they have to and manage to stay afloat but not to finance major new initiatives. The economy, still suffering from a shortage of saving and relatively high real interest rates, continues to limp along.

Second is the "liberal" scenario or "Back to the 1960s." A double-dip recession or some other calamity propels an activist Democrat into the White House with a supportive majority in the Congress. As the economy turns around and begins growing again, significant tax increases are enacted to finance not only national health insurance and deficit reduction but also big new federal grant programs for the federal schools initiative, the housing initiative, etc. The combination of federal grants and relief from rising medicaid costs enables states and localities to reduce taxes a little. The federal share of GNP rises, the state and local share declines a little. More important, policy action shifts back to Washington, along with intense lobbying by myriad interest groups, including state and local governments, for additional federal spending.

The third scenario, which I believe to be both more realistic than Back to the 1960s, and more desirable than either of the other two, is called "Dividing the Job." It has three main new elements. First, the federal government takes responsibility for health care financing. It enacts some system that covers everyone for basic health services. Fees and reimbursement rates are set according to a nationally negotiated formula. Cost controls halt the increase in health care spending as a percent of GNP. The system requires some new federal taxes dedicated to health financing.

Second, the states, not the federal government, take charge of accomplishing a productivity agenda of reforms designed to revitalize the economy and raise incomes. These include education and skills training, child care, housing, and infrastructure and economic development. Federal programs in these areas are devolved to the states or just wither away Once clearly in charge, the states compete vigorously with each other to improve services and to attract business by offering high quality education, infrastructure, and other services. Some specific programs where federal action is needed are retained, even expanded; for example, higher education scholarships for low income students and federal support for scientific research.

Third, the states, with the blessing and perhaps the assistance of the federal government, strengthen their revenue systems by adopting one or more common taxes (same base, same rate) and sharing the proceeds. Common shared taxes are an attempt to offset two of the major disadvantages of relying on states to finance needed improvements in public services. States have unequal resources and poorer states are unable to finance high quality services even with higher than average tax rates. Moreover, states compete with each other in an increasingly mobile and interlinked society for private sector employment and sales, as well as for higher income residents. Increasingly, they lose revenue on cross-border transactions and worry about tax increases causing them to lose more. Moreover, as business becomes national and international, the plethora of state taxes becomes an increasing headache for corporate and even individual taxpayers.

Many variations are possible on the theme of common shared taxes. Two seem to me most attractive. One is a single, state corporate income tax, perhaps collected by the Internal Revenue Service (IRS) along with the federal tax, and shared on a formula basis. The other is a uniform value-added tax (VAT), shared on a per capita basis and substituted for state retail sales taxes.

There are several arguments for a shared VAT. All but five states have sales taxes, but most are increasingly concerned about mail order and other cross-border sales escaping taxation. Moreover, most are trying to find ways of extending their sales taxes to services, which are a growing portion of sales. Many services are hard to tax because they can be performed at a distance. Moreover, taxing business services under a retail sales tax tends to involve double counting or tax pyramiding. Substituting a VAT for a retail sales tax would make it possible to tax services more easily and without pyramiding. A common tax would eliminate cross-border escapes, and sharing the revenue on a per capita basis would be both simple and somewhat redistributive toward poorer states.

The advantages of the Dividing-the-Jobs scenario are several. The task of improving public services is allocated to the level of government most likely to be able to respond, and citizens will be clear who is in charge, where to pressure for performance, and whom to blame for bad results. New tax revenues injected at the federal level through the health insurance tax are clearly associated with a desired benefit, and some impediments to state revenue increases are mitigated.

The federal government can move its budget into surplus, thanks to devolution of some domestic programs to the states and to medical cost control, as well as a decline in defense requirements. The NHI subsumes Medicaid and medicare and eliminates their upward pressure on the budget deficit. Social Security surpluses can be used to reduce the federal debt held by the public—a shift that will channel these savings into private investment and put downward pressure on interest rates.

Meanwhile, at the state level, budget pressure is reduced by the elimination of Medicaid. New demands for services are added by state assumption of the productivity agenda, but these can be funded more easily than before from the proceeds of common shared taxes or in the case of some infrastructure, from well-designed user charges.

Despite its name, the Dividing-the-Job scenario is not a return to dual federalism. There are important areas—for example, environmental protection—in which cooperative federalism is necessary and desirable. At one time, I favored federal takeover of cash assistance to the poor, but I have come to believe that retaining joint federal-state involvement is important, in part to give both levels of government incentives to try a variety of means of reducing welfare dependency. To this end, the states should improve education, training, and child care for welfare mothers, and the federal government should adjust the income tax to improve incentives for low-income families to work.

Conclusion

I hope I have convincingly demonstrated two important points. One is that there are ways out of the current deadlock that are worth earnest consideration. We do not need to be stuck in this particular political swamp forever. The other is that the assignment of roles and revenues to state and federal government is an important part of the discussion of which way to go.

Debating the Issues: Opposing Views

IS THE SEPARATION OF POWERS OBSOLETE?

See text p. 94–95

Fragmenting power among separate institutions provides an effective check on the improper accumulation of power by any single branch, but it is a cumbersome method of governing. Conflict between the branches is inevitable, and no institution is likely to willingly surrender authority to the others.

During the 1992 election campaign, both Governor Clinton and President Bush talked about gridlock resulting from conflicts between a Democratic Congress and a Republican President. In fact, President Clinton utilized that image effectively to suggest that a Democratic President and Congress could work hand-in-hand to efficiently resolve a number of domestic problems. But as President Clinton is learning, the problems of gridlock cannot be dismissed as a problem of party politics; they are equally attributable to conflicts between institutions of political authority themselves. This institutional dispute surfaced early in the Clinton presidency, as the President sought to exercise control over the federal budget through the assertion of a power to veto budget items on his own initiative. As Adam Clymer points out in the following article, power over the federal purse strings will not be lightly surrendered by Congress.

Michael Kinsley, writing for Time Magazine, *suggests that the conflicts are not necessary. Granting the president the authority to veto line-item budget requests should not generate the kind of conflicts pointed out by Adam Clymer. The line-item veto, far from undercutting congressional authority, would increase the responsibility of both Congress and the Executive branch: Congress would be forced to assume responsibility for submitting a balanced budget, Kinsley argues, and the president would be denied "the luxury of blaming Congress for excessive spending."*

Adam Clymer
"Politics Fuels Debate on Budget Power"*

The renewed arguments over whether President Bill Clinton should have what President Bush wanted—devices he could use to cut spending, like the "line-item veto" and its feebler cousin "enhanced rescission authority"—are not really about cutting the deficit.

Nobody, not even Mr. Clinton, argues that either device would affect the deficit very much, even though they would allow a President to strike individual items from spending bills without having to veto the entire measure.

Instead, the engine behind this discussion is perceived political necessity, an urgent need to convey to constituents that lawmakers are willing to take a bold step to curb Federal spending.

For opponents of both notions, the issue is as old as the Republic, the contest for power between the executive and legislative branches. And the foremost opponent is the chairman of the Senate Appropriations Committee, Senator Robert C. Byrd of West Virginia, who has said Congress would have to be crazy to surrender any of the power of the purse to any President of either party.

So even though Mr. Clinton can expect support from the House and from most Senate Republicans, he has a formidable battle ahead if he is serious about this issue. Simply put, he will have to get about 20 Democratic Senators to shift their positions and vote with him and against Mr. Byrd, a Senate power in the traditional mold.

*"Politics Fuels Debate on Budget Power," Adam Clymer, *New York Times* (November 18, 1992).

Limits on the President

But Mr. Clinton's fight is no more formidable than that of normal people trying to fight their way through the jargon this issue attracts, from impoundment to rescission to line-item veto.

Tough Presidents from Thomas Jefferson through Richard Nixon sometimes impounded, or refused to spend, money appropriated by Congress. But Watergate so weakened Mr. Nixon that Congress took away that authority in the Budget and Impoundment Control Act of 1974.

Now the President can still rescind spending approved by Congress, but only if both houses vote to go along with his request for taking back previously appropriated money. And they do not have to bring his precise proposal to a vote. Last year, Mr. Bush called for $6.9 billion in rescissions. Congress took out some, added others, and eventually voted for $8.2 billion in cuts.

On Oct. 3 the House voted on a bill that would guarantee that a President's proposals for specific cuts come to a vote; a majority would be required to enforce them. This "enhanced rescission" measure passed 312 to 97, with the knowledge that the Senate had no intention of considering it before adjournment.

That proposal is the one that Speaker Thomas S. Foley has been advocating in recent days and the one that Mr. Clinton on Monday called an "intriguing suggestion." Mr. Foley and other supporters in the House have favored it as a less sweeping transfer of power than a true line-item veto and as a strategic retreat that would curb appetites for a Constitutional amendment to require a balanced Federal budget.

Roadblock in the Senate

The full-fledged line-item veto measure most recently put to a vote, in the Senate, would allow the President to kill spending he disliked and require Congress to pass it again as a new bill, which he could veto. It would then take two-thirds votes in both houses to force the spending to go ahead.

That measure was shelved, 54 to 44, after Mr. Byrd assailed it for hours last February, going back to Anglo-Saxon kings and the entire history of English battles over spending, and forward to the Bush Administration.

"The power over the purse is the taproot of the tree of Anglo-Saxon liberty," Mr. Byrd said. "The item-veto debate, when shorn of all of its fancy trappings, is a debate about power, and control of the purse is the bone and sinew of power."

And to illustrate the point, Mr. Byrd suggested that the President, with this power, might have sought his vote on another issue by saying there was a spending item White House his budget officials disapproved of. The Senator imagined Mr. Bush telling him: "I kind of hate to veto your item. How are you going to vote on Clarence Thomas?"

While it is clear that the measure Mr. Foley and Mr. Clinton like does not go as far as the bill that Mr. Byrd attacked, the West Virginia Senator came out flatly against it after the House passed it, calling the differences between the two superficial.

Months earlier, in that same February debate, Mr. Byrd said, "Surely, Congress would have to be infected with a collective madness to seriously contemplate handing to any President such a blackjack, even though it be clothed with the velvet-sounding name, enhanced rescissions."

One Senator's Power

Perhaps out of politeness to Mr. Clinton, Mr. Byrd has declined to comment on the issue in recent days, but there is no reason to think his opposition has softened.

While Mr. Byrd is hardly alone in his fears, his opposition is especially formidable. The Senator's control of the Appropriations Committee gives him real influence over his colleagues. But even more, he is the Congress's leading champion against slights from the executive branch on all sorts of issues. No one who knows him well doubts he would oppose these spending proposals even if he was not on the Appropriations Committee, much less its chairman.

In the House, the situation is very different. First of all, it feels the hot breath of public anger over apparently silly spending more than does the Senate with its six-year terms. The House Appropriations Committee has no leader to match Mr. Byrd, and House leaders have given ground on the issue to appease conservative Democrats and fend off budgetary solutions they consider too drastic.

An enhanced-rescission bill will almost surely pass the House fairly early next year. The test will come in the Senate, though perhaps not quickly, and it will be a measure of how much political capital Mr. Clinton is prepared to spend on a war with the Senate's senior Democrat. He will not want to lose such a war, but neither is he likely to want to retreat from a fight.

Michael Kinsley
"The Case for a Big Power Swap"*

Bitter arguments between the president and the Congress are built into our constitutional system. What isn't necessarily built in are the bitter arguments of recent years over the constitutional division of labor itself. Controversies over a wide range of issues—independent-counsel prosecutions, Supreme

*Michael Kinsley, "The Case for a Big Power Swap," *Time Magazine* (March 5, 1993.) Reprinted with permission.

Court nominees, funding of the Nicaraguan *contras*, the Persian Gulf War, the federal budget deficit—all turned into fights about the separation of powers between the Legislative and Executive branches.

During the era of divided government, conservatives developed an enormous and historically uncharacteristic enthusiasm for presidential power. Conservative legal scholars produced elaborate theories establishing to their own satisfaction that the independent counsel is unconstitutional; that the President not only needs but already has a line-item veto over congressional appropriations; and so on. This trend culminated in President Bush's breathtaking assertion—never put to the test—that he could send half a million American troops into battle halfway around the globe without so much as a nod to Congress's constitutional power to "declare war."

Now divided government is gone. And already we can see the Republican enthusiasm for Executive authority fading and a new respect growing for the prerogatives of the legislature.

But Democrats also face a test of their principles. And with control of both branches, the Democrats are in a position to put their principles into practice. Democrats could serve the Constitution and the country by making a "grand bargain" between Congress and the White House. In foreign policy, the President should acknowledge and begin honoring Congress's war power. In domestic and budgetary policy, Congress should restore meaning to the President's veto power by giving him the line-item veto. Fair enough?

Congress's war power has become the most flagrantly disregarded provision in the Constitution. There have always been debates over the extent of the President's authority to respond to unexpected emergencies. But the real erosion began after World War II. During the cold war era, there were claims that the hair-trigger nuclear stalemate made the notion of consulting Congress obsolete. From Vietnam through the invasion of Panama, there were arguments about what was and was not a "war." In the 1980s the issue was usually whether Congress was trying to "micromanage" foreign-policy issues short of actually sending in the troops. By 1991, however, President Bush could claim with a straight face that he didn't need congressional approval for Operation Desert Storm: a deliberate, unhurried, post-cold war decision to start a war.

In the end, Congress approved Desert Storm. But only after America's prestige and hundreds of thousands of troops had been committed and the President had made clear he would go ahead with or without that approval. And since then there has been no talk of asking Congress's approval for further adventures in Somalia and Bosnia. As legal scholar John Hart Ely explains in a forthcoming book on this subject, restoring the war power is no special favor to the Legislative Branch. "The legislative surrender was a self-interested one: accountability is pretty frightening stuff." It's been too easy for members of Congress to play the hindsight game, supporting military adventures that turn out well and blaming the President for ones that turn out badly.

President Clinton faces the challenge of creating a post-cold war foreign policy. He seems to want it to be activist, including the possibility of military action in support of democracy and human rights. Especially given his own lack of military experience, he should be happy to abandon any claim to the right to commit U.S. troops unilaterally (except in genuine emergencies)—a right he does not possess under the Constitution in any event.

The line-item veto is also a matter of forcing a delinquent branch of government to take responsibility for its actions (or rather, its inactions). In this case, the guilty party is the Executive Branch. For 12 years we have been hearing from Presidents that the budget deficit is the legislature's fault because "Congress appropriates every dime." That's true. But Presidents submit an annual budget, and neither Bush nor Ronald Reagan ever came close to submitting a balanced one.

Critics of Congress have a point when they say the legislature has eviscerated the President's constitutional veto power by submitting gigantic, combination-platter spending bills, often at the last minute. The President then has a Hobson's choice of signing on to the whole thing or shutting down the government. The line-item veto, which 43 Governors (including the Governor of Arkansas) have in one form or another, would give the President authority to approve or disapprove individual spending proposals. It would also, thereby, deny him the luxury of blaming Congress for excessive spending.

A genuine line-item veto would require a constitutional amendment. But Congress could achieve the same result by agreeing to submit every appropriation and tax item as a separate bill for the President to sign or veto. Senator Bill Bradley has suggested adopting this practice as a two-year experiment. The Democratic-controlled Congress should have tried this experiment back when Republicans controlled the White House. It would have been a sparkling exercise in bluff calling. Now they can grant the power to one of their own. Politically, it would be no special favor to Clinton. But if he is serious about leading us out of the deficit, it is a burden he should be willing to accept.

QUESTIONS

1. In *The Federalist No. 49* Madison assures Antifederalists that the power of the federal government will not overshadow those retained by the states and thus displace the states as the locus of citizens' primary political attachment. What kinds of powers were retained by the states, and why would those powers be effective in securing the attachments of citizens?
2. In *Marbury v. Madison* Chief Justice Marshall outlines two important constitutional principles: first, that the U.S. Constitution and laws made under its authority are superior to the laws of the states, and second, that Congress may make all laws "necessary and proper" to give effect to those powers it is expressly granted. How does Marshall explain that the estab-

lishment of a national bank is a necessary and proper extension of Congress's taxing power? In what ways would Maryland's imposition of a tax on operations of the Bank of the United States make state law prevail over federal law in violation of the Supremacy Clause?

3. Alice Rivlin argues that the American system needs to revitalize the concept of federalism. In what ways has the concept been eroded over the last 200 years? At a time when federal authority is pervasive, what advantages might be gained from re-inventing federalism along the lines suggested by Rivlin?
4. How has the separation of powers principle contributed to the current problems with creating a balanced budget and dealing with the federal deficit? Is the problem simply a matter of stubborness and animosity between Congress and the Executive branch, or are there genuine institutional barriers to resolving the conflict?

CHAPTER 4

The Constitutional Framework and the Individual: Civil Liberties and Civil Rights

CIVIL LIBERTIES: NATIONALIZING THE BILL OF RIGHTS

See text p. 104

The declaration made in Barron v. Baltimore *(1833) that citizenship had a dual aspect—state and national—set the terms of the Supreme Court's interpretation of the Bill of Rights for nearly 150 years. The reasoning of the case proved persuasive even after the adoption of the Fourteenth Amendment, as the federal courts refused to extend the protections of the federal Constitution to citizens aggrieved by the actions of state or local governments.*

Barron v. *Baltimore* (1833)*

[Barron brought suit in a federal court claiming that the city of Baltimore had appropriated his property for a public purpose without paying him just compensation. He asserted that the Fifth Amendment to the Constitution operated as a constraint upon both state and federal governments.]

CHIEF JUSTICE JOHN MARSHALL delivered the opinion of the court.

. . . The question presented is, we think, of great importance, but not of much difficulty. The constitution was ordained and established by the people of the United States for themselves, for their own government, and not for the government of the individual states. Each state established a constitution for itself, and in that constitution, provided such limitations and restrictions on the powers of its particular government, as its judgment dictated. The people of the United States framed such a government for the United States as they supposed best adapted to their situation and best calculated to promote their interests. The powers they conferred on this government were to be exercised by itself; and the limitations on power, if expressed in general terms, are naturally, and, we think, necessarily, applicable to the government created by the instrument. They are limitations of power

*Barron v. Baltimore, 32 U.S. 243, 1833.

granted in the instrument itself; not of distinct governments, framed by different persons and for different purposes.

If these propositions be correct, the fifth amendment must be understood as restraining the power of the general government, not as applicable to the states. In their several constitutions, they have imposed such restrictions on their respective governments, as their own wisdom suggested; such as they deemed most proper for themselves. It is a subject on which they judge exclusively, and with which others interfere no further than they are supposed to have a common interest. . . .

Had the people of the several states, or any of them, required changes in their constitutions; had they required additional safe-guards to liberty from the apprehended encroachments of their particular governments; the remedy was in their own hands, and could have been applied by themselves. A convention could have been assembled by the discontented state, and the required improvements could have been made by itself.

. . . Had congress engaged in the extraordinary occupation of improving the constitutions of the several states, by affording the people additional protection from the exercise of power by their own governments, in matters which concerned themselves alone, they would have declared this purpose in plain and intelligible language.

But it is universally understood, it is a part of the history of the day, that the great revolution which established the constitution of the United States, was not effected without immense opposition. Serious fears were extensively entertained, that those powers which the patriot statesmen, who then watched over the interests of our country, deemed essential to union, and to the attainment of those unvaluable objects for which union was sought, might be exercised in a manner dangerous to liberty. In almost every convention by which the constitution was adopted, amendments to guard against the abuse of power were recommended. These amendments demanded security against the apprehended encroachments of the general government—not against those of the local governments. In compliance with a sentiment thus generally expressed, to quiet fears thus extensively entertained, amendments were proposed by the required majority in congress, and adopted by the states. These amendments contain no expression indicating an intention to apply them to the state governments. This court cannot so apply them.

We are of opinion, that the provision in the fifth amendment to the constitution, declaring that private property shall not be taken for public use, without just compensation, is intended solely as a limitation on the exercise of power by the government of the United States, and is not applicable to the legislation of the states. We are, therefore, of opinion, that there is no repugnancy between the several acts of the general assembly of Maryland, given in evidence by the defendants at the trial of this cause, in the court of that state, and the constitution of the United States. This court, therefore, has no jurisdiction of the cause, and it is dismissed.

This cause came on to be heard, on the transcript of the record from the court of appeals for the western shore of the state of Maryland, and was argued by counsel: On consideration whereof, it is the opinion of this court, that there is no repugnancy between the several acts of the general assembly of Maryland, given in evidence by the defendants at the trial of this cause in the court of that state, and the constitution of the United States; whereupon, it is ordered and adjudged by this court, that this writ of error be and the same is hereby dismissed, for the want of jurisdiction.

See text p. 109

The process by which the Bill of Rights was extended to protect citizens from abuses of state and local governmental powers, in addition to abuses by federal authorities, was called "incorporation." Over a period of approximately fifty years beginning in 1921, the Supreme Court found that the Fourteenth Amendment, which prohibits states from denying their citizens due process and equal protection of the laws, had "absorbed" virtually all of the provisions of the first eight amendments to the Constitution. For example, the Fourteenth Amendment does not expressly prohibit states from passing laws that inhibit free speech, and the First Amendment states only that Congress shall pass no laws inhibiting free speech. Nonetheless, the Court found in Gitlow v. New York *(1925) that the protection of free expression was a fundamental liberty that could not be abridged by a state.*

While the Supreme Court was more reluctant to incorporate other provisions from the Bill of Rights, which in large measure protect the rights of the accused, beginning in the early 1960s, most of the protections concerning criminal procedure contained in the Fourth, Fifth, Sixth, and Eighth Amendments were incorporated into the Fourteenth Amendment. The incorporation of these provisions dramatically changed the face of state criminal proceedings. While persons accused of crimes had always been entitled, under the Fourth Amendment, to protection against unreasonable searches and seizures when the offense was charged as a violation of federal law, no such protections were in place when a suspect was accused of violating a state criminal statute—and only a tiny fraction of criminal violations involve federal law. The case of Gideon v. Wainwright *(1963) was groundbreaking, both because it heralded a concern for the rights of criminal defendants and because it continued to break down the divisions between rights as a federal citizen and rights as a state citizen.*

Today, virtually all of the protections outlined in the Bill of Rights have been applied to the states through the Fourteenth Amendment. Exceptions, however, still remain. In recent years, for example, the meaning of the "reasonable bail" requirements in the Bill of Rights have been open to debate: for poor defendants, the amount of bail that may be considered reasonable will be significantly different than what may be considered reasonable for a wealthy defendant.

Gideon v. *Wainwright* (1963)*

JUSTICE BLACK delivered the opinion of the Court, saying in part:

Petitioner was charged in a Florida state court with having broken and entered a poolroom with intent to commit a misdemeanor. This offense is a felony under Florida law. Appearing in court without funds and without a lawyer, petitioner asked the court to appoint counsel for him, whereupon the following colloquy took place:

"The Court: Mr. Gideon, I am sorry, but I cannot appoint Counsel to represent you in this case. Under the laws of the State of Florida, the only time the Court can appoint Counsel to represent a Defendant is when that person is charged with a capital offense. I am sorry, but I will have to deny your request to appoint Counsel to defend you in this case.

"The Defendant: The United States Supreme Court says I am entitled to be represented by Counsel."

Put to trial before a jury, Gideon conducted his defense about as well as could be expected from a layman. He made an opening statement to the jury, cross-examined the State's witnesses, presented witnesses in his own defense, declined to testify himself, and made a short argument "emphasizing his innocence to the charge contained in the Information filed in this case." The jury returned a verdict of guilty, and petitioner was sentenced to serve five years in the state prison.

. . . The Sixth Amendment provides, "In all criminal prosecutions, the accused shall enjoy the right . . . to have the Assistance of Counsel for his defence." We have construed this to mean that in federal courts counsel must be provided for defendants unable to employ counsel unless the right is competently and intelligently waived. [In *Betts* v. *Brady* (1942), a case identical on its facts, but decided aversely to the defendant], Betts argued that this right is extended to indigent defendants in state courts by the Fourteenth Amendment. In response the Court stated that, while the Sixth Amendment laid down "no rule for the conduct of the States, the question recurs whether the constraint laid by the Amendment upon the national courts expresses a rule so fundamental and essential to a fair trial, and so, to due process of law, that it is made obligatory upon the States by the Fourteenth Amendment." In order to decide whether the Sixth Amendment's guarantee of counsel is of this fundamental nature, the Court in *Betts* set out and considered "[r]elevant data on the subject . . . afforded by constitutional and statutory provisions subsisting in the colonies and the States prior to the inclusion of the Bill of Rights in the national Constitution, and in the constitutional, legislative, and judicial history of the States to the present date." On the basis of this historical data the Court concluded that "appointment of counsel is not a fundamental right, essential to a fair trial."

*Gideon v. Wainwright, 372 U. S. 335, 1963.

[The Court then reviewed the cases and decided that the rights contained in the Sixth Amendment are fundamental.]

. . . In 1938 this Court said: "[The assistance of counsel] is one of the safeguards of the Sixth Amendment deemed necessary to insure fundamental human rights of life and liberty. . . . The Sixth Amendment stands as a constant admonition that if the constitutional safeguards it provides be lost, justice will not 'still be done.' " . . .

In light of these many other prior decisions of the Court, it is not surprising that the Betts Court, when faced with the contention that "one charged with crime, who is unable to obtain counsel, must be furnished counsel by the State," conceded that "[e]xpressions in the opinions of this court lend color to the argument. . . ." The fact is that in deciding as it did—that "appointment of counsel is not a fundamental right, essential to a fair trial"—the Court in Betts v. Brady made an abrupt break with its own well-considered precedents. In returning to these old precedents, sounder we believe than the new, we but restore constitutional principles established to achieve a fair system of justice. Not only these precedents but also reason and reflection require us to recognize that in our adversary system of criminal justice, any person haled into court, who is too poor to hire a lawyer, cannot be assured a fair trial unless counsel is provided for him. This seems to us to be an obvious truth. Governments, both state and federal, quite properly spend vast sums of money to establish machinery to try defendants accused of crime. Lawyers to prosecute are everywhere deemed essential to protect the public's interest in an orderly society. Similarly, there are few defendants charged with crime, few indeed, who fail to hire the best lawyers they can get to prepare and present their defenses. That government hires lawyers to prosecute and defendants who have the money hire lawyers to defend are the strongest indications of the widespread belief that lawyers in criminal courts are necessities, not luxuries. The right of one charged with crime to counsel may not be deemed fundamental and essential for fair trials in some countries, but it is in ours. From the very beginning, out state and national constitutions and laws have laid great emphasis on procedural and substantive safeguards designed to assure fair trials before impartial tribunals in which every defendant stands equal before the law. This noble ideal cannot be realized if the poor man charged with crime has to face his accusers without a lawyer to assist him. A defendant's need for a lawyer is nowhere better stated than in the moving words of Mr. Justice Sutherland in Powell v. Alabama:

"The right to be heard would be, in many cases, of little avail if it did not comprehend the right to be heard by counsel. Even the intelligent and educated layman has small and sometimes no skill in the science of law. If charged with crime, he is incapable, generally, of determining for himself whether the indictment is good or bad. He is unfamiliar with the rules of evidence. Left without the aid of counsel he may be put on trial without a proper charge, and convicted upon incompetent evidence, or evidence irrelevant to the issue or otherwise inadmissible. He lacks both the skill and knowledge adequately to prepare his defense, even though he have a perfect one. He requires the guiding hand of counsel at every step in the proceedings against him. Without it, though he be not guilty, he faces the danger of conviction because he does not know how to establish his innocence."

. . . The judgment is reversed and the cause is remanded to the Supreme Court of Florida for further action not inconsistent with this opinion. Reversed.

See text p. 114

One of the most significant changes in constitutional interpretation in the last twenty-five years has been the Court's willingness to look beyond the explicit language of the Bill of Rights to find unenumerated rights, such as the right to privacy. In discovering such rights, the Court has engaged in what is known as substantive due process analysis—defining and articulating fundamental rights—distinct from its efforts to define the scope of procedural due process, when it decides what procedures the state and federal governments must follow to be fair in their treatment of citizens. The Court's move into the substantive due process area has generated much of the political discussion over the proper role of the Court in constitutional interpretation, as discussed in further detail in Chapter 8 of your textbook.

The case that has been the focal point for this debate is Roe v. Wade, *the 1972 case which held that a woman's right to privacy protected her decision to have an abortion. The right to privacy in matters relating to contraception and childbearing had been recognized in the 1965 decision of* Griswold v. Connecticut, *and was extended in subsequent decisions culminating in* Roe. *The theoretical issue of concern here relates back to the incorporation issue: Should the Supreme Court be able to prohibit the states not only from violating the express guarantees contained in the Bill of Rights, but its implied guarantees as well?*

Roe v. *Wade* (1973)*

[Texas law prohibited abortions except for "the purpose of saving the life of the mother." Plaintiff challenged the constitutionality of the statute, claiming that it infringed upon her substantive due process right to privacy.]

JUSTICE BLACKMUN delivered the opinion of the Court.

. . . [We] forthwith acknowledge our awareness of the sensitive and emotional nature of the abortion controversy, of the vigorous opposing views, and the deep and seemingly absolute convictions that the subject inspires. One's philosophy, one's experiences, one's exposure to the raw edges of human existence, one's religious training, one's attitudes toward life and

*Roe v. Wade, 410 U.S. 113, 1973.

family and their values, and the moral standards one establishes and seeks to observe, are all likely to affect one's thinking [about] abortion. In addition, population growth, pollution, poverty, and racial overtones tend to complicate and not to simplify the problem. Our task, of course, is to resolve the issue by constitutional measurement, free of emotion and of predilection. We seek earnestly to do this, and, because we do, we have inquired into, and in this opinion place some emphasis upon, medical and medical-legal history and what that history reveals about man's attitudes toward the abortion procedure over the centuries. . . .

[The Court here reviewed ancient and contemporary attitudes toward abortion, observing that restrictive laws date primarily from the late nineteenth century. The Court also reviewed the possible state interests in restricting abortions, including discouraging illicit sexual conduct, limiting access to a hazardous medical procedure, and the states' general interests in protecting fetal life. The Court addressed only the third interest as a current legitimate interest of the state.]

. . . The Constitution does not explicitly mention any right of privacy. In a line of decisions, however, . . . the Court has recognized that a right of personal privacy, or a guarantee of certain areas or zones of privacy, does exist under the Constitution. . . . This right of privacy, whether it be founded in the Fourteenth Amendment's concept of personal liberty and restrictions upon state action, as we feel it is, or, as the District Court determined, in the Ninth Amendment's reservation of rights to the people, is broad enough to encompass a woman's decision whether or not to terminate her pregnancy. The detriment that the State would impose upon the pregnant woman by denying this choice altogether is apparent. Specific and direct harm medically diagnosable even in early pregnancy may be involved. Maternity, or additional offspring, may force upon the woman a distressful life and future. Psychological harm may be imminent. Mental and physical health may be taxed by child care. There is also the distress, for all concerned, associated with the unwanted child, and there is the problem of bringing a child into a family already unable, psychologically and otherwise, to care for it. In other cases, as in this one, the additional difficulties and continuing stigma of unwed motherhood may be involved. All these are factors the woman and her responsible physician necessarily will consider in consultation.

On the basis of elements such as these, appellants and some amici argue that the woman's right is absolute and that she is entitled to terminate her pregnancy at whatever time, in whatever way, and for whatever reason she alone chooses. With this we do not agree. Appellants' arguments that Texas either has no valid interest at all in regulating the abortion decision, or no interest strong enough to support any limitation upon the woman's sole determination, is unpersuasive. The Court's decisions recognizing a right of privacy also acknowledge that some state regulation in areas protected by that right is appropriate. As noted above, a State may properly assert important interests in safeguarding health, in maintaining medical standards, and in protecting potential life. At some point in pregnancy, these respective interests become sufficiently compelling to sustain regulation of the factors that govern the abortion decision. The privacy right involved, therefore, cannot be said to be absolute. In fact, it is not clear to us that the claim asserted by some amici that one has an unlimited right to do with one's body as one pleases bears a close relationship to the right of privacy previously articulated in the Court's decisions. . . .

We therefore conclude that the right of personal privacy includes the abortion decision, but that this right is not unqualified and must be considered against state interests in regulation.

Where certain "fundamental rights" are involved, the Court has held that regulation limiting these rights may be justified only by a "compelling state interest," and that legislative enactments must be narrowly drawn to express only the legitimate state interests at stake.

. . . The District Court held that the appellee failed to meet his burden of demonstrating that the Texas statute's infringement upon Roe's rights was necessary to support a compelling state interest. . . . Appellee argues that the State's determination to recognize and protect prenatal life from and after conception constitutes a compelling state interest. As noted above, we do not agree fully with either formulation.

The appellee and certain amici argue that the fetus is a "person" within the language and meaning of the Fourteenth Amendment. In support of this they outline at length and in detail the well-known facts of fetal development. If this suggestion of personhood is established, the appellant's case, of course, collapses, for the fetus' right to life is then guaranteed specifically by the Amendment. The appellant conceded as much on reargument. On the other hand, the appellee conceded on reargument that no case could be cited that holds that a fetus is a person within the meaning of the Fourteenth Amendment.

The Constitution does not define "person" in so many words. Section 1 of the Fourteenth Amendment contains three references to "person." The first, in defining "citizens," speaks of "persons born or naturalized in the United States." The word also appears both in the Due Process Clause and in the Equal Protection Clause. "Person" is used in other places in the Constitution. . . . But in nearly all these instances, the use of the word is such that it has application only postnatally. None indicates, with any assurance, that it has any possible pre-natal application.

All this, together with our observation, that throughout the major portion of the 19th century prevailing legal abortion practices were far freer than they are today, persuades us that the word "person," as used in the Fourteenth Amendment, does not include the unborn.

. . . The pregnant woman cannot be isolated in her privacy. She carries an embryo and, later, a fetus, if one accepts the medical definitions of the developing young in the human uterus. . . . The situation therefore is inherently different from marital intimacy, or bedroom possession of obscene material, or marriage, or procreation, or education, with which [earlier cases defining the right to privacy] were concerned. As we have intimated above, it is reasonable and appropriate for a State to decide that at some point in time another interest, that of health of the mother or that of potential human life, becomes significantly involved. The woman's privacy is no longer sole and any right of privacy she possesses must be measured accordingly.

Texas urges that, apart from the Fourteenth Amendment, life begins at conception and is present throughout pregnancy, and that, therefore, the State has a compelling interest in protecting that life from and after conception. We need not resolve the difficult question of when life begins. When those trained in the respective disciplines of medicine, philosophy, and theology are unable to arrive at any consensus, the judiciary, at this point in the development of man's knowledge, is not in a position to speculate as to the answer.

. . . In view of all this, we do not agree that, by adopting one theory of life, Texas may override the rights of the pregnant woman that are at stake. We repeat, however, that the State does have an important and legitimate interest in preserving and protecting the health of the pregnant woman, whether she be a resident of the State or a nonresident who seeks medical consultation and treatment there, and that it has still *another* important and legitimate interest in protecting the potentiality of human life. These interests are separate and distinct. Each grows in substantiality as the woman approaches term and, at a point during pregnancy, each becomes "compelling."

With respect to the State's important and legitimate interest in the health of the mother, the "compelling" point, in the light of present medical knowledge, is at approximately the end of the first trimester. This is so because of the now established medical fact . . . that until the end of the first trimester mortality in abortion is less than mortality in normal childbirth. It follows that, from and after this point, a State may regulate the abortion procedure to the extent that the regulation reasonably relates to the preservation and protection of maternal health. Examples of permissible state regulation in this area are requirements as to the qualifications of the person who is to perform the abortion; as to the licensure of that person; as to the facility in which the procedure is to be performed, that is, whether it must be a hospital or may be a clinic or some other place of less-than-hospital status; as to the licensing of the facility; and the like.

This means, on the other hand, that, for the period of pregnancy prior to this "compelling" point, the attending physician, in consultation with his patient, is free to determine, without regulation by the State, that in his medical judgment the patient's pregnancy should be terminated. If that decision is reached, the judgment may be effectuated by an abortion free of interference by the State.

With respect to the State's important and legitimate interest in potential life, the "compelling" point is at viability. This is so because the fetus then presumably has the capability of meaningful life outside the mother's womb. State regulation protective of fetal life after viability thus has both logical and biological justifications. If the State is interested in protecting fetal life after viability, it may go so far as to proscribe abortion during that period except when it is necessary to preserve the life or health of the mother.

Measured against these standards, the Texas Penal Code, in restricting legal abortions to those "procured or attempted by medical advice for the purpose of saving the life of the mother," sweeps too broadly. The statute makes no distinction between abortions performed early in pregnancy and those performed later, and it limits to a single reason, "saving" the mother's life, the legal justification for the procedure. The statute, therefore, cannot survive the constitutional attack made upon it here. . . .
Reversed.

See text p. 118

During the Reagan and Bush presidencies, five Supreme Court Justices were appointed: Justice Scalia, Justice O'Connor, Justice Kennedy, Justice Souter, and Justice Thomas. By the beginning of 1992 the Court was considered to be a solidly conservative institution, bent on curtailing the expansion of civil liberties and civil rights initiated by the Warren Court and continued under the Burger Court. While positions among the Justices varied on specific issues, it seemed to be a foregone conclusion that the Court would uphold the judgments of state and federal legislatures more than it had in the previous thirty years.

In the last two years, however, a strong centrist bloc, consisting of Justices O'Connor, Kennedy, and Souter has emerged. Although clearly willing to impose limits on a number of previously articulated civil rights and civil liberties, this bloc has not been willing to abandon many of those rights and liberties outright. Moreover, the extent to which the Court will redraw the contours of the rights and liberties currently guaranteed is an open question, since the judicial philosophy of any new appointees may have a significant effect on the direction the Court will take.

In the following article, written before President Clinton had nominated a replacement for retiring Justice Byron White, Supreme Court commentator John Moore canvasses the Court's work to look at how various Justices have approached civil liberties and civil rights questions.

W. John Moore
"Sizing Up the Court's 'Gang of Three' "*

Like a spectacular fireworks display, the Supreme Court, in its 1991–92 term, left its most dazzling performance to the end. The Court's grand finale elicited oohs and ahs from even the most jaded Court-watchers; many prognosticators, in fact, were fooled by the last batch of decisions. In abortion, church-state and death penalty cases, the Court declined to make the dramatic changes that some experts had predicted.

Court-watchers reversed their interpretations. Even with five Justices appointed by Presidents Reagan and Bush, the Court refused to make a sharp turn to the right. Such hard-core conservatives as Justices Antonin Scalia and Clarence Thomas were blocked by the Court's moderates. The "Gang of Three"—Anthony M. Kennedy, Sandra Day O'Connor and David H. Souter—prevailed. The middle held.

"The three Justices seem to have formed a surprising new force reasserting a traditional legal attitude toward constitutional interpretation, a force that has so far partially frustrated the right-wing's desire" to remake the Court, Ronald Dworkin, a scholar at Harvard Law School, wrote recently in *The New York Review of Books.*

Some critics, however, maintain that both the analysis and the applause are a wee bit premature. There has been "a counter-revolution in Supreme Court jurisprudence," warned Ira Glasser, the executive director of the American Civil Liberties Union (ACLU) in New York City. "The Court increasingly defers to the majoritarian excesses it is supposed to curb."

Other legal experts noted that the centrist bloc has played a key role in moving the Court to the right in such key areas as civil rights and criminal law. The trio has been part of the majority in limiting access to federal courts.

"There is no center," John A. Powell, the ACLU's legal director, added at a recent briefing on the Court's new term. "The cases that did test the judiciousness of the Justices have largely come and gone, and the center did not hold." The centrists only blunted the impact of the right-wing judges in what should have been easy cases to decide—*Planned Parenthood of Southeastern Pennsylvania v. Casey,* for instance. [In *Planned Parenthood v. Casey,* the Court upheld the majority of the provisions of a Pennsylvania law restricting access to abortions, holding that they did not amount to an "undue burden" on women's right to an abortion. Pro-choice activists claimed that the restrictions substantially undercut the right to an abortion, while anti-abortion activists berated the Court for failing to overturn *Roe v. Wade* outright.]

"If you took a poll among women denied abortions, or blacks in the

*W. John Moore, "Sizing Up the Court's 'Gang of Three,' " *National Journal* (October 10, 1992).

inner cities, or gays," Glasser said, "I don't think they would say the Court is moderate."

The ACLU lawyers emphasize that public access to the courts and civil rights are two areas of the law in which conservatives have seemingly triumphed. In the civil rights cases, the Gang of Three has had no problem scaling back affirmative action. The three Justices, along with the other six, ruled last term in *Board of Education of Oklahoma City Public Schools v. Dowell* that after school districts have eliminated any vestiges of illegal segregation, they have no duty to remedy racial imbalances that have been caused by demographic shifts.

For plaintiffs' lawyers, the Justices appointed by Reagan and Bush have erected sturdy procedural barriers that limit access to the courts. Last term, the Court, in *Lujan v. Defenders of Wildlife,* restricted the ability of environmental groups to challenge an Interior Department regulation and also ruled in *Suter v. Artist M* that there was no private right to bring suit under the 1980 Adoption Assistance Act, which was supposed to protect the parental rights of natural parents. And finally the Court, with only the three remaining liberals dissenting, barred certain indigent plaintiffs from requesting a waiver of the Court's filing fees when asking the Court to hear their cases. These new restrictions come as the Bush Administration's agenda at the Court has become far more important.

"The Solicitor General takes a larger and larger role in the Court's business," E. Barrett Prettyman Jr., a partner at the Washington law firm of Hogan & Hartson, said at a press briefing sponsored by the pro-business Washington Legal Foundation. The Solicitor General has filed briefs in 48 of the first 65 cases the Court has agreed to hear this term, Prettyman said.

Most conservatives would cheer the recent Court rulings that the ACLU found most abhorrent, especially those limiting the power of the courts to protect minority rights that run contrary to majority will. On the other hand, many conservatives have groaned the loudest about a centrist troika that's unwilling to overturn abortion or church-state precedent.

The [1992 election] could determine how long any such bloc exists, with legal experts saying that . . . President [Clinton] could name one to perhaps four or even five new Justices. The Court's 1992–93 term should also give a better sense of the power held by Kennedy, O'Connor and Souter. One of the key cases, *Bray v. Alexandria Women's Health Clinic,* has to do with an abortion protest. At issue is whether women seeking an abortion should be protected from protesters under a Reconstruction Era civil rights law. The case was heard last year before Clarence Thomas joined the Court. The speculation has been that the voting was 4–4, meaning that Thomas would be the fifth vote. But the moderates could decide this case.

"I believe that what the centrist court did in *Casey* gives us cause to be optimistic," said Helen R. Neuborne, the executive director of the NOW Legal Defense and Education Fund in New York City. But the case could be decided on different legal grounds than was the last abortion case, Neuborne added.

Another key test could be a religious freedom case, *Church of the Lukumi*

Babalu Aye v. Hialeah, Fla. At issue is what city ordinances constitute an abridgement of religion. O'Connor and Scalia have clashed on this issue. In the area of criminal law, the moderates must decide whether a death row prisoner with new evidence of his innocence is entitled to a federal review of his conviction. Criminal law and civil rights experts see this as a major test for the Court's moderates. Other pending cases examine whether judicial decisions should be retroactive and whether lower courts can refuse to hear civil liberties cases merely because the plaintiffs have included too little information in their complaints. These decisions may reveal whether the Court is truly in the middle, or just in a muddle.

CIVIL RIGHTS

See text p. 125

Brown v. Board of Education *(1954) was a momentous opinion, invalidating the system of apartheid that had been established under* Plessy v. Ferguson *(1896). As the text points out, however, the constitutional pronouncement only marked the beginning of the struggle for racial equality, as federal courts got more and more deeply involved in trying to prod recalcitrant state and local governments into taking steps to end racial inequalities. The* Brown *decision follows.*

Brown v. *Board of Education* (1954)*

[The Brown *case involved appeals from several states. In each case, the plaintiffs had been denied access to public schools designated only for white children under a variety of state laws. They challenged the* Plessy *v.* Ferguson *(1896) "separate but equal" doctrine, contending that segregated schools were by their nature unequal.*

Chief Justice Warren first discussed the history of the Fourteenth Amendment's equal protection clause, finding it too inconclusive to be of assistance in determining how the Fourteenth Amendment should be applied to the question of public education.]

Chief Justice Warren writing for the majority.

. . . The doctrine of "separate but equal" did not make its appearance in this Court until 1896, in the case of Plessy v. Ferguson, involving not education but transportation. American courts have since labored with the doctrine for over half a century. In this Court, there have been six cases involving the "separate but equal" doctrine in the field of public education. . . .

*Brown v. Board of Education of Topeka, Kansas, 347 U.S. 483, 1954.

In the instant cases, [the question of the application of the separate but equal doctrine to public education] is directly presented. Here, . . . there are findings below that the Negro and white schools involved have been equalized, or are being equalized, with respect to buildings, curricula, qualifications and salaries of teachers, and other "tangible" factors. Our decision, therefore, cannot turn on merely a comparison of these tangible factors in the Negro and white schools involved in each of the cases. We must look instead to the effect of segregation itself on public education.

In approaching this problem, we cannot turn the clock back to 1868 when the [Fourteenth] Amendment was adopted, or even to 1896 when Plessy v. Ferguson was written. We must consider public education in the light of its full development and its present place in American life throughout the Nation. Only in this way can it be determined if segregation in public schools deprives these plaintiffs of the equal protection of the laws.

Today, education is perhaps the most important function of state and local governments. Compulsory school attendance laws and the great expenditures for education both demonstrate our recognition of the importance of education to our democratic society. It is required in the performance of our most basic public responsibilities, even service in the armed forces. It is the very foundation of good citizenship. Today it is a principal instrument in awakening the child to cultural values, in preparing him for later professional training, and in helping him to adjust normally to his environment. In these days, it is doubtful that any child may reasonably be expected to succeed in life if he is denied the opportunity of an education. Such an opportunity, where the state has undertaken to provide it, is a right which must be made available to all on equal terms.

We come then to the question presented: Does segregation of children in public schools solely on the basis of race, even though the physical facilities and other "tangible" factors may be equal, deprive the children of the minority group of equal educational opportunities? We believe that it does.

In Sweatt v. Painter, in finding that a segregated law school for Negroes could not provide them equal educational opportunities, this Court relied in large part on "those qualities which are incapable of objective measurement but which make for greatness in a law school." In McLaurin v. Oklahoma State Regents, the Court, in requiring that a Negro admitted to a white graduate school be treated like all other students, again resorted to intangible considerations: ". . . his ability to study, to engage in discussions and exchange views with other students, and, in general, to learn his profession." Such considerations apply with added force to children in grade and high schools. To separate them from others of similar age and qualifications solely because of their race generates a feeling of inferiority as to their status in the community that may effect their hearts and minds in a way unlikely ever to be undone. The effect of this separation on their educational opportunities was well stated by a finding in the Kansas case by a court which nevertheless felt compelled to rule against the Negro plaintiffs:

"Segregation of white and colored children in public schools has a detrimental effect upon the colored children. The impact is greater when it has the sanction of the law; for the policy of separating the races is usually interpreted as denoting the inferiority of the Negro group. A sense of inferiority affects the motivation of a child to learn. Segregation with the sanction of law, therefore, has a tendency to [retard] the educational and mental development of Negro children and to deprive them of some of the benefits they would receive in a racial[ly] integrated school system." Whatever may have been the extent of psychological knowledge at the time of Plessy v. Ferguson, this finding is amply supported by modern authority. Any language in Plessy v. Ferguson contrary to this finding is rejected.

We conclude that in the field of public education the doctrine of "separate but equal" has no place. Separate educational facilities are inherently unequal. Therefore, we hold that the plaintiffs and others similarly situated for whom the actions have been brought are, by reason of the segregation complained of, deprived of the equal protection of the laws guaranteed by the Fourteenth Amendment. This disposition makes unnecessary any discussion whether such segregation also violates the Due Process Clause of the Fourteenth Amendment.

Because these are class actions, because of the wide applicability of this decision, and because of the great variety of local conditions, the formulation of decrees in these cases presents problems of considerable complexity. On reargument, the consideration of appropriate relief was necessarily subordinated to the primary question—the constitutionality of segregation in public education. We have now announced that such segregation is a denial of the equal protection of the laws.

Debating the Issue: Opposing Views

AFFIRMATIVE ACTION

See text p. 136–37

As the text notes, government-sponsored affirmative action programs have generated enormous controversy across the nation. In the following two pieces, Evan Kemp, former chair of the Equal Employment Opportunity Commission (EEOC) under President Bush, and Paul Starr, a Princeton University sociologist and coeditor of the American Prospect *look at the continued viability of affirmative action programs.*

Kemp argues that, in practice, affirmative action policies have led to race norming and quota systems that ultimately undercut the goals behind those policies. Efforts to increase the numbers of women and people of color in the workforce and elsewhere have resulted in hiring practices that look only at numbers, not merit. Calls for diversity, according to Kemp, have become a blind for "politically correct . . . group entitlements." Kemp argues that the only way out of the dilemma is to abandon the practice of "discount[ing] the importance of merit in the guise of fairness."

Paul Starr agrees that current affirmative action policies should be re-examined, but disagrees with the premise that merit alone should be a determining factor in allocating resources; he contends that the United States has a singular obligation to assist the African-American community. Starr looks at the question in light of the conservative shift on the United States Supreme Court over the last decade, and the suggestion that the Court will reverse its earlier decisions approving affirmative action. Starr argues that affirmative action policies as currently structured have never been a good tool for changing the structure of opportunity in this country, and proposes instead a two-pronged program involving colorblind social policies and significant, broad-based support for minority communities.

Evan J. Kemp, Jr.
"Rights and Quotas, Theory and Practice"*

Finally, thanks to [the *Washington*] *Post*'s editorial "Looking Like America" [Nov. 29], the real debate on civil rights has begun. In my speech Nov. 24 [1992] to the National Press Club—"Have Civil Rights Become Group Rights?"—I called for such a beginning, for an honest discussion of the state of civil rights. I emphasized we must examine the effects of policies—race norming, quotas, goals, timetables—designed to facilitate affirmative action but resulting in insidious and pervasive racial, ethnic and gender preferences. I asked that we take a hard look at what is producing tensions among groups and fostering division in our society.

I have seen how the group approach feeds these tensions. As a leader of the disability rights movement, I fought for the guarantee of individual rights in the Americans With Disabilities Act. I knew group entitlement fails when applied to disability; employers do the minimum necessary under law to meet quotas, and never fill a quota with individuals with serious disabilities. As chairman of the EEOC I have found protection on the basis of group status also fails when applied to race, ethnicity and gender.

President-elect Clinton has recognized these tensions and resentments, and has been widely praised for doing so. He courageously told whites and blacks that division is unhealthy and must be healed. But the challenge to the Clinton administration will be to take the next step and examine whether the prescriptions to cure the disease of racial, ethnic and gender discrimination are outdated, even producing a counter-reaction.

According to the *Post*'s editorial, President-elect Clinton "can have a

*Evan J. Kemp, Jr., "Rights and Quotas, Theory and Practice," *Washington Post* (December 8, 1992).

diverse administration and the country *still* [Kemp's emphasis] be safe from quotas. . . . [T]he achievement of diversity in an administration or student body or faculty or work force does not require a resort to quotas."

In theory, no, but in practice, yes. Even after 12 years of Reagan-Bush policies, employers large and small, governments, universities and the non-profit sector all labor under a regulatory regime that results in the wide-spread use of quotas.

Here's how the system actually works: The Labor Department requires federal contractors to report the race, ethnic and gender composition of its work force. Failure to reflect a "correct" composition risks loss of federal contracts. Employers also must grapple with "business necessity" and the Uniform Guidelines on Employee Selection Procedures)—the government regulation that requires businesses to prove any selection procedure that has a "disparate impact" on racial, ethnic or gender groups is absolutely necessary. "Disparate impact" means if your payroll doesn't meet the government's prescription for racial, ethnic or gender mix, you may be sued.

Thus, the Uniform Guidelines have become the arbiter of individual merit in American employment. An employer who prefers high school graduates over nongraduates, for example, would risk a discrimination charge because of possible differences in graduation rates among different racial and ethnic groups. But even when an employer successfully defends the "business necessity" of employment decisions, the Uniform Guidelines burden the employer to continue to search for "alternative selection procedures" producing less of a disparate impact (i.e., producing equality of results when comparing groups).

To avoid expensive litigation, prudent employers "hire by the numbers" ensuring their work force's "bottom line" reflects the racial, ethnic and gender composition of their labor market. More important, "hiring by the numbers" satisfies the Office of Federal Contract Compliance (and for that matter, EEOC field investigators), even though the Supreme Court has held Title VII of the Civil Rights Act of 1964 protects individuals, not groups.

While "hiring by the numbers" has become de facto civil rights policy, it begs the question of whose "numbers." According to historian Stephan Thernstrom of Harvard University, there are at least 106 ethnic groups in the American labor force.

Here we get to the issue of "diversity," which the media treat as the Holy Grail but which in practice has too often come to mean group entitlement in the workplace and in our universities. President-elect Clinton's desire to make his administration "look like America" is laudable. But how to get there? The Clinton administration can be expected to report this "diversity" in terms of the percentage of race, ethnicity and gender for some, but not all, of these groups. "Diversity," which used to bring to mind the image of the melting pot, is today a politically correct call for group entitlements—the very quotas a majority of Americans oppose. . . .

Recently I heard divergent definitions of affirmative action voiced by two journalists, one black and one white. The black journalist believed affirmative action means dismantling illegal barriers to equal opportunity.

Her white colleague described affirmative action as preferential treatment. These insights were not the political hyperbole or euphemism of Bush-Reagan policy makers or, for that matter, *Post* editorial writers. These were citizens telling the truth as they saw it. And their truths reveal the lack of consensus, the myth of the "middle ground" that characterizes the debate about civil rights.

Where is [a] middle ground[?] . . . If by middle ground we mean consensus, that can only be reached by continuing to ask the tough questions—questions such as: In today's highly competitive world can we afford to discount the importance of merit in the guise of fairness? Do we owe something special to present-day African Americans—as opposed to Korean Americans, Chinese Americans, Hispanic Americans, Irish Americans—because blacks have suffered a history of slavery and discrimination? And if the answer is yes, can that debt ever be repaid in the devalued coin of racial preference? We must not be satisfied with facile or simplistic answers that bear little relationship to the reality of the workplace, the universities, indeed, of society as a whole.

The [Clinton] administration . . . must face that fact that if "diversity" is used to mask a regime of quotas, we will tear the fabric of this national along ethnic, racial and gender lines. Surely none of us wants that.

Paul Starr
"Race and Reparations: A New Road to Healing Black America"*

The rightward shift of the U.S. Supreme Court—likely to result in the reversal of earlier decisions upholding affirmative action—makes it imperative for Americans to find a new road to racial equality.

I propose that we move in two directions—toward the reconstruction of civil society in minority communities and the promotion of broad, nonracial policies for economic opportunity and security.

By civil society, I mean the "intermediate" institutions between the state and the individual—community associations, schools, local media, independent social agencies—that have always been critical to community economic and political development. Because of the legacy of slavery and discrimination, black institutions have never had the capital resources of comparable, predominantly white institutions.

A renewal of minority institutions, backed by fresh capital support, would have a potentially large "multiplier" effect on social development

*Paul Starr, "Race and Reparations: A New Road to Healing Black America," *Washington Post* (April 19, 1992). Copyright 1992 by The Washington Post. Reprinted with permission.

over generations because it would represent a lasting contribution to the stock of community wealth, not just to an individual's advantage.

Yet such institution-building would have limited impact unless complementary efforts addressed under economic and social problems. Scarce employment opportunities, eroding incomes in lower brackets and lack of access to health care hit minority groups with particular force. But rather than rely on racially targeted efforts, a post-affirmative-action strategy should emphasize broad-based, nonracial policies that make sense on their own—for example, national health reform, financing for training and higher education, family leave and other policies benefiting families with young children.

As William Julius Wilson and others have argued, broad-based policies that promote the interests of lower- and middle-income Americans—and that deliver substantial benefits to minorities on the basis of their economic condition—will do more to reduce minority poverty than narrowly based, and hence poorly funded, measures for minority groups or the poor alone. These efforts can also be designed to dovetail with strengthened intermediate institutions and thereby to contribute to the overall process of civil reconstruction and renewal.

Neither minority institution-building nor nonracial social policy implies any diminished commitment to fight racial discrimination. Given the judicial realities, however, discrimination will generally have to be fought with means provided by civil rights law other than preferential hiring and similar practices adopted under the rubric of affirmative action.

Originally, affirmative action meant outreach for minority candidates for college admissions, jobs and contracts. But it has also come to mean use of racial preferences to remedy a historic pattern of discrimination either in a particular institution or in society at large, or to achieve balance or diversity in line with demographic patterns. The constitutional and political problems concern affirmative action in this broadened use.

For many, affirmative action in the extended sense has become a litmus test of loyalty to civil rights and minority interests. Yet it has never been a good test. Affirmative action—that is, racial preference, above and beyond antidiscrimination enforcement—has had only a modest impact on the structure of opportunity and little, if any, effect on the ghetto poor.

And while it has improved minority representation in the professions and at some corporations, universities and public agencies, these gains have not come without cost. Affirmative-action policies have insidiously helped to perpetuate racism, as whites are inclined to believe that blacks have gotten positions despite having lower scores and lesser abilities—and accordingly expect blacks to perform less ably than whites.

There is no case currently on the court calendar likely to result in a decision overturning precedents for affirmative action. The departure of Justices William Brennan and Thurgood Marshall and the addition of Clarence Thomas, however, make likely a reversal of earlier decisions upheld by narrow majorities. In the wake of such a ruling, many liberals will want Congress to undo the court's action, as recent civil rights legislation reverses several court decisions regarding job discrimination.

But should the court overturn *Bakke* (the 1978 decision upholding affirmative action in public institutions), it may virtually preclude any congressional reversal by ruling that racial preferences are constitutionally impermissible, except as a narrowly tailored remedy in specific cases of discrimination. On the other hand, in restricting or overturning *United Steelworkers v. Weber* (a key 1979 decision approving private affirmative-action plans), the court would be revising its interpretation of a civil rights statute. Congress, to be sure, could respond by giving explicit approval to private affirmative-action plans. But, with opinion polls showing overwhelming majorities against affirmative action, this seems highly unlikely.

Nonetheless, the curtailment of affirmative action may mean less than is generally expected. Much of what is conventionally attributed to affirmative action will be sustained under antidiscrimination law, including the 1991 civil rights legislation (although this may be complicated if the court unleashes a wave of reverse-discrimination lawsuits). Furthermore, affirmative action is now a firmly established practice of many university, corporate and political decision makers. Just as discrimination did not end with formal rulings against it, neither will affirmative action end with formal rulings.

Some institutions may adopt more general, nonracially defined policies promoting diversity. In university admissions, there is already a move afoot to adopt affirmative action for the socio-economically disadvantaged of all races. Blacks could benefit because they form a higher proportion of the disadvantaged. But because low-income Asians and whites now outperform low-income blacks academically, such a policy would help blacks only when they make greater educational progress at earlier ages. That is surely where the chief emphasis should be—along with a broad, progressive program of financial support for post-secondary education and new capital for historically black institutions.

Here, as elsewhere, we need complementary strategies—nonracial social policy and community self-development.

Strengthening communal self-development in minority communities could appeal to conservatives, because it emphasizes nongovernmental means; to minority communities, because it conveys respect and provides support for their autonomous and indigenous institutions; and to the public at large, because it favors the kinds of institutions that promise to bring order and stability to violence-torn ghettoes.

Some may worry that support for community self-development is tantamount to an acceptance of separatism. But other ethnic and religious groups have strong communal institutions—Catholic, Protestant and Jewish philanthropies, social agencies, hospitals, newspapers and magazines—without anyone raising the specter of separatism. Those institutions have facilitated the integration of immigrant minorities into American society. Even if some black institutions, such as Afrocentric schools, do have a separatist philosophy, the history of the black community and inescapable economic realities strongly suggest that separatism will fail to command general support from black Americans.

The more practical question is this: Does white America owe black

America resources for community self-development? I think it does. Slavery and its aftermath deprived blacks as a community of opportunities to accumulate wealth. Today, a wide economic gulf separates even the black middle class from the white middle class. Overall, according to a study by Melvin L. Oliver and Thomas M. Schapiro based on 1984 data, black households have only one quarter the net worth and 11 percent of the net financial assets of white households. Astonishingly, white households with annual incomes between $7,500 and $15,000 in 1984 had higher mean net worth and net financial assets than black households making $45,000 to $60,000. Not just individuals, but the black community as a whole stands to inherit relatively little wealth from one generation to the next.

Still, I am under no illusion that American voters are ready to accept—let us use the correct term—reparations. But private philanthropy could recognize such obligations and lay the groundwork for a new National Endowment for Black America. This fund would receive capital contributions from industry and charitable foundations and individuals and would support a variety of social and cultural organizations in the black community. (It could also aid the formation of minority businesses with programs aimed at fostering entrepreneurship.) Once in operation, the endowment might receive public as well as private funds, which it could disburse in the form of "challenge" grants, requiring additional fund-raising to leverage its own resources and to reinforce practices of communal savings and investment.

My use of the word "black" rather than "minority" here is not accidental. While strengthening intermediate institutions among Hispanics and other minorities would also be worthwhile, I believe the obligations of the United States to black Americans are historically singular. And because the problems of social isolation and decline of civil society are more acute in the black ghettoes, civil reconstruction in black America is especially urgent.

Would a National Endowment for Black America be subject to the same criticism as affirmative action? The crucial difference is that this approach provides resources to institutions rather than individuals and thereby sidesteps charges that compensatory programs undermine merit-based standards. Unlike affirmative action, it does not affect decisions about individual careers and thereby avoids generating the sense of personal grievance that affirmative action has produced among some whites. The National Endowment for Black America would be a private institution—the private, race-specific branch of a strategy whose public branches are race-neutral.

Yet community development efforts, even with greater capital support, will fail unless combined with broader social and economic policies benefiting low- and middle-income Americans. Capital endowments provide institutions a margin of independence, often vital to developing their own long-term mission. But without strong, complementary systems of public financing for education, social services and child care—to mention three of the most critical areas—a strong independent sector in minority communities will not emerge.

The shift of the Supreme Court to the right is, I believe, an ominous development. But on affirmative action, it could be a blessing in disguise, forcing Americans to come up with answers to racial inequality that are more effective in liberating minorities from poverty and more successful in generating the broad coalitions needed to carry out a wider progressive reform. When the Supreme Court overturns racial preferences, those committed to racial justice should seize the occasion to mark a new beginning in the struggle.

QUESTIONS

1. As the result of the Court's decision in *Barron v. Baltimore,* was Barron left without any means of recovering compensation for the loss of his property? What avenues of relief might Barron have pursued after the Supreme Court dismissed his case?
2. According to the Supreme Court in *Gideon,* treating an accused person fairly serves not only the interests of the accused, but broader interests in governmental authority and legitimacy. In what ways might the authority of the government be undermined if the rights of criminal defendants are not protected?
3. According to the holding in *Roe v. Wade,* is a fetus a person endowed with rights under the Constitution? What is the "trimester approach" endorsed by Justice Blackmun? How might opponents of the Court's decision in *Roe* argue that the decision was not simply wrong on the merits, but represented an improper expansion of the Court's authority in a federal constitutional system?
4. How did the Supreme Court support its decision that segregated school systems are "inherently unequal" in *Brown v. Board of Education?* What kind of evidence did the Court consider in reaching that conclusion?
5. Is it realistic to suggest that women and people of color will have access to equal work and educational opportunities without affirmative-action programs? What does Kemp suggest are the pitfalls of affirmative-action programs? What modifications to the present system are suggested by Paul Starr?
6. Observers of the Supreme Court have expressed concern that the Rehnquist Court will turn the tide on expanding civil liberties under the Constitution. To what extent does it appear that the Court will reverse itself, and in what areas is retrenchment likely?

CHAPTER 5

Congress: The First Branch

REPRESENTATION

See text p. 152

In The Federalist No. 10, *the most important of* The Federalist Papers *(also reprinted as an appendix to the text), James Madison outlined the theory of representation that was to serve as the foundation for the American political system. Madison argued that faction was inevitable in a democracy, and that the only way to mitigate the effects of faction was to set up a representative system through which the passions of the people could be "refine[d] and filter[ed] . . . by passing them through the medium of a chosen body of citizens, whose wisdom may best discern the true interest of their country."*

This concept of a filter was critical to Federalist thought, and provided a key point of contention between the Federalists and the Antifederalists. The Antifederalists objected strongly to the idea that the views of the people ought to be screened by an elite representative body; they argued instead that representatives ought to mirror their constituents' views. Responding to the criticism about elite control, Madison propounded his views on a bicameral system in The Federalist No. 57 *and* The Federalist No. 62. *Madison argued that the structure and composition of the House of Representatives would provide the necessary link to the people, while the structure and composition of the Senate would insure that intemperate actions proposed by the House would not be too readily adopted.*

These institutional differences lead to differences in the way that law is made, as the text notes. Peter Carlson, writing in the Washington Post Magazine *in 1990, described the resulting distinctions between the House and the Senate as follows: "The Senate is a gentleman's [sic] club. The House is a fraternity. The Senate is the* New York Times. *The House is the* New York Post. *The Senate is 'Washington Week in Review.' The House is 'The Morton Downey Show.' " Whatever the merit of this description, it is very clear from reading the following selections that the differences were designed into the system.*

James Madison
*The Federalist No. 57**

[There is a] charge against the House of Representatives . . . that it will be taken from that class of citizens which will have least sympathy with the mass of the people, and be most likely to aim at an ambitious sacrifice of the many to the aggrandizement of the few.

Of all the objections which have been framed against the federal Consti-

*James Madison, *The Federalist No. 57.*, ed. Clinton Rossiter (New York: NAL, 1961).

tution, this is perhaps the most extraordinary. Whilst the objection itself is leveled against a pretended oligarchy, the principle of it strikes at the very root of republican government.

The aim of every political constitution is, or ought to be, first to obtain for rulers men who possess most wisdom to discern, and most virtue to pursue, the common good of the society; and in the next place, to take the most effectual precautions for keeping them virtuous whilst they continue to hold their public trust. The elective mode of obtaining rulers is the characteristic policy of republican government. The means relied on in this form of government for preventing their degeneracy are numerous and various. The most effectual one is such a limitation of the term of appointments as will maintain a proper responsibility to the people.

Let me now ask what circumstance there is in the constitution of the House of Representatives that violates the principles of republican government, or favors the elevation of the few on the ruins of the many? Let me ask whether every circumstance is not, on the contrary, strictly conformable to these principles, and scrupulously impartial to the rights and pretensions of every class and description of citizens?

Who are to be the electors of the federal representatives? Not the rich, more than the poor; not the learned, more than the ignorant; not the haughty heirs of distinguished names, more than the humble sons of obscure and unpropitious fortune. The electors are to be the great body of the people of the United States. They are to be the same who exercise the right in every State of electing the corresponding branch of the legislature of the State.

Who are to be the objects of popular choice? Every citizen whose merit may recommend him to the esteem and confidence of his country. No qualification of wealth, of birth, of religious faith, or of civil profession is permitted to fetter the judgment or disappoint the inclination of the people.

If we consider the situation of the men on whom the free suffrages of their fellow-citizens may confer the representative trust, we shall find it involving every security which can be devised or desired for their fidelity to their constituents.

In the first place, as they will have been distinguished by the preference of their fellow-citizens, we are to presume that in general they will be somewhat distinguished also by those qualities which entitle them to it, and which promise a sincere and scrupulous regard to the nature of their engagements.

In the second place, they will enter into the public service under circumstances which cannot fail to produce a temporary affection at least to their constituents. There is in every breast a sensibility to marks of honor, of favor, of esteem, and of confidence, which, apart from all considerations of interests, is some pledge for grateful and benevolent returns. . . .

In the third place, those ties which bind the representative to his constituents are strengthened by motives of a more selfish nature. . . . [A] great proportion of the men deriving their advancement from their influence with the people would have more to hope from a preservation of the favor than from innovations in the government subversive of the authority of the people.

All these securities, however, would be found very insufficient without the restraint of frequent elections. Hence, in the fourth place, the House of Representatives is so constituted as to support in the members an habitual recollection of their dependence on the people. Before the sentiments impressed on their minds by the mode of their elevation can be effaced by the exercise of power, they will be compelled to anticipate the moment when their power is to cease, when their exercise of it is to be reviewed, and when they must descend to the level from which they were raised; there forever to remain unless a faithful discharge of their trust shall have established their title to a renewal of it.

I will add, as a fifth circumstances in the situation of the House of Representatives, restraining them from oppressive measures, that they can make no law which will not have its full operation on themselves and their friends, as well as on the great mass of the society. . . . It creates between [the rulers and the people] that communion of interests and sympathy of sentiments of which few governments have furnished examples; but without which every government degenerates into tyranny. If it be asked, what is to restrain the House of Representatives from making legal discriminations in favor of themselves and a particular class of the society? I answer: the genius of the whole system; the nature of just and constitutional laws; and, above all, the vigilant and manly spirit which actuates the people of America—a spirit which nourishes freedom, and in return is nourished by it.

If this spirit shall ever be so far debased as to tolerate a law not obligatory on the legislature, as well as on the people, the people will be prepared to tolerate anything but liberty.

Such will be the relation between the House of Representatives and their constituents. Duty, gratitude, interest, ambition itself, are the cords by which they will be bound to fidelity and sympathy with the great mass of the people. It is possible that these may all be insufficient to control the caprice and wickedness of men. But are they not all that government will admit, and that human prudence can devise? Are they not the genuine and the characteristic means by which republican government provides for the liberty and happiness of the people? Are they not the identical means on which every State government in the Union relies for the attainment of these important ends? . . . What are we to say to the men who profess the most flaming zeal for republican government, yet boldly impeach the fundamental principle of it; who pretend to be champions for the right and the capacity of the people to choose their own rulers, yet maintain that they will prefer those only who will immediately and infallibly betray the trust committed to them?

PUBLIUS

James Madison
*The Federalist No. 62**

Having examined the constitution of the House of Representatives, and answered such of the objections against it as seemed to merit notice, I enter next on the examination of the Senate. . . .

The qualifications proposed for senators, as distinguished from those of representatives, consist in a more advanced age and a longer period of citizenship. . . . The propriety of these distinctions is explained by the nature of the senatorial trust, which, requiring greater extent of information and stability of character, requires at the same time that the senator should have reached a period of life most likely to supply these advantages; and which, participating immediately in transactions with foreign nations, ought to be exercised by none who are not thoroughly weaned from the prepossessions and habits incident to foreign birth and education. . . .

It is equally unnecessary to dilate on the appointment of senators by the State legislatures. . . . It is recommended by the double advantage of favoring a select appointment, and of giving to the State governments such an agency in the formation of the federal government as must secure the authority of the former, and may form a convenient link between the two systems.

The equality of representation in the Senate is another point which, being evidently the result of compromise between the opposite pretensions of the large and the small States, does not call for much discussion. . . . In a compound republic, partaking both of the national and federal character, the government ought to be founded on a mixture of the principles of proportional and equal representation. . . .

In this spirit it may be remarked that the equal vote allowed to each State is at once a constitutional recognition of the portion of sovereignty remaining in the individual States and an instrument for preserving that residuary sovereignty. So far the equality ought to be no less acceptable to the large than to the small States; since they are not less solicitous to guard, by every possible expedient, against an improper consolidation of the States into one simple republic.

Another advantage accruing from this ingredient in the constitution of the Senate is the additional impediment it must prove against improper acts of legislation. No law or resolution can now be passed without the concurrence, first, of a majority of the people, and then of a majority of the States. It must be acknowledged that this complicated check on legislation may in some instances be injurious as well as beneficial; and that the peculiar defense which it involves in favor of the smaller States would be more rational if any interests common to them and distinct from those of the other States would otherwise be exposed to peculiar danger. But as the larger States will always be able, by their power over the supplies, to defeat

*James Madison, *The Federalist No. 62,* ed. Clinton Rossiter (New York: NAL, 1961).

unreasonable exertions of this prerogative of the lesser States, and as the facility and excess of law-making seem to be the diseases to which our governments are most liable, it is not impossible that this part of the Constitution may be more convenient in practice than it appears to many in contemplation.

The number of senators and the duration of their appointment come next to be considered. . . . It will be proper to inquire into the purposes which are to be answered by a senate; and in order to ascertain these it will be necessary to review the inconveniences which a republic must suffer from the want of such an institution.

First. It is a misfortune incident to republican government . . . that those who administer it may forget their obligations to their constituents and prove unfaithful to their important trust. In this point of view a senate, as a second branch of the legislative assembly distinct from and dividing the power with a first, must be in all cases a salutary check on the government. It doubles the security of the people by requiring the concurrence of two distinct bodies in schemes of usurpation or perfidy, where the ambition or corruption of one would otherwise be sufficient. . . .

Second. The necessity of a senate is not less indicated by the propensity of all single and numerous assemblies, to yield to the impulse of sudden and violent passions, and to be seduced by factious leaders into intemperate and pernicious resolutions. . . . A body which is to correct this infirmity ought itself to be free from it, and consequently ought to be less numerous. It ought, moreover, to possess great firmness, and consequently ought to hold its authority by a tenure of considerable duration.

Third. Another defect to be supplied by a senate lies in a want of due acquaintance with the objects and principles of legislation. It is not possible that an assembly of men called for the most part from pursuits of a private nature continued in appointment for a short time and led by no permanent motive to devote the intervals of public occupation to a study of the laws, the affairs, and the comprehensive interests of their country, should, if left wholly to themselves, escape a variety of important errors in the exercise of their legislative trust. . . .

A good government implies two things: first, fidelity to the object of government, which is the happiness of the people; secondly, a knowledge of the means by which that object can be best attained. . . . The federal Constitution avoids this error; and what merits particular notice, it provides for the last in a mode which increases the security for the first.

Fourth. The mutability in the public councils arising from a rapid succession of new members, however qualified they may be, points out, in the strongest manner, the necessity of some stable institution in the government. Every new election in the States is found to change one half of the representatives. From this change of men must proceed a change of opinions; and from a change of opinions, a change of measures. But a continual change even of good measures is inconsistent with every rule of prudence and every prospect of success. The remark is verified in private life, and becomes more just, as well as more important, in national transactions.

. . . [If the nation's government changes too often], it forfeits the respect and confidence of other nations, and all the advantages connected with national character. . . . Every nation, . . . whose affairs betray a want of wisdom and stability, may calculate on every loss which can be sustained from the more systematic policy of its wiser neighbors. But the best instruction on this subject is unhappily conveyed to America by the example of her own situation. She finds that she is held in no respect by her friends; that she is the derision of her enemies; and that she is a prey to every nation which has an interest in speculating on her fluctuating councils and embarrassed affairs.

The internal effects of a mutable policy are still more calamitous. It poisons the blessings of liberty itself, it will be of little avail to the people that the laws are made by men of their own choice if the laws be so voluminous that they cannot be read, or so incoherent that they cannot be understood; if they be repealed or revised before they are promulgated, or undergo such incessant changes that no man, who knows what the law is today, can guess what it will be tomorrow. Law is defined to be a rule of action; but how can that be a rule, which is little known, and less fixed?

Another effect of public instability is the unreasonable advantage it gives to the sagacious, the enterprising, and the moneyed few over the industrious and uniformed mass of the people. Every new regulation concerning commerce or revenue, or in any manner affecting the value of the different species of property, presents a new harvest to those who watch the change, and can trace its consequences; a harvest, reared not by themselves, but by the toils and cares of the great body of their fellow-citizens. This is a state of things in which it may be said with some truth that laws are made for the *few,* not for the *many.*

In another point of view, great injury results from an unstable government. The want of confidence in the public councils camps every useful undertaking, the success and profit of which may depend on a continuance of existing arrangements. . . . In a word, no great improvement or laudable enterprise can go forward which requires the auspices of a steady system of national policy.

But the most deplorable effect of all is that diminution of attachment and reverence which steals into the hearts of the people towards a political system which betrays so many marks of infirmity, and disappoints so many of their flattering hopes. No government, any more than an individual, will long be respected without being truly respectable; nor be truly respectable without possessing a certain portion of order and stability.

PUBLIUS

Making Law

THE COMMITTEE SYSTEM: THE CORE OF CONGRESS

See text p. 177

As the text notes, committees have traditionally been the backbone of Congress, providing the structure upon which the actual work of legislating is carried out. The importance of committees lies largely in their function as a forum in which legislative proposals can be brought forth and discussed by members of both parties with expertise in the particular subject matter at issue.

In recent years, however, the power of committees has been dramatically undercut. As Kenneth Shepsle has pointed out in The Changing Textbook Congress, *Congress in the 1940s and 1950s operated on a committee-based equilibrium. Beginning in the 1970s, however, broad, demographic changes created a different external environment, while internal changes in rules governing seniority allowed less experienced congressional members to chair committees. Subcommittees proliferated, draining power from committee chairs, legislation became increasingly complex, and deep divisions developed both within the parties and between Congress and the executive branch. Each of these factors contributed to the decreasing efficiency of the committee system. The result, according to Richard Cohen, a political commentator for the* National Journal, *is that committees have proved largely unable to initiate and move along legislative proposals, shifting that responsibility to party leaders by default.*

Richard E. Cohen
"Crumbling Committees"*

Woodrow Wilson would hardly recognize Congress these days.

"Congress in its committee rooms is Congress at work," the 32nd President, while a graduate student in 1885, wrote in *Congressional Government.*

Wilson's book, still a political science classic a century later, talked of how Congress handled most legislation through a hierarchical system dominated by committee chairmen.

In recent years, however, internal changes have quietly revolutionized the sources of legislative power on Capitol Hill, eroding the influence of once all-powerful committees and of their bosses. Today, committees are often irrelevant or, worse yet, obstacles.

Congress has turned to these new arrangements, in part, to ease the lawmakers' burden. "The erosion of the committee process has made life more difficult in the Senate," said a former top Senate aide who is now a corporate lobbyist. But the informal, closed-door sessions that have resulted

*Richard E. Cohen, "Crumbling Committees," *National Journal* (August 4, 1990).

from this erosion "may be an attribute for Senators working in a fish-bowl, where every lobbyist knows what is happening before he does."

There are other reasons for the new procedures, including the reforms of the 1970s that some blame for exacerbating committee turf battles and producing too many subcommittee chairmen. The move away from committee dominance is also driven by nonlegislative concerns: On some politically volatile issues, party leaders have simply concluded that the committee process doesn't work.

. . . [C]ongress, especially the Senate [repeatedly went] outside the committee system to handle key legislation during [1990]. . . . [Through] informal arrangements, [legislation] took shape behind closed doors, with party leaders controlling the process. In at least one aspect, therefore, Wilson's portrayal of Congress remains valid. "One very noteworthy result of this system," he wrote, "is to shift the theater of debate upon legislation from the floor of Congress to the privacy of the committee rooms."

Shifting Power

This topsy-turvy handling of major issues reflects some broader internal changes. They include the breakdown of the seniority system, an erosion of party discipline, the paralysis resulting from divided party control of the White House and Congress, increased partisan sloganeering and the growing influence of 30-second campaign spot commercials.

The new, less formal procedures have led to other shortcomings in the legislative work product. "The committee process is designed to weed out problems," J. Thomas Sliter, a former top Senate Democratic aide, said. "But when bills are put together on an ad hoc basis, the trouble can be that there are no hearings and more staff control, which increases the risk of unintended consequences."

Members of Congress have complained that they have little idea what they are voting on when they are presented on the floor with an anticrime or an environmental bill, for example, that runs several hundred pages. Although tax bills are typically written inside the Ways and Means and Finance Committees, even those panels assign the task of writing the details to the committee staffs. The committees have been embarrassed occasionally when they have learned about the impact of the bills that have emerged.

. . . "In the not-distant past, the hallmark of the Senate was weak leaders and strong chairmen," said Robert G. Liberatore, who was staff director of the Senate Democratic Policy Committee from 1981–84. "The loss of power by committee chairmen and the increased chaos in the use of Senate rules to promote a Senator's views have required leadership to be more involved in keeping things going."

The altered power relationships have come in response to the often tumultuous political changes of the 1980s—notably, the division of political power between the White House and Congress and the shifts in control of the Senate in 1980 and again in 1986.

"The institution is groping to find ways to get things done when it's difficult to do anything," said Norman J. Ornstein, a congressional scholar at the American Enterprise Institute for Public Policy Research.

Congress is resorting more frequently to the informal procedures in part because the Bush Administration has been "more aggressive in arguing its views," Sen. Wendell H. Ford, D-Ky., said. "With the Administration leading the [Senate] Republicans almost in lockstep, that means that even if a bill is reported by a committee, the bill often won't move" without further negotiations. The President's effective use of the veto . . . has enhanced his influence at Congress's expense.

In the Senate more than in the House, Democrats have been forced to improvise because of turnover in the ranks of committee chairmen and party leaders. "Prior to 1980, there was an entrenched senior member staff structure in the Senate that had been there for more than a decade," said Leon G. Billings, a lobbyist who was a top aide to then-Senator Edmund S. Muskie, D-Maine. "That was seriously disrupted for Democrats in the six year hiatus [of 1981–87, when the GOP controlled the Senate]. More junior Senators, who were less well versed on specific issues, took over."

. . . "The problems we face are becoming more complex, and the solutions don't fit neatly into the baskets represented by the committee system," said David E. Johnson, a former top aide to [Senate Majority Leader George J.] Mitchell who is now a Washington lobbyist and an informal adviser to the Majority Leader. "When I started working for Muskie in 1973, the Senate was a much different place. There was more respect for seniority and learning your committee assignment. Now, it seems that there is more of an entrepreneurial spirit in the Senate and in politics, generally."

Constituent Committees

Wilson's observation in 1885 that committees predominate because "the House is conscious that time presses" remains apt.

Congress functions most smoothly when bills are written in committee with bipartisan support. On most committees, the members generally seek that approach, if only because what they produce is more likely to win support on the House or Senate floor if a consensus has developed.

"Task forces usually are created only after a committee has run into a problem moving a bill," said Thomas A. Daschle of South Dakota, the co-chairman with Mitchell of the Senate Democratic Policy Committee. "They may enhance the influence of a chairman if they can improve his ability to move a bill through the floor."

Members often seek assignments to committees that deal with the issues in which they and their constituents are most interested. And that means that the committees can become captives of the interest groups most affected by their work. Seats on the Agriculture Committees tend to be filled by lawmakers representing farmers, for example, and western and southern Senators gravitate toward the Energy and Natural Resources Committee.

"On the key committees that Senators want to be on—Finance, Appropriations, Armed Services—there tend to be more balanced views," said Liberatore, who is a lobbyist for Chrysler Corp. "Many of the others are constituent committees, which generally have more staff control, and there is less interest by members in the details of programs."

. . . "There is no concerted effort to bypass committees," said Senator Wyche Fowler Jr., D-Ga., whom Mitchell tapped as assistant floor leader. "That's much more difficult for leadership to manage." The need for informal mechanisms, in part, "has to do with the personalities and effectiveness" of chairmen, Fowler added.

Even seemingly routine action on bills can often become snarled. When the Senate in June 1989 acted on the child care bill—one of the Democrats' top domestic priorities—it was initially written by Labor and Human Resources Committee Democrats, who are mostly sympathetic to organized labor and child care groups. Before the measure could win Senate passage, however, Mitchell was forced to file a floor substitute that substantially watered down the original version and added provisions that the Finance Committee had prepared. Because most Republicans opposed the measure, the support of Orrin G. Hatch of Utah, the Labor Committee's senior Republican, was vital to Senate passage.

Hatch took a more traditional minority role when his strong opposition triggered an angry debate on the pending Civil Rights Act, which the Labor Committee drafted. As a result, committee chairman Edward M. Kennedy, D-Mass., sought but ultimately failed to work out differences directly with White House chief of staff John H. Sununu. Kennedy and Sununu had conducted similar negotiations a year ago to expedite Senate passage of landmark legislation expanding the rights of disabled persons.

. . . Some committees and committee chairmen have been ill-equipped to deal with . . . controversial topics requiring quick action and a sensitivity to partisan implications.

Pay raise and campaign finance bills, for example, have become known as "leadership issues." They require party leaders' extensive participation because "they involve the Members themselves and need bipartisan support," said Rep. Martin Frost, D-Texas, who has served on informal leadership panels dealing with both issues. . . .

"These are issues that require the leadership to play a critical role to overcome the parochial interests of individual Members," Common Cause president Fred Wertheimer said. "After 15 years of the parties' battling each other and incumbents benefiting from the current system, that makes it harder to resolve. . . . On these issues, accountability is not with the committee system, it's with the party leaders."

. . . Sometimes, overlapping committee jurisdictions are obstacles to moving legislation to the floor. Issues such as education, trade and drug control may be in the jurisdiction principally of a single committee of the House or Senate. But several other committees can and often do argue for a share of the jurisdiction so that their members can get a piece of the action.

"There are so many overlapping jurisdictions, which create difficulties in working out problems," Daschle said. "And many more Members desire to be involved, even though they are not on the committee with jurisdiction." That helps to explain, for example, why eight Senate committees and nine House committees worked on parts of the 1988 Trade Act.

Reformers made several efforts in the 1970s to overhaul committee jurisdiction but failed, for the most part, because of opposition from Members who feared a loss of influence. . . .

"It's not possible for many bills to go through the committee system until Congress redoes itself," said Bolling, who has become an adviser to Gephardt. "It's nutty now. But this is not the time to reform, either strategically or politically."

Other major changes in the mid-1970s, which were the culmination of lengthy efforts by Bolling and other Democratic reformers, served to weaken the roles of the once-autocratic committee chairmen. They included the adoption of the new congressional budget process; the election in 1974 of the "Watergate babies," nationally oriented House Democrats with little respect for their elders or for House traditions; and the strengthening of the House Democratic Caucus, which demonstrated its new muscle in 1975 by ousting three senior committee chairmen. Intentionally or not, these changes contributed to Congress's internal gridlock. . . .

"Congress prefers strong chairmen," Fowler said. "But the proliferation of chairmen has weakened the committee system. You no longer have the whales on any complex issues. You usually have two to three committee chairmen and eight or nine subcommittee chairmen, all jealous of their turf.". . .

Flexible Leaders

New procedures intended to supplement the work of the committees may enhance the power of congressional leaders, especially those in the Senate. "By picking who is on the team and putting a spin on the outcome, leadership can exert more control," a Senate Democratic source said.

At the same time, the added responsibilities can complicate the lives of party leaders, who already have to balance a range of legislative and political demands. Increasingly, however, Members are selecting leaders—such as Mitchell, Gephardt, Dole and House Minority Whip Newt Gingrich—who have demonstrated that they can not only speak to national constituencies but can also deal with internal pressures.

In addition, Bush and top White House officials have been more interested in resolving legislative details with congressional leaders than their recent predecessors have—in part, congressional sources suggest, because Bush spends less time than other Presidents did developing a White House legislative agenda.

Until recent years, active Presidents did not have to contend with strong congressional leaders seeking their own podiums. Sam Rayburn of Texas, who was House Speaker in 17 of the years from 1940–61 and was probably the century's most skillful lawmaker, prided himself on his ability to work closely with Presidents and committee chairmen. But to the public at large, he was not very well known.

"Rayburn had half the power" of later Speakers, said Bolling, whom many regarded as Rayburn's protege. "But he had enormous prestige from the ability to understand what could be done and how to tell a President."

Mitchell may be setting a new model for Senate leaders as he tries to combine the roles of legislative agenda-setter and national party spokesman. Last fall, for example, he engaged in public and private lobbying to kill, virtually single-handedly, Bush's proposed cut in the capital gains tax rate, which was backed by a majority of Senators, including members of the Finance Committee.

"George Mitchell takes a much more flexible approach to leadership," Ornstein said. "This is an era when leaders use whatever tools work and seek new ones, where necessary. . . . They have to be more creative and improvisational." . . .

Whether it is the budget or other issues, party leaders have often said that they do not want to put their own "stamp" on issues. In an increasing number of cases, however, they have found that if they don't no one else can.

See text p. 179

As the text notes, the size of the Congressional staff has increased dramatically in recent decades. In the following article Eric Felton, an editorial writer for the Washington Times *and author of* The Ruling Class: Inside the Imperial Congress, *takes aim at the power of Congressional staffers. Felton argues that in an increasingly complex Congressional arena, staffers have unwarranted power, a vested interest in enlarging governmental programs, and are wholly unaccountable to the public.*

Eric Felten
"Little Princes: The Petty Despotism of Congressional Staff"*

"People asked me how I felt about being elected to Congress, and I told them I never thought I'd give up that much power voluntarily."

—Representative Norman Dicks (D-WA), on his election to Congress after spending eight years as an aide to Senator Warren Magnuson (D-WA)

Neil Sigmon is one of the most powerful people in Congress. But Sigmon is neither a senator nor a representative. A staff member for the House

*Eric Felten, "Little Princes: The Petty Despotism of Congressional Staff" *Policy Review* (Winter 1993). Reprinted with permission.

Appropriations Interior Subcommittee, he exercises de-facto control over a sizable corner of the federal government. Members of Congress leave most of the details in handling taxpayers' money to legislative aides such as Sigmon. With the purse-strings comes power.

Sigmon's job is to write the final version of the Interior Department's appropriation, fleshing out in legislative language the broad agreements made by the lawmakers. This gives Sigmon great discretion in how the taxpayers' money is spent: dropping or adding a few words can move tens of thousands of dollars into or out of a government program. No surprise, then, that Sigmon sometimes pursues his own policy preferences, or even acts to punish those who have displeased him.

Gerry Tays is one bureaucrat unlucky enough to have displeased Sigmon. Tays used to write the "Notes from the Hill" column in the National Park Service magazine, the *Courier*. One day Tays inserted a little jab against Congress into his column. "Having assured themselves a significant pay increase while retaining many of the 'perks' attendant to being a member of Congress," he wrote, "they made the nation safe again by recessing for the Christmas holidays in late December."

Harmless, you might think, even trite. Yet Sigmon didn't think so. He felt that his bosses had been slighted and launched a personal crusade against Tays. According to the *Washington Post,* Sigmon dressed down no fewer than four Park Service officials, including Deputy Director Herbert S. Cables Jr., spokesman George Berklacy, *Courier* Editor Mary Maruca, and Tays himself. All of them grovelled, apologizing to Sigmon for that most unpardonable of sins, criticizing Congress. To appease Sigmon's wrath, Tays was sacked from his job at the paper and reassigned to a position where he wouldn't get into trouble. The Park Service assumed this would be the end of the matter.

But even all this kowtowing was not enough to assuage Sigmon's outrage. When he got his hands on the next year's appropriations bill, he slashed $75,000 from the budget of the Park Service's Public Affairs Office—the precise amount used by that office to publish the *Courier.* Sigmon's congressional bosses never even noticed his petty act of revenge, and the Park Service survived: ultimately it found funds elsewhere to continue the publication. Still, Sigmon had sent his message. As an unnamed staffer told the *Post,* "From time to time, signals are sent to the agencies when they've been bad." You can bet that the *Courier* will have no more criticisms, however trivial, of Congress.

Sigmon's vendetta may have been particularly mean-spirited, but it is by no means unique. Senators and representatives have little time, and even less inclination, to read the thousands of bills that are produced each session. In 1991 4,702 bills were introduced in the House, of which 248 were enacted. Of the 2,136 bills introduced in the Senate that year, 182 were approved. With so much activity, members are forced to rely on people such as Sigmon, whom they trust to represent their best political interests. In exchange, committee staffers become what congressional scholar Michael Malbin calls "unelected representatives," making decisions routinely affecting hundreds of millions of dollars.

Scripting the Senator

Members of Congress tolerate the arrogance of their minions for a variety of reasons. For one thing, many are arrogant themselves, and their staffs' actions and attitude seem innocuous by contrast. Even more important, many lawmakers have become products of their staffs. When legislators ask questions at hearings, more often than not, their every remark has been scripted in advance by staff aides. What about follow-ups? Look for a staffer to lean over and whisper them into the member's ear. Most legislation gets its start at staffers' desks. Even when lawmakers give their aides broad outlines, the staff fills in the text. And when it comes time for that text to be voted on, few lawmakers will have read it, though again their aides will be there to tell them whether they ought to vote yes or no. It is not uncommon to see legislators, rushing in for a roll call, looking for a staffer to flash a thumbs-up or -down so they will know how to vote.

The reason most often given for the growth and influence of staff is that Congress is just trying to match the executive branch, datum for datum. Once upon a time, Congress relied almost completely on the Department of Defense for estimates of military costs, and the Office of Management and Budget for estimates on economic growth. After Watergate, Congress moved to seize power back from what was characterized as an imperial presidency, and one of the key sources of presidential power Congress attacked was the executive's virtual monopoly on detailed information about government programs.

Congress might have cut back on the president's informational and bureaucratic resources. It chose instead to compete by erecting a parallel congressional bureaucracy. There were only 2,030 members of the House and Senate staff in 1947, a number that grew to 3,556 within 10 years. By 1972 there were 7,706 staffers, and in the short space of four years that number leapt to 10,190. Much of this increase was in committee staff. In 1965 the House had 571 aides working on committees. By 1985 that number had reached 2,009. On the Senate side the number rose from 509 to 1,080. The crowd of Capitol Hill assistants stabilized by the late 1970s, and in 1989 the total number of staff aides was at 11,406.

Many of these new staffers were deployed in members' offices, including district offices to drum up constituent service work. But much of the staff went to the burgeoning committees, creating a shadow bureaucracy, one that helps explain why cutting spending is so hard in Washington: for every corner of every federal program, there is not only a gaggle of bureaucrats desperate to protect and expand their turf, there are also one or more congressional staffers who have a stake in the program's existence. The bigger a program a staff aide oversees, the more power and importance he has. No aide, then, wants to allow, let alone propose, cutting spending in a program under his control. Lawmakers, at least, have their fingers in many pies, and thus are not necessarily threatened personally by the reduction or eradication of a program they are involved with. For many staffers, though, the particular program they oversee is their whole political existence. They protect this power jealously. . . .

Legislative Minutiae

The power of committee staffers comes primarily from their control of the minutiae of legislation. If members themselves had to draft legislation, it would likely be less complicated and abstruse than it is today, for the simple reason that members have neither the time nor the patience to put together thousand-page bills. Staffers, on the other hand, have both. Legislation consequently becomes a creature of staff, with twists and turns that only they understand and details that only they know how to exploit.

Members also rely on the committee staff to keep a bill moving forward. If a would-be law fails to pass during its first session, as most do, it is largely up to staff to keep the measure on the agenda, by scheduling meetings and hearings about the bill, gauging support and opposition, and working out compromises and forming coalitions.

So powerful are committee staffs that senators have personal aides on each committee on which they serve. These operatives are called "S. Res. 60" aides, after the 1975 bill that created them. The arrangement is often criticized because it politicizes the committees with a new, partisan layer between committee staff and the members. But the need for committee aides responsible directly to senators is a result of the legislators' recognition that they have handed perhaps too much power to staffs. To get control of those staffs they—what else?—add another layer of staff, this time a layer more responsible to individual lawmakers. But the extra layer only reinforces the tendency of delegating responsibility to aides. With each senator having his own man on the committee staff, those staffers then conduct the debates and work out the compromises that senators, once upon a time, would have fought out themselves. The result is, of course, even more power for the unelected and invisible staff.

The 1987 Highway Bill is a typical result of this process, too long for individual consumption or comprehension. The hot political aspects of the $88 billion bill were easily reduced to evening news sound bites. But when the bill reached a conference committee there were hundreds of points of contention. Of these, staffers recommended that members deal directly with 18 major ones. Sixty smaller issues were highlighted for consideration by members with a particular interest. That meant there were 200 to 300 points to be negotiated by staff alone.

Packed Like Sardines

Members of Congress have put up with this explosion of staff not only to compete with the executive branch but also because it helped break apart the seniority system that put power in the hands of a few lawmakers. The old system was not without its advantages; congressional policies were more unified and coherent, and the White House could negotiate with Capitol Hill more easily, having to deal with only a limited number of people. The drawback was that congressional decisions were made in smoke-filled rooms by gerontocrats and their bureaucrat and lobbyist buddies. Younger lawmakers played along, rubber-stamping the decisions of the elder powers, hoping that they would be around long enough to someday assume the positions of power themselves.

The reforms of the 1970s demolished that system. Power was wrested from entrenched committee structures and spread around to individual members; individual members consequently took on more staff. In the new system, knowledge, not longevity, was at the core of power. The more staff a member had at his disposal, the more power he could wrest from the old congressional establishment and the executive branch. Thus the constant addition of ever-more staff, to the point where it has outstripped even the explosion of congressional office space, leading to sardine-like conditions in most Hill offices.

These newly expanded staffs have in turn facilitated the diffusion of power in Congress. Almost every member, for example, now has an aide responsible for foreign affairs; thus, lawmakers don't have to rely on the Foreign Affairs Committee. Indeed, the growth of staff has so helped to fragment power in Congress that there are over 100 different committees and subcommittees claiming jurisdiction over the Department of Defense alone. At least 74 have some influence in drug abuse policy. More than 110 committees and subcommittees have some jurisdiction over the Department of Housing and Urban Development (HUD). Those committees are full of staffers pushing for projects their bosses favor. True oversight gets lost in the shuffle. How else can we explain the failure of Congress to expose the HUD scandal—in which sweetheart deals were packaged for friends of the agency's officials—until after the fact, even though HUD was receiving 2,400 telephone calls a month from members of Congress and their staffs.

The growth of staff has been expensive in budgetary terms as well. As former Senator William Proxmire, the Wisconsin Democrat, pointed out in awarding his famous "Golden Fleece" to Congress, "Added staff is . . . used to justify new buildings, more restaurants, added parking spaces, and greater support personnel." The legislative branch budget has soared by more than 3,000 percent since 1946 and is now well over $2 billion.

Faux Pas by Conyers

With all this staff, and all these resources, it might seem that Congress has no excuse for not doing its job well. In fact, the expansion of staff has had an inverse effect on efficiency. As members and senior staffers pursue their interests, basic oversight tasks are often left to junior staffers, sometimes high school or college interns. Take a February 4, 1992, letter to the Defense Department. President Bush had just announced a moratorium on all new regulations pending a review of existing rules to see if they should be revised or revoked. Representative John Conyers, head of the Committee on Government Operations, did not want the administration to think it could start playing around with regulations without hearing from Congress. The Michigan Democrat thus sent vaguely threatening letters to the head of every department and agency demanding the names and titles of any employees who were to be a part of the President's regulatory review.

The letter arriving at the Department of Defense, however, was addressed, not to Defense Secretary Dick Cheney, but to "The Honorable John G. Tower, Secretary of Defense." Although former Senator Tower had been nominated for that position at the beginning of the Bush administration, after a nasty battle he was not confirmed. More to the point, Tower had been killed in 1991 in a plane crash. A Conyers spokesman says it was a simple mistake: the intern drawing up the letters got the wrong mailing list (which means that several other letters were misaddressed as well). What makes it more telling is that these letters were intended to ensure that only Congress control regulatory law. The rulers on the Hill who want to micromanage the federal government can't even get the right name for the Secretary of Defense.

In fact, as committee staff has grown in influence, they have imitated their bosses in looking to turn the hard work over to others. Often this means using statistics that have conveniently been provided by advocates of one policy or another. Sometimes it means letting special interests write the first draft of a piece of legislation. The more staffers there are, the more legislation they end up proposing, to justify their existence if nothing else. But this means they never get ahead of the work curve. Always understaffed, aides are all too often beholden to lobbyists of diverse stripes for help in putting bills together. In addition, because staffers are far more accessible than members, the more staffers there are, the more access special interests can get (especially if the lobbyists are, as is usually the case, themselves ex-staffers).

As Mark Bisnow, once an aide to Senator Robert Dole, has pointed out, "The presence of specialized aides on each representative's staff has multiplied contact points for peddlers of influence . . . the thousands of lobbyists in Washington, many former staffers, would have little to do if they depended on personal audiences with Congressmen."

Gifts from Perot

Indeed, lobbyists and special-interest representatives sometimes court staffers more assiduously than they do members. Washington restaurants do a booming business on all the lunches bought for aides who have a direct say on legislation. Special interests and corporate lobbies fly congressional staffers around the globe on exotic "fact finding" missions. To be sure, these trips usually include a series of meetings and tours of relevant areas. But it's remarkable how often they coincide with, say, an NCAA basketball tournament.

Until recently most staffers faced even fewer limits than their bosses on accepting gifts and honoraria from interest groups. Although most staffers like to keep a low profile, that doesn't mean they don't jump at the chance to get on the lucrative lecture circuit. There are groups, such as Washington Campus, that regularly book speaking engagements for key aides.

William Pitts is a good example. An aide to House Minority Leader Robert Michel, he was profiled in 1989 by the *Wall Street Journal.* In 1988, the aide to the Illinois Republican had accepted $17,000 in honoraria. Just prior to the *Journal* interview he swore off accepting any more speaking fees. But the list of corporate contributors to Pitts was nonetheless interesting, including $2,000 from H. Ross Perot's oil company, H.R. Petroleum, and another $2,000 from Perot himself. If honoraria are ethically dubious for members of Congress, they should be all the more so for staffers, who, after all, are the only ones who actually know what is in many of those bills that members pass without ever having read them.

But free trips, lunches, and speaking fees are not the only ways staffers cash in. They may not make much money while on the Hill, but the pay is sweet when they leave to join a Washington lobbying firm. Even better, staffers planning to leave the Hill can create jobs for themselves by writing legislation so complex that only legislative experts, for a consulting fee, can unravel it.

Section 89 of the 925-page tax reform act is an example of legislation that provided employment for one who wrote it. A Capitol Hill lawyer named Kent Mason wrote the section, which imposed tax penalties on companies that didn't include low-paid and part-time employees in their health and pension plans. The measure was bound in so much red tape that it virtually promised full-time employment for those who could advise businesses on how to collect, analyze, and present the data needed to comply with the law. Nor was all that effort a one-time expense. The data had to be provided every year. One estimate concluded that American businesses would have to assign 2,000 full-time workers per year to comply.

So huge and complex was the Tax Reform Act that no one even noticed Section 89. The chairman of the Small Business Committee, Representative John LaFalce, a New York Democrat, organized a hearing only after it had become law and several small business owners complained they had to spend $24,000 to $60,000 in consulting fees just to figure out what Section 89 meant. Mason, who three months before the law was to take effect joined the Washington law firm Caplin and Drysdale, was eager to direct some of those fees his way. Had Section 89 not been repealed, Mason would have made a small fortune counselling businesses on how to comply with the law he had devised.

The Mayor of HUD

The greatest cost to the political system, however, is not from staffers getting rich. It's the way staff power perverts the legislative process and intrudes into the daily operations of executive agencies. One aide notorious for wielding his power to control the tiniest details of the executive branch is Kevin Kelly, the top staffer on the Senate Appropriations Subcommittee that approves spending for the Department of Housing and Urban Development (HUD). Kelly, who answers to Maryland Democratic Senator Barbara Mikulski, is effectively the author of the annual appropriations bill for HUD and several other agencies. Such is Kelly's power that, not only do executive branch employees hesitate to tangle with him, most House members also take pains not to offend him.

Over the last few years Kelly was at odds with HUD Secretary Jack Kemp, who came to HUD with the mandate to clean it up after a particularly embarrassing scandal. The previous secretary and some of his assistants had used HUD's discretionary fund to dole out juicy favors and pet projects to cronies and friends. Secretary Kemp moved to eliminate the kind of discretion that was abused, making all decisions involving HUD funds competitive rather than political. A point system with performance goals was set up to evaluate applications for funding. The projects with the most points were to be the only ones funded. This also meant there would be no room for pork projects back in the home district. Congress complained; Kevin Kelly went to work.

Kelly agreed to Kemp's plan to eliminate discretionary spending by the secretary. But, instead of eliminating the funding altogether, he turned it to his own use, becoming the gatekeeper for congressional pork projects. When members asked Kelly for money for their districts, he did not write the pork projects into the actual appropriations bill. Instead, he slipped them into the committee report that accompanied the legislation, a report that no one could change once it left Kelly's hands.

Secretary Kemp resisted Kelly's first attempt to control his budget through the report, which is never actually voted on. Because committee reports are not officially binding, HUD's General Counsel, Frank Keating, advised Kemp that he could ignore the line-item projects in the committee report. Kemp did just that. The following year, Kelly placed an item in the appropriations bill requiring the secretary to adhere to recommendations in the accompanying committee report. To make his point, Kelly also punished Keating for giving the secretary the advice about ignoring line-item projects by deleting the funding requested for nearly 50 lawyers that were to have been added to his staff. Several years later, Keating was still in trouble in the Senate. Despite a long record of civil-rights activity, his nomination to be a federal judge was held up over transparently absurd charges of insensitivity. . . .

. . . Lawmakers come and go, but key staffers like Kevin Kelly rarely leave, thus becoming the institutional memory of their committees. If Senator Mikulski loses or gives up her position as chairman of the subcommittee, her successor will inherit Kelly. And he will be happy to do so. Kelly is the only person who, practically speaking, can write his subcommittee's appropriations bill. Along with the power that comes from being the only mechanic who understands the machinery, staffers like Kelly enjoy leverage over pet projects and the power to put people out of jobs. If this doesn't make them the most important people in Washington, it at least makes them *think* they are. . . .

Clinton Fumbles

. . . Unlike senators or representatives, who are accountable at the ballot box, staffers work behind the curtains. They are the new rulers on Capitol Hill, a nameless, faceless mandarinate that pulls the strings and feeds off the worst impulses of the institution it claims to serve.

The remedy is obvious: cut staff. Fearing a confrontation with Capitol Hill, President-elect Bill Clinton now seems to be backing down from his campaign pledge to cut congressional staff by 25 percent. This gives other politicians an extraordinary opportunity to run with the ball he has fumbled.

Debating the Issues: Opposing Views

CONGRESSIONAL TERM LIMITS: REMEDY OR SNAKE OIL?

See text p. 194–95

As the text points out, Americans have become increasingly concerned that Congress is controlled by an entrenched elite of Senators and Representatives who are beholden to special interests and whose only aim is their own re-election. Across the country in 1992 proposals surfaced to limit the terms that elected representatives may serve, and fourteen states voted to enact such limits.

The following two articles provide arguments for and against term limits. In the first article Bill Frenzel, a guest scholar at The Brookings Institution, argues that term limits would serve an attractive and necessary function. Strong—and contested—elections provide the accountability that is needed in a democratic system; unless elections are "unrigged" in favor of incumbents, there is little reason to place any faith in the system as a whole.

Thomas Mann, also from The Brookings Institution, disagrees. He argues that term limits will not substantially increase competition, nor will they alter the failing public images of Congress. Real reforms, he contends, require more expansive changes, including reforms in campaign financing laws that will encourage strong competitors to run. Moreover, term limits will not necessarily increase accountability among elected officials. Mann argues that the only way to increase the quality and performance of those officials is to "cajole, shame, and threaten politicians into doing the right thing."

Bill Frenzel and Thomas E. Mann "Term Limits for Congress: Arguments Pro and Con"*

Bill Frenzel

The idea of limiting the number of terms a member of Congress may serve has been rattling around since the Constitution was a gleam in the eye of the framers. But until 1990 it was just another idea whose time had not come.

In 1990 California, Colorado, and Oklahoma all passed referendums providing severe term limits on their state legislatures. One of them, Colorado, also set limits on the terms of its representatives in the U.S. Congress. Only in California, where ballot initiative contests have become a major contact sport, was there any real resistance. There a well-organized $5 million opposition campaign kept the vote close. In the two other states, term limits was a runaway winner.

The referendums were a stentorian wake-up call for state and federal legislators who had slumbered through earlier warnings and who had somehow failed to notice that their collective popular approval rating had sunk to levels usually reserved for used car salesmen. For some time, polls had been showing strong popular support for term limits. Nearly a year before the 1990 election one poll had shown 70 percent support running uniformly through regions, parties, sexes, and ages.

With latent enthusiasm for term limits ignited across the country, fledgling state term limits movements arose. They quickly became active everywhere, hyperactive in states that provide for ballot access for initiatives. Term limit bills were introduced in most states, and campaigns got under way in most of the initiative states.

Then last November a funny thing happened. Term limits suffered an unexpected, serious setback. The voters of Washington state defeated a ballot initiative with retrospective effect that would have limited congressional service almost immediately. Opposition forces, thought to be disheartened by unpleasant publicity about the lax personal banking habits of U.S. House members, rallied under the leadership of House Speaker Tom Foley, himself a Washingtonian, to defeat the initiative.

The Washington initiative proved that the term limits juggernaut was not irresistible. It gave the counterforces strong momentum going into the 1992 elections, which are expected to produce about a dozen initiatives. But the term limits forces are still powerful. With both sides gearing up, 1992 is certain to be a lively election year.

*Bill Frenzel and Thomas E. Mann, "Term Limits for Congress: Arguments Pro and Con," *Current* (July/August 1992). Copyright 1992 by *The Brookings Review*, The Brookings Institution. Reprinted with permission.

Incumbent Reelection Success

The appeal of term limits, most often proposed as a limit of 12 years, springs from the extraordinarily high, and rising, reelection rates of congressional incumbents. Historically, U.S. House incumbents have never had much trouble getting reelected, but from the middle of the nineteenth century, the reelection rate has crept up steadily to its current average of better than 94 percent in the past ten elections and better than 97 percent in the past three elections.

Until 1914 senators were spared the indignity of elections. Since then they have generally done less well than House members. Even so, their increasing success has produced a reelection rate of better than 88 percent in the past five elections and an astounding 97 percent in the last election. Congress has become almost immortal.

Winning margins are increasing too. Nowadays most members of Congress face only token opposition, if any. In 1990 only one in twenty races for U.S. House seats could be described as competitive—that is, with a winning margin of less than 4 percent. That year four out of five House incumbents got more than 60 percent of the votes in their districts. Sixty-nine incumbents, or 16 percent, had either no major party opposition or no opposition at all. Four senators (12 percent) were so blessed.

The growing victory margins mean that reelection rates have not peaked yet. It is impossible to break the House record of 1792, when 100 percent of House incumbents who sought reelection were successful (thankfully, 37 percent did not run), but we are headed in that direction. Meanwhile, challengers are not stupid. As long as they know 97 percent of them will lose, their campaigns will be token. Good challengers simply will not file. They know the odds are better at Las Vegas.

Accountability is the heart of our system. Yet the 97 percent success rate has decimated congressional accountability. In days of yore, when members of Congress went home to face the voters, some of them would face the music. The music has stopped. The principal check and balance on the House was its election contests. Today there are no contests.

Congressional Turnover

Election defeats have always represented the smallest fraction of congressional turnover. In the first 100 years of our republic, House reelection rates were in the 70–90 percent range, but a quarter to a half of all incumbents did not seek reelection. That high rate of voluntary retirement kept total turnover in the 40–50 percent range. Each new House was about half rookie and half veteran. By the turn of the century retirement turnover had already declined to about 15 percent, and it continued to decline thereafter. In the past four elections, retirement turnover averaged about 31 members, about 7 percent. Total House turnover, including election defeats, was about 10 percent, an historic low.

In the Senate, retirement turnover is even lower. Senators must love their jobs. On average, over the past five elections, about four senators retired. Last year one retired. Total turnover for the Senate, including election defeats, over the past five elections was about 8 percent. For 1990 it was 2 percent.

The turnover that supplied vitality and inhibited rigidity in the early days of the House is gone, a victim of the incentives of the seniority system, and, more recently, of sure-fire reelection.

Declining Voter Participation

In 1990 the United States held an election party, but only one-third of the voting age population showed up. One-half showed up for the presidential election of 1988. Both those figures are the lowest in 60 years, and voting participation has been headed down for the past 30 years. The drop has come at a time when the United States and the individual states have made substantial efforts to lower barriers to voting (the Voting Rights Act, improved registration systems, better access to voting sites, absentee ballots, lowering the voting age to 18).

Even Americans who can tolerate 97 percent reelection rates with high voter turnout blanch when they understand that Congress is being immortalized by one-third of the eligible voters. As long as reelection certainty is being sustained by a small and declining fraction of the voters, protests are inevitable.

The Term Limits Protagonists

In the states, proponents of term limits belong to all parties and to none. They are liberal and conservative, often close to the ends of the spectrum. They are bound together by the common feeling that they are outsiders, estranged from a system that is rigged against them.

The opponents of term limits are easier to identify. They are the ins and their friends—incumbents, staff, lobbyists, and close observers. They have a stake in the present system or know it and are comfortable with it. They do not believe "their" system is broken, and they see dangers in fixing it.

Congressmen and ex-congressmen, by huge margins, oppose term limits regardless of party affiliation. (A few former members of Congress dot the letterheads of national term limits groups, but they are overwhelmed by the long, prestigious list of opponents.) A powerful opposition force, the group was an idle resource until awakened by the Foley campaign in Washington state.

If one believes party platforms, Republicans are for term limits. A canvass of GOP members of Congress, past and present, however, would reveal little fidelity to that platform. In the states, some Republicans think that term limits might make their party a majority in the legislatures. Even so, party activity has not been encouraged by Republican members of Congress.

Although polls generally show equal ratios of Democrats and Republicans opposing and supporting term limits, the Democratic party actively and officially opposed initiatives in California and Washington. It may not believe that control of the legislatures will change, but, as the majority party, it sees no reason to take either the trouble or the risk to find out.

Arguments Pro and Con

Enthusiasm often overwhelms reason on both sides of the term limits debate. Much of the campaign rhetoric is speculative. Some of it is specious. Those who favor term limits claim miraculous powers for it. Those who oppose it see in it the demise of the republic.

Reasonable people are probably not going to be persuaded that term limits is the magic bullet that will produce smarter congressmen, better ideas, improved oversight, a balanced budget, or affordable health care, or that it will put "our" side (either liberal or conservative) in control of Congress. Neither are they likely to be convinced by counterarguments that the present system provides ample challenger opportunity, that there is insufficient talent in the United States to service higher turnover, that incumbents are the only ones who can do the job, or that legislative rookies will be pushovers for staff, lobbyists, and bureaucrats.

The simple, essential reason for congressional term limits is to unrig a rigged system, end automatic reelection, and make Congress mortal again.

Citizen-Legislator

Many Americans cling to the now lost idea of the citizen-legislator. Term limits can't completely recreate this extinct creature. But it will take us a couple of paces backward and away from the professional congressman-for-life. It will also allow more citizens to serve in Congress, and it could reduce some of the advantages of incumbency, even during the 12-year term.

Predicting the inner workings of Congress is highly speculative, but, at the least, the seniority system will be truncated and weakened by term limits. At best, it may yield to another system that could provide more equal opportunities for leadership for all members and less entrenched regionalism.

Known retirement dates would allow challengers to get their affairs in order and plan their campaigns in advance. That would mean better campaigns, better candidates, and more competition. Incumbents could continue to give themselves more reelection insurance in the form of greater perks and new campaign laws, but competition cannot get worse. If it improves, accountability will also improve.

Voter participation is a complicated subject, but more competition ought to improve it too. Congressional term limits would also restore balance to our system by extending to the legislative branch the noble precedent of term limits applied by the 22nd Amendment to the executive branch only. Both branches need limits.

With less career time to be consumed with the petty details of legislative work and less time to ponder the defense of turf, Congress may begin to look at the forest again, rather than each leaf. The now-compelling urge to micro-manage and extend one's own power and programs far past their usefulness to the republic will be reduced.

Perhaps the essential objection to term limits is that it restricts voter choice. For the purist, that will be a problem, but, alas, there are few purists in politics. A 12-year limit is surely a tiny restriction. The Constitution already contains three other small restrictions on voting for Congress, as well as the presidential term limit. Congressional term limits would be a mere scratch on the body politic compared with the running sore of current congressional immortality.

Opponents worry that Congress will lose good members. It will. But it will also gain good members. All the titans of Congress were pea-green freshmen once. They were good when they got there. Experience (seniority) did not make them smarter. It just gave them more staff and made them harder to say no to. There is plenty of talent that can't get to Congress under the present rules. Today Congress survives the infrequent retirement of its titans. It can survive an accelerated process too.

There are complaints that the legislative branch will lose power to the executive. That is possible, but not necessarily probable and certainly not inevitable. There is no rule forcing one branch to grow long whiskers before it can stand up to another.

Lame ducks, it is said, are not accountable. Yet studies of lame ducks show no substantial changes in voting patterns. There is no evidence to show unbeatable ducks are more accountable than lame ones.

Finally, opponents suggest that "other changes" will cure the system. That is probably true, but no such changes are in eminent danger of enactment. Usually the "other changes" are reforms in campaign law. That won't help because no legislature has ever passed a campaign law that made it harder for incumbents to get reelected.

The Future

Term limits enjoy wide popular support. But that does not mean that they will see the light of day. The Balanced Budget Amendment and the Line Item Veto, both of which enjoyed majority public support and yet were not adopted, are testament to Congress's ability to defend itself. Congress merely toyed with them until the intensity of their supporters petered out. Possessed of nearly infinite staying power and an irresistible urge for self-preservation, Congress is prepared to dally term limits to death too.

Following the Washington state defeat, proponents will have to prove that they can regain their lost momentum. Even if they can succeed in their initiative strategy, most constitutional scholars suggest that states cannot limit the terms of their congressmen, and that a constitutional amendment is required. If so, a term limits strategy must be a very long-term proposition.

If the term limits movement can recapture its successes in the states, it can elect some pro-term limits congressmen, just as it has begun to seat some friendly state legislators. Making a majority in Congress is a long process, but other factors will help. State limits will give state legislators more incentive to run for Congress, and more incentive to create districts in which their success is more likely. This process will create a new class of more credible challengers in primaries as well as general elections.

It is also possible, but unlikely at present, that Congress will be pressured to cure some of the irritants that are bugging the American people. Only if there is a strong anti-incumbent reaction in the 1992 elections will Congress be forced to begin making changes. Remember, it is just as distasteful to give away immortality piece by piece as it is to surrender it all in one lump.

Wagering the rent money on term limits for Congress is surely not in order now. The movement is for real, and it is making an impact. However, it must match its high intensity with unprecedented staying power before it can achieve the muscle to force Congress to begin stripping away elements of its own immortality.

In some sort of national debate, Americans must decide what kind of representation they want. The framers wisely made system changes difficult to achieve. It's not enough for Americans to want term limits badly. To get them, they have to want them over the long haul.

Thomas E. Mann

Bill Frenzel's case for congressional term limits is disarmingly attractive. No fire and brimstone about the corruption of Congress. No grandiose claim that limits will produce higher quality members or more effective national policymaking. No expedient assertion that states can limit congressional terms without a constitutional amendment. Instead, Frenzel embraces term limits as the only available means of achieving an important but limited objective—namely, restoring competition, turnover, and accountability to an electoral system that has essentially lost all three.

But Frenzel's judicious approach to term limits should not obscure the radical character of his proposed reform. The burden of proof—diagnosing the problem and demonstrating that the cure is likely to work without debilitating side effects—properly falls on those who would alter the constitutional order. My view is that a persuasive case for term limits has not been made.

Legislatures Under Siege

Congress and state legislatures are suffering from extraordinarily (if not unprecedentedly) low levels of popular support. With only a fourth of the electorate approving of the job these representative bodies are doing, the soil is fertile for the burgeoning term limit movement. But it would be a mistake to infer that declining competition and turnover in legislatures are responsible for the drop in public esteem, that the public's embrace of term limits is in any way novel, or that the term limit movement reflects a spontaneous uprising by the public to restore accountability in legislative elections.

Public confidence in legislatures is low because the news coming out of Washington and state capitals has been bad. Recent stories on state legislatures by Alan Ehrenhalt in *Governing* and on Congress by Richard Cohen in the *National Journal* are remarkably parallel in this respect. A stagnant economy, declining real wages and limits on upward mobility for many working-class Americans, suffocating budget deficits, and chronic crime and poverty in our cities have constrained effective policymaking and frustrated citizens. At the same time several developments in the political system have further damaged the reputation of legislatures. Divided government, now the norm in two-thirds of the states as well as in Washington, invites public squabbling between the branches, which diminishes the stature of both. The increasing focus on scandal, fueled by ethics and public disclosure statutes, tough law enforcement against public officials, and a press inclined toward feeding frenzies, leads the public to believe (incorrectly) that legislatures and politicians are more and more corrupt. And the situation is made even worse by negative campaigning—the growing tendency of politicians to cast their electoral and legislative opponents in the worst possible light.

Uncompetitive elections and low turnover are at most sidebars to the big story of the public loss of confidence in Congress and state legislatures. Using term limits to increase competition and turnover is unlikely to alter the public image of these institutions.

Indeed, the public's support for term limits predates the contemporary disrepute of Congress and state legislatures. Polls taken 40 years ago found roughly the same level of support as exists today. No surprise here. Term limits are irresistible to poll respondents: they provide a simple, no-cost means of registering skepticism and unhappiness with politics and politicians in general.

What's different today is that activists have mobilized to bring term limit initiatives before the electorate. Frenzel portrays these activists as Democrats and Republicans, liberals and conservatives, united only in their status as outsiders, "estranged from a system that is rigged against them." My own view of the term limit movement is slightly less benign. The energy and resources of the movement come overwhelmingly from conservative, libertarian business and ideological interests who share a strong distaste for government and a wish to control or weaken legislatures now dominated by Democrats.

Politics does make strange bedfellows, and there are a handful of Democrats and liberals who are working on behalf of term limits. But I believe any fair accounting would reveal that the struggle for term limits is more about political power than good government. We are in the midst of a national campaign to limit legislative terms not because the public is in open revolt against a rigged electoral system but because the intense ideological and partisan battles of our time have been moved to a new venue.

What's Wrong with Congressional Elections?

Frenzel correctly notes the incredibly high reelection rates of congressional incumbents and their substantial margins of victory. The study of the "vanishing marginals" and the advantages of incumbency has been a cottage industry in political science, and Frenzel is not alone in his concern that the threat of defeat is no longer real for congressional incumbents.

The problem is greater in the House than in the Senate. Although there has been a long-term decline in competitiveness in Senate elections and only one incumbent was defeated in 1990, a third to a half of senators running for reelection routinely attract strong, well-funded challengers. Large-scale defeat of Senate incumbents led to a change in party control of the chamber twice in the 1980s, something that had not been seen since the 1950s.

House elections lack credible challengers. More and more House elections go uncontested; most of the others feature relatively unknown and woefully underfinanced challengers. Fundraising by House challengers has declined precipitously since 1984 while the cost of campaigning and incumbent spending has sharply increased. As the minority party in the House, the Republicans have suffered disproportionately but Democratic opposition to Republican incumbents is also increasingly anemic.

The absence of credible challengers in the 1990 elections kept House incumbent losses to 15, in spite of an unprecedented drop in the vote margins of both parties' incumbents. A slightly stronger field of opponents could easily have converted the expressed public discontent with Congress into double or triple the number of incumbent defeats.

The 1990 experience highlights an important lesson about congressional elections. Robust competition requires both strong, well-financed challengers and public antipathy to the status quo. The quiescent House elections after 1982 reflected in large part the relatively benign national political environment. From "It's morning again in America" in 1984 to "Keep the recovery going" in 1988, there was no clarion call to throw the rascals out. Absent a scandal or serious political misstep, voters had little incentive to reject their representative. At the same time, potential challengers had no reason to believe that conditions were ripe for a political upset. Their reluctance to run reinforced the public passivity and ensured good times for congressional incumbents.

But it would be a mistake to conclude that these conditions are permanent, that the recent pattern of competition and turnover in congressional elections will continue. No simple linear trend line fits the history of congressional elections. Between 1974 and 1982 the membership of the House and Senate was almost entirely replaced as a result of retirements and incumbent defeats. By the early 1980s three-fourths of senators and representatives had served fewer than 12 years. That tumultuous decade in congressional elections was followed by the placid years after 1982, which saw a drop in voluntary retirements and election defeats and therefore a much more stable membership.

Rapid Turnover

We are about to enter another period of rapid membership turnover. Redistricting, a surge in retirements, more successful candidate recruitment, and a high level of public angst may well produce 80 to 100 new members of the House in 1992, with 30 to 40 reaching office by defeating an incumbent. The volatile Senate class of 1992 could see a dozen of its members replaced in the November elections. And it is easy to imagine conditions under which rapid turnover continues in the 1994 midterm elections. A massive increase in competitiveness is not prerequisite to a healthy flow of new blood into the legislature.

But what of the charge that the incredibly high success rate of incumbents has destroyed the system of accountability essential to a democracy? There are ample grounds for concern here. Uncontested elections and halfhearted challengers are unlikely to have a bracing effect on incumbents and over time may breed an unhealthy feeling of invulnerability and arrogance. Yet most members of Congress remain unbelievably insecure about their political futures and highly responsive to the interests of their constituencies. One big reason incumbents are so successful is that electoral accountability is alive and well: representatives conform to the wishes of their constituents and are in turn rewarded with reelection.

The problem is not individual accountability. Voters show no signs of suffering from inattentive or unresponsive representatives. If anything, members of Congress are too solicitous of their constituencies and insufficiently attentive to broader national interests, too consumed with their personal standing in their district or state and too little dependent on their political party.

What's needed is a change in the electoral system that once again allows the outcome of hundreds of congressional elections to cumulate to a meaningful national decision. We should aspire to elections that are more party-based, less candidate-centered—and capable, on occasion, of changing the majority party in the House and of putting a single party in control of the government in Washington.

Term Limits in Congressional Elections

If my analysis is correct, term limits are the wrong medicine for what ails the congressional election system. There is no compelling reason to insist on 100 percent turnover in Congress every 12 years when 50 to 75 percent of the members of the House and Senate are routinely replaced every decade. Natural turnover (from voluntary retirement, progressive ambition, and election defeat) is preferable to an arbitrary scheme that unnecessarily restricts a democratic electoral process.

Would term limits increase the competitiveness of congressional elections? If more competitiveness means lower reelection rates for incumbents, the answer is clearly no. A term limit would very likely turn into a floor, with would-be candidates deferring their challenge and awaiting the involuntary retirement of the incumbent. If a norm of deference to the term-limited incumbent took root, elections would be contested only in open seats, and then only those not safe for one political party or the other.

Indeed, there is little reason to think that congressional term limits would produce anything approaching a surge in high-quality, well-financed challengers, which is essential for increased competitiveness. More targeted interventions are required to produce that result. (On the other hand, term limits for state legislators, however harmful their effects on state government, would increase the supply of experienced politicians seeking election to Congress.)

Finally, would congressional term limits increase accountability? Would the personal standing of representatives and senators become less important and their political party more so? Would Republicans have a better shot at taking control of Congress when they won the presidency? Having more open seats might marginally increase the ties between presidential and congressional voting. And Republicans would have a better chance of climbing out of their near permanent minority status in the House if the cohort of veteran Democratic legislators were forced to give up their seats without a fight.

Yet reformers would be disappointed by the likely consequences of term limits. The candidate-centered character of our elections would not disappear in a world of shortened congressional careers. The personal vote for incumbents materializes in their first reelection campaign. And while Republicans fare better in open seats than in those contested by an incumbent, even here their performance falls short of the Democrats'.

Term limits just won't get the job done. What's needed are a Republican party determined to build from the bottom up rather than the top down, with a public philosophy that encourages men and women to seek legislative office under the Republican banner; a reformed campaign finance system that puts more resources (money, cheaper mail, less expensive access to television) into the hands of the challengers; additional restrictions on franked mail and other advantages of incumbency; and creative strategies to shift the focus of officeholders and voters from position-taking on parochial matters to collective efforts that grapple with serious national problems.

Frenzel is skeptical that any such changes will ever be achieved. I believe we have no choice but to cajole, shame, and threaten politicians into doing the right thing.

Side Effects

These other measures should be pursued not only because they have a better chance of making congressional elections more competitive, but also because they lack term limits' potentially debilitating side effects.

Frenzel is surely correct to note the inflated rhetoric of proponents and opponents of term limits. The republic has survived the limit on presidential terms imposed by the 22nd Amendment and is unlikely to perish if congressional term limits are added to the Constitution.

Nonetheless, it is not unreasonable to be concerned that term limits might eliminate many of the members most inclined to legislate in the national interest; shift power from elected politicians to unelected officials and private interests; and strengthen the executive branch at the expense of Congress. These questions are not easily answered, but they should not be summarily dismissed.

The road to constitutional change, Frenzel approvingly observes, is long and difficult. Let's hope the journey enlightens the public and channels its energy into more productive forms of political participation.

QUESTIONS

1. *The Federalist No. 10* outlines the basic theory of representation upon which the American political system rests. According to Madison, how are the problems of faction resolved in a representative democracy? Moreover, how does the representative system proposed check the excesses of a purely democratic system?
2. How do the structural differences between the House of Representatives and the Senate carry out Madison's ideas in *The Federalist No. 10*?
3. In what ways does the power of Congressional staff distort the system of representative government? Given the complexity of the problems that members of Congress must attempt to resolve, what alternatives exist that could provide representatives with the information necessary to enact adequate laws and stay informed about the various issues they face?
4. As the text notes, reforms in the 1970s dramatically altered the committee structure in Congress, as power was diverted away from a few dominant committees and into a number of subcommittees and less experienced subcommittee chairs. Richard E. Cohen suggests that the result has been the fragmentation of power, which makes it ever more difficult

to generate consensus for any legislative program. Should the old system be reinstated? Why or why not?

5. During the 1992 national election, voters approved term-limit initiatives in a number of states. What kinds of problems are term limits intended to remedy? Will they accomplish their goals? What theoretical concerns about the nature of representative democracy are implicated, and how significant are those concerns?

CHAPTER 6

The President: From Chief Clerk to Chief Executive

THE CONSTITUTIONAL BASIS OF THE PRESIDENCY

See text p. 208

Wary of the power of the monarchy represented by Great Britain's rule, the founders of the American Constitution voiced grave concerns about the scope of power conferred upon a chief executive. Different proposals were suggested, including the idea that power should be distributed among two or more chiefs of state. Later, having accepted the idea of a single head of state, the problem lay in designing a system to insure that the chief executive could be an active and effective leader while restraining his or her ability to usurp more power than was warranted, given the republican structure of the American system.

Alexander Hamilton, author of several of the Federalist Papers, supported a strong central government headed by a single, powerful executive official. "Energy in the executive is a leading character in the definition of good government," he argued, and that energy could be sustained only by vesting authority in a single individual whose actions could then be carried out with "[d]ecision, activity, secrecy, and dispatch."

Alexander Hamilton
*The Federalist No. 70**

There is an idea, which is not without its advocates, that a vigorous executive is inconsistent with the genius of republican government. . . . Energy in the executive is a leading character in the definition of good government. It is essential to the protection of the community against foreign attacks; it is not less essential to the steady administration of the laws; to the protection of property against those irregular and high-handed combinations which sometimes interrupt the ordinary course of justice; to the security of liberty against the enterprises and assaults of ambition, of faction, and of anarchy. . . .

A feeble executive implies a feeble execution of the government. A feeble execution is but another phrase for a bad execution; and a government ill executed, whatever it may be in theory must be, in practice, a bad government.

*Alexander Hamilton, *The Federalist No. 70,* ed. Clinton Rossiter (New York: NAL, 1961).

Taking it for granted, therefore, that all men of sense will agree in the necessity of an energetic executive, it will only remain to inquire, what are the ingredients which constitute this energy? How far can they be combined with those other ingredients which constitute safety in the republican sense? And how far does this combination characterize the plan which has been reported by the convention?

The ingredients which constitute energy in the executive are unity; duration; an adequate provision for its support; and competent powers.

The ingredients which constitute safety in the republican sense are a due dependence on the people, and a due responsibility.

Those politicians and statesmen who have been the most celebrated for the soundness of their principles and for the justness of their views have declared in favor of a single executive and a numerous legislature. They have, with great propriety, considered energy as the most necessary qualification of the former, and have regarded this as most applicable to power in a single hand; while they have, with equal propriety, considered the latter as best adapted to deliberation and wisdom, and best calculated to conciliate the confidence of the people and to secure their privileges and interests.

That unity is conducive to energy will not be disputed. Decision, activity, secrecy, and dispatch will generally characterize the proceedings of one man in a much more eminent degree than the proceedings of any greater number; and in proportion as the number is increased, these qualities will be diminished.

This unity may be destroyed in two ways: either by vesting the power in two or more magistrates of equal dignity and authority, or by vesting it ostensibly in one man, subject in whole or in part to the control and cooperation of others, in the capacity of counselors to him. . . .

[A]ttaching ourselves purely to the dictates of reason and good sense, we shall discover much greater cause to reject than to approve the idea of plurality in the executive, under any modification whatever.

Whenever two or more persons are engaged in any common enterprise or pursuit, there is always danger of difference of opinion. If it be a public trust or office in which they are clothed with equal dignity and authority, there is peculiar danger of personal emulation and even animosity. From either, and especially from all these causes, the most bitter dissensions are apt to spring. Whenever these happen, they lessen the respectability, weaken the authority, and distract the plans and operations of those whom they divide. If they should unfortunately assail the supreme executive magistracy of a country, consisting of a plurality of persons, they might impede or frustrate the most important measures of the government in the most critical emergencies of the state. And what is still worse, they might split the community into the most violent and irreconcilable factions, adhering differently to the different individuals who composed the magistracy. . . .

Upon the principles of a free government, inconveniences from the source just mentioned must necessarily be submitted to in the formation of the legislature; but it is unnecessary, and therefore unwise, to introduce them into the constitution of the executive. It is here too that they may be most pernicious. In the legislature, promptitude of decision is oftener an evil than a benefit. The differences of opinion, and the jarring of parties in that department of the government, though they may sometimes obstruct salutary plans, yet often promote deliberation and circumspection, and serve to check excesses in the majority. When a resolution too is once taken, the opposition must be at an end. That resolution is a law, and resistance to it punishable. But no favorable circumstances palliate or atone for the disadvantages of dissension in the executive department. Here they are pure and unmixed. There is no point at which they cease to operate. They serve to embarrass and weaken the execution of the plan or measure to which they relate, from the first step to the final conclusion of it. They constantly counteract those qualities in the executive which are the most necessary ingredients in its composition—vigor and expedition, and this without any counterbalancing good. In the conduct of war, in which the energy of the executive is the bulwark of the national security, everything would be to be apprehended from its plurality. . . .

[O]ne of the weightiest objections to a plurality in the executive, and which lies as much against the last as the first plan is that it tends to conceal faults and destroy responsibility. Responsibility is of two kinds—to censure and to punishment. The first is the more important of the two, especially in an elective office. Men in public trust will much oftener act in such a manner as to render them unworthy of being any longer trusted, than in such a manner as to make them obnoxious to legal punishment. But the multiplication of the executive adds to the difficulty of detection in either case. It often becomes impossible, amidst mutual accusations, to determine on whom the blame or the punishment of a pernicious measure, or series of pernicious measures, ought really to fall. It is shifted from one to another with so much dexterity, and under such plausible appearances, that the public opinion is left in suspense about the real author. . . .

It is evident from these considerations that the plurality of the executive tends to deprive the people of the two greatest securities they can have for the faithful exercise of any delegated power, *first,* the restraints of public opinion, which lose their efficacy, as well on account of the division of the censure attendant on bad measures among a number as on account of the uncertainty on whom it ought to fall; and, *second,* the opportunity of discovering with facility and clearness the misconduct of the persons they trust, in order either to their removal from office or to their actual punishment in cases which admit of it. . . .

I clearly concur in opinion, . . . with a writer whom the celebrated Junius pronounces to be "deep, solid, and ingenious," that "the executive power is more easily confined when it is one"; that it is far more safe there should be a single object for the jealousy and watchfulness of the people; and, in a word, that all multiplication of the executive is rather dangerous than friendly to liberty.

PUBLIUS

See text p. 210

The Supreme Court has had few occasions to rule on the constitutional limits of executive authority. As discussed in Chapters 4 and 8 of the text, the Court is understandably reluctant to articulate the boundaries of presidential and legislative power, given the Court's own somewhat ambiguous institutional authority. In the case that follows, however, the Court looked at one of the ways in which the Constitution circumscribes the exercise of presidential prerogative.

United States v. Nixon *(1974) involves claims to executive authority. President Richard Nixon had been implicated in a conspiracy to cover up a burglary of the Democratic Party Headquarters at the Watergate Hotel in Washington, D.C., during the 1972 re-election campaign. The Special Prosecutor assigned to investigate the break-in and file appropriate criminal charges asked the trial court to order the President to disclose a number of documents and tapes related to the cover-up in order to determine the scope of the President's involvement. The President produced edited versions of some of the materials, but refused to comply with most of the trial court's order, asserting that he was entitled to withhold the information under a claim of "executive privilege."*

United States v. *Nixon* (1974)*

CHIEF JUSTICE BURGER delivered the opinion of the Court.

In the District Court, the President's counsel argued that the court lacked jurisdiction to issue the subpoena because the matter was an intra-branch dispute between a subordinate and superior officer of the Executive Branch and hence not subject to judicial resolution. That argument has been renewed in this Court with emphasis on the contention that the dispute does not present a "case" or "controversy" which can be adjudicated in the federal courts. The President's counsel argues that the federal courts should not intrude into areas committed to the other branches of Government. He views the present dispute as essentially a "jurisdictional" dispute within the Executive Branch which he analogizes to a dispute between two congressional committees. Since the Executive Branch has exclusive authority and absolute discretion to decide whether to prosecute a case, it is contended that a President's decision is final in determining what evidence is to be used in a given criminal case.

. . . Although his counsel concedes the President has delegated certain specific powers to the Special Prosecutor, he has not "waived nor delegated to the Special Prosecutor the President's duty to claim privilege as to all materials which fall within the President's inherent authority to refuse to disclose to any executive officer." The Special Prosecutor's demand for the items therefore presents, in the view of the President's counsel, a political question since it involves a "textually demonstrable" grant of power under Art. II. . . .

*United States v. Nixon, 418 U.S. 683, 1974.

The demands of and the resistance to the subpoena present an obvious controversy in the ordinary sense, but that alone is not sufficient to meet constitutional standards. In the constitutional sense, controversy means more than disagreement and conflict; rather it means the kind of controversy courts traditionally resolve. Here at issue is the production or nonproduction of specified evidence deemed by the Special Prosecutor to be relevant and admissible in a pending criminal case. It is sought by one official of the Government within the scope of his express authority; it is resisted by the Chief Executive on the ground of his duty to preserve the confidentiality of the communications of the President. Whatever the correct answer on the merits, these issues are "of a type which are traditionally justiciable." . . .

. . . We turn to the claim that the subpoena should be quashed because it demands "confidential conversations between a President and his close advisors that it would be inconsistent with the public interest to produce." The first contention is a broad claim that the separation of powers doctrine precludes judicial review of a President's claim of privilege. The second contention is that if he does not prevail on the claim of absolute privilege, the court should hold as a matter of constitutional law that the privilege prevails over the subpoena *duces tecum*. . . .

[The Court discussed its authority to interpret the Constitution, concluding that it had full power to interpret a claim of executive privilege.]

In support of his claim of absolute privilege, the President's counsel urges two grounds one of which is common to all governments and one of which is peculiar to our system of separation of powers. The first ground is the valid need for protection of communications between high government officials and those who advise and assist them in the performance of their manifold duties; the importance of this confidentiality is too plain to require further discussion. Human experience teaches that those who expect public dissemination of their remarks may well temper candor with a concern for appearances and for their own interests to the detriment of the decisionmaking process. Whatever the nature of the privilege of confidentiality of presidential communications in the exercise of Art. II powers the privilege can be said to derive from the supremacy of each branch within its own assigned area of constitutional duties. Certain powers and privileges flow from the nature of enumerated powers; the protection of the confidentiality of presidential communications has similar constitutional underpinnings.

The second ground asserted by the President's counsel in support of the claim of absolute privilege rests on the doctrine of separation of powers. Here it is argued that the independence of the Executive Branch within its own sphere, insulates a president from a judicial subpoena in an ongoing criminal prosecution, and thereby protects confidential presidential communications.

However, neither the doctrine of separation of powers, nor the need for confidentiality of high level communications, without more, can sustain an absolute, unqualified presidential privilege of immunity from judicial process under all circumstances. The President's need for complete candor and objectivity from advisers calls for great deference from the courts. However, when the privilege depends solely on the broad, undifferentiated claim of public interest in the confidentiality of such conversations, a confrontation with other values arises. Absent a claim of need to protect military, diplomatic or sensitive national security secrets, we find it difficult to accept the argument that even the very important interest in confidentiality of presidential communications is significantly diminished by production of such material for *in camera* inspection with all the protection that a district court will be obliged to provide.

The impediment that an absolute, unqualified privilege would place in the way of the primary constitutional duty of the judicial branch to do justice in criminal prosecutions would plainly conflict with the function of the courts under Art. III. In designing the structure of our Government and dividing and allocating the sovereign power among three coequal branches, the Framers of the Constitution sought to provide a comprehensive system, but the separate powers were not intended to operate with absolute independence. To read the Art. II powers of the President as providing an absolute privilege as against a subpoena essential to enforcement of criminal statutes on no more than a generalized claim of the public interest in confidentiality of nonmilitary and nondiplomatic discussions would upset the constitutional balance of "a workable government" and gravely impair the role of the courts under Art. III.

Since we conclude that the legitimate needs of the judicial process may outweigh presidential privilege, it is necessary to resolve those competing interests in a manner that preserves the essential functions of each branch. The right and indeed the duty to resolve that question does not free the judiciary from according high respect to the representations made on behalf of the President. The expectation of a President to the confidentiality of his conversations and correspondence, like the claim of confidentiality of judicial deliberations, for example, has all the values to which we accord deference for the privacy of all citizens and added to those values the necessity for protection of the public interest in his responsibilities against the inroads of such a privilege on the fair administration of criminal justice. The interest in preserving confidentiality is weighty indeed and entitled to great respect. However we cannot conclude that advisers will be moved to temper the candor of their remarks by the infrequent occasions of disclosure because of the possibility that such conversations will be called for in the context of a criminal prosecution.

On the other hand, the allowance of the privilege to withhold evidence that is demonstrably relevant in a criminal trial would cut deeply into the guarantee of due process of law and gravely impair the basic function of the courts. A President's acknowledged need for confidentiality in the communications of his office is general in nature, whereas the constitutional need for production of relevant evidence in a criminal proceeding is specific and central to the fair adjudication of a particular criminal case in the administration of justice. Without access to specific facts a criminal prosecution may be totally frustrated. The President's broad interest in confidentiality of communications will not be vitiated by disclosure of a limited number of conversations preliminarily shown to have some bearing on the pending criminal cases.

We conclude that when the ground for asserting privilege as to subpoenaed materials sought for use in a criminal trial is based only on the generalized interest in confidentiality, it cannot prevail over the fundamental demands of due process of law in the fair administration of criminal justice. The generalized assertion of privilege must yield to the demonstrated, specific need for evidence in a pending criminal trial. . . .

In this case the President challenges a subpoena served on him as a third party requiring the production of materials for use in a criminal prosecution on the claim that he has a privilege against disclosure of confidential communications. He does not place his claim of privilege on the ground they are military or diplomatic secrets. As to these areas of Art. II duties the courts have traditionally shown the utmost deference to presidential responsibilities. No case of the Court, however, has extended this high degree of deference to a President's generalized interest in confidentiality. Nowhere in the Constitution, as we have noted earlier, is there any explicit reference to a privilege of confidentiality; yet to the extent this interest relates to the effective discharge of a President's powers, it is constitutionally based. . . .

[The Court distinguished this case from cases involving claims against the president while acting in an official capacity.]

Mr. Chief Justice Marshall sitting as a trial judge in the *Burr* case was extraordinarily careful to point out that: "[I]n no case of this kind would a Court be required to proceed against the President as against an ordinary individual." Marshall's statement cannot be read to mean in any sense that a President is above the law, but relates to the singularly unique role under Art. II of a President's communications and activities, related to the performance of duties under that Article. Moreover, a President's communications and activities encompass a vastly wider range of sensitive material than would be true of any "ordinary individual." It is therefore necessary in the public interest to afford presidential confidentiality the greatest protection consistent with the fair administration of justice. The need for confidentiality even as to idle conversations with associates in which casual reference might be made concerning political leaders within the country or foreign statesmen is too obvious to call for further treatment. We have no doubt that the District Judge will at all times accord to presidential records that high degree of deference suggested in *United States v. Burr,* and will discharge his responsibility to see to it that until released to the Special Prosecutor no *in camera* material is revealed to anyone. This burden applies with even greater force to excised material; once the decision is made to excise, the material is restored to its privileged status and should be returned under seal to its lawful custodian.

Affirmed.

Debating the Issues: Opposing Views

PRESIDENTIAL POWER: BROAD OR NARROW?

See text p. 221

"Presidential government" is a term that would have sounded foreign to the Founders, who were careful to design a governmental system in which the legislative branch firmly held the upper hand. Beginning in the 1930s, however, the power of the presidency grew, so that by the 1960s, some scholars were inclined to refer to the "imperial presidency." This growth in power created an imbalance in the constitutional system, as the power of Congress seemed to wane in the face of ascending executive authority.

In recent years, the concern has shifted somewhat. Scholars and commentators, while still interested in the sum of power held by the president, have become equally concerned with the inability of anyone to function effectively in the office, given both the expectations placed upon the position and the overwhelming complexity of the modern state. The shape of the institution is discussed in the following two pieces.

In the first, Steven Stark argues that the presidency is no longer the exalted position it once was. The president can no longer control either foreign or domestic affairs—he or she faces stalemate and gridlock on every front. Moreover, changes in media and technology have made it more difficult for presidents to become prime opinion movers: the voice of the president is simply one among many on the political scene as he or she struggles to maintain control over an increasingly fragmented state. The result, Stark argues, is that over time the president will become more and more irrelevant, and the presidency itself will command less attention as an institution.

George Will, on the other hand, argues that the role of the president is not to try to compete with other voices in a simple-minded and futile attempt to mold public opinion; presidents should direct their actions to encouraging thoughtfulness in Congress. According to Will, a president should not act "as a handmaiden of public opinion but as an 'example' elevating that opinion."

Steven Stark
"The First Modern Presidency: Bill Clinton"*

Everyone agrees that Bill Clinton faces Herculean tasks in trying to reduce the deficit and improve the nation's health-care system. According to several prominent presidential scholars and corporate theorists, however, the toughest job of all for Clinton—and the one that could determine to what degree his term is a success—will be to redefine the very office of the presidency. Because of the end of the Cold War and recent changes in mass communication, the role Clinton assumes in the government and culture is far different from that played by Franklin Roosevelt, John F. Kennedy, or

*Steven Stark, "The First Modern Presidency: Bill Clinton," *The Atlantic Monthly* (April 1993). Reprinted with permission.

even Ronald Reagan. Though politicians, the media, and the public continue to treat the presidency as the cynosure of American life, in important ways Clinton has inherited a diminished office.

Abroad, the President's role as a foreign-policy leader has receded. From the end of the Second World War until roughly the middle of the Bush presidency, the threat of communism and nuclear war created a sense of continuing crisis, fueling demand for a strong presidency. Just as other wars led to increases in executive power throughout our history, so did the Cold War.

Moreover, because foreign policy is the one area in which a President can act with relatively little interference from Congress and the press, chief executives have tended to be absorbed by it. Even Jimmy Carter, a candidate elected without much of an international agenda, found himself spending an increasing amount of his presidency on foreign-policy issues, where it was easier to get things done. This ease of action in foreign affairs was aided by the fact that the Cold War coincided with a period of almost total American dominance of the international scene. Since Franklin Roosevelt's third term our Presidents have been primarily foreign-policy Presidents.

Those days are now fading. The world may still be a dangerous place, and foreign policy remains a presidential dominion. But if the end of the Cold War did nothing else, it reduced the public's fear of nuclear annihilation and thus its interest in foreign policy. The recent presidential campaign was the first since 1936 in which foreign-policy issues played virtually no role. What's more, the President's ability to shape the world has been greatly curtailed by the rise of the global economy. Richard Rose, a presidential scholar at the University of Strathclyde, in Scotland, describes a postmodern chief executive as one who, among other things, not only can no longer dominate the world but also finds that what happens abroad, in trade or monetary policy, often dictates what happens in the United States. As Rose puts it in his book The Postmodern President (1988), Presidents used to face stalemate and interference only at home. Now, as part of a so-called new world order, they can look forward to them abroad as well.

At the same time that these shifts have occurred, Presidents have learned dramatic new ways of using their office as a bully pulpit. Since the Administrations of Theodore Roosevelt and Woodrow Wilson, Presidents have increasingly used the media to "go over the heads" of Congress on domestic matters, creating a cult of presidential personality and power—a "rhetorical presidency," in the words of the presidential scholar Jeffrey Tulis. In The Decline of American Political Pardo (1990), Martin Wattenberg documents how the role of political parties has diminished in the past few decades, in large part because Presidents and other politicians have learned to communicate directly with voters through the mass media. Candidates increasingly run campaigns stressing their personal qualities rather than their party ties. That development inevitably has given the President increased visibility as the most powerful individual on the national scene.

Meanwhile, the rise of national mass media—first network radio and then three-network television—has allowed the President to speak in unmediated fashion to virtually the whole nation at once. Many recent presidential scholars have been writing about a similar phenomenon, as Samuel Kernell's "going public" and Theodore Lowi's "the personal president" together suggest: from Franklin Roosevelt to John Kennedy to Ronald Reagan, the history of the past sixty years has often been the story of how Presidents used the mass media to become our prime political movers, appropriating roles once held by Congress or the parties.

That era may be drawing to a close. The ability of a President to draw the mass audience that broadcasting once afforded has been dramaticaly diminished by the rise of cable television. The political conventions draw roughly two thirds of the audience they did twelve years ago; many presidential news conferences are no longer covered by the three major networks. As Samuel Kernell has documented, when the major networks do cover a presidential appearance, it tends to get lower ratings than in the past because of cable competition. Sixty percent or more of all households with television watched the first televised addresses of Presidents Nixon, Carter, and Reagan, in the days before cable's ascendancy. George Bush never even broke 40 percent except with one speech—during the Gulf War. In this environment it becomes far more difficult for a President to mobilize the nation. The once all-powerful national megaphone of the presidency competes with many amplified voices in a diverse, atomized culture.

So what's Bill Clinton to do? One idea Clinton seems likely to pursue, as he did in the campaign, is that of a cable-TV-style marketing strategy. Instead of appearing ten or fifteen times a year on prime-time network television, where he would give a traditional formal speech or hold a press conference, Clinton may well appear far more often in a variety of different forums before smaller audiences—on the morning shows, C-SPAN, local television, talk radio, and even MTV. Marketers have found that generic mass-market advertising no longer works as effectively as targeted communication—so President Clinton would deliver his message, to borrow a phrase from his predecessor, as a thousand points of light. Occasional Clinton advisers such as Doug Ross, the former Michigan secretary of commerce, and David Osborne, a co-author of Reinventing Government, spent time between Election Day and the Inauguration designing a presidential communication strategy that, if adopted, could eventually include extensive use of such direct-marketing expedients as video and audio cassettes, direct mail, and 800 numbers.

Ross sees this "direct relationship" as the key part of a broader effort to redefine the presidency. "If Clinton acts like just another FDR or JFK," Ross says, "he will at best end up making only marginal improvements that are unable to transport America successfully into the future." Describing Clinton's new mission, Ross cites not the scholars whom Presidents have often sought out in the past but popular business theorists, such as Max De Pree, the author of two highly impressionistic books on corporate leadership, Leadership Jazz and Leadership Is an Art, and the management guru Tom Peters. According to Ross, the world has entered an era of decentralization, in which large bureaucracies—whether General Motors or the federal government—are increasingly incapable of dealing in broad, programmatic ways with individual customer or constituent demands. Ross describes, in almost evangelical terms, a "new paradigm"—as applicable to Clinton as it is to CEOs—in which consumers and voters are looking to leaders to provide them with "broad visions and values rather than top-down commands and elaborate rule books." Borrowing a metaphor from De Pree, Ross says that a President is no longer like an autocratic symphony conductor, leading everyone together. Instead, he's more like a jazz musician, setting the tempo for each player to do his own thing. Evidently there was more to that picture of Clinton the saxophone player than met the eye.

For example, Ross foresees that Clinton might announce a new initiative dealing with educational standards after holding a public meeting with education experts, much like the December [1992] economic summit in Little Rock. Or he might give a speech to discuss the issue, using videotapes to provide viewers with a clear picture of the problem. Interested voters would be encouraged to respond to questionnaires; they might then be put on a list to receive an audio tape or a series of mailings, or to attend a town meeting. Afterward the Secretary of Education might announce a series of pilot projects to test new ideas. The eventual goal, Ross says, would be to provide local school districts with good information that they could apply individually, consistent with a national approach. It's a vision of customer-driven government which appears strangely similar to Ross Perot's concept of an electronic town hall.

Related ideas have been outlined by other corporate theorists, among them Peter Block, the author of The Empowered Manager (1987). "There's a new model for corporate leadership now," Block says. "The whole patriarchal concept of a charismatic leader to whose authority you submit so he will take care of you is disappearing, in favor of a model in which partnership and service are dominant ideas." If Clinton can redefine the presidency to be more consistent with that model, Block says, he won't have to worry much about his TV ratings. "You don't turn up the volume in response to the new age," he says. "You change the station."

If this all sounds a bit ethereal and imbued with New Age spirituality, it is. Moreover, even if the goals of advisers like Ross and Osborne can be reduced to a blueprint, enormous problems would arise in trying to implement such a vision of the presidency in other than peripheral ways. Using an innovative communication strategy to deal with a few creative aspects of education policy is one thing; using the same method to come up with defense or trade proposals is quite another. Some question the relevance of "CEO models" to the presidency at all—with respect to communication or anything else. A CEO typically has the power to move workers around and even lay them off; a President has very little control over the federal work force. "What's the incentive for anyone who's not on the White House staff to do anything?" asks James Pinkerton, who was a counselor to President Bush and was known for trying to get his boss to think about the "new paradigm." Jeffrey Tulis, the acting chair of the Department of Government at the University of Texas at Austin, sees another problem. "Political leadership and business leadership are not the same," he says. "In business, the bottom line is money. In politics, the whole point is to figure out what the bottom line even is." In other words, without an initial firm agreement on the chord changes, the jazz is likely to turn into nothing more than loud noise.

Others find fault with a model that has the President continually on the road, or running from studio to studio. Sixteen years ago Jimmy Carter developed a communication strategy similar to the one proposed for Clinton, albeit on a smaller scale, when he scheduled town meetings in distant places and joined Walter Cronkite in order to take questions by phone. This approach hardly helped him. Moreover, for a President—as for any public figure—there is a danger of overexposure. "If the Carter administration were a television show," Russell Baker wrote in December of 1977, "it would have been cancelled months ago." Franklin Roosevelt never averaged more than two Fireside Chats a year until the war. In contrast, even Bush—who was hardly known for a concerted communication strategy—made fifty-six television appearances of various sorts during his first nineteen months in office.

Tulis is one of several presidential scholars who maintain that what Clinton needs to do with the presidency is something quite different from running a perpetual campaign, as he apparently intends to do. "Teledemocracy has weakened the presidency," Tulis says. "A President needs some distance from the people to reflect, to slow down passionate ideas, and to protect minority rights against the tyranny of the majority." If Presidents have often been more successful in the international arena than in the domestic one, he says, it is because the conduct of foreign policy doesn't lend itself to public campaigning.

Theodore Lowi, a professor of government at Cornell, says that Presidents inevitably create other problems for themselves when they establish a close relationship with the electorate by means of television. Such a "personal presidency" helps to set expectations so high that they cannot but be dashed when the President and the public find, inevitably, that the chief executive's powers to change the nation's domestic life are limited. "As visibility goes up," Lowi says, "so do expectations and vulnerability. There's more of a chance to make really big mistakes. It's a treadmill to oblivion. It's why modern history is filled with so many failed presidencies."

For that reason Lowi recommends that Clinton try to avoid a personal presidency. With the rise of "narrowcasting" and a diminishing media role for the President, Lowi sees a historic opportunity for Clinton to reduce the heroic expectations that have encumbered the office. He thinks that Clinton should reduce his visibility and resist efforts to accumulate presidential influence—getting rid of regulatory reforms that increase executive power and vetoing bills that impose conditions he can't meet.

Lowi's views have a correlate in the private sector. Many CEOs have successfully reformed their businesses by decentralizing power, giving far more authority and visibility to people who are closer to customers. The problem is that a CEO disperses power to other employees in his organization, whereas a President who gives up power along the lines Lowi suggests often gives it to another branch of government, Congress, which is considered more a competitor than part of the team.

Another problem, of course, is that Clinton probably didn't spend his life planning a run for the presidency so that he could diminish its importance. In the popular mind, and most likely in Clinton's own, the great Presidents were the strong and visible ones who accumulated power—the Abraham Lincolns, not the Calvin Coolidges. And in the end there is only so much that Clinton himself can do, even if he were to agree with Lowi and like-minded scholars. News coverage revolves around strong personas: in the Weltanschauung of the Washington press corps, the President must be the focus of events. The press would likely rebel against any moves that dictated otherwise. Moreover, if the rise of the Cold War and the age of broadcasting contributed to the growth of the executive branch, they were hardly the only factors. The rise of the regulatory and social-welfare state which began in the Roosevelt Administration has played a major role too.

Still, the presidency seems headed toward a different role in American life, though it may take years for that progress to be effected and assessed. Horace W. Busby, once an aide to Lyndon Johnson and now the publisher of a Washington newsletter, foresees an era in which the President will be a kind of "governor of the fifty states." "The President will become more of an irrelevancy," he says. "The old image of the powerful President wasn't due only to the Cold War. It was the product of a more primitive era. People today have far more education and exposure to the outside world. They don't need to attach that importance and responsibility to the office anymore." Indeed, in the new age of fragmentation, when it's tougher to assemble a mass following, virtually all colossal entities and authority figures of the old age have seen their prestige and power recede. There are no centers of the universe anymore: if Dan Rather is no Walter Cronkite, and Jay Leno is no Johnny Carson, it's not necessarily because the people got smaller; it's because, metaphorically speaking, the pictures did too. It's no coincidence that George Bush was no Ronald Reagan and Bill Clinton is no Jack Kennedy. Their successors won't be either.

George Will
"Rhetorical Presidency"*

The Constitution requires only that the president "shall from time to time give to the Congress information on the State of the Union" and recommend measures for improving it. Although Washington and Adams had

*George Will, "Rhetorical Presidency," *Newsweek* (February 8, 1993)

delivered their messages orally, Jefferson in 1801 sent a written message, a practice continued until Wilson went up to Congress in 1913, his first year as president. Jefferson's and Wilson's decisions expressed sharply contrasting understandings of the presidency.

In 1801, in his first giving of "information," Jefferson told Congress that recent "wars and troubles" were largely surmounted, so taxes could be cut and government pruned. As used to be customary, Jefferson put his remarks in a context of constitutional interpretation, stressing that "the states have themselves principal care of our persons, our property, and our reputation, constituting the great field of human concerns." Enterprise flourishes most when most free, and the federal government should feel strictly inhibited by the "limits of our constitutional powers." The idea of such limits now seems quaint, but not more so than Jefferson's concluding pledge: "Nothing shall be wanting on my part to inform, as far as in my power, the legislative judgment, nor to carry that judgment into faithful execution." Jefferson envisioned a modest role for presidents. They are primarily to execute the judgments of the First Branch, and secondarily to help "inform" that branch's deliberations.

It would have been in character if Jefferson, having economized time by not traipsing up to Capitol Hill, had spent the time reading a book. Clinton could profit by doing that, and a particularly pertinent book is "The Rhetorical Presidency" by Jeffrey K. Tulis of the University of Texas at Austin.

Tulis identifies Wilson as the principal progenitor of the modern presidency, the office that has broken many of its occupants, including Wilson. Wilson, who regarded the separation of powers not as the Constitution's genius but as its defect, articulated in theory and vivified in practice what has become the unexamined premise of contemporary politics. It is that the president's primary function is to exercise rhetorical leadership to mobilize the public's "opinion" in order to shatter the gridlock to which a large and pluralistic society, with a government of checks and balances, is prone.

It was grimly apposite that Wilson's health collapsed beneath the weight of this duty, during his Western tour to arouse opinion against congressional opposition to the League of Nations. Wilson cast presidents in a crushing role, one demanding skills that few presidents have in a sufficiency for the post-Wilson office. Tulis warns of, and Clinton should worry about, "an increasing lack of 'fit' between institution and occupant" in the era of the rhetorical presidency. Increasingly "presidential abilities and institutional requirements diverge," now that those requirements involve constant exhortation of an—inevitably—jaded public.

Clinton, who has been campaigning unceasingly since 1974 (20 campaigns since then), vows not to stop, promising more bus trips and the like. The presidency has become a seamless extension of campaigning, at a cost to the deliberative processes of government. Management of the dynamics of public opinion takes precedence over the rhythms of deliberation in representative institutions.

Bugle Call. The toll that rhetorical style can take on substantive policy is illustrated by Tulis's analysis of President Johnson's 1964 State of the

Union declaration: "This administration today, here and now, declares unconditional war on poverty." War. Unconditional. That bugle call launched the nation on a hurried march to disillusionment.

Johnson promised to "pursue poverty" with "pinpointed" attacks. It would not be an easy "struggle"; no single "weapon" or "strategy" would suffice "in the field." Rather than make a reasoned, deliberative presentation, persuasive about why eliminating poverty should be considered possible and an "unconditional" imperative, Johnson used a metaphor—"war'-'—as a substitute for argument. Indeed, it truncated debate. The premise—we were at war—drove policy: frantic urgency, quick mobilization. Johnson's subsequent message to Congress bristled with martial metaphors. Poverty is the "enemy" to be "driven from the land," not by "a single attack on a single front" but by all our "weapons" in "many battles," just as in "war against foreign enemies."

The metaphor "worked." Hearings in the poverty program were hasty; dissent seemed like a shirking of wartime duty. But the public's understanding of what it had embarked upon was superficial. And when the "war" bogged down, the public's commitment to it proved to be slight.

The "rhetorical presidency," continuously trying to mold the public mind, suits the temperament of the hyperkinetic persons who prosper by means of peripatetic campaigning. But one result is the loss of indirectness in government—representation, separation of powers. As Congress comes to accept the terms of competition with the "rhetorical presidency," it, too, tries to become a molder of "opinion," but in the unequal struggle Congress becomes a marionette of opinion, a role devoid of dignity. (Witness senators telling Zoë Baird their counts of telegrams and telephone calls.)

There is a tension between rhetoric written to a deliberative assembly and rhetoric spoken to an audience of scores of millions. The former seeks to "inform"—Jefferson's word—the reasoning within an assembly's walls. The latter seeks to inspirit the populace. Prior to this century, Tulis says, presidents preferred written communication with Congress rather than oral addresses to the public. This preference derived from an idea—the Founders'—of the proper functioning of the government. After Jefferson vowed "to inform . . . the legislative judgment," he continued: "The prudence and temperance of your discussions will promote, within your own walls, that conciliation which so much befriends national conclusion; and by its example will encourage among our constituents that progress of opinion which is tending to unite them in object and in will."

That is representative government, elegantly understood not as a handmaiden of public opinion but as an "example" elevating that opinion. It is still worth trying.

PRESIDENTIAL GOVERNMENT

See text p. 229

Early in the Clinton administration, the influence of Hillary Rodham Clinton became an object of public concern. The president openly and enthusiastically acknowledged that he sought advice and assistance from Mrs. Clinton in virtually every aspect of policy making. Within days of his inauguration, the president appointed Mrs. Clinton to head a task force charged with examining the scope of the health care crisis in America and with drafting a proposed policy response—a major position, given the importance of health care reform as an issue during the 1992 election.

Critics who claimed that Mrs. Clinton was exercising undue influence initiated a suit in federal court to determine the propriety of Mrs. Clinton's position. On June 21, 1993, shortly after the task force completed its work, the federal Court of Appeals ruled that Mrs. Clinton's appointment violated no federal laws. This decision, explained in the New York Times *article reprinted below, marks an important step in recognizing the political significance of the First Lady's role.*

Robert Pear
"Court Rules That First Lady Is 'De Facto' Federal Official"*

Ruling that Hillary Rodham Clinton was a fulltime Government official, a Federal appeals court today approved the secrecy of her task force on health care and essentially acquiesced in Mrs. Clinton's views about the role and powers of the First Lady.

The ruling, by the United States Court of Appeals for the District of Columbia, came in a case filed by doctors and others seeking to force the panel, the Task Force on National Health Care Reform, to conduct its business in public.

Redefines Role of First Lady

The judges ruled that the secrecy was legal, but the practical effect of the ruling is uncertain, because the task force and its staff of more than 500, which did most of the work, were disbanded last month. The court sent the case back to a Federal district judge to determine whether the staff might have to make its voluminous records and working papers public.

The decision on Mrs. Clinton's status represents a victory for the Administration and may remove a potential obstacle if the President wants to appoint his wife to head other advisory groups. She has, for instance, been mentioned as a possible leader of the Administration's effort to overhaul the welfare system.

*Robert Pear, "Court Rules That First Lady Is 'De Facto' Federal Official," *New York Times* (June 22, 1993).

But the rationale of the ruling is not limited to Mrs. Clinton. It would seem to permit any Presidential spouse to engage in official and semiofficial activities of a type normally performed by Government employees.

Mrs. Clinton is more powerful than many of her predecessors, and she is certainly more open in exercising that power. Her role has been a matter of debate since early 1992, when Mr. Clinton boasted of her talents, saying "Vote for one, get one free."

'De Facto Officer or Employee'

The appeals court acknowledged that it was stretching the definition of "officer or employee" of the Government to include Mrs. Clinton in her role as First Lady. But it said such a strained interpretation of the law was necessary to avoid the difficult constitutional problems that would arise if she had no official status.

Moreover, it said, "Congress itself has recognized that the President's spouse acts as the functional equivalent of an assistant to the President."

The court added: "We see no reason why a President could not use his or her spouse to carry out a task that the President might delegate to one of his White House aides." Therefore, the judges said, it is reasonable to treat the President's spouse as "a de facto official or employee" of the Government.

In March, Federal District Judge Royce C. Lamberth ruled that Mrs. Clinton was not a Government official, officer or employee. As a result, he said, the task force she headed was a Federal advisory committee. Under a 1972 law, the Federal Advisory Committee Act, such panels, when not composed wholly of Government officials, must conduct their meetings in public and must make their work papers available to the public.

The appeals court rejected Judge Lamberth's logic and said that the First Lady's status, though ambiguous, qualified her as a Government official. Thus, it said, "the task force is a committee wholly composed of Government officials."

The case was heard by a three-judge panel of the appeals court. Judge Laurence H. Silberman wrote the main opinion, and Judge Stephen F. Williams concurred.

The appellate court said there was "a longstanding tradition of public service by First Ladies—including, we are told, Sarah Polk, Edith Wilson, Eleanor Roosevelt, Rosalynn Carter and Nancy Reagan—who have acted (albeit in the background) as advisers and personal representatives of their husbands."

The court added: "We are not confident that this traditional perception of the President's wife, as a virtual extension of her husband, is widely held today. As this very case suggests, it may not even be a fair portrayal of Mrs. Clinton, who certainly is performing more openly than is typical of a First Lady."

Judge James L. Buckley wrote a separate opinion asserting that Mrs.

Clinton was not a Government officer or employee. But he concluded that the 1972 law was "unconstitutional as applied to the task force," because it interfered excessively with the President's right to receive confidential communications from his advisers.

Judge Buckley observed that Mrs. Clinton was greeted like a head of state, guarded by the Secret Service and allowed to spend Federal money. But he said, "She has been neither appointed to nor confirmed in the position of First Lady, she has taken no oath of office and she neither holds a statutory office nor performs statutory duties."

'Staff' Not Yet Defined

Mr. Clinton appointed the 12-member task force on Jan. 25, in the hope that it would help him prepare legislation for submission to Congress by May 1. The task force, which included six Cabinet Secretaries and several White House officials, held more than 20 meetings, at which it developed options and recommendations for the President. Mr. Clinton allowed the task force to expire May 30. Aides have said he now plans to offer a national plan to control health costs before the end of September.

The appeals court said it needed more information to determine whether the staff of the task force was subject to the 1972 law. The lawsuit was filed by the Association of American Physicians and Surgeons, a doctors' group; the American Council for Health Care Reform, a consumer group, and the National Legal and Policy Center, which seeks to promote ethics in government.

Kent Masterson Brown, a lawyer for the plaintiffs, said tonight that they had not decided whether to appeal. But he said he would proceed with taking depositions from people who had worked for the task force and would try to obtain the records of their deliberations.

QUESTIONS

1. According to *The Federalist No. 70* what are the differences in the functions of the legislative and executive branches that warrant structuring the two branches differently? How does the unified structure of the executive branch proposed by Hamilton promote responsibility in that branch?
2. If Hamilton argued persuasively in *The Federalist No. 70* that a president must be empowered to act with "[d]ecision, activity, secrecy and dispatch," how can the Supreme Court's decision in *United States v. Nixon* be justified? What test does the Court articulate to distinguish between permissible and impermissible confidentiality in the executive branch?
3. According to Steven Stark the days of strong presidential leadership have

come and gone. What factors have diminished the ability of a president to act as an effective leader? What are the pitfalls for any president who attempts to take a strong leadership position?

4. Unlike Steven Stark, George Will argues that presidents can continue to exercise effective leadership. According to Will what changes in the presidential role are necessary to recapture the loss of presidential power and competence?
5. Presidents are influenced by a number of individuals—staff, cabinet members, and spouses, to name a few. What problems are raised by the President's reliance on advisors of this type? Should all presidential advisors have some kind of electoral accountability, or do other safeguards exist?

CHAPTER 7

The Executive Branch: Bureaucracy in a Democracy

THE BUREAUCRATIC PHENOMENON

See text p. 266

Until the late nineteenth century, almost no one paid attention to the manner in which the government actually worked. Government positions were generally filled by elected officials, and there was little systematic management of government programs; indeed, at least at a national level, there were few governmental programs. There was, however, a great deal of governmental largesse to distribute—at least at a national level—and as scandals mounted over the manner in which this largesse was distributed, the demand for accountability grew.

In the wake of calls for civil service reform, some commentators began to argue in favor of a broader approach to public management. One of the earliest pieces in the field was written by President Woodrow Wilson. Nearly thirty years before his ascent to the presidency, Wilson, a professor at Bryn Mawr College, wrote an article for the Political Science Quarterly *arguing that political scientists had neglected the study of public administration. Wilson noted that the great questions in political science had revolved around what power the state ought to hold and how it was legitimated with no attention to how that power should be exercised. Wilson argued that public administration should be carried out in accordance with scientific principles of management and efficiency, an argument that can be heard in contemporary debates over the need for reforming public administration. After reading this chapter, you should consider whether you agree with Wilson's central proposition that politics and administration are separate phenomena.*

Woodrow Wilson
"The Study of Administration"*

. . . It is the object of administrative study to discover, first, what government can properly and successfully do, and, secondly, how it can do these proper things with the utmost possible efficiency and at the least possible cost either of money or of energy. On both these points there is obviously much need of light among us; and only careful study can supply that light. . . .

*Woodrow Wilson, "The Study of Administration," in *Classics in Public Administration, 2d ed.*, Shafritz and Hyde, eds. (Belmont: Dorsey Press, 1986). Originally in *Political Science Quarterly* (June 2, 1887). Reprinted with permission.

I

The science of administration is the latest fruit of that study of the science of politics which was begun some twenty-two hundred years ago. It is a birth of our own century, almost of our own generation.

Why was it so late in coming? Why did it wait till this too busy century of ours to demand attention for itself? Administration is the most obvious part of government; it is government in action; it is the executive, the operative, the most visible side of government, and is of course as old as government itself. It is government in action, and one might very naturally expect to find that government in action had arrested the attention and provoked the scrutiny of writers of politics very early in the history of systematic thought.

But such was not the case. No one wrote systematically of administration as a branch of the science of government until the present century had passed its first youth and had begun to put forth its characteristic flower of systematic knowledge. Up to our own day all the political writers whom we now read had thought, argued, dogmatized only about the *constitution* of government; about the nature of the state, the essence and seat of sovereignty, popular power and kingly prerogative; about the greatest meanings lying at the heart of government, and the high ends set before the purpose of government by man's nature and man's aims. . . . The question was always: Who shall make law, and what shall that law be? The other question, how law should be administered with enlightenment, with equity, with speed, and without fiction, was put aside as "practical detail" which clerks could arrange after doctors had agreed upon principles.

. . . [However,] if difficulties of government action are to be seen gathering in other centuries, they are to be seen culminating in our own.

This is the reason why administrative tasks have nowadays to be so studiously and systematically adjusted to carefully tested standards of policy, the reason why we are having now what we never had before, a science of administration. The weightier debates of constitutional principle are even yet by no means concluded; but they are no longer of more immediate practical moment than questions of administration. It is getting to be harder to *run* a constitution than to frame one. . . .

There is scarcely a single duty of government which was once simple which is not now complex; government once had but a few masters; it now has scores of masters. Majorities formerly only underwent government; they now conduct government. Where government once might follow the whims of a court, it must now follow the views of a nation.

And those views are steadily widening to new conceptions of state duty; so that at the same time that the functions of government are every day becoming more complex and difficult, they are also vastly multiplying in number. Administration is everywhere putting its hands to new undertakings. . . . Seeing every day new things which the state ought to do, the next thing is to see clearly how it ought to do them.

This is why there should be a science of administration which shall seek to straighten the paths of government, to make its business less businesslike, to strengthen and purify its organization, and to crown its dutifulness. This is one reason why there is such a science.

But where has this science grown up? Surely not on this side [of] the sea. Not much impartial scientific method is to be discerned in our administrative practices. The poisonous atmosphere of city government, the crooked secrets of state administration, the confusion, sinecurism, and corruption ever and again discovered in the bureaux at Washington forbid us to believe that any clear conceptions of what constitutes good administration are as yet very widely current in the United States. . . .

. . . American political history has been a history, not of administrative development, but of legislative oversight—not of progress in governmental organization, but of advance in law-making and political criticism. Consequently, we have reached a time when administrative study and creation are imperatively necessary to the well-being of our governments saddled with the habits of a long period of constitution-making. . . . We have reached . . . the period . . . when the people have to develop administration in accordance with the constitutions they won for themselves in a previous period of struggle with absolute power. . . .

. . . It is harder for democracy to organize administration than for monarchy. The very completeness of our most cherished political successes in the past embarrasses us. We have enthroned public opinion; and it is forbidden us to hope during its reign for any quick schooling of the sovereign in executive expertness or in the conditions of perfect functional balance in government. The very fact that we have realized popular rule in its fulness has made the task of *organizing* that rule just so much the more difficult. . . . An individual sovereign will adopt a simple plan and carry it out directly: he will have but one opinion, and he will embody that one opinion in one command. But this other sovereign, the people, will have a score of differing opinions. They can agree upon nothing simple: advance must be made through compromise, by a compounding of differences, by a trimming of plans and a suppression of too straightforward principles. There will be a succession of resolves running through a course of years, a dropping fire of commands running through a whole gamut of modifications.

. . . Wherever regard for public opinion is a first principle of government, practical reform must be slow and all reform must be full of compromises. For wherever public opinion exists it must rule. . . .

II

The field of administration is a field of business. It is removed from the hurry and strife of politics; it at most points stands apart even from the debatable ground of constitutional study. It is a part of political life only as the methods of the counting-house are a part of the life of society; only as machinery is part of the manufactured product. But it is, at the same time, raised very far above the dull level of mere technical detail by the fact that through its greater principles it is directly connected with the lasting maxims of political wisdom, the permanent truths of political progress.

The object of administrative study is to rescue executive methods from the confusion and costliness of empirical experiment and set them upon foundations laid deep in stable principle.

. . . [A]dministration lies outside the proper sphere of *politics.* Administrative questions are not political questions. Although politics sets the tasks for administration, it should not be suffered to manipulate its offices. . . .

There is another distinction which must be worked into all our conclusions, which, though but another side of that between administration and politics, is not quite so easy to keep sight of: I mean the distinction between *constitutional* and administrative questions, between those governmental adjustments which are essential to constitutional principle and those which are merely instrumental to the possibly changing purposes of a wisely adapting convenience. . . .

A clear view of the difference between the province of constitutional law and the province of administrative function ought to leave no room for misconception; and it is possible to name some roughly definite criteria upon which such a view can be built. Public administration is detailed and systematic execution of public law. Every particular application of general law is an act of administration. The assessment and raising of taxes, for instance, the hanging of a criminal, the transportation and delivery of the mails, the equipment and recruiting of the army, and navy, etc., are all obviously acts of administration; but the general laws which direct these things to be done are as obviously outside of and above administration. The broad plans of governmental action are not administrative; the detailed execution of such plans is administrative. Constitutions, therefore, properly concern themselves only with those instrumentalities of government which are to control general law. Our federal constitution observes this principle in saying nothing of even the greatest of the purely executive offices, and speaking only of that President of the Union who was to share the legislative and policy-making functions of government, only of those judges of highest jurisdiction who were to interpret and guard its principles, and not of those who were merely to give utterance to them. . . .

There is, [however,] one point at which administrative studies trench on constitutional ground—or at least upon what seems constitutional ground. The study of administration, philosophically viewed, is closely connected with the study of the proper distribution of constitutional authority. To be efficient it must discover the simplest arrangements by which responsibility can be unmistakably fixed upon officials; the best way of dividing authority without hampering it, and responsibility without obscuring it. And this question of the distribution of authority, when taken into the sphere of the higher, the originating functions of government, is obviously a central constitutional question. . . .

To discover the best principle for the distribution of authority is of greater importance, possibly, under a democratic system, where officials serve many masters, than under others where they serve but a few. All sovereigns are suspicious of their servants, and the sovereign people is no exception to the rule; but how is its suspicion to be allayed by *knowledge?* If that suspicion could be clarified into wise vigilance, it would be altogether salutary; if that vigilance could be aided by the unmistakable placing of responsibility, it would be altogether beneficient. Suspicion in itself is never healthful either in the private or in the public mind. *Trust is strength* in all relations of life; and, as it is the office of the constitutional reformer to create conditions of trustfulness, so it is the office of the administrative organizer to fit administration with conditions of clear-cut responsibility which shall insure trustworthiness.

And let me say that large powers and unhampered discretion seem to me the indispensable conditions of responsibility. Public attention must be easily directed, in each case of good or bad administration, to just the man deserving of praise or blame. There is no danger in power, if only it be not irresponsible. If it be divided, dealt out in shares to many, it is obscured; and if it be obscured, it is made irresponsible. But if it be centered in heads of the service and in heads of branches of the service, it is easily watched and brought to book. If to keep his office a man must achieve open and honest success, and if at the same time he feels himself intrusted with large freedom of discretion, the greater his power the less likely is he to abuse it, the more is he nerved and sobered and elevated by it. The less his power, the more safely obscure and unnoticed does he feel his position to be, and the more readily does he relapse into remissness.

Just here we manifestly emerge upon the field of that still larger question—the proper relations between public opinion and administration.

To whom is official trustworthiness to be disclosed, and by whom is it to be rewarded? Is the official to look to the public for his meed of praise and his push of promotion, or only to his superior in office? Are the people to be called in to settle administrative discipline as they are called in to settle constitutional principles? These questions evidently find their root in what is undoubtedly the fundamental problem of this whole study. That problem is: What part shall public opinion take in the conduct of administration?

The right answer seems to be, that public opinion shall play the part of authoritative critic.

But the *method* by which its authority shall be made to tell? Our peculiar American difficulty in organizing administration is not the danger of losing liberty, but the danger of not being able or willing to separate its essentials from its accidents. Our success is made doubtful by that besetting error of ours, the error of trying to do too much by vote. Self-government does not consist in having a hand in everything, any more than housekeeping consists necessarily in cooking dinner with one's own hands. The cook must be trusted with a large discretion as to the management of the fires and the ovens. . . .

The problem is to make public opinion efficient without suffering it to be meedlesome. Directly exercised, in the oversight of the daily details and in the choice of the daily means of government, public criticism is of course a clumsy nuisance, a rustic handling delicate machinery. But as superintending the greater forces of formative policy alike in politics and administration, public criticism is altogether safe and beneficent, altogether indispensable. Let administrative study find the best means for giving public criticism this control and for shutting it out from all other interference.

But is the whole duty of administrative study done when it has taught the people what sort of administration to desire and demand, and how to get what they demand? Ought it not to go on to drill candidates for the public service?

. . . If we are to improve public opinion, which is the motive power of government, we must prepare better officials as the *apparatus* of government. . . . It will be necessary to organize democracy by sending up to the competitive examinations for the civil service men definitely prepared for standing liberal tests as to technical knowledge. A technically schooled civil service will presently have become indispensable.

I know that a corps of civil servants prepared by a special schooling and drilled, after appointment, into a perfected organization, with appropriate hierarchy and characteristic discipline, seems to a great many very thoughtful persons to contain elements which might combine to make an offensive official class—a distinct, semi-corporate body with sympathies divorced from those of a progressive, free-spirited people, and with hearts narrowed to the meanness of a bigoted officialism. . . .

But to fear the creation of a domineering, illiberal officialism as a result of the studies I am here proposing is to miss altogether the principle upon which I wish most to insist. That principle is, that administration in the United States must be at all points sensitive to public opinion. A body of thoroughly trained officials serving during good behavior we must have in any case: that is a plain business necessity. But the apprehension that such a body will be anything un-American clears away the moment it is asked, What is to constitute good behavior? For that question obviously carries its own answer on its face. Steady, hearty allegiance to the policy of the government they serve will constitute good behavior. That *policy* will have no taint of officialism about it. It will not be the creation of permanent officials, but of statesmen whose responsibility to public opinion will be direct and inevitable. Bureaucracy can exist only where the whole service of the state is removed from the common political life of the people, its chiefs as well as its rank and file. Its motives, its objects, its policy, its standards, must be bureaucratic. . . .

The ideal for us is a civil service cultured and self-sufficient enough to act with sense and vigor, and yet so intimately connected with the popular thought, by means of elections and constant public counsel, as to find arbitrariness or class spirit quite out of the question.

III

Having thus viewed in some sort the subject-matter and the objects of this study of administration, what are we to conclude as to the methods best suited to it—the points of view most advantageous for it?

Government is so near us, so much a thing of our daily familiar handling, that we can with difficulty see the need of any philosophical study of it, or the exact point of such study, should it be undertaken. We have been on our feet too long to study now the art of walking. We are a practical people, made so apt, so adept in self-government by centuries of experimental drill that we are scarcely any longer capable of perceiving the awkwardness of the particular system we may be using, just because it is so easy for us to use any system. We do not study the art of governing: we govern. But mere unschooled genius for affairs will not save us from sad blunders in administration. Though democrats by long inheritance and repeated choice, we are still rather crude democrats. Old as democracy is, its organization on a basis of modern ideas and conditions is still an unaccomplished work. The democratic state has yet to be equipped for carrying those enormous burdens of administration which the needs of this industrial and trading age are so fast accumulating. . . .

We can borrow the science of administration [developed elsewhere] with safety and profit if only we read all fundamental differences of condition into its essential tenets. We have only to filter it through our constitutions, only to put it over a slow fire of criticism and distil away its foreign gases. . . .

Our own politics must be the touchstone for all theories. The principles on which to base a science of administration for America must be principles which have democratic policy very much at heart. And, to suit American habit, all general theories must, as theories, keep modestly in the background, not in open argument only, but even in our own minds—lest opinions satisfactory only to the standards of the library should be dogmatically used, as if they must be quite as satisfactory to the standards of practical politics as well. Doctrinaire devices must be postponed to tested practices. Arrangements not only sanctioned by conclusive experience elsewhere but also congenial to American habit must be preferred without hesitation to theoretical perfection. In a word, steady, practical statesmanship must come first, closet doctrine second. The cosmopolitan what-to-do must always be commanded by the American how-to-do-it.

Our duty is to supply the best possible life to a *federal* organization, to systems within systems; to make town, city, county, state, and federal governments live with a like strength and an equally assured healthfulness, keeping each unquestionably its own master and yet making all interdependent and co-operative, combining independence with mutual helpfulness. The task is great and important enough to attract the best minds.

This interlacing of local self-government with federal self-government is quite a modern conception. . . . The question for us is, how shall our series of governments within governments be so administered that it shall always be to the interest of the public officer to serve, not his superior alone but the community also, with the best efforts of his talents and the soberest service of his conscience? How shall such service be made to his commonest interest by contributing abundantly to his sustenance, to his dearest interest by furthering his ambition, and to his highest interest by advancing his honor and establishing his character? And how shall this be done alike for the local part and for the national whole?

If we solve this problem we shall again pilot the world. . . .

AGENCIES AND THEIR POLITICS

See text p. 272

Every president in recent decades has sworn to decrease waste in government—to cut unnecessary programs and to make the bureaucracy accountable. Few have succeeded: agencies are created with their own missions and those aims may not coincide precisely with the aims of the President.

When President Clinton took office, he promised to "reinvent government," and appointed Vice President Al Gore to head a policy group that would look at instituting a system of performance reviews to evaluate governmental function. The following article, written shortly after the election and before any significant efforts at reform could be initiated, looks at the perennial problems that beset reform efforts. The article notes that some critics argue that efforts to reshape agencies and improve performance are just "buzzword[s]" that "allow[] Clinton to redefine tough political issues as bureaucratic problems. . . ."

Stephen Barr
"The Promise to Transform Government"*

The worries are familiar: Government is sluggish, suffering from bureaucratic bloat. It is full of rules and regulations and chains of command. It can't keep up in the real world. Now, more than ever, change is mandatory.

For Bill Clinton, the remedy is "reinventing government." The words served not only as a campaign slogan but as the foundation for his promise "to change the way the federal government operates."

How that promise can be carried out is under study by the transition's domestic policy team. Its leading advocate, David Osborne, has been asked to take part in the Little Rock, Ark., economic summit beginning today, focusing, he said, on "the connection between reinventing government and creating job growth."

*Stephen Barr, "The Promise to Transform Government," *Washington Post* (December 14, 1992).

The transition team's work has been guided in many ways by Osborne, who wrote a chapter on the topic in "Mandate for Change," a policy blueprint for the Clinton administration released last week by the Progressive Policy Institute, a think tank that has helped shape several Clinton initiatives. In his chapter, Osborne urges the next president to "create a high-level reinventing government group within the White House."

The phrase "reinventing government" covers almost everything that Clinton talked about during the campaign. It's a way to raise money and cut costs, a way to link government management and systems to big issues like health care and "fair share" taxation. It includes Clinton's pledge to cut 100,000 federal jobs through attrition and to require federal executives to achieve a 3 percent across-the-board administrative saving in every agency.

It's also how Clinton can change the behavior of the bureaucracy by injecting it with an entrepreneurial spirit that provides new incentives for federal workers.

To skeptics, however, "reinventing government" is just a buzzword that allows Clinton to redefine tough political issues as bureaucratic problems and to beguile taxpayers with visions of more government for less money.

"When we can't deal with the big issues, we start dealing with the management," said H. George Frederickson, a University of Kansas public administration professor. "The big issues are housing and health care. It takes dedication and political consensus-building and dollars and skills with federalism to deal with those problems. What you've got in Washington is the wrong-problems problem."

But Osborne and his supporters say they believe it is time to concentrate on how government works, because they view this as central to helping solve the nation's long-term economic problems.

For example, Osborne said, the government has set up job training, vocational education and welfare systems that began decades ago. Because of the way the government provides money for vocational education, he said, "you get a system that continues to teach things in some cases long after those skills become fairly irrelevant to the marketplace."

The government's systems can be restructured only by "changing the basic incentives that drive public institutions," Osborne said in an interview. "The budget system rewards waste and encourages waste, because if you don't spend every penny every fiscal year you lose it and get less next year. So if you're smart, you spend it."

As he explains in his "Mandate for Change" chapter: "Most public programs are monopolies whose customers cannot go elsewhere for a better deal. Most are funded according to their inputs—how many children are eligible for a given program, how many families are poor enough to qualify for public assistance—rather than according to their outcomes, or results."

Osborne doesn't fault government workers so much as he does the way government manages. "The marching orders given to the bureaucracy often require them to suspend common sense," he said. "If your personnel system makes it difficult to move people around as needs change, it won't move them around."

Ralph Whitehead, a University of Massachusetts professor who studies the nation's work force, said he thinks the Clinton administration can use "reinventing government" efforts as "an experimental showcase for new ways of organizing work."

If the federal government becomes an innovator, "it can gain new stature in the country. If it doesn't step up, it will be one more sign that the Beltway is out of touch," he said.

The erosion of the middle class over the last decade shows why it is important to think about how work is organized, Whitehead said. "The various levels of the public sector spend hundred of millions of dollars on manpower, mainly for education, and hundreds of millions on technology," he said, "but spend very little on establishing the work systems that make sure that the manpower and the technology will get hooked up to one another in ways that are efficient and equitable."

Osborne's proposed solutions have been outlined in detail in a book, "Reinventing Government," that he wrote with Ted Gaebler, a former city manager of Visalia, Calif., and Vandalia, Ohio. The book gives examples of innovative government at the local and state levels and concludes that "the central failure of government today is one of means, not ends."

Under Osborne's framework, a "mission-driven government," for example, would overhaul its budget system and adopt performance-based budgeting. Performance measures would be developed for all federal programs, and the budget would specify performance targets and reward agencies that exceeded those targets.

"Politically, it requires a change of mindset on the part of people in Congress," Osborne said. "They're used to controlling the inputs—you'll spend so much on this base or that base—and they're used to distributing pork. A performance-based system eliminates some of the micro-management up front."

Congress, however, has seen several similar overhaul proposals before. For example, Osborne urges a "sunset law" that would require reapproval of all government regulations—a practice that could create political chaos when such popular programs as Social Security came up for renewal.

And Congress has been moving to foster better management in the government. Sen. William V. Roth Jr. (R-Del.) expects to reintroduce legislation next year that would require federal agencies to develop program performance plans, specify goals and report on the results. Sen. John Glenn (D-Ohio), chairman of the Governmental Affairs Committee, has helped create new agency financial officers and reviews and strengthened the role of inspectors general.

James Colvard, a former deputy director of the Office of Personnel Management, said there is "some real profit to be made" by rethinking many of the current bureaucratic premises.

"The federal system is highly overstructured at the moment," he said, leading to situations where the official interpreting a federal rule effectively makes decisions for line managers and employees but "is not held accountable." He added, "It's the kind of thing that occurs when you have complex processes. . . . There are no villains, and that's the part that makes it so frustrating."

See text p. 283

If the key activity of regulatory agencies during the 1980s was deregulation, the watchword of the 1990s is likely to be regulation. Despite perennial complaints about government interference in the free operation of the market, regulation has often facilitated business, especially at the federal level, where it has provided a uniform set of standards that allow companies to operate in several different states at the same time. In the wake of declining federal regulatory programs, many states have stepped in to regulate commerce on a local level, creating a confusing patchwork of standards that businesses are finding difficult to work with—a consequence of the federalist nature of the American system discussed in Chapter 3. In a February 1991 article, commentator John Holusha points out that the 1990s may be marked by increasing requests for "the good old days of . . . federal control." Of course, the extent to which a corporation will seek federal regulation will depend upon how it perceives a particular administration—whether Democrat or Republican—and whether that administration is likely to be sympathetic to its own interests.

John Holusha
"Some Corporations Plead for the Firm Hand of Uncle Sam"*

The pace of regulatory activity in Washington slowed sharply after President Ronald Reagan promised to get big government off the back of industry in the 1980s. Budgets were cut and top officials emphasized a free market approach. But now, faced with a patchwork of conflicting regulations at the state level, a broad coalition of companies that produce and sell consumer products is deciding that maybe uniform Federal regulations wouldn't be such a bad thing after all. In some cases, companies are actually going to Washington and asking for a return to the good old days of broader Federal control.

"It may be that, after the fact, nationwide marketers are becoming opposed to the trend and are moving to stem the onrush to deregulation," said Susan Edelman, a professor at the Columbia University Business School.

For those who have felt that in many cases deregulation went too far, the idea of executives asking for regulation is a welcome twist.

*John Holusha, "Some Corporations Plead for the Firm Hand of Uncle Sam," *New York Times* (February 24, 1991).

"With environmental issues, it is not clear that the invisible hand will optimize," said John Meyer, a professor at the Kennedy School of Government at Harvard University. "There are too many external factors that have high public costs. So it would appear that the benefits of government action would exceed the costs."

States are increasingly moving to fill the void left by the Federal Government by imposing their own regulations on packaging, hazardous waste, automotive emissions and other environmentally related activities. With no sign that the Federal Government was interested in decreeing when a company can claim that a product is "recyclable" or "recycled"—designations that consumer products manufacturers want to be able to use on their packages because surveys have shown that buyers feel better about products that appear to be environmentally sound—New York, Rhode Island and California have enacted their own conflicting rules. Other states are considering their own measures.

Executives for companies like Proctor & Gamble and Lever Brothers, which manufacture products in large centralized factories and distribute them across the country, say that contradictory state laws can be a nightmare. For example, California requires that 10 percent of a product consist of recovered material before it can be labeled "recycled." In New York, the requirement varies from product to product; paper towels need 40 percent recycled content, while for aluminum packaging the requirement is 15 percent. Some industry officials say the companies might reluctantly drop the environmental claims rather than try to meet different requirements in different states.

"The states moved into a vacuum," said Robert M. Viney, a environmental marketing specialist at Proctor & Gamble. "There were no Federal standards or guidelines for labeling."

Looking to Washington

Many manufacturers fear they will be victimized by politically ambitious state officials seeking to exploit the environmental issue. Last year several state attorneys general accused a subsidiary of Mobile Oil of false advertising when it labeled its Hefty plastic trash bags "degradable." The company had agreed to remove the claim. Last November, 10 attorneys general, 7 of them Democrats, appeared to be trying to seize control of the labeling issue when they issued a report of "recommendations for responsible environmental advertising."

Hoping that the Republican Bush Administration would give them standards that were not only uniform but more lenient, Proctor & Gamble, Lever Brothers, Kraft Foods and a number of trade associations, including the National Retail Federation, the Grocery Manufacturers Association and the Food Marketing Institute, asked the Federal Trade Commission on Feb. 14 to issue guidelines regulating the use of environmental claims. Officials of the agency have indicated they are receptive to such an approach.

Officials of some of the companies involved concede that it is unusual for them to seek direction from Washington. "This is an anomaly," said Melinda Sweet, the director of environmental affairs for Lever Brothers. "Normally we would shout and fight."

But she said many of the same companies and associations may be back in Washington later this year if states start imposing limits on packaging, requiring, for example, that it contain a certain percentage of recycled material. This, too, is an issue that Federal regulators have never addressed.

Fighting Back

"Modifying package designs state by state would be impractical and uneconomical," Ms. Sweet said. "Distribution would be impossible." Since the Resource Conservation and Recovery Act, which deals with solid waste, is due for reauthorization this year, it could become the vehicle for attempts to pre-empt state actions.

Packaging manufacturers and consumer goods companies have good reason to be worried about state action. Legislators in Maine last year voted to ban single-serving juice boxes made with layers of plastic, aluminum and paper on the ground that they are difficult to recycle.

Model legislation developed by the Coalition of Northeast Governors and adopted by eight states, which would limit the amount of heavy metals in printing inks, is on its way to becoming a national standard. The coalition has been working on developing rules to make packaging more recyclable, although the process has been slowed recently by infighting between environmental groups and state officials.

Some industry representatives say the Reagan Administration's reluctance to do anything that smacked of regulation is the reason for the unwanted upsurge in activity by the states. "You have a maturing environmental movement that was blocked in Washington, so they went to the states," said Jeffrey Nedelman, a vice president of Grocery Manufacturers of America. "The Reagan Administration stiff-armed them for eight years."

Susan Birmingham, a lobbyist for the United States Public Interest Research Group, an umbrella organization of state environmental and consumer groups, said that ideally the Federal Government should take a leadership role. "But the political reality is that you have to be successful at the state level before you can start persuading Congress," she said. "We have much more room to maneuver in the states."

Debating the Issues: Opposing Views

THE FEDERAL BUREAUCRACY: WHO SHOULD CONTROL IT?

See text pp. 302–3

As the text points out, controlling the size and power of administrative agencies is a complex problem. Governmental bureaucracies are easy targets, and vows to cut red tape are easily made. Every president in recent decades has come to office promising reform; very few are able to make significant changes.

Most people agree, regardless of political affiliation, with the basic issues—that agencies should be responsible for their actions and that waste and duplication should be reduced—but finding a way of achieving those ends remains elusive. In the following two articles, both David Broder, a political columnist for the Washington Post *and William Ruckelshaus, a former director of the Environmental Protection Agency, argue that regulators must be regulated. Ruckelshaus argues that reform efforts must be based in the White House in some form of regulatory oversight and review procedure, while Broder suggests that the administration's reform efforts need to be directed at breaking up special interest groups and their colluders in Congress.*

David S. Broder
"To Slim Down the Federal Goliath"*

During last year's [1992] campaign, it became known as The Speech He Never Gave. It was a speech on "entrepreneurial government," a new way of organizing the bureaucracy to cut down on wasteful spending and excessive staffing—and improve the delivery of services.

It was always somewhere just over the horizon in Bill Clinton's campaign—a subject of humor to some insiders and of regret to others. Some blamed the influence of public employee unions, which endorsed early in the game, for inhibiting Clinton from suggesting that government was an overstuffed couch. Others said that talk of big reorganization plans smacked too much of Jimmy Carter and would divert voters from the desired focus on economic issues.

Whatever the case, the speech was never given. And the theme seems to have disappeared so far from public discussion of the plans of the new administration. And that's a real loss.

The inertial forces in government are enormously powerful. Programs, once launched, tend to go on forever. Agencies are immortal. Unless a president comes to town determined to shake up the system, he will usually

*David S. Broder, "To Slim Down the Federal Goliath," *Washington Post* (January 13, 1993).

find that the only way to energize it is to add new layers on top of the old. Clinton has done that already. Despite his promise to streamline the White House staff, he has added a new National Economic Council, of unknown dimensions, to the preexisting Council of Economic Advisers, the Treasury, the Office of Management and Budget and all the other bureaucracies that have an oar in economic policy-making.

That same thing is likely to happen in government programs, from health care to high-tech development, unless Clinton deliberately searches out places to slim down and redesign the federal Goliath.

A good place for him to start might be the chapter on the "new federal compact" in "Mandate for Change," the volume of proposals issued by the Progressive Policy Institute, Clinton's favorite think tank. The chapter was written by David Osborne, whose books on state and local experiments in "reinventing government" have been influential in shaping Clinton's thinking.

Osborne argues, with great vehemence, that Clinton should launch a serious effort to sort out and rationalize the responsibilities of the three levels of government—national, state and local—with a view to saving money, slashing layers of bureaucracy and, most important, getting the citizens better results.

That sounds like Republican talk; in fact, both Richard Nixon and Ronald Reagan did start such efforts. But they stalled well short of success, stymied by the suspicion in Congress, state legislatures and city halls that these conservatives were just looking for ways to sabotage vital social services.

Presumably, Clinton's credentials with the governors and mayors are good enough to spare him from that cynical suggestion. The starting point, Osborne rightly suggests, has to be an examination of the 557 separate grant programs that funnel almost $160 billion a year into states and local communities. Although almost all the services are rendered locally, people on the receiving end must satisfy the minuscule eligibility standards and detailed regulations that Congress and the bureaucracy attach to the money. That means thousands of federal and state bureaucrats are kept busy writing the regs and seeing that they are complied with.

Osborne suggests that easily 100 of the grant-in-aid programs could be eliminated and another 400 consolidated into what he calls "challenge grants"—block grants with built-in rewards for those who demonstrate they are getting results. He also endorses the plea governors and mayors have made for years for more flexibility in the use of these funds.

That sounds so sensible you would think it would be easy. But it is not. Each of those programs has a history that involves some organized constituency and some senator or representative colluding to create a categorical grant that will serve the particular need that they regard for the moment as specially compelling. It's not easy to strip them of their pet playthings—the programs, the agencies, the line-item appropriations they feel they own.

The only way that gets done is if a president is willing to use some of his political capital and persuasive powers to do it. Plenty of people can draw him the map of what needs to be done; indeed, Alice Rivlin, Clinton's . . .

deputy director of the Office of Management and Budget, has written a book that spells out many of the same restructuring ideas that Osborne suggests. But only the president has the muscle it will take to overcome congressional, bureaucratic and interest-group opposition.

We don't know if Clinton has his heart in that battle.

William D. Ruckelshaus "Who Will Regulate the Regulators?"*

The public believes Republican administrations oppose environmental, health and safety regulations because of their ties to big business. This belief was fueled by the Bush Administration's Council on Competitiveness, which was abolished right after the Clinton Administration took office.

Beginning in 1970, Democratic Congresses gradually stripped regulatory discretion from Republican Presidents when reauthorizing old laws and enacting new ones. They vested this power in independent agencies like the Environmental Protection Agency and Occupational Safety and Health Administration.

Congress hampered Presidents by writing more and more regulatory requirements and deadlines into laws. This set up the agencies for failure. The agencies, in turn, issued rules that were flawed from the start because the consequences were unknown, and they missed deadlines because they lacked time to gather necessary data.

One result has been further criticism from members of Congress and still more prescriptive legislation. Another has been continuing erosion of trust in the Government, reinforced by our leaders' use of the regulatory agencies as whipping boys. Small wonder the nation despairs of Federal solutions to the problems of a modern industrial state.

There is no doubt that the President needs to coordinate regulatory policy. Each one since Richard Nixon has tried. The issue is how it can best be done.

Since the new Administration offers the prospect of improvement, Congress should restore the President's powers to issue regulations. This would clearly fix regulatory and economic accountability, now diffused.

President Clinton needs to create a White House oversight and review mechanism that allows him to coordinate environmental, health and safety regulations with his economic policies, particularly since his main concern is economic rebuilding.

This mechanism could address E.P.A. standards aimed, for example, at

*William D. Ruckelshaus, "Who Will Regulate the Regulators?" *New York Times* (February 3, 1993).

reducing pollutants discharged into water from pulp mills. The impact of the standards on the worldwide competitiveness of our pulp industry is not an E.P.A. issue. The President should be the Congressionally mandated authority to weigh the environmental and economic effects of such a regulation.

Apparently the Administration is on the right track. Mr. Clinton has directed the drafting of an executive order that would give Vice President Al Gore authority for reviewing regulatory decisions.

This was the function of the much criticized Bush Council on Competitiveness, led by Vice President Dan Quayle. The council, established to review the cost to business of regulations, came to be perceived as a back door for disgruntled special interests to obtain exemptions from regulations, especially environmental ones.

In laying out a clear, comprehensive strategy, the Administration need not cite every action contemplated but should state the criteria for its legislative initiatives and regulatory decisions. It could have applied such criteria to the new E.P.A. Administrator's decision, reported yesterday, to ask Congress to relax a law prohibiting trace amounts of cancer-causing pesticides in food. The Administrator, Carol Mr. Browner, called the law a scientific anachronism.

Regulatory review has to be accessible and understandable to the public. We need these questions answered: When will the public have access? Who will make the final decisions? How will the public be informed? If they are not answered, the exercise will be suspect.

Fortunately, a Gore spokesman has said the Administration plans to pursue a much more open process for reviewing environmental, health and safety regulations.

QUESTIONS

1. According to Woodrow Wilson, "administration lies outside the proper sphere of *politics.*" Do you agree? Can government programs be administered scientifically? Should concern for efficiency be the guiding principle for the administration of governmental programs, or might other factors enter into a management plan?
2. President Clinton's advisors in his plan for "reinventing government" have argued that bureaucratic reform can be accomplished only by altering "the incentives that drive public institutions." What are the current incentives, and in what ways can those incentives be altered to increase governmental effectiveness?
3. The article by Holusha suggests that some firms seek federal regulation. What factors motivate such requests? Is the issue simply one of striving for consistency in regulatory programs in the face of inconsistent state programs, or are other factors at work?

4. Does the problem with bureaucratic accountability originate with agencies themselves? What is the locus of the problem—are agencies simply too quick to generate rules, or are the rules generated in response to outside pressures? Depending upon whether the problems are internally or externally generated, what kinds of policy changes will increase accountability and efficiency?
5. While the president has a great deal of management authority as the chief executive, Congress exercises authority as well. In recent decades, however, Congressional control over agencies has not been particularly effective. What kinds of tools does Congress have at its disposal to manage agency activity, and why has it been unable to utilize those tools effectively? What reforms might improve Congressional performance in this area?

CHAPTER 8

The Federal Courts: Least Dangerous Branch or Imperial Judiciary?

THE JUDICIAL PROCESS

See text p. 312

This section of the text discusses the types of cases courts consider and the types of law with which they deal, but it also raises the central question, discussed throughout this chapter, of how *courts make their decisions. Interpreting the law is at best an imperfect art, and the credibility of the courts as an institution rests on their ability to justify their decisions in reasoned opinions.*

As this chapter explains, courts are constrained by a number of explicit and implicit principles of interpretation. One of those limitations, mentioned on page 312 of the text, is the principle of stare decisis, *which instructs judges to draw from earlier decisions and render their pronouncements consistent. That principle requires courts to make decisions about what is settled law and how the facts in subsequent cases justify altering or amending those settled decisions. While the following decision,* Planned Parenthood v. Casey *(1992), could be read in conjunction with a number of sections of this chapter and in chapter Four, it is particularly noteworthy for the ways in which the Supreme Court utilized the principle of* stare decisis.

As discussed in Chapter Four, in Roe v. Wade *(1973), the Court held that the right to privacy encompassed a woman's right to choose to have an abortion. In the twenty years since* Roe *was decided, a number of states have passed statutes attempting to limit that right and the Court indicated that it would uphold regulations on abortions so long as they did not place an "undue burden" upon a woman's right to choose an abortion, which was a less restrictive test for evaluating the constitutionality of the regulations than might have been applied, and which allowed for a broad interpretation by the states. Therefore, when a Pennsylvania law imposing significant restrictions on abortion "on demand" was passed in the early 1990s, Planned Parenthood of SEPA sued the state's Governor, Tom Casey, for violating a woman's right to an abortion.*

The Court in Planned Parenthood v. Casey *reaffirmed* Roe *by a bare majority. A prominent factor in the majority's opinion was the extent to which the Court should be willing to upset a prior holding. The majority opinion discussed in detail the conditions under which a departure from a settled interpretation ought to be considered, and expressed concern about perceptions of institutional legitimacy that might result if it acted too precipitously to overturn a prior decision. The dissent argued just as strongly that the Court was not compelled to save* Roe, *since the initial decision was ill-considered.*

Planned Parenthood of Southeastern Pennsylvania v. *Casey* (1992)*

JUSTICE O'CONNOR, JUSTICE KENNEDY, and JUSTICE SOUTER announce the judgment of the Court.

I

After considering the fundamental constitutional questions resolved by *Roe* [*v. Wade,* . . .], principles of institutional integrity, and the rule of *stare decisis,* we are led to conclude this: the essential holding of *Roe v. Wade* should be retained and once again reaffirmed.

It must be stated at the outset and with clarity that *Roe*'s essential holding, the holding we reaffirm, has three parts. First is a recognition of the right of the woman to choose to have an abortion before viability and to obtain it without undue interference from the State. Before viability, the State's interests are not strong enough to support a prohibition of abortion or the imposition of a substantial obstacle to the woman's effective right to elect the procedure. Second is a confirmation of the State's power to restrict abortions after fetal viability, if the law contains exceptions for pregnancies which endanger a woman's life or health. And third is the principle that the State has legitimate interests from the outset of the pregnancy in protecting the health of the woman and the life of the fetus that may become a child. These principles do not contradict one another; and we adhere to each. . . .

II

Our law affords constitutional protection to personal decisions relating to marriage, procreation, contraception, family relationships, child rearing, and education. Our cases recognize "the right of the individual, married or single, to be free from unwarranted governmental intrusion into matters so fundamentally affecting a person as the decision whether to bear or beget a child." *Eisenstadt v. Baird,* . . . . Our precedents "have respected the private realm of family life which the state cannot enter." *Prince v. Massachusetts,* . . . . These matters, involving the most intimate and personal choices a person may make in a lifetime, choices central to personal dignity and autonomy, are central to the liberty protected by the Fourteenth Amendment. At the heart of liberty is the right to define one's own concept of existence, of meaning, of the universe, and of the mystery of human life. . . .

While we appreciate the weight of the arguments made on behalf of the State in the case before us, arguments which in their ultimate formulation

*Planned Parenthood of Southeastern Pennsylvania v. Casey, 112 S.Ct. 2791.

conclude that *Roe* should be overruled, the reservations any of us may have in reaffirming the central holding of *Roe* are outweighed by the explication of individual liberty we have given combined with the force of *stare decisis.* We turn now to that doctrine.

III

A [W]hen this Court reexamines a prior holding, its judgment is customarily informed by a series of prudential and pragmatic considerations designed to test the consistency of overruling a prior decision with the ideal of the rule of law, and to gauge the respective costs of reaffirming and overruling a prior case. Thus, for example, we may ask whether the rule has proved to be intolerable simply in defying practical workability; whether the rule is subject to a kind of reliance that would lend a special hardship to the consequences of overruling and add inequity to the cost of repudiation; whether related principles of law have so far developed as to have left the old rule no more than remnant of abandoned doctrine; or whether facts have so changed or come to be seen so differently, as to have robbed the old rule of significant application or justification[.]

Although *Roe* has engendered opposition, it has in no sense proven "unworkable," representing as it does a simple limitation beyond which a state law is unenforceable[.]

We have seen how time has overtaken some of *Roe*'s factual assumptions: advances in maternal health care allow for abortions safe to the mother later in pregnancy than was true in 1973, and advances in neonatal care have advanced viability to a point somewhat earlier. But these facts go only to the scheme of time limits on the realization of competing interests, and the divergences from the factual premises of 1973 have no bearing on the validity of *Roe*'s central holding, that viability marks the earliest point at which the State's interest in fetal life is constitutionally adequate to justify a legislative ban on nontherapeutic abortions. The soundness or unsoundness of that constitutional judgment in no sense turns on whether viability occurs at approximately 28 weeks, as was usual at the time of *Roe,* at 23 to 24 weeks, as it sometimes does today, or at some moment even slightly earlier in pregnancy, as it may if fetal respiratory capacity can somehow be enhanced in the future. Whenever it may occur, the attainment of viability may continue to serve as the critical fact, just as it has done since *Roe* was decided; which is to say that no change in *Roe*'s factual underpinning has left its central holding obsolete, and none supports an argument for overruling it.

B In a less significant case, *stare decisis* analysis could, and would, stop at the point we have reached. But the sustained and widespread debate *Roe* has provoked calls for some comparison between that case and others of comparable dimension that have responded to national controversies and taken on the impress of the controversies addressed. . . .

[The Court reviewed two earlier lines of cases involving major reversals of doctrine, holding that there had been no similar changes in the factual assumptions underpinning the decision here.]

. . . In constitutional adjudication as elsewhere in life, changed circumstances may impose new obligations, and the thoughtful part of the Nation could accept each decision to overrule a prior case as a response to the Court's constitutional duty.

Because the case before us presents no such occasion it could be seen as no such response. Because neither the factual underpinnings of *Roe*'s central holding nor our understanding of it has changed (and because no other indication of weakened precedent has been shown) the Court could not pretend to be reexamining the prior law with any justification beyond a present doctrinal disposition to come out differently from the Court of 1973[.]

. . . In the present case, . . . as our analysis to this point makes clear, [a] terrible price would be paid for overruling. Our analysis would not be complete, however, without explaining why overruling *Roe*'s central holding would not only reach an unjustifiable result under principles of *stare decisis,* but would seriously weaken the Court's capacity to exercise the judicial power and to function as the Supreme Court of a Nation dedicated to the rule of law[.]

The underlying substance of [the Court's] legitimacy is . . . expressed in the Court's opinions, and our contemporary understanding is such that a decision without principled justification would be no judicial act at all. But even when justification is furnished by apposite legal principle, something more is required. Because not every conscientious claim of principled justification will be accepted as such, the justification claimed must be beyond dispute. The Court must take care to speak and act in ways that allow people to accept its decisions on the terms the Court claims for them, as grounded truly in principle, not as compromises with social and political pressures having, as such, no bearing on the principled choices that the Court is obliged to make. Thus, the Court's legitimacy depends on making legally principled decisions under circumstances in which their principled character is sufficiently plausible to be accepted by the Nation. . . .

The Court's duty in the present case is clear. In 1973, it confronted the already-divisive issue of governmental power to limit personal choice to undergo abortion, for which it provided a new resolution based on the due process guaranteed by the Fourteenth Amendment. Whether or not a new social consensus is developing on that issue, its divisiveness is no less today than in 1973, and pressure to overrule the decision, like pressure to retain it, has grown only more intense. A decision to overrule *Roe*'s essential holding under the existing circumstances would address error, if error there was, at the cost of both profound and unnecessary damage to the Court's legitimacy, and to the Nation's commitment to the rule of law. It is therefore imperative to adhere to the essence of *Roe*'s original decision, and we do so today.

IV

From what we have said so far it follows that it is a constitutional liberty of the woman to have some freedom to terminate her pregnancy. We conclude that the basic decision in *Roe* was based on a constitutional analysis which we cannot now repudiate. The woman's liberty is not so unlimited, however, that from the outset the State cannot show its concern for the life of the unborn, and at a later point in fetal development the State's interest in life has sufficient force so that the right of the woman to terminate the pregnancy can be restricted.

That brings us, of course, to the point where much criticism has been directed at *Roe,* a criticism that always inheres when the Court draws a specific rule from what in the Constitution is but a general standard. . . . And it falls to us to give some real substance to the woman's liberty to determine whether to carry her pregnancy to full term.

We conclude the line should be drawn at viability, so that before that time the woman has a right to choose to terminate her pregnancy. We adhere to this principle for two reasons. First, as we have said, is the doctrine of *stare decisis.* Any judicial act of line-drawing may seem somewhat arbitrary, but *Roe* was a reasoned statement, elaborated with great care. We have twice reaffirmed it in the face of great opposition. Although we must overrule those parts of *Thornburgh* and *Akron I* which, in our view, are inconsistent with *Roe*'s statement that the State has a legitimate interest in promoting the life or potential life of the unborn, the central premise of those cases represents an unbroken commitment by this Court to the essential holding of *Roe.* It is that premise which we reaffirm today.

The second reason is that the concept of viability, as we noted in *Roe,* is the time at which there is a realistic possibility of maintaining and nourishing a life outside the womb, so that the independent existence of the second life can in reason and all fairness be the object of state protection that now overrides the rights of the woman. Consistent with other constitutional norms, legislatures may draw lines which appear arbitrary without the necessity of offering a justification. But courts may not. We must justify the lines we draw. And there is no line other than viability which is more workable. . . .

The woman's right to terminate her pregnancy before viability is the most central principle of *Roe v. Wade.* It is a rule of law and a component of liberty we cannot renounce. . . .

Though the woman has a right to choose to terminate or continue her pregnancy before viability, it does not at all follow that the State is prohibited from taking steps to ensure that this choice is thoughtful and informed. Even in the earliest stages of pregnancy, the State may enact rules and regulations designed to encourage her to know that there are philosophic and social arguments of great weight that can be brought to bear in favor of continuing the pregnancy to full term and that there are procedures and institutions to allow adoption of unwanted children as well as a certain degree of state assistance if the mother chooses to raise the child herself. "The Constitution does not forbid a State or city, pursuant to democratic processes, from expressing a preference for normal childbirth." *Webster v. Reproductive Health Services* [(1989)]. It follows that States are free to enact laws to provide a reasonable framework for a woman to make a decision that has such profound and lasting meaning. This, too, we find consistent with *Roe*'s central premises, and indeed the inevitable consequence of our holding that the State has an interest in protecting the life of the unborn.

We reject the trimester framework, which we do not consider to be part of the essential holding of *Roe*. . . . The trimester framework suffers from these basic flaws: in its formulation it misconceives the nature of the pregnant woman's interest; and in practice it undervalues the State's interest in potential life, as recognized in *Roe*. . . .

Because we set forth a standard of general application to which we intend to adhere, it is important to clarify what is meant by an undue burden.

A finding of an undue burden is a shorthand for the conclusion that a state regulation has the purpose or effect of placing a substantial obstacle in the path of a woman seeking an abortion of a nonviable fetus. . . . [W]e answer the question, left open in previous opinions discussing the undue burden formulation, whether a law designed to further the State's interest in fetal life which imposes an undue burden on the woman's decision before fetal viability could be constitutional. The answer is no.

Some guiding principles should emerge. What is at stake is the woman's right to make the ultimate decision, not a right to be insulated from all others in doing so. Regulations which do no more than create a structural mechanism by which the State, or the parent or guardian of a minor, may express profound respect for the life of the unborn are permitted, if they are not a substantial obstacle to the woman's exercise of the right to choose. Unless it has that effect on her right of choice, a state measure designed to persuade her to choose childbirth over abortion will be upheld if reasonably related to that goal. Regulations designed to foster the health of a woman seeking an abortion are valid if they do not constitute an undue burden.

Even when jurists reason from shared premises, some disagreement is inevitable. . . . We do not expect it to be otherwise with respect to the undue burden standard. We give this summary:

(a) To protect the central right recognized by *Roe v. Wade* while at the same time accommodating the State's profound interest in potential life, we will employ the undue burden analysis as explained in this opinion. An undue burden exists, and therefore a provision of law is invalid, if its purpose or effect is to place a substantial obstacle in the path of a woman seeking an abortion before the fetus attains viability.

(b) We reject the rigid trimester framework of *Roe v. Wade*. To promote the State's profound interest in potential life, throughout pregnancy the State may take measures to ensure that the woman's choice is informed, and measures designed to advance this interest will not be invalidated as long as their purpose is to persuade the woman to choose childbirth over abortion. These measures must not be an undue burden on the right.

(c) As with any medical procedure, the State may enact regulations to further the health or safety of a woman seeking an abortion. Unnecessary health regulations that have the purpose or effect of presenting a substantial obstacle to a woman seeking an abortion impose an undue burden on the right.

(d) Our adoption of the undue burden analysis does not disturb the central holding of *Roe v. Wade,* and we reaffirm that holding. Regardless of whether exceptions are made for particular circumstances, a State may not prohibit any woman from making the ultimate decision to terminate her pregnancy before viability.

(e) We also reaffirm *Roe*'s holding that "subsequent to viability, the State in promoting its interest in the potentiality of human life may, if it chooses, regulate, and even proscribe, abortion except where it is necessary, in appropriate medical judgment, for the preservation of the life or health of the mother."

These principles control our assessment of the Pennsylvania statute, and we now turn to the issue of the validity of its challenged provisions.

[The Court upholds several provisions of the Pennsylvania law.]

JUSTICE BLACKMUN concurring in part, concurring in the judgment in part, and dissenting in part.

. . . I remain steadfast in my belief that the right to reproductive choice is entitled to the full protection afforded by this Court before *Webster.* And I fear for the darkness as four Justices anxiously await the single vote necessary to extinguish the light.

Make no mistake, the joint opinion of Justices O'Connor, Kennedy, and Souter is an act of personal courage and constitutional principle. In contrast to previous decisions in which Justices O'Connor and Kennedy postponed reconsideration of *Roe v. Wade,* the authors of the joint opinion today join Justice Stevens and me in concluding that "the essential holding of *Roe* should be retained and once again reaffirmed." In brief, five Members of this Court today recognize that "the Constitution protects a woman's right to terminate her pregnancy in its early stages." . . .

Today, no less than yesterday, the Constitution and decisions of this Court require that a State's abortion restrictions be subjected to the strictest of judicial scrutiny. Our precedents and the joint opinion's principles require us to subject all non-de minimis abortion regulations to strict scrutiny. Under this standard, the Pennsylvania statute's provisions requiring content-based counseling, a 24-hour delay, informed parental consent, and reporting of abortion-related information must be invalidated. . . .

If there is much reason to applaud the advances made by the joint opinion today, there is far more to fear from the Chief Justice's opinion.

The Chief Justice's criticism of *Roe* follows from his stunted conception of individual liberty. While recognizing that the Due Process Clause protects more than simple physical liberty, he then goes on to construe this Court's personal-liberty cases as establishing only a laundry list of particular rights, rather than a principled account of how these particular rights are grounded in a more general right of privacy. This constricted view is reinforced by the Chief Justice's exclusive reliance on tradition as a source of fundamental rights. He argues that the record in favor of a right to abortion is no stronger than the record in *Michael H. v. Gerald D.*, . . . where the plurality found no fundamental right to visitation privileges by an adulterous father, or in *Bowers v. Hardwick*, . . . where the Court found no fundamental right to engage in homosexual sodomy, or in a case involving the "firing of a gun . . . into another person's body." In the Chief Justice's world, a woman considering whether to terminate a pregnancy is entitled to no more protection than adulterers, murderers, and so-called "sexual deviates." Given the Chief Justice's exclusive reliance on tradition, people using contraceptives seem the next likely candidate for his list of outcasts. . . .

The Chief Justice's narrow conception of individual liberty and *stare decisis* leads him to propose the same standard of review proposed by the plurality in *Webster.* "States may regulate abortion procedures in ways rationally related to a legitimate state interest. *Williamson v. Lee Optical Co.*, . . . cf. *Stanley v. Illinois*" . . .

But, we are reassured, there is always the protection of the democratic process. While there is much to be praised about our democracy, our country since its founding has recognized that there are certain fundamental liberties that are not to be left to the whims of an election. A woman's right to reproductive choice is one of those fundamental liberties. Accordingly, that liberty need not seek refuge at the ballot box.

In one sense, the Court's approach is worlds apart from that of the Chief Justice and Justice Scalia. And yet, in another sense, the distance between the two approaches is short—the distance is but a single vote.

I am 83 years old. I cannot remain on this Court forever, and when I do step down, the confirmation process for my successor well may focus on the issue before us today. That, I regret, may be exactly where the choice between the two worlds will be made. . . .

CHIEF JUSTICE REHNQUIST, with whom JUSTICE WHITE, JUSTICE SCALIA, and JUSTICE THOMAS join, concurring in the judgment in part and dissenting in part.

The joint opinion, following its newly-minted variation on *stare decisis,* retains the outer shell of *Roe v. Wade*, . . . but beats a wholesale retreat from the substance of that case. We believe that *Roe* was wrongly decided, and that it can and should be overruled consistently with our traditional approach to *stare decisis* in constitutional cases. We would adopt the approach of the plurality in *Webster v. Reproductive Health Services*, . . . and uphold the challenged provisions of the Pennsylvania statute in their entirety. . . .

We think . . . that the Court was mistaken in *Roe* when it classified a woman's decision to terminate her pregnancy as a "fundamental right" that could be abridged only in a manner which withstood "strict scrutiny." . . . We believe that the sort of constitutionally imposed abortion code of the type illustrated by our decisions following *Roe* is inconsistent "with the notion of a Constitution cast in general terms, as ours is, and usually speaking in general principles, as ours does." *Webster v. Reproductive Health Services* . . . The Court in *Roe* reached too far when it analogized the right to abort a fetus to the rights involved in *Pierce* [*v. Society of Sisters*, . . .], *Meyer* [*v. Nebraska*, . . .], *Loving* [*v. Virginia*, . . .] and *Griswold* [*v. Connecticut*, . . .], and thereby deemed the right to abortion fundamental.

The joint opinion of Justices O'Connor, Kennedy, and Souter cannot bring itself to say that *Roe* was correct as an original matter, but the authors are of the view that "the immediate question is not the soundness of *Roe*'s resolution of the issue, but the precedential force that must be accorded to its holding." Instead of claiming that *Roe* was correct as a matter of original constitutional interpretation, the opinion therefore contains an elaborate discussion of *stare decisis*. This discussion of the principle of *stare decisis* appears to be almost entirely dicta, because the joint opinion does not apply that principle in dealing with *Roe*. *Roe* decided that a woman had a fundamental right to an abortion. The joint opinion rejects that view. *Roe* decided that abortion regulations were to be subjected to "strict scrutiny" and could be justified only in the light of "compelling state interests." The joint opinion rejects that view. *Roe* analyzed abortion regulation under a rigid trimester framework, a framework which has guided this Court's decision-making for 19 years. The joint opinion rejects that framework.

Stare decisis is defined in *Black's Law Dictionary* as meaning "to abide by, or adhere to, decided cases." Whatever the "central holding" of *Roe* that is left after the joint opinion finished dissection it is surely not the result of that principle. While purporting to adhere to precedent, the joint opinion instead revises it. *Roe* continues to exist, but only in the way a storefront on a western movie set exists: a mere facade to give the illusion of reality. Decisions following *Roe*, such as *Akron v. Akron Center for Reproductive Health, Inc.*, . . . and *Thornburgh v. American College of Obstetricians and Gynecologists*, . . . are frankly overruled in part under the "undue burden" standard expounded in the joint opinion.

In our view, authentic principles of *stare decisis* do not require that any portion of the reasoning in *Roe* be kept intact. . . .

The joint opinion discusses several *stare decisis* factors which, it asserts, point toward retaining a portion of *Roe*. Two of these factors are that the main "factual underpinning" of *Roe* has remained the same, and that its doctrinal foundation is no weaker now than it was in 1973. Of course, what might be called the basic facts which gave rise to *Roe* have remained the same women become pregnant, there is a point somewhere, depending on medical technology, where a fetus becomes viable, and women give birth to children. But this is only to say that the same facts which gave rise to *Roe* will continue to give rise to similar cases. It is not a reason, in and of itself, why those cases must be decided in the same incorrect manner as was the first case to deal with the question. And surely there is no requirement, in considering whether to depart from stare decisis in a constitutional case, that a decision be more wrong now than it was at the time it was rendered. If that were true, the most outlandish constitutional decision could survive forever, based simply on the fact that it was no more outlandish later than it was when originally rendered[.]

The joint opinion also points to the reliance interests involved in this context in its effort to explain why precedent must be followed for precedent's sake. . . . But, as the joint opinion apparently agrees, any traditional notion of reliance is not applicable here. The Court today cuts back on the protection afforded by *Roe,* and no one claims that this action defeats any reliance interest in the disavowed trimester framework. Similarly, reliance interests would not be diminished were the Court to go further and acknowledge the full error of *Roe,* as "reproductive planning could take virtually immediate account of" this action[.]

. . . [T]he joint opinion's argument is based solely on generalized assertions about the national psyche, on a belief that the people of this country have grown accustomed to the *Roe* decision over the last 19 years and have "ordered their thinking and living around" it. As an initial matter, one might inquire how the joint opinion can view the "central holding" of *Roe* as so deeply rooted in our constitutional culture, when it so casually uproots and disposes of that same decision's trimester framework. Furthermore, at various points in the past, the same could have been said about this Court's erroneous decisions that the Constitution allowed "separate but equal" treatment of minorities, or that "liberty" under the Due Process Clause protected "freedom of contract." The "separate but equal" doctrine lasted 58 years after *Plessy,* and *Lochner's* protection of contractual freedom lasted 32 years. However, the simple fact that a generation or more had grown used to these major decisions did not prevent the Court from correcting its errors in those cases, nor should it prevent us from correctly interpreting the Constitution here.

Apparently realizing that conventional *stare decisis* principles do not support its position, the joint opinion advances a belief that retaining a portion of *Roe* is necessary to protect the "legitimacy" of this Court.

. . . [T]he joint opinion goes on to state that when the Court "resolves the sort of intensely divisive controversy reflected in *Roe* and those rare, comparable cases," its decision is exempt from reconsideration under established principles of *stare decisis* in constitutional cases. This is so, the joint opinion contends, because in those "intensely divisive" cases the Court has "called the contending sides of a national controversy to end their national division by accepting a common mandate rooted in the Constitution," and must therefore take special care not to be perceived as "surrendering to political pressure" and continued opposition. This is a truly novel principle. . . . Under this principle, when the Court has ruled on a divisive issue, it is apparently prevented from overruling that decision for the sole reason that it was incorrect, unless opposition to the original decision has died away. . . .

Taking the joint opinion on its own terms, we doubt that its distinction between *Roe,* on the one hand, and *Plessy* and *Lochner,* on the other, withstands analysis. The joint opinion acknowledges that the Court improved its stature by overruling *Plessy* in *Brown* on a deeply divisive issue. And our decision in *West Coast Hotel,* which overruled *Adkins v. Children's Hospital* and *Lochner,* was rendered at a time when Congress was considering President Franklin Roosevelt's proposal to "reorganize" this Court and enable him to name six additional Justices in the event that any member of the Court over the age of 70 did not elect to retire. It is difficult to imagine a situation in which the Court would face more intense opposition to a prior ruling than it did at that time, and, under the general principle proclaimed in the joint opinion, the Court seemingly should have responded to this opposition by stubbornly refusing to reexamine the *Lochner* rationale, lest it lose legitimacy by appearing to "overrule under fire."

The joint opinion agrees that the Court's stature would have been seriously damaged if in *Brown* and *West Coast Hotel* it had dug in its heels and refused to apply normal principles of *stare decisis* to the earlier decisions. But the opinion contends that the Court was entitled to overrule *Plessy* and *Lochner* in those cases, despite the existence of opposition to the original decisions, only because both the Nation and the Court had learned new lessons in the interim. This is at best a feebly supported, post hoc rationalization for those decisions[.]

There are other reasons why the joint opinion's discussion of legitimacy is unconvincing as well. In assuming that the Court is perceived as "surrendering to political pressure" when it overrules a controversial decision, the joint opinion forgets that there are two sides to any controversy[.] But a decision to adhere to prior precedent is subject to the same criticism, for in such a case one can easily argue that the Court is responding to those who have demonstrated in favor of the original decision. The decision in *Roe* has engendered large demonstrations, including repeated marches on this Court and on Congress, both in opposition to and in support of that opinion. A decision either way on *Roe* can therefore be perceived as favoring one group or the other. But this perceived dilemma arises only if one assumes, as the joint opinion does, that the Court should make its decisions with a view toward speculative public perceptions. If one assumes instead, as the Court surely did in both *Brown* and *West Coast Hotel,* that the Court's legitimacy is enhanced by faithful interpretation of the Constitution irrespective of public opposition, such self-engendered difficulties may be put to one side. . . .

The sum of the joint opinion's labors in the name of *stare decisis* and "legitimacy" is this: *Roe v. Wade* stands as a sort of judicial Potemkin Village, which may be pointed out to passers by as a monument to the importance of adhering to precedent. But behind the facade, an entirely new method of analysis, without any roots in constitutional law, is imported to decide the constitutionality of state laws regulating abortion. Neither *stare decisis* nor "legitimacy" are truly served by such an effort.

For the reasons stated, we therefore would hold that each of the challenged provisions of the Pennsylvania statute is consistent with the Constitution.

JUSTICE SCALIA, concurring in the judgment in part and dissenting in part.

My views on this matter are unchanged from those I set forth in my separate opinions in *Webster v. Reproductive Health Services,* . . . and *Ohio v. Akron Center for Reproductive Health,* . . . The States may, if they wish, permit abortion-on-demand, but the Constitution does not require them to do so. The permissibility of abortion, and the limitations upon it, are to be resolved like most important questions in our democracy: by citizens trying to persuade one another and then voting. . . . A State's choice between two positions on which reasonable people can disagree is constitutional even when (as is often the case) it intrudes upon a "liberty" in the absolute sense. Laws against bigamy, for example—which entire societies of reasonable people disagree with—intrude upon men and women's liberty to marry and live with one another. But bigamy happens not to be a liberty specially "protected" by the Constitution.

That is, quite simply, the issue in this case. . . . The issue is whether [a woman's claim to a constitutional right to have an abortion] is liberty protected by the Constitution of the United States. I am sure it is not. I reach that conclusion not because of anything so exalted as my views concerning the "concept of existence, of meaning, of the universe, and of the mystery of human life." Rather, I reach it for the same reason I reach the conclusion that bigamy is not constitutionally protected—because of two simple facts: (1) the Constitution says absolutely nothing about it, and (2) the longstanding traditions of American society have permitted it to be legally proscribed. . . .

The Court's reliance upon *stare decisis* can best be described as contrived. It insists upon the necessity of adhering not to all of *Roe,* but only to what it calls the "central holding." It seems to me that *stare decisis* ought to be applied even to the doctrine of *stare decisis,* and I confess never to have heard of this new, keep-what-you-want-and-throw-away-the-rest version. . . .

I am certainly not in a good position to dispute that the Court has saved the "central holding" of *Roe,* since to do that effectively I would have to know what the Court has saved, which in turn would require me to understand (as I do not) what the "undue burden" test means. I must confess, however, that I have always thought, and I think a lot of other people have always thought, that the arbitrary trimester framework, which the Court today discards, was quite as central to *Roe* as the arbitrary viability test, which the Court today retains. It seems particularly ungrateful to carve the trimester framework out of the core of *Roe,* since its very rigidity (in sharp contrast to the utter indeterminability of the "undue burden" test) is probably the only reason the Court is able to say, in urging *stare decisis,* that *Roe* "has in no sense proven unworkable. "I suppose the Court is entitled to call a "central holding" whatever it wants to call a "central holding"—which is, come to think of it, perhaps one of the difficulties with this modified version of *stare decisis*. . . .

. . . *Roe* fanned into life an issue that has inflamed our national politics in general, and has obscured with its smoke the selection of Justices to this Court in particular, ever since. And by keeping us in the abortion-umpiring business, it is the perpetuation of that disruption, rather than of any pax Roeana, that the Court's new majority decrees.

JUDICIAL REVIEW

See text p. 324

The power of judicial review—the authority of the federal courts to determine the constitutionality of state and federal legislative acts—was established early in the nation's history in the case of Marbury v. Madison *(1803). While the doctrine of judicial review is now firmly entrenched in the American judicial process, the outcome of* Marbury *was by no means a sure thing. The doctrine had been outlined in* The Federalist No. 78, *and had been relied upon implicitly in earlier, lower federal court cases, but there were certainly sentiments among some of the Founders to suggest that only Congress ought to be able to judge the constitutionality of its acts.*

Marbury v. *Madison* (1803)*

[The facts leading up to the decision in Marbury v. Madison *tell an intensely political story. Efforts to reform the federal judiciary had been ongoing with the Federalist administration of President Adams. Following the defeat of the Federalist party in 1800, and the election of Thomas Jefferson as president, the Federalist Congress passed an act reforming the judiciary. The act gave outgoing President Adams authority to appoint several Federalist justices of the peace* before *Jefferson's term as president began. This would have enabled the Federalist party to retain a large measure of power.*

Marbury was appointed to be a justice of the peace by President Adams, but his commission, signed by the president and sealed by the secretary of state, without which he could not assume office, was not delivered to him before President Jefferson took office March 4, 1803. Jefferson refused to order James Madison, his secretary of state, to deliver the commission. Marbury, in turn, filed an action in the U.S. Supreme Court seeking an order—called a writ of mandamus—directing the secretary of state to compel the delivery of the commission.

The Constitution grants the Supreme Court original jurisdiction in only a limited number of cases—those involving ambassadors, public ministers, and those in which a state is a party; in the remaining cases, the Court has authority only as

*Marbury v. Madison, 5 U.S. 137, 1803.

an appellate court. When it acts according to its original jurisdiction, the Court exercises initial authority over a controversy, just like a trial court, as distinguished from the more limited authority it exercises when a case is presented as an appeal from a lower court's decision.

In 1789, Congress passed legislation setting up the federal courts, called the Judiciary Act of 1789. That legislation gave the Supreme Court the original authority to "issue writs of mandamus in cases warranted by the principles and usage of law. . . ." Thus, the ultimate question in Marbury *v.* Madison *was whether Congress could, by statute, enlarge the original jurisdiction of the Court.*

The Court first considered whether Marbury's appointment was complete—and therefore irrevocable—before Jefferson took office. Under the law, the appointment was deemed complete when the president signed the commission and the secretary of state sealed it; the appointment was a completed fact at that time, and was not dependent upon delivery. Therefore, the Court found that Marbury was entitled to his commission. The Court then decided that by withholding the commission, Secretary of State Madison was violating Marbury's legal rights. The remaining question was whether the Supreme Court could issue an order compelling the delivery of the commission.]

CHIEF JUSTICE MARSHALL DELIVERED THE OPINION OF THE COURT.

. . . It is, then, the opinion of the Court,

1st. That by signing the commission of Mr. Marbury, the President of the United States appointed him a justice of peace for the county of Washington, in the District of Columbia; and that the seal of the United States, affixed thereto by the Secretary of State, is conclusive testimony of the verity of the signature, and of the completion of the appointment, and that the appointment conferred on him a legal right to the office for the space of five years.

2d. That, having this legal title to the office, he has a consequent right to the commission; a refusal to deliver which is a plain violation of that right, for which the laws of his country afford him a remedy.

It remains to be inquired whether,

3d. He is entitled to the remedy for which he applies. This depends on,

1st. The nature of the writ applied for; and,

2d. The power of this court. . . .

This . . . is a plain case for a mandamus, either to deliver the commission, or a copy of it from the record; and it only remains to be inquired,

Whether it can issue from this court.

The act to establish the judicial courts of the United States authorizes the Supreme Court "to issue writs of mandamus in cases warranted by the principles and usages of law, to any courts appointed, or persons holding office, under the authority of the United States."

The Secretary of State, being a person holding an office under the authority of the United States, is precisely within the letter of the description, and if this court is not authorized to issue a writ of mandamus to such an officer, it must be because the law is unconstitutional, and therefore absolutely incapable of conferring the authority, and assigning the duties which its words purport to confer and assign.

The constitution vests the whole judicial power of the United States in one Supreme Court, and such inferior courts as congress shall, from time to time, ordain and establish. This power is expressly extended to all cases arising under the laws of the United States; and, consequently, in some form, may be exercised over the present case; because the right claimed is given by a law of the United States.

In the distribution of this power it is declared that "the Supreme Court shall have original jurisdiction in all cases affecting ambassadors, other public ministers and consuls, and those in which a state shall be a party. In all other cases, the Supreme Court shall have appellate jurisdiction." . . .

To enable this court, then, to issue a mandamus, it must be shown to be an exercise of appellate jurisdiction, or to be necessary to enable them to exercise appellate jurisdiction. . . .

It is the essential criterion of appellate jurisdiction, that it revises and corrects the proceedings in a cause already instituted, and does not create that cause. . . . [Y]et to issue such a writ to an officer for the delivery of a paper, is in effect the same as to sustain an original action for that paper, and, therefore, seems not to belong to appellate, but to original jurisdiction.

The authority, therefore, given to the Supreme Court, by the act establishing the judicial courts of the United States, to issue writs of mandamus to public officers, appears not to be warranted by the constitution; and it becomes necessary to inquire whether a jurisdiction so conferred can be exercised.

The question, whether an act, repugnant to the constitution, can become the law of the land, is a question deeply interesting to the United States; but, happily, not of an intricacy proportioned to its interest. It seems only necessary to recognize certain principles, supposed to have been long and well established, to decide it.

That the people have an original right to establish, for their future government, such principles, as, in their opinion, shall most conduce to their own happiness is the basis on which the whole American fabric has been erected. The exercise of this original right is a very great exertion; nor can it, nor ought it, to be frequently repeated. The principles, therefore, so established, are deemed fundamental. And as the authority from which they proceed is supreme, and can seldom act, they are designed to be permanent.

This original and supreme will organizes the government, and assigns to different departments their respective powers. It may either stop here, or establish certain limits not to be transcended by those departments.

The government of the United States is of the latter description. The powers of the legislature are defined and limited; and that those limits may not be mistaken, or forgotten, the constitution is written. To what purpose are powers limited, and to what purpose is that limitation committed to writing, if these limits may, at any time, be passed by those intended to be restrained? The distinction between a government with limited and unlimited powers is abolished, if those limits do not confine the persons on whom they are imposed, and if acts prohibited and acts allowed, are of equal obligation. It is a proposition too plain to be contested, that the constitution controls any legislative act repugnant to it; or, that the legislature may alter the constitution by an ordinary act.

Between these alternatives there is no middle ground. The constitution is either a superior paramount law, unchangeable by ordinary means, or it is on a level with ordinary legislative acts, and, like other acts, is alterable when the legislature shall please to alter it.

If the former part of the alternative be true, then a legislative act contrary to the constitution is not law: if the latter part be true, then written constitutions are absurd attempts, on the part of the people, to limit a power in its own nature illimitable.

Certainly all those who have framed written constitutions contemplate them as forming the fundamental and paramount law of the nation, and, consequently, the theory of every such government must be, that an act of the legislature, repugnant to the constitution, is void.

This theory is essentially attached to a written constitution, and, is consequently, to be considered, by this court, as one of the fundamental principles of our society. It is not therefore to be lost sight of in the further consideration of this subject.

If an act of the legislature, repugnant to the constitution, is void, does it, notwithstanding its invalidity, bind the courts, and oblige them to give it effect? Or, in other words, though it be not law, does it constitute a rule as operative as if it was a law? This would be to overthrow in fact what was established in theory; and would seem, at first view, an absurdity too gross to be insisted on. . . .

It is emphatically the province and duty of the judicial department to say what the law is. Those who apply the rule to particular cases, must of necessity expound and interpret that rule. If two laws conflict with each other, the courts must decide on the operation of each.

So if a law be in opposition to the constitution; if both the law and the constitution apply to a particular case, so that the court must either decide that case conformably to the law, disregarding the constitution; or conformably to the constitution, disregarding the law; the court must determine which of these conflicting rules governs the case. This is of the very essence of judicial duty.

If, then, the courts are to regard the constitution, and the constitution is superior to any ordinary act of the legislature, the constitution, and not such ordinary act, must govern the case to which they both apply.

Those, then, who controvert the principle that the constitution is to be considered, in court, as a paramount law, are reduced to the necessity of maintaining that courts must close their eyes on the constitution, and see only the law.

This doctrine would subvert the very foundation of all written constitutions. It would declare that an act which, according to the principles and theory of our government, is entirely void, is yet, in practice, completely obligatory. It would declare that if the legislature shall do what is expressly forbidden, such act, notwithstanding the express prohibition, is in reality effectual. It would be given to the legislature a practical and real omnipotence, with the same breath which professes to restrict their powers within narrow limits. It is prescribing limits, and declaring that those limits may be passed at pleasure.

That it thus reduces to nothing what we have deemed the greatest improvement on political institutions, a written constitution, would of itself be sufficient, in America, where written constitutions have been viewed with so much reverence, for rejecting the construction. But the peculiar expressions of the constitution of the United States furnish additional arguments in favour of its rejection.

The judicial power of the United States is extended to all cases arising under the constitution.

Could it be the intention of those who gave this power, to say that in using it the constitution should not be looked into? That a case arising under the constitution should be decided without examining the instrument under which it arises?

This is too extravagant to be maintained.

In some cases, then, the constitution must be looked into by the judges.

. . . [I]t is apparent, that the framers of the constitution contemplated that instrument as a rule for the government of courts, as well as of the legislature.

Why otherwise does it direct the judges to take an oath to support it? This oath certainly applies in an especial manner, to their conduct in their official character. How immoral to impose it on them, if they were to be used as the instruments, and the knowing instruments, for violating what they swear to support!

The oath of office, too, imposed by the legislature, is completely demonstrative of the legislative opinion on this subject. . . .

Why does a judge swear to discharge his duties agreeably to the constitution of the United States, if that constitution forms no rule for his government? If it is closed upon him, and cannot be inspected by him?

If such be the real state of things, this is worse than solemn mockery. To prescribe, or to take this oath, becomes equally a crime.

It is also not entirely unworthy of observation, that in declaring what shall be the supreme law of the land, the constitution itself is first mentioned; and not the laws of the United States generally, but those only which shall be made in pursuance of the constitution, have that rank.

Thus, the particular phraseology of the constitution of the United States confirms and strengthens the principle, supposed to be essential to all written constitutions, that a law repugnant to the constitution is void; and that courts, as well as other departments, are bound by that instrument.

Debating the Issues: Opposing Views

INTERPRETING THE CONSTITUTION AND ORIGINAL INTENT

See text pp. 354–55

As the text points out, the ways in which Supreme Court Justices interpret the Constitution are influenced in large measure by a particular Justice's own jurisprudential theory. The Warren Court was dominated by a number of justices who adhered to what has become known as an activist model, as discussed in the text. Proponents of that model argued that constitutional principles must evolve with changes in values over time; the document, according to these justices, is a "living organism." The first piece that follows is a profile of Justice William Brennan, who retired from the Court in 1990. As the article points out, Justice Brennan articulated a set of principles that attempted to draw upon underlying moral precepts; he based his interpretive approach upon a set of moral principles that he believed provided the bedrock upon which the Constitution was built. In short, that approach to interpretation holds that there are certain principles of human dignity built into the Constitution, and that those principles may not only change over time, but may be above ordinary political discourse. That philosophy led the Court, when it was headed by Chief Justice Warren, into expansive readings of the guarantees of individual rights and liberties across a broad spectrum of cases, from criminal defendant's rights to rights of privacy for women.

The profile of Chief Justice Rehnquist illustrates the opposite judicial philosophy, one that is far more deferential to purely democratic principles. As the article notes, Justice Rehnquist adheres to a position that major questions of rights and liberties should be decided in representative forums, Congress, and state legislatures. The Court should not, according to Rehnquist and those who agree with his outlook, appropriate to itself the role of setting the nation's fundamental values by reading them into the Constitution. The Constitution provides a blueprint for the structure of government, according to this view, and as long as the process of formulating laws complies with the Constitution, the substantive result arrived at by legislative bodies should be accepted. If the people feel that those laws are unfair, the remedy lies in the legislative sphere through the election of new representatives.

Fred Barbash
"With Brennan, The Old Order's Power Endured"*

This one is not just another Supreme Court retirement.

It is not just another new vote, not just another chance to tip the court's balance this way or that on one issue or another.

Justice William J. Brennan Jr., who announced his retirement Friday,

*Fred Barbash, "With Brennan, The Old Order's Power Endured," *Washington Post* (July 22, 1990). Copyright 1990 by The Washington Post. Reprinted with permission.

July 20, 1990, was the chief living practitioner of a style, an approach, a method of judging that reached out to right perceived wrongs, wore its values on its sleeve and changed the course of American history.

Call it "humanist." Call it "activist." Call it the "Warren Court" approach.

Love it or hate it, Brennan perfected it, and helped it endure two decades beyond the retirement of Chief Justice Earl Warren. From it flowed the principle of "one man, one vote," constitutional protection for women; a ban on public aid to religious schools; the legalization of abortion; protections for welfare recipients and prison inmates, and for purveyors of rudeness, lewdness and nudity; for killers, flag-burners, whistle-blowers and fire-breathers of every imaginable stripe. It opened doors in the federal judiciary for arguments and issues once flatly barred from entry.

Brennan's retirement signals the ascension of a very different approach. "Reaching out," to its adherents, is the business of legislatures, not judges. They believe values should be expressed through the ballot box, not at the bench, and they confront cases asking fundamentally different questions leading to fundamentally different conclusions. The conflict between the two schools is as old as the judiciary, ebbing and flowing with the times and presidential appointments.

The current transition, now well underway, may never be complete. The approach cultivated by the Warren Court has penetrated too deeply into case law and the skulls of generations of law students, lawyers, judges and politicians.

Brennan, even to those who disagree with the Warren approach, has had a profound impact on more than just American jurisprudence. "Brennan is in a different league than other judges," said Charles J. Cooper, assistant attorney general in the Reagan administration and an architect of much conservative Reagan legal policy. "In the time frame of this half century, he towers above every other individual who has been in public life. There's no president who has had the influence on public policy" that Brennan has had.

"I can think of no one on the court who had more influence in shaping the modern Supreme Court than Bill Brennan," said A.E. Dick Howard, University of Virginia law professor.

The genius of Brennan—the skill that made him more equal than his equals on the court—was that as he crafted his opinions he worried about the analysis, knowing that it would endure longer than the result, and would be applied over and over again at all levels of the judiciary.

His battle to give constitutional protection to women is illustrative. Until Brennan's rulings in the 1970s, states could, and did, treat women differently than men in a variety of ways, imposing varying requirements for everything from beer drinking to alimony.

Though nothing in the Constitution explicitly prevented this, Brennan held that distinctions based on gender could survive only if "substantially related to the achievement of an important governmental objective." This subjected gender distinctions to a higher level of court scrutiny.

Brennan's theory, fumed Justice William H. Rehnquist, "apparently comes out of thin air. . . . I would have thought that if this court were to leave anything to decision by the popularly elected branches of the government, it would be this."

Although the court did not go as far as Brennan would have liked, the theory became the law, and discriminatory statutes were overturned across the nation—without ratification of any Equal rights Amendment.

It is "an approach to judging that will be losing its most important practitioner," said Cooper, a former Rehnquist clerk. "It is understandable why liberals are rending their garments and conservatives are respectfully applauding."

Even when Brennan lost, he often won something. He waged war against the death penalty throughout his 34 years on the court, but was never able to get a court majority to agree with him that capital punishment is unconstitutional. Still, he and his allies slowed the process to a relative crawl by erecting so many procedural hurdles for states that even today less than 5 percent of the thousands of people sentenced to death in the past two decades have been executed.

Brennan's approach to capital punishment illustrates the difference between his approach to judging and that now in ascendance. He never argued that any specific language in the Constitution even hinted that capital punishment should be banned. Rather, the Eighth Amendment's ban on cruel and unusual punishment, he wrote, "embodies in unique degree moral principles restraining the punishments that our civilized society may impose on those persons who transgress its laws." The court "inescapably has the duty" to bring "moral concepts" to bear on the issue, he wrote.

To judicial conservatives, the "inescapable" duty of the court, when it lacks explicit guidance from the Constitution, is to defer to the elected branches of government rather than to "moral concepts." To do otherwise, they say, is the very essence of activism.

Even judicial moderates, like Howard, raise their eyebrows at some of Brennan's views. "I've had hours and hours of interviews with him for a public television series, Howard said. "I thought it [his death penalty stand] was his longest stretch. These cases came nearest to reflecting an a priori judgment on Brennan's part . . . asserting a value and saying this is what the Constitution means."

No one is pure in this long-running struggle over judicial philosophy, and activists abound on all sides. But the gap in outlook between the liberal and conservative approaches is nonetheless vast and of enormous consequence for litigants and for the nation. Warren-era judges, like Brennan, ask whether anything in the Bill of Rights explicitly prevents them from offering its protection to the individual. The burden is on the government to show that someone said "no."

Judges who take pride in "judicial restraint" ask whether anything in the Constitution or in the precedents explicitly permits them to extend protection. The burden is on the individual to show that someone said "yes."

When it comes to government power, on the other hand, the liberal activist judges reverse the coin. They tend to ask, when state power is challenged, whether such power draws its authority from any explicit constitutional or statutory declaration. If not, they look askance. The conservative judges ask whether anything in the law prevents government from bringing its power to bear. If not, it is permissible.

Brennan and the other Warren-era judges were not afraid to cross boundaries into areas previously considered off-limits for the federal courts. Before 1962, for example, the fairness of legislative apportionment in the states was considered a "political question"—the business of elected leaders, not judges. In *Baker v. Carr,* an opinion that may be Brennan's most important, the court stepped across that line.

Nothing, Brennan concluded for the majority, prevents us from doing so.

The pure "strict constructionists" wade through the Constitution, along with the laws, the debates of the nation's founders and the precedents, to find guidance. They say they go by the book, and if it's not there, they rule accordingly.

But Brennan, especially in his writings and speeches, confesses unabashedly to a humanist approach. The Bill of Rights, he said in a 1966 speech, is not just words. It's "an arsenal for achieving human brotherhood."

"Our task," Brennan said in an interview long ago, "is to interpret and apply the Constitution faithfully to the wisdom and understanding of the Founding Fathers. But often it is impossible to make a constitutional decision without basing certain findings on data drawn from the social sciences, from history, geography, economics and the like."

Brennan had brains, skill, single-mindedness of purpose and powerful ideas. There is no debate about that. But virtually all who knew him or worked with him attribute his singular role on the court to something more visceral as well, something they say cannot be understated and is not mere tribute.

"I don't think you can account for Justice Brennan's influence without saying this," Howard said. "He was a warm, charming, gregarious, universally loved member of the court. I've known a lot of justices," said Howard, who clerked at the court for two terms, "and I can think of no justice who has enjoyed more respect and affection. Coupled with his tactical skill, his uncanny mechanical skills and his political instincts, one gets a most effective justice."

"He is a lovable man," said Cooper, an ideological archenemy of Brennan. "You cannot dislike this man on a personal level, no matter how destructive he's been to the values you hold dear.

"He was grasping my arm tight against his chest as we walked to lunch one day when I was a law clerk." It is pure charm, said Cooper, and "one of the reasons he's been so awesomely successful at influencing others."

David G. Savage
"The Rehnquist Court"*

On Friday morning, Nov. 2, 1990, the buzzer sounded at 9:25 on the second floor of the Supreme Court, signaling that the weekly conference of the nine justices would start in five minutes. It was a summons to the most important deliberation of the term. The case of Dr. Irving Rust, the director of a family-planning clinic in New York City, versus Dr. Louis W. Sullivan, the secretary of Health and Human Services, was not only a key abortion dispute but also an important test of the First Amendment. The question before the court was this: Can the government prohibit doctors from telling their pregnant patients about abortion as a medical option?

Yes, the Bush Administration had said. In 1988, during his last year in office, Ronald Reagan had ordered an abrupt change in the regulations governing an 18-year-old federal-subsidy program for family-planning clinics. In setting up the program, Congress had said these clincs should provide contraceptives, pregnancy tests and medical advice to poor women and teen-agers but should not use abortion "as a method of family planning." Between 1970 and 1988, several administrations, Republican and Democratic, interpreted that to mean that, while clinic doctors and nurses could not "encourage or promote" abortion, they could refer pregnant patients to doctors who perform abortions. Why use federal funds to send "unborn children" to their deaths? asked Reagan. His aides issued new regulations that said clinic doctors could not even mention the word *abortion.* They were required to refer *all* pregnant patients for prenatal care to "promote the welfare of . . . the unborn child." Clinic directors, women's-rights advocates and many members of Congress labeled the directive a "gag rule" and vowed to fight it. In February, 1988, a lawsuit was filed on behalf of Rust and his patients. His lawyers argued that the new regulations violated the intent of the law, stifled the free-speech rights of doctors and infringed on the abortion rights of women. Upon taking office, George Bush and his Justice Department took up the defense of the regulations.

Now, behind the closed doors of their conference room, the nine justices would decide whether Reagan's regulations would stand. The Administration's case rested in reliable hands. At the head of the long, rectangular table sat the chief justice of the United States, 66-year-old William H. Rehnquist. No other member of the court in recent decades had been as faithful in backing the government. No other justice so regularly turned thumbs down when individuals contended their constitutional rights had been violated. During a legal career spanning nearly 40 years, Rehnquist had made his mark as a steadfast conservative. He supported official prayers in schools and opposed school desegregation. He opposed the Equal Rights Amendment for women, saying it would "turn holy wedlock into holy dead-

*David G. Savage, "The Rehnquist Court," *Los Angeles Times* (September 29, 1991). Reprinted with permission.

lock" and "hasten the dissolution of the family." He contended that the Constitution's guarantee of the "equal protection of the laws" did not forbid sex discrimination because the 14th Amendment was designed to protect blacks, not females. And he dissented, along with Justice Byron R. White, when the court in 1973 ruled, in Roe vs. Wade, that women had a constitutional right to abortion. No wonder the Bush Administration attorneys were confident. Although he controlled only one vote—his own—the chief justice could use his powers of persuasion to sway the outcome. As is customary, Rehnquist led off the discussion by summarizing the background of the abortion-clinic dispute and the legal issues involved. He then announced he would vote to uphold the government. But "the chief," as he is known around the court, knew he had a problem. He needed four votes besides his own if his opinion was to prevail, and, as the meeting opened, he seemed certain of only three.

Now-retired Justice William J. Brennan Jr. used to call "the rule of five" the most important principle of American law. His new law clerks were usually stumped when he asked them about it; no one had ever taught them about the rule of five in law school. Brennan would then hold up his hand, palm open and fingers outstretched, and say, "You can do anything you want at the Supreme Court with five votes." The corollary was just as true. With only *four* votes, you did nothing but write dissents. During his more than three decades on the court, Brennan had been the master of the rule of five. Somehow, year after year, despite a procession of new Republican appointees, Brennan managed to piece together five-vote majorities to rule in favor of civil rights and civil liberties.

But by October, 1990, Brennan was gone, having retired at age 84 after suffering a stroke. Rehnquist now expected that his job of "counting to five" would be easier. But on this case, the numbers weren't adding up. Though Rehnquist's fellow conservatives—White, Antonin Scalia and Anthony M. Kennedy—voted with him to uphold the new regulations, the court's only woman justice, Sandra Day O'Connor, balked.

She had done the same in 1989 in Webster vs. Reproductive Health Services, the much publicized Missouri abortion case that attempted to overturn Roe vs. Wade. There, Rehnquist had tried to sway her with an opinion that quoted from her earlier writings. With her vote, Rehnquist could have cleared the way for broad state regulation of abortion—although the basic right to choose abortion would have survived.

But, to his surprise, O'Connor refused to sign his opinion in the Missouri case. Instead, she wrote a separate, narrow opinion that permitted Missouri to halt abortions in its public hospitals—but no more. She refused to tamper with the *Roe* decision at all. Rehnquist had a majority to rule for Missouri but no majority to cut back on Roe vs. Wade. The case set off a loud political reverberation, but it had little legal significance.

Once again, in Rust vs. Sullivan, O'Connor refused to go along with Rehnquist, who had been her friend and classmate at Stanford Law School. Instead, she cast her vote with the liberals—Thurgood Marshall, Harry A. Blackmun and John Paul Stevens—to strike down the gag rule.

So Rehnquist turned his attention on David H. Souter. Souter had replaced Brennan just three weeks earlier, and he was still unsure of himself. Because he had spent most of his career as a state attorney and state judge in New Hampshire, he did not have a thorough grounding in the intricacies of federal law. Suddenly he was faced each month with deciding the 24 most divisive cases before the federal judiciary. In addition, 100 new appeals arrived at the court each week. He said he felt as if he had been hit "by a tidal wave."

With O'Connor's vote, the score was 4 to 4. The new justice was on the spot. And Rehnquist was prepared to help him out.

Souter was a conservative picked for the court because the Bush Administration believed he could be trusted to uphold the government most of the time. But he seemed to be troubled by one point in this case. His concern had surfaced three days earlier when John Paul Stevens, from the bench, challenged the Bush Administration's top courtroom attorney, Solicitor General Kenneth W. Starr, during oral arguments. What if a doctor concludes "from a purely medical point of view" that an abortion would be advisable? Stevens wanted to know. Can the doctor recommend an abortion to his patient?

No, Starr said. Abortion is outside "the scope" of the family-planning clinics. The woman must go elsewhere for advice and assistance.

Souter, at the far end of the bench, had leaned toward his microphone. He spoke deliberately, with a distinctive New England accent. But what if the pregnant woman "is in some imminent danger to her health," perhaps because of heart trouble or high blood pressure? Can the doctor then refer her to a hospital for an abortion?

Yes and no, Starr said. He can refer her to a hospital for emergency care, but not for an abortion. That is outside the scope of the program, he reiterated, at least as determined by the Reagan and Bush administrations.

Souter sounded unswayed. "In those circumstances, the physician cannot perform a normal professional responsibility," he said. "I think you are telling us that in that circumstance, [the government] may in effect preclude professional speech."

That was exactly the argument put forth by those challenging the rules. The government need not pay for abortion, Harvard Law School Professor Laurence H. Tribe conceded in his oral argument, and the clinics may be prevented from "promoting or encouraging" abortion. But the government cannot stop doctors from telling their patients "the whole truth," Tribe had argued on behalf of Dr. Rust.

Later, at their conference, Souter seemed torn. But Rehnquist had come into this meeting with a solution that would not only help his new colleague make a decision but also ensure that the chief got his five votes. Rehnquist could, he told Souter, draft an opinion simply making clear that a clinic doctor who faces a medical emergency can do what he thinks best, including recommending abortion. Rehnquist would just ignore the contrary view voiced by the Administration's attorney.

Souter decided to go along with the chief.

On May 23, 1991, Rehnquist announced from the bench to a full courtroom that he would deliver the opinion of the court in Rust vs. Sullivan. His five-vote majority had not faltered. He upheld the government on all points.

Tucked into Rehnquist's 27-page opinion was his concession to Souter: one pragmatic paragraph on doctors and medical emergencies. The lawyers challenging the regulations "rely heavily on the claim that the regulations would not, in the circumstance of a medical emergency, permit a [clinic] to refer a woman whose emergency places her life in imminent peril to a provider of abortions or abortion-related services," he wrote. "On their face, we do not read the regulations to bar abortion referral or counseling in such circumstances. Abortion counseling as a 'method of family planning' is prohibited, and it does not seem that a medically necessitated abortion in such circumstances would be the equivalent of its use as a 'method of family planning.'

"The government has no affirmative duty to commit any resources to facilitating abortions," the chief justice said. If a poor woman or a pregnant teen-ager cannot find an affordable abortion, that is "the product not of government restrictions on abortion but rather of her indigency."

The opinion, like the bulk of the decisions the court is likely to issue in the years to come, was vintage Rehnquist. He upheld the powers of the government and dismissed any claims that it has special responsibilities toward the poor.

Under Rehnquist, the Supreme Court no longer sees itself as the defender of civil rights and civil liberties, the champion of the individual. Gone is the court majority that breathed new life into the Bill of Rights, dismantled Southern segregation, disciplined police who violated the rights of citizens, removed religion from the public schools, pushed a President into resignation and swept aside the laws forbidding women to end their pregnancies. Instead, the court shaped by Ronald Reagan and George Bush has become an institution that sees its duty as upholding the will of the majority. Whether the issue is local rent control, prayer in the public schools, drug testing of public employees or the death penalty for mentally retarded murderers, Rehnquist takes the same view: Government officials exercise the will of the citizens who elected them; they may do as they choose and should be shown deference by the courts.

And, more and more, the Supreme Court's prevailing philosophy mirrors that of the affable but solidly conservative man who presides as its head. The Supreme Court has become the Rehnquist court, just as the court of the 1950s and 1960s was widely known as the Warren court, after the influential chief justice of that era, Earl Warren. And Rehnquist, the dominant figure in American law, is clearly the most powerful member of the Supreme Court since Warren retired in 1969. Unlike anyone since Warren, Rehnquist has firm control of the court majority and a commitment to rewriting constitutional law.

[Biographical details of Justice Rehnquist's life are omitted here.]

Lawyers of the post-World War II Generation were shaped by their perception of the 1930s Supreme Court. By a slim majority, the "nine old men" of the court blocked a number of Roosevelt's New Deal programs, rejecting laws such as those setting a minimum wage and maximum hours on the grounds that these measures violated an individual's supposed "right to contract." The minimum wage, they said, takes away one's right to work for *less* than the minimum wage.

For liberals such as Brennan and the late William O. Douglas, the lesson to be drawn from the era of the discredited nine old men was that the court must protect civil rights and individual liberties, not economic and property rights. Nothing in the Constitution or its history necessarily endorses such a distinction, but that has been the prevailing consensus since the 1940s.

But conservatives drew a quite different lesson from the decisions of the nine old men: The court should not become involved in economic matters or in social policy. According to Rehnquist, the court errs when it tries to do too much, when it "legislates." Better to uphold the laws of the state legislatures, he says, rather than striking them down as potentially unconstitutional. As a committee of undetected lawyers, the justices do not have "a roving commission to second-guess Congress, state legislatures and state and federal administrative officers concerning what is best for the country," he said in a 1976 speech.

He first laid out his philosophy in his 1952 memo to Justice Jackson on the groundbreaking Brown vs. Board of Education school-desegregation case. Throughout its history, the justices had erred, he said, when they sought to protect individual rights. For example, in 1857, the court helped spark the Civil War when it ruled, in the infamous Dred Scott case, that the Constitution protected the rights of slaveholders. In the early decades of the 20th Century, the court blocked progressive measures by ruling that the Constitution protected the rights of businessmen.

"One hundred and fifty years of attempts on the part of this court to protect minority rights of any kind—whether those of business, slaveholders or the Jehovah's Witnesses—have all met the same fate. One by one, the cases establishing such rights have been sloughed off and [have] crept silently to rest," he wrote as a 27-year-old law clerk.

On matters involving the Constitution, Rehnquist's hands-off approach has been extraordinarily consistent. There is, however, one major exception: affirmative action. Repeatedly, and without exception, he has voted to strike down laws—city, state or federal—that give preferences to blacks, women, Latinos or other minorities. Whether it is the University of California giving an edge in admissions to minority students, the Federal Communications Commission giving a slight preference to minorities in competing for new broadcast licenses or the Richmond, Va., City Council setting aside a percentage of its city contracts for minorities, Rehnquist says those laws are unconstitutional. White males are entitled to "the equal protection of the laws," too, he says.

While that stand is not odd in itself—many legal scholars and most Americans think the Constitution forbids any distinctions based on race or sex—it is slightly peculiar for a conservative like Rehnquist. In the early 1950s, he did not think the segregation of black school children was unconstitutional. In the 1970s, he did not think discrimination against women violated the Constitution. Now, he insists that any discrimination against white males violates the Constitution. It is also somewhat odd because Rehnquist rarely strikes down any law on the ground that it violated the Constitution.

Under Rehnquist's view of the Constitution, state officials may execute juveniles for murder, may arrest gays for homosexual acts in their homes and may prohibit women from having abortions, but they may *not* give a slight preference to African-American students seeking admission to a state university.

During the 1988–89 term, when the court was badly split on scores of constitutional cases involving, for example, flag burning, the death penalty, drug testing, abortion and religion, Rehnquist voted against the government only once to strike down the Richmond city ordinance benefiting minority businesses.

His willingness to abandon his usual hands-off approach in order to overturn liberal civil-rights laws points up the most troubling side of Rehnquist's decision making. It leads his critics to say that he is result-oriented, that he is not governed by any consistent philosophy but, like the liberals he excoriated in the 1950s, makes his own preferences the law of the land.

Take, for example, his decisions in cases involving women and pregnancy. In 1976, Rehnquist wrote an opinion for the court declaring that the General Electric Company did not violate federal sex-discrimination laws when it excluded pregnant women from its otherwise all-encompassing disability coverage. The company treated men and women equally, Rehnquist said. Yes, the dissenters commented sarcastically, if men got pregnant, they would not be covered, either.

In response, Congress passed the Pregnancy Discrimination Act of 1978, requiring that employers treat pregnant women "the same" as men and insisting that women be evaluated only on their "ability or inability to work." That same year, the California Legislature said employers must allow pregnant women up to four months of unpaid leave to recover from childbirth and guaranteed that they would get their jobs back after maternity leave. When california employers challenged this law in the Supreme Court in 1987, Rehnquist sided with them, showing no deference to the California Legislature. Rehnquist argued that the law discriminates in favor of women and therefore must be invalidated under the Pregnancy Discrimination Act. However, Rehnquist was on the losing side in that decision because Scalia and O'Connor voted with the liberals to uphold California's law.

So, can an employer whose factory contains toxic lead exclude women because they may get pregnant and their fetuses may be damaged? Yes, said Rehnquist in an March, 1991, decision in the case of Auto Workers Union vs. Johnson Controls Co. But once again, Scalia and O'Connor joined with the liberals to strike down these "fetal-protection" policies. The Pregnancy Discrimination Act may not be wise, Scalia wrote, but it is clear: A woman's "ability or inability to work" governs employers, not the potential impact on the fetus.

In each of those cases, spanning 15 years, Rehnquist steadfastly refused to invoke the federal laws against discrimination based on sex or pregnancy to protect women. He invoked them only in the 1987 case to argue that California's law that gave extra leave to pregnant women should be struck down.

"He is very much the ideologue," USC Law Center Professor Erwin Chemerinsky says of Rehnquist. In a 1989 Harvard Law Review article on the Rehnquist court, Chemerinsky showed that the chief justice almost never votes to strike down laws—unless the laws happen to benefit minorities or women. "He writes decisions to get the results he wants. He is not consistent on a principle of law."

Scalia is certainly as conservative as Rehnquist, Chemerinsky noted, but he also votes on occasion for what is considered a "liberal" result. "Scalia lays out a principle and follows it, even if he doesn't like where it goes," Chemerinsky commented. By contrast, Rehnquist knows where he wants to go and doesn't let an adherence to legal principle get in the way. . . .

When the court takes the bench on the first Monday in October, its most liberal members will be two Midwestern Republicans: Harry Blackmun and John Paul Stevens. All the rest will be conservatives, most of whom were appointed by Presidents Reagan and Bush.

With an unquestioned majority, Rehnquist may move aggressively to throw out established doctrines of constitutional law. For example, Rehnquist has long disputed Thomas Jefferson's view that the Constitution demands a "separation of church and state." Rehnquist has called this "a misleading metaphor" that is "based on bad history." Although most historians disagree with him, Rehnquist says the government should be allowed to support and encourage religion, including group prayers in school. If the court's newest members, Souter and Thurgood Marshall's replacement are willing to join him, Rehnquist may move to overturn the 1962 decision outlawing state-sponsored school prayers.

Given an opportunity, Rehnquist would probably also overturn the best known of the Warren court's criminal-law rulings: Miranda vs. Arizona. As most TV cop-show viewers know, it is because of the Miranda decision that police officers warn suspects that they have the right to remain silent and the right to speak with a lawyer. Though the Miranda warnings have become standard police practice, on occasion a criminal conviction is overturned because the suspect was questioned before he waived his rights. Two years ago, during an oral argument in just such a case, a defense attorney began a sentence by saying, "Well, your honor, Miranda requires that. . . ."

Rehnquist cut him off. "Miranda doesn't require anything," he snapped. "All of Miranda is dicta, the meaningless verbiage in a court opinion.

The addition of Souter [in 1989] entrenched a pro-police, pro-prosecution majority, one that moved too fast even for Byron White, a John F. Kennedy appointee who is usually a hard-liner on crime. Twice during the last term, White wrote impassioned dissents in criminal cases. The first came when the 5-4 majority said for the first time that a coerced confession can be used during a trial. The second came on the term's final day when the same 5-4 majority ruled that it is not cruel and unusual punishment to impose a life prison term without parole for a first-time conviction for drug possession.

The abortion issue again stands as a major test for Rehnquist and his leadership of the court. Even those who have sat around the table and argued the issue for years are not sure what will happen. Brennan thinks the constitutional right to abortion will survive. Blackmun, the author of the majority opinion in Roe vs. Wade, thinks it will not. And Rehnquist is not predicting. The outcome may depend on Souter and on Marshall's replacement [Clarence Thomas].

Clearly, the justices will allow the states to regulate abortion—but how far will the states be permitted to go? Will the Supreme Court allow states to make abortion a crime—as Louisiana and Utah have—and to send doctors to prison for performing abortions? The court will be forced to address those questions in the next two years.

Some legal experts believe the doctrine of *stare decisis*—Latin for letting a matter stand as decided—will prevent the court from overturning the right to abortion. But Rehnquist seemed to shatter that view on June 27, the last day of the 1990–91 term. In overturning two recent precedents on the death penalty, the chief justice said, "*Stare decisis* is not an inexorable command." When a new majority sees old decisions as "unworkable or badly reasoned," it will overturn them, he said. Legal precedent is most important "in cases involving property and contract rights" but less so in matters of individual constitutional rights, he added. For supporters of the constitutional right to abortion and the right to free speech, Rehnquist's opinion in the Rust vs. Sullivan case and his expressed disregard for *stare decisis* seemed ominous.

Rehnquist would caution that, over time, the political system will supply the final answer, either by writing new laws or by changing the makeup of the Supreme Court. As Rehnquist wrote nearly 40 years ago, "In the long run, it is the majority who will determine what the constitutional rights of the minority are." And, at least for now, Rehnquist has five votes in his pocket and the power to interpret what the majority wants.

JUDICIAL POWER AND POLITICS

See text p. 351

As this chapter has discussed, courts must always be aware of the limits to their authority. Because federal judges are not elected, courts walk a fine line between interpreting the law and substituting their own judgments for those of representative officials. They are guided in this task by several traditional restraints, discussed on pages 351 and 352 of the text. They are also constrained by traditional rules of interpretation that dictate the kinds of evidence they should consider when reaching a decision. One of the traditional rules of interpretation that constrains the power of federal courts is the reliance upon legislative history to help resolve ambiguities concerning the scope of federal laws. Examining the legislative history behind a particular enactment can shed light on what Congress actually meant when it was passing a statute. The court's use of legislative history also helps to legitimate a judicial decision, by filling in gaps with reference to specific evidence rather than simply substituting its own judgment for that of Congress.

In recent years, Justice Antonin Scalia, one of the most outspoken members of the court, has debunked this tradition. According to Scalia, legislative history has very little merit. There is some truth to his view, since legislative history can be contradictory and sometimes is simply placed in the record, as the article that follows notes, to "lace committee reports and the Congressional Record with [a particular member's] spin on a law's intent." Nonetheless, Justice Scalia's approach has been widely criticized, both by commentators and fellow justices. Justice Scalia has often claimed superior moral ground for exercising judicial restraint, for paying scrupulous attention to text and history, and for his concerns for consistency. Yet, as Jeffrey Rosen pointed out in a January 1993 article in The New Republic, *"[t]here is an apparent tension . . . between Scalia's insistence on consulting extrinsic evidence of the framers' intentions and his refusal to consult extrinsic evidence of Congress's intentions[,]" and argues that Justice Scalia has utilized his own "plain meaning" test, described in the article from the* Washington Post *that follows, in ways that sometimes thwarts the express intention of Congress.*

Joan Biskupic
"Scalia Sees No Justice in Trying to Judge Intent of Congress on a Law"*

Antonin Scalia is the most opinionated and outspoken of the Supreme Court justices. He has a quick wit and a knack for words. And when he seizes on an idea or argument, there is no letup.

The argument he has seized upon most vigorously concerns the way federal courts determine how Congress wanted a particular law to be used. It is a key question in many lawsuits: when the government denies a worker a tax break or a convict challenges his prison sentence or an environmental group sues a chemical company.

Scalia rejects the traditional, decades-old approach of using congressional committee reports, floor speeches and other components of legislative history to decipher the statute at the heart of a case.

Legislative history "is not merely a waste of research time and ink," Scalia wrote in a March opinion, "it is a false and disruptive lesson in the law. . . . We are governed by laws, not by the intentions of legislators."

This has become his crusade.

"Justice Scalia is clearly an *agent provocateur* for thinking about the

*Joan Biskupic, "Scalia Sees No Justice in Trying to Judge Intent of Congress on a Law," *Washington Post* (May 11, 1993).

relationship between the legislative branch and judicial branch," said Judge Abner J. Mikva of the U.S. Court of Appeals in Washington, who disagrees with Scalia but nonetheless is fascinated by his views.

To some, the concept of "legislative history" may seem abstract. But to judges, it is the judicial equivalent of the meaning of life, the key to the universe, the yin and yang.

That is because the laws Congress passes, while often voluminous, can be vague. So, when the use of a federal law is challenged and the justices try to divine the intent of Congress, they turn to committee reports and floor speeches.

Since he joined the court seven years ago, Scalia has been urging the justices to ignore all that and look only to the actual words in the statute and to other relevant statutes.

Each year he gets more persistent and makes a few more inroads. The court's newest justice, Clarence Thomas, subscribes to Scalia's method.

While the debate over how to interpret a statute comes up several times a term, it is likely to be most in focus on a case the justices recently took—a test of whether Congress wanted the 1991 Civil Rights Act, an anti-discrimination employment law, to apply to cases pending at the time of enactment.

The language of the law is not clear, and during floor debate Democrats said that it should cover pending cases. Republicans said it should apply only to cases brought after the bill was signed into law. In one section of the legislation, members of Congress actually tried to dictate just what the courts should use as legislative history. But that "exclusive legislative history," too, is vague.

"The greatest defect of legislative history is its illegitimacy," Scalia wrote in the March 31 concurring opinion in *Conroy v. Aniskoff.* He joined the majority in its judgment on a tax dispute but not in its reliance on legislative history.

Scalia dismisses committee reports, which accompany a bill to the floor, as merely the work of staff and not representative of a sense of Congress. Floor speeches by members, he believes, are just one man or one woman's view, not to be taken for the majority.

That Scalia, 57, is so bold and articulate has almost as much to do with the attention he gets as the strength of his ideas. In a 1992 opinion, he called legislative history "the last hope of lost interpretive causes, that St. Jude of the hagiology of statutory construction."

That prompted Justice David H. Souter to rejoin in a footnote, "Justice Scalia upbraids us for reliance on legislative history, his 'St. Jude of the hagiology of statutory construction.' The shrine, however, is well peopled (though it has room for one more) and its congregation has included such noted elders as Mr. Justice [Felix] Frankfurter."

Souter then quoted Frankfurter, who sat on the court from 1939–1962, that, "A statute, like other living organisms, derives significance and sustenance from its environment. . . . The meaning of such a statute cannot be gained by confining inquiry within its four corners. Only the historic process . . . can yield its true meaning."

The difference in methods, while sounding theoretical, has real life significance. It can determine how far legal rights, benefits and penalties go.

Last year, when the Scalia approach prevailed, it meant that a man who fled Guatemala was not eligible for U.S. asylum because he did not meet a statutory definition for a "fear of persecution on account . . . of political opinion"; that a bankruptcy trustee trying to recover money wrongly paid to the Internal Revenue Service could not sue the government; and that a 1978 law preempted states from regulating airline advertising to try to ensure consumers are not misled about discount fares.

In earlier years, Scalia has won narrow majorities, while rejecting legislative history, to limit attorney and expert witness fees in civil rights cases and to rule that welfare recipients cannot appeal when the government offsets an underpayment of benefits with prior overpayments.

If the Scalia majority had looked to legislative history in the latter case, from 1990, Justice John Paul Stevens argued in a dissent, it would have decided that Congress did not intend to deny people on welfare a chance to persuade the government to waive its claim to the overpayment.

While Scalia is arguably the most judicially conservative of the Supreme Court justices and his narrow approach to the reading of statutes might be a byproduct of that philosophy, other conservatives who now dominate the federal courts have not followed Scalia's lead. On the Supreme Court, only Thomas regularly joins Scalia in his arguments against legislative history.

Further, the reality is that the unwieldy and political nature of the legislative process yields gaps in statutes. Omissions happen. And when partisan differences cannot be reconciled, details give way to broad principles.

Yet, while there are reasons to turn to legislative history, it is not without pitfalls. Knowing that courts rely on it, members of Congress often lace committee reports and the Congressional Record with their particular spin on a law's intent.

"Every time we have a tax bill we try to do that," Sen. John C. Danforth (R-Mo.) has said. "I remember one night literally following one of my colleagues around the floor of the Senate for fear that he would slip something into the Congressional Record, and I would have to slip something else in."

It is rare for members of Congress to admit to the practice, and Danforth's comments were made during a heated floor debate in late 1991 as Republicans and Democrats were trying to influence the record on how courts should interpret the Civil Rights Act.

"Justice Scalia was correct," Danforth said. "Any judge who tries to make legislative history out of the free-for-all that takes place on the floor of the Senate is on very dangerous grounds. . . . It is a muddle."

Kenneth S. Geller, a former deputy solicitor general, said recently that Scalia has "sensitized" the legal community to the drawbacks of some legislative history. "There are degrees of legislative history," said Geller, who often represents clients before the high court. "Committee reports can be impressive. Floor statements are less impressive. And some legislative history is, frankly, garbage."

But Geller quickly added, "I don't know of any brief that our firm has filed that failed to rely on legislative history. First, Justice Scalia is the minority up there, and second, it can't hurt to use legislative history if it helps your case."

If Scalia were ever to truly change the way courts interpret laws, it could diminish Congress's authority. Under a 1984 Supreme Court ruling, courts defer to administration interpretations of statutes in the absence of clear evidence of a contrary congressional intent. That is what happened in the 1991 *Rust v. Sullivan* case, in which a narrow statutory reading led the court to adopt a Bush administration position that allowed a ban on abortion counseling at publicly financed clinics.

Scalia has said that if the court interprets a statute in a way that Congress disapproves, it can always go back and change the law.

But Stevens, who engages Scalia most in opinions on the topic, wrote in a case last term that the "stubborn insistence on 'clear statements' burdens the Congress with unnecessary reenactment of provisions that were already plain enough."

If Scalia's approach were widely adopted, Rep. Barney Frank (D-Mass.) said recently, "we would have a new category of legislation: the 'No, we really meant it' statute." Frank, a member of the House Judiciary Committee, has tracked Scalia's approach and reactions to it.

Two years ago during committee negotiations on an anti-crime bill, Frank warned colleagues not to resolve a dispute by putting explanatory language in a committee report. He used just two words: "Justice Scalia," then said the committee report might ultimately be judged irrelevant.

But Frank said Scalia is less "dangerous" today to the Democratic-controlled Congress because a Democrat is in the White House. When a statute is ambiguous and a court defers to administration views, they will be Democratic views, he noted.

Former representative Robert W. Kastenmeier (D-Wis.), now chairman of a national commission on judicial impeachment, said Scalia's theories have stimulated thinking, but have not taken root.

"Most judges seek better relations with Congress," he said, "and rather than curse the darkness, they would rather light a candle."

QUESTIONS

1. A number of unwritten rules guide the Supreme Court's interpretation of the constitutionality of a particular statute or action. In the *Casey* decision, the Court discussed the importance of the rule of *stare decisis,* or adherence to precedence. According to Justices O'Connor, Kennedy, and Souter, what considerations of institutional legitimacy are implicated by the *stare decisis* rule? Why do Justices Thomas, Rehnquist, and Scalia argue that *stare decisis* does not require affirmance of the Court's earlier holding in *Roe v. Wade*?

2. Does the power of judicial review give the Court too much authority vis-a-vis other branches of government? If *Marbury v. Madison* had not vested the Supreme Court with authority to determine whether statutes are constitutional, what institution would make those determinations? What objections might be raised if, for example, Congress had final authority to decide whether the laws it passed were constitutional?
3. The profiles of Chief Justice Rehnquist and Justice Brennan illustrate very different philosophies of judicial interpretation. How might Justice Brennan's philosophy be categorized?
4. Does the Supreme Court lose credibility when it attempts to articulate fundamental principles like the right of privacy? Does Chief Justice Rehnquist's philosophy adequately protect minority rights against majority tyranny?
5. To what extent should the Supreme Court's interpretations of legislation be guided by legislative history? If the Court does not accord any weight to legislative history, is it simply substituting its own judgment for that of Congress when it interprets the law?

CHAPTER 9

Public Opinion

See text p. 364

The concept of a marketplace of ideas was first articulated by Justice Oliver Wendell Holmes in his dissent to the Supreme Court's decision in Abrams v. United States *(1919). The* Abrams *dissent set the tone for the unfolding of the First Amendment's free speech doctrine that followed; to understand the impact of the dissent, it is important to remember that at the time that Abrams was written, the First Amendment's free speech guarantees had barely begun to be tested. In the* Abrams *dissent, Holmes lays out a position that contemporary commentators often take for granted as the cornerstone of the American political structure: that an open struggle among competing ideas is essential to any effort to discover truth in a democratic society.*

Abrams v. *United States* (1919)*

[In 1918, during the First World War, the United States sent a small force of marines into the Soviet Union, ostensibly as part of strategic operations against Germany. In response to this action, Jacob Abrams and four associates—Russian immigrants who characterized themselves as rebels, anarchists, or socialists—distributed two leaflets criticizing the United States and calling upon workers to unite and defeat what they viewed as capitalist aggression against the Soviet Union. The Supreme Court upheld the convictions of Abrams and his associates for conspiring to violate the Espionage Act of 1917, which prohibited, among other things, the publication of materials encouraging disloyalty to the United States or containing language intended to invite scorn of or incite resistance to the United States during the war. In an earlier case, Schenck v. United States, *the Court had formulated what was called the clear and present danger test, holding that the extent of protection afforded to public expression of ideas depended upon the context in which the opinion was uttered, and that language intended to likely to generate a public disturbance was not shielded by the Constitution's guarantee of free expression.]*

JUSTICE HOLMES, dissenting.

. . . The first of these leaflets says that the President's cowardly silence about the intervention in Russia reveals the hypocrisy of the plutocratic gang in Washington. It intimates that 'German militarism combined with allied

*Abrams v. United States, 250 U.S. 616, 1919.

capitalism to crush the Russian revolution'—goes on that the tyrants of the world fight each other until they see a common enemy—working class enlightenment. . . . It says that there is only one enemy of the workers of the world and that is capitalism; that it is a crime for workers of America, etc., to fight the workers' republic of Russia. . . .

The other leaflet, headed 'Workers—Wake Up,' with abusive language says that America together with the Allies will march for Russia to help the Czecko-Slovaks [*sic*] in their struggle against the Bolsheviki, and that this time the hypocrites shall not fool the Russian emigrants and friends of Russia in America. It tells the Russian emigrants that they now must spit in the face of the false military propaganda by which their sympathy and help to the prosecution of the war have been called forth and says that with the money they have lent or are going to lend 'they will make bullets not only for the Germans but also for the Workers Soviets of Russia,' and further, 'Workers in the ammunition factories, you are producing bullets, bayonets, cannon to murder not only the Germans, but also your dearest, best, who are in Russia fighting for freedom.' It then appeals to the same Russian emigrants at some length not to consent to the 'inquisitionary expedition in Russia,' and says that the destruction of the Russian revolution is 'the politics of the march on Russia.' The leaflet winds up by saying 'Workers, our reply to this barbaric intervention has to be a general strike!' and after a few words on the spirit of revolution, exhortations not to be afraid, and some usual tall talk ends 'Woe unto those who will be in the way of progress. Let solidarity live! The Rebels.' . . .

I do not doubt for a moment that . . . the United States constitutionally may punish speech that produces or is intended to produce a clear and imminent danger that it will bring about forthwith certain substantive evils that the United States constitutionally may seek to prevent. The power undoubtedly is greater in time of war than in time of peace because war opens dangers that do not exist at other times.

But as against dangers peculiar to war, as against others, the principle of the right to free speech is always the same. It is only the present danger of immediate evil or an intent to bring it about that warrants Congress in setting a limit to the expression of opinion where private rights are not concerned. Congress certainly cannot forbid all effort to change the mind of the country. Now nobody can suppose that the surreptitious publishing of a silly leaflet by an unknown man, without more, would present any immediate danger that its opinions would hinder the success of the government arms or have any appreciable tendency to do so. . . .

In this case sentences of twenty years imprisonment have been imposed for the publishing of two leaflets that I believe the defendants had as much right to publish as the Government has to publish the Constitution of the United States now vainly invoked by them. . . . [T]he defendants are to be made to suffer not for what the indictment alleges but for the creed that they avow—a creed that I believe to be the creed of ignorance and immaturity when honestly held, as I see no reason to doubt that it was held here. . . .

. . . [I] think that we should be eternally vigilant against attempts to check the expression of opinions that we loathe and believe to be fraught with death, unless they so imminently threaten immediate interference with the lawful and pressing purposes of the law that an immediate check is required to save the country. I wholly disagree with the argument of the Government that the First Amendment left the common law as to seditious libel in force. History seems to me against the notion. I had conceived that the United States through many years had shown its repentance for the Sedition Act of 1798, by repaying fines that it imposed. Only the emergency that makes it immediately dangerous to leave the correction of evil counsels to time warrants making any exception to the sweeping command, 'Congress shall make no law abridging the freedom of speech.' Of course I am speaking only of expressions of opinion and exhortations, which were all that were uttered here, but I regret that I cannot put into more impressive words my belief that in their conviction upon this indictment the defendants were deprived of their rights under the Constitution of the United States.

SHAPING PUBLIC OPINION

See text p. 372

As opportunities expand for getting public opinion before public officials, so do the opportunities for manipulating that opinion. The nature of the opinion poll—the way that it tames or domesticates public opinion—has allowed modern governments to transform public opinion from a tool for objecting to governmental actions into something that can be manipulated to generate support for state policies, as Professor Benjamin Ginsberg argues in the following article on shaping public opinion.

Benjamin Ginsberg
"How Polling Transforms Public Opinion"*

The "will of the people" has become the ultimate standard against which the conduct of contemporary governments is measured. In the democracies, especially in the United States, both the value of governmental programs and the virtue of public officials are typically judged by the extent of their popularity. . . .

Much of the prominence of opinion polling as a civic institution derives from the significance that present-day political ideologies ascribe to the will of the people. Polls purport to provide reliable, scientifically derived information about the public's desires, fears and beliefs, and so to give concrete expression to the conception of a popular will. The availability of accurate

*Excerpts from *The Captive Public: How Mass Opinion Promotes State Power,* by Benjamin Ginsberg.

information certainly is no guarantee that governments will actually pay heed to popular opinions. Yet, it has always been the belief of many students and practitioners of survey research that an accurate picture of the public's views might at least increase the chance that governments' actions would be informed by and responsive to popular sentiment.

Unfortunately, however, polls do more than simply measure and record the natural or spontaneous manifestation of popular belief. The data reported by opinion polls are actually the product of an interplay between opinion and the survey instrument. As they measure, the polls interact with opinion, producing changes in the character and identity of the views receiving public expression. The changes induced by polling, in turn, have the most profound implications for the relationship between public opinion and government. In essence, polling has contributed to the domestication of opinion by helping to transform opinion from a politically potent, often disruptive, force into a more docile, plebiscitary phenomenon.

Publicizing Opinion

Over the past several decades, polling has generally come to be seen as the most accurate and reliable means of gauging the public's sentiments. Indeed, poll results and public opinion are terms that are used almost synonymously. But, despite this general tendency to equate public opinion with survey results, polling is obviously not the only possible source of knowledge about the public's attitudes.

[A] presumption in favor of the polls . . . [however] stems from both the scientific and representative character of opinion polling. Survey research is modeled after the methodology of the natural sciences and at least conveys an impression of technical sophistication and scientific objectivity. Occasional press accounts of deliberate bias and distortion of survey findings only partially undermine this impression.

At the same time, the polls can claim to offer a more representative view of popular sentiment than any alternative source of information is likely to provide. Group spokespersons sometimes speak only for themselves. The distribution of opinion reflected by letters to newspapers and public officials is notoriously biased. Demonstrators and rioters, however sincere, are seldom more than a tiny and unrepresentative segment of the populace. The polls, by contrast, at least attempt to take equal account of all relevant individuals. And, indeed, by offering a representative view of public opinion the polls have often served as antidotes for false spokespersons, correctives for mistaken politicians, and guides to popular concerns that might never have been mentioned by the individuals writing letters to legislators and newspaper editors.

Nevertheless, polling does more than offer a scientifically derived and representative account of popular sentiment. The substitution of polling for other means of gauging the public's views also has the effect of changing several of the key characteristics of public opinion. Critics of survey research have often noted that polling can affect both the beliefs of individuals asked to respond to survey questions and the attitudes of those who subsequently read a survey's results. However, the most important effect of the polls is not a result of their capacity to change individuals' beliefs. The major impact of polling is, rather, on the cumulation and translation of individuals' private beliefs into collective public opinion. Four fundamental changes in the character of public opinion can be traced to the introduction of survey research.

Changing the Character of Public Opinion

First, polling alters both what is expressed and what is perceived as the opinion of the mass public by transforming public opinion from a voluntary to an externally subsidized matter. Second, polling modifies the manner in which opinion is publicly presented by transforming public opinion from a behavioral to an attitudinal phenomenon. Third, polling changes the origin of information about public beliefs by transforming public opinion from a property of groups to an attribute of individuals. Finally, polling partially removes individuals' control over the subject matter of their own public expressions of opinion by transforming public opinion from a spontaneous assertion to a constrained response.

Individually and collectively, these transformations have profound consequences for the character of public opinion and, more important, for the relationship of opinion to government and policy. To the extent that polling displaces alternative modes of gauging popular sentiment, these four transformations contribute markedly to the domestication or pacification of public opinion. Polling renders public opinion less dangerous, less disruptive, more permissive and, in some instances, more amenable to governmental control.

Polling does not make public opinion politically impotent. Nor, as the recent failure of the Reagan administration's efforts to "disinform" the American public on the government's policies toward Iran and Central America indicate, does the availability of polling guarantee that governments will be able to successfully manipulate public beliefs for an indefinite length of time. Nevertheless, polling helps to diminish the danger that public opinion poses to those in power and helps to increase the potential for government management of mass beliefs.

From Voluntarism to Subsidy

In the absence of polling, the cost and effort required to organize and publicly communicate an opinion are normally borne by one or more of the individuals holding the opinion. . . . The polls, by contrast, organize and publicize opinion without necessitating any initiative or action on the part of individuals. . . .

This displacement of costs from the opinion-holder to the polling agency has important consequences for the character of the opinions likely to receive public expression. In general, the willingness of individuals to bear the costs of publicly asserting their views is closely tied to the intensity with which they hold those views. . . . So long as the costs of asserting opinions are borne by opinion-holders themselves, those with relatively extreme viewpoints are also disproportionately likely to bring their views to the public forum.

The polls weaken this relationship between the public expression of opinion and the intensity or extremity of opinion. The assertion of an opinion through a poll requires little effort on the part of the opinion-holder. As a result, the beliefs of those who care relatively little or even hardly at all, are as likely to be publicized as the opinions of those who care a great deal about the matter in question. Similarly, individuals with moderate viewpoints are as likely as those taking extreme positions to publicly communicate their opinions through a survey. The upshot is that the distribution of public opinion reported by the polls generally differs considerably from the distribution that emerges from forms of public communication initiated by citizens. . . .

This difference between polled and voluntarily expressed opinion can have important implications for the degree of influence or constraint that public opinion is likely to impose upon administrators and policymakers. The polls, in effect, submerge individuals with strongly held views in a more apathetic mass public. The data reported by the polls are likely to suggest to public officials that they are working in a more permissive climate of opinion than might have been thought on the basis of alternative indicators of the popular mood. A government wishing to maintain some semblance of responsiveness to public opinion would typically find it less difficult to comply with the preferences reported by the polls than to obey the opinion that might be inferred from letters, strikes, or protests. Indeed, relative to these other modes of public expression, polled opinion could be characterized as a collective statement of permission.

Certainly, even in the era of polling, voluntary expressions of public opinion can still count heavily. In recent years, for example, members of Congress were impressed by calls, letters, and telegrams from constituents—and threats from contributors—regarding President Reagan's various tax reform proposals. Of course, groups like the National Rifle Association are masters of the use of this type of opinion campaign. Nevertheless, contradiction by the polls tends to reduce the weight and credibility of other sources of public opinion. This effect of polling can actually help governments to resist the pressure of constituent opinion. Constituency polls, for example, are often used by legislators as a basis for resisting the demands of political activists and pressure groups in their districts.

Polling is especially useful when voluntary expressions of public opinion indicate severe opposition to a government and its programs. The relatively permissive character of polled opinion can allow a government faced with demonstrations, protests, and other manifestations of public hostility a basis for the claim that its policies are compatible with true public opinion and opposed only by an unrepresentative group of activist malcontents. A notable contemporary illustration of this role of the polls is the case of the "silent majority" on whose behalf Richard Nixon claimed to govern. The notion of a silent majority was the Nixon administration's answer to the protestors, who demanded major changes in American foreign and domestic policies. Administration spokespersons frequently cited poll data, often drawing upon Scammon and Wattenberg's influential treatise, *The Real Majority* (1970) to question the popular standing of the activist opposition. According to the administration's interpretation, its activist opponents did not represent the views of the vast majority of "silent" Americans who could be found in the polls but not on picket lines, marches, or in civil disturbances. . . .

From Behavior to Attitude

Prior to the advent of polling, public opinion could often only be inferred from political behavior. Before the availability of voter survey data, for example, analysts typically sought to deduce electoral opinion from voting patterns, attributing candidates' electoral fortunes to whatever characteristics of the public mood could be derived from election returns. Often, population movements served as the bases for conclusions about public preferences. Even in recent years, the movement of white urbanites to the metropolitan fringe, dubbed "white flight," has been seen as a key indicator of white attitudes toward racial integration. Particularly, however, where the least articulate segments of the populace were concerned, governments often had little or no knowledge of the public's mood until opinion manifested itself in some form of behavior. Generally, this meant violent or disruptive activity. . . .

From Assertion to Response

In the absence of polling, individuals typically choose for themselves the subjects of any public assertions they might care to make. Those persons or groups willing to expend the funds, effort, or time needed to acquire a public platform, normally also select the agenda or topics on which their views will be aired. The individual writing an angry letter to a newspaper or legislator generally singles out the object of his or her scorn. The organizers of a protest march typically define the aim of their own wrath. Presumably, 19th-century mobs of "illuminators" determined of their own accord the matters on which the larger public would be enlightened.

The introduction of opinion surveys certainly did not foreclose individuals' opportunities to proffer opinions on topics of their own choosing. Indeed, in the United States, a multitude of organizations, groups, and individuals are continually stepping forward to present the most extraordinary notions. Nevertheless, the polls elicit subjects' views on questions which have been selected by an external agency—the survey's sponsors—rather than by the respondents themselves. Polling thus erodes individuals' control over the agenda of their own expressions of opinion. With the use of surveys, publicly expressed opinion becomes less clearly an assertion of individuals' own concerns and more nearly a response to the interests of others.

The most obvious problem stemming from this change is that polling can create a misleading picture of the agenda of public concerns. The matters which appear significant to the agencies sponsoring polls may be quite different from the concerns of the general public. Discrepancies between the polls' agenda and the general public's interests were especially acute during the political and social turmoil of the late 1960s and early 1970s. Though, as we saw, polling was used by the government during this period to help curb disorder, the major commercial polls took little interest in the issues which aroused so much public concern. The year 1970, for example, was marked by racial strife and antiwar protest in the United States. Yet, the 1970 national Gallup Poll devoted only 5 percent of its questions to American policy in Vietnam and only 2 of 162 questions to domestic race relations.

But, whatever the particular changes polling may help to produce in the focus of public discourse, the broader problem is that polling fundamentally alters the character of the public agenda of opinion. So long as groups and individuals typically present their opinions on topics of their own choosing, the agenda of opinion is likely to consist of citizens' own needs, hopes, and aspirations. A large fraction of the opinion which is publicly expressed will involve demands and concerns that groups and individuals wish to bring to the attention of the government. Opinions elicited by the polls, on the other hand, mainly concern matters of interest to government, business, or other poll sponsors. Typically, poll questions have as their ultimate purpose some form of exhortation. Businesses poll to help persuade customers to purchase their wares. Candidates poll as part of the process of convincing voters to support them. Governments poll as part of the process of inducing citizens to obey. Sometimes several of these purposes are combined. In 1971, for example, the White House Domestic Council sponsored a poll dealing with a host of social issues designed both to assist the administration with policy planning and to boost the president's reelection efforts.

In essence, rather than offer governments the opinions that citizens want them to learn, the polls tell governments—or other sponsors—what they would like to learn about citizens' opinions. The end result is to change the public expression of opinion from an assertion of demand to a step in the process of persuasion.

Making Opinion Safer for Government

Taken together, the changes produced by polling contribute to the transformation of public opinion from an unpredictable, extreme, and often dangerous force into a more docile expression of public sentiment. Opinion stated through the polls imposes less pressure and makes fewer demands upon government than would more spontaneous or natural assertions of popular sentiment. Though opinion may be expressed more democratically via the polls than though alternative means, polling can give public opinion a plebescitary character—robbing opinion of precisely those features that might maximize its impact upon government and policy. . . .

Government: From Adversary to Manager of Opinion

Because it domesticates public opinion, polling has contributed to one of the 20th century's major political transformations—the shift from an adversarial to a managerial relationship between government and popular opinion. . . .

On a day-to-day basis, the 20th-century state depends upon considerable support, cooperation, and sacrifice from its citizens in forms ranging from military service and large tax payments, through popular adherence to a multitude of rules and regulations. The scope and technical complexity of the modern state's activities, moreover, render governmental administration extremely sensitive to popular opposition. In the short term, opposition can often be forcibly quelled and a populace forcibly compelled to obey its rulers' edicts, pay taxes, and serve in the military. But, over long periods, even many of those governments commanding both the requisite armed might and appropriate lack of scruples have come to appreciate the wisdom of the Napoleonic dictum that one "may do anything with a bayonet but sit on it." By cultivating favorable public opinion, present-day rulers hope to

MEASURING PUBLIC OPINION

See text p. 385

While public opinion polling techniques have become highly sophisticated, many polls that get reported are conducted with little to no scientific accuracy. In the following article Richard Morin, the director of polling for the Washington Post *takes call-in polls to task. Called SLOP surveys—self-selected listener opinions—by one leading pollster, these surveys were first touted by tabloid news media, and have now gained a foothold among more traditional media. Call-in surveys have some appeal among those who argue that the nation should move to more direct democracy, but as the article notes, they are no less subject to abuse and manipulation than any other kind of public opinion measuring system.*

Richard Morin
"Numbers from Nowhere: The Hoax of the Call-In 'Polls' "*

It's hard to imagine television getting much worse, what with Geraldo, "American Gladiators" and the Fox network. But it had. Under the pretense of seeking out public opinion, CBS recently created a public nuisance. And in the process, the network became another willing victim of call-in polls, the research equivalent of what Millie leaves on the White House lawn.

CBS seems proud of the show "America on the Line" and its featured attraction, a call-in survey that followed Bush's State of the Union address. And they're reportedly thinking about doing it again, perhaps as part of a weekly show, and perhaps as early as March.

"Oh no, I'd hope they'd never do it again," said Norman Bradburn, director of the National Opinion Research Center at the University of Chicago. "But I suppose it's fantasy to think that they won't."

Bradburn has a name for this kind of pseudo-polls. He calls them SLOP surveys, an acronym for "self-selected listener opinion polls."

Like radio talk shows, they attract a slice of America that is anything but representative of the country, painting a distorted picture of public attitudes—and possibly even helping to shape those attitudes—on any issue they touch.

For those who missed it, CBS's "America on the Line" featured two surveys conducted immediately after Bush's State of the Union speech. A total of 314,786 viewers managed to connect to CBS. They heard a recording of Charles Kuralt asking a series of survey questions, which they answered by pushing buttons on their phone. The second poll was a more scientific survey of 1,241 adults that served as a kind of modest check and balance on the other effort.

But the call-in poll was the real star, hogging air time and generating swoons from Dan Rather, Connie Chung and Kuralt. "A unique experiment in television, something brand-new," Rather told his viewers.

Wrong, at least in part. Call-in polls are nothing new. And unfortunately, they appear to be increasingly popular. Newspapers, television and radio stations, even politicians and agencies of state and local governments use them to show they "care"—in that cynical, disengaged '90s sort of way—about what their audiences or constituents think.

Such polls have amassed quite a track record. It may not be good, but it is amusing. Some examples:

A June 1990 phone-in poll conducted by *USA Today* asked callers to

*Richard Morin, "Numbers From Nowhere: The Hoax of the Call-In 'Polls' ", *Washington Post* (February 9,1992).

choose which statement came closest to their view: "Donald Trump symbolizes what made the USA a great country" or "Donald Trump symbolizes the things that are wrong with this country."

The results: 81 percent of the 6,406 respondents said Trump was what's right with America; 19 percent said he was what was wrong.

"You like him! You really like him! Despite the hype, Trump's a hero to many," read the headline in the June 11 issue of *USA Today.*

One problem: The telephone ballot box had been electronically stuffed.

"Two telephone numbers in a single insurance company accounted for 72 percent of the favorable calls," said Jim Norman, who directs polls—real polls—for the newspaper and was not involved in the call-in project.

USA Today subsequently was told by the owner of the insurance company that he made the calls simply because he admired Trump.

"You can definitely put us in with those people who have been burned by one-900 number polls," Norman said.

A *Parade* magazine call-in poll on abortion in August 1990 found that the "overwhelming majority of the nearly 300,000 respondents who participated . . . were opposed to abortion.

That's a remarkable finding, since national surveys consistently show that a majority of Americans favor abortion under most circumstances. But it became less remarkable when *Parade* acknowledged in a press release that its "records indicate that 21 percent of the callers may have voiced their opinions more than once."

Last week, West Virginia's Gov. Gaston Caperton scored big over his rivals for the gubernatorial nomination when his own aides flooded a Charleston TV station's phone-in poll with votes for their boss.

And early-rising conspiracy theorists weighed in heavily Friday in a "Today" show call-in poll on NBC, fingering the CIA as JFK's probable assassin.

CBS wasn't the first network to use call-in polls. ABC's "Nightline" was briefly smitten in the early 1980s. They abandoned the effort after conducting five tests in 1983 in which the results of call-in polls fared poorly when compared to scientific surveys done at the same time.

One "Nightline" call-in poll asked Americans whether the United Nations should be kicked out of the United States. Two out of three callers said give the U.N. the boot. But on the scientific survey, seven out of 10 said precisely the opposite: Keep the U.N. in the United States.

Despite some good-faith efforts by CBS to step on the results of its SLOP survey, many viewers were left with the distinct and decidedly incorrect impression that the results of the phone-in poll and the scientific survey were virtually the same.

Even the *Washington Post* reported, in a favorable review of the show, that "by and large the two polls produced the same or similar results."

In fact, on two of the nine questions asked in both polls, the results differed by more than 20 percentage points. On another five, the differences were 10 percentage points or more.

For example, polls asked participants whether they were better or worse off than they were four years ago, an important election-year question. In the scientific survey, 32 percent said they were worse off.

But 54 percent of those who participated in the phone-in poll said they were worse off—a whopping 22 percentage point credibility gap.

When asked to predict the "future for the next generation of Americans," 36 percent in the scientific survey predicted it would be worse, compared to 57 percent in the phone-in poll.

And when asked whether they were worried that they or someone in their family might lose their job in the next year, 48 percent in the scientific poll but 64 percent in the call-in survey said yes. And so on.

The CBS project does have one modest benefit. The huge differences in the two polls again support researchers' claims that call-in participants are a generally sour crowd.

"It does confirm the hypothesis that people who take this action are more motivated, more angered, more extreme, and the differences vary from question to question," said Kathy Frankovic, the widely respected director of surveys at CBS, who directed the scientific poll.

But really, what's so wrong with a few hundred thousand Americans venting their spleen and then pretending it's a "poll"? Is it really any more harmful than, say, the pretense that pro wrestling is sports, or that "A Current Affair" is news?

Maybe it is. There's evidence that many Americans do believe the results of call-in polls. A scientific survey conducted in 1990 by Bruskin Associates found that 45 percent of the adults interviewed said results of call-in polls were believable. About 24 percent said such polls were "scientific." And four out of 10 said "results of a call-in poll should be believed if thousands of people participated in it."

The bogus results of call-in polls may thus work to shape others' reactions, because they can encourage a "bandwagon" effect. That is, those with no opinions of their own may begin to parrot the line that they perceive to be popular sentiment.

Frankovic acknowledges that the network could have done a better job highlighting the differences between the real poll and the call-in effort.

"Everybody agreed afterward that it would have been a little clearer if there had been more direct comparisons, and we should have been putting comparative numbers on the screen at the same time," she said. As it was, the call-in results were displayed visually, while the often contradictory poll findings were merely spoken but never visually reinforced.

Overall, CBS defends the effort. The phone-in poll attracted an estimated 24.5 million calls to its toll-free number.

"People even called the next day, and they called an 800 number in Wisconsin that sounded like our number; I even got letters from people answering our questions," Frankovic said. "Why are people doing this?"

Frankovic, the incoming president of American Association for Public Opinion Research (AAPOR), defends the project as a worthy experiment.

"We can do it better," she said. "The important thing is that we were engaging people."

Bradburn, AAPOR's current president, and others report Frankovic fought the methodologically good fight inside CBS. One result was the scientific poll that ran concurrent with the call-in survey, which Bradburn said "kept CBS from making a total fool of itself."

"I didn't have to make that fight," she said. "It was always assumed there would be a polling component. Even the president of CBS News said we can't do this unless" it is done in conjunction with a real poll.

Despite the problems, CBS appears ready to do more such slop. The *Post*'s TV critic Tom Shales reports that "America on the Line" was a pilot for a planned weekly show.

"The fundamental problem is that it's a good show," Bradburn said. "And who's going to give up a good show just for the truth?"

Debating the Issues: Opposing Views

THE POWER OF PUBLIC OPINION

See text p. 398–99

The ultimate question concerning public opinion is "Who affects who?" With our current system, it matters in a number of ways, as the text points out: opinion movers respond to and manipulate opinion as a matter of course. Changes in technology that make it easier to generate public opinion about a variety of issues, however, cast an entirely new light on concerns about public opinion in recent years, raising questions that run to the heart of representative government itself.

In his surprisingly strong third-party bid for the presidency in 1992, candidate Ross Perot talked at length about an idea he called the "electronic town hall," in which citizens could participate in a "teledemocracy," registering their opinions about everything from reducing the deficit to gays in the military simply by pressing a button on their TV sets or telephones. These technological developments have begun to create a new form of plebiscitary democracy, one that the Federalists would be wary of.

The following two pieces discuss this new form of democratic rule. The first piece, written by a techno-democrat whose legal name is FM-2030, argues that the American political process, with its representative politics, is an anachronism in this brave new technological world. He argues that the use of computer referenda would eliminate the need for elected officials altogether, and that politics could move toward objective decision making in which the focus would be on issues, not on candidates whose moves are always mediated by a desire for reelection.

Anthony Lewis, a political observer for the New York Times, *is apprehensive about this move to a mass-participatory democracy. Acknowledging that a new technological age has dawned, he urges Americans to consider the concerns of the Framers: those concerns—about the caprice of public opinion and the capacity for a majority to tyrannize minorities—have lost none of their salience today, and we should not allow that system of representative government to be easily supplanted.*

FM-2030
"Our Political Process Suits the 18th Century"*

News flashes across the planet in seconds. Electronic transfer zips billions of dollars from continent to continent in minutes. Entire professions and industries and nations dis-exist and coalesce overnight. The world is streaming ahead faster and faster—but the American election process creeps along slower and slower.

We are in the middle of another volatile election year. Month after endless month, candidates for the presidency and Congress wake up at agrarian hours to stand on street corners shaking hands and pleading for votes. Tens of millions of dollars are frittered away on predatory media blitzes.

What is endlessly called a "democracy" is actually a 200-year-old system of decision-making, a representative form of government totally out of sync with the realities of this late-20th Century. It is slow, costly, exclusionary, undemocratic and often trivial.

Specifically, elective government is an anachronism because:

—Modern generations are more self-reliant and less power-oriented than previous generations. Imagine asking them who the "head of household" is or who should "lead" on the dance floor. In my seminars for industry, older executives often complain that young employees don't know how to take orders: young, educated personnel insist that senior officers are too "controlling" and out of touch with new ways of doing things.

—Information has been one of the principal tools of power. As information decentralizes, the relative power of governments declines. It is not an accident that in recent years the most profound transformations in North America—the civil-rights movement, the consumer and environmental movements, the women's movement—have been spearheaded by activists outside government. Governments are less able to control events. Telecommunication is the powerful tool that enables these peoples' initiatives.

—Elective governments may have worked well in the agrarian and early industrial ages, when change unfolded slowly. But this plodding process of electioneering for months is now absurdly slow. Pressing national and international policy decisions, for example the current peace talks in the combustible Arab-Israeli conflict, have to be put on hold for months.

The people of North America have changed, the technology has

*FM-2030, Our Political Process Suits the 18th Century, *Los Angeles Times* (May 15, 1992). Reprinted with permission.

changed, the pace of events has changed—but the basic manner in which national decisions are made has not.

In the United States, nearly half of the eligible voters persistently do not vote. This may only be partly due to chronic apathy. There is abundant evidence that people also feel left out by the exclusionary nature of this political process. North Americans are actually more activist than ever, but are no longer content to be juvenilized by an antiquated paternalism.

The future doesn't come with blueprints, but here's a sketch of one possible postindustrial civic decision-making process.

Once a month, or as frequently as is necessary, a list of issues would be submitted to the people in a referendum. A certain number of "signatures," written or electronic, would be necessary to get an issue on the referendum. All sides of an issue would get equal time in the electronic and print media. When possible, computer projections of probable consequences of each option would be aired.

People would participate in referendums by telephone or computer, logging on with personal code number to select from a menu of options. Televoting could be done from anywhere: home, office, beach, car. The maybe-candidate, Ross Perot, has nodded in this direction with his proposal for weekly opinion referendums.

An ad hoc referendum committee comprised of people selected at random by computer, somewhat as in jury duty today, could serve for a month or two at time. This committee could see to the drafting of ballot measures, supervise the voting and oversee implementation of the referendum decisions. Leaders and representatives are superfluous—we need facilitators.

Without leadership struggles, the decision-making process would be depoliticized, freeing it of the wasteful personal ambitions and partisan politics that hobble elective government. Referendums focus on the merits of different plans instead of calculating their effect on a candidate's electability. Computer testing of consequences of each option further helps objectify the process.

The modern path to genuine democracy is to create mechanisms empowering people to vote not for leaders but directly on issues. This at last is government by the people and for the people.

Anthony Lewis
"Not a Rose Garden"*

After the election, Republicans charged that the press was biased against George Bush. A conservative think tank produced a solemn report to the same effect.

Well, ladies and gentlemen, look at the press now and think again. Reporters and commentators are savaging Bill Clinton. They are doing what comes naturally to a free press: criticizing those in authority.

The battering the new President is taking arises from two episodes of his first 10 days in office: the forced withdrawal of his nominee for Attorney General, and his forced compromise on homosexuals in the armed forces. Those episodes carry important lessons on the problem of governing in contemporary America.

We have moved rapidly in this country toward a form of mass-participatory democracy. The American public learns instantly what happens in Washington, and members of that public massively and almost as instantly tell their leaders what they think.

The public awareness and response are a product of technology but also of something else: the discontent with government that was so evident in the 1992 election campaign. The sour feelings that brought Ross Perot 19 percent of the vote are still there, and focused on the new President.

The idea of participatory democracy is quite different from the political system that the founders of this country meant to create. James Madison and the other Framers of the Constitution feared the whim—the tyranny—of passing majorities. They tried to construct a system insulated from the winds of public passion.

But here we are, in a new age and a new reality with which every President will have to deal, starting with Bill Clinton. Doing so means not just yielding to instant public emotions but working to keep alive the Framers' constitutional design for a more reflective, more considered form of government.

The danger of mass participatory democracy is that it can be manipulated: shaped by ideologues and demagogues. That was the concern when Ross Perot proposed his "electronic town hall," which he said would make "the White House and Congress, like a ballet," pirouette around the stage. And the danger has been evident in these first days of the Clinton Administration.

The negative public reaction to Zoë Baird's past use of illegal aliens for child care—the telephone calls to senators—seemed genuine. Sensitized by the scandals of recent years, the public did not want an Attorney General who had violated a law.

But the protests against President Clinton's plan to end the ban on gay

*Anthony Lewis, "Not a Rose Garden," *New York Times* (February 1, 1993).

men and women in the services were different. To a considerable degree they were orchestrated by the religious right and conservative extremists.

Randall Terry of Operation Rescue, the group that tries to terrorize women out of having abortions, turned to the homosexual issue. He said, "We're avalanching [Congress] with phone calls and letters," because "sodomy is against God's law." The extreme-right talk show hosts on Thug Radio also denounced the Clinton plan.

So it is important to have some perspective on manifestations of public emotion. Randall Terry, Pat Robertson and others in the religious right opposed Bill Clinton in the election, as did the talk show hosts. They lost.

In such turbulent and dangerous conditions, it is harder than ever to be an effective President. And quite plainly Bill Clinton was insufficiently prepared for the storm. He misjudged the public temper, and he failed to pay due deference to Congressional egos.

One necessary corrective is obvious. President Clinton needs some aides with political sensitivity. He had picked one of the best, Harold Ickes, to be deputy chief of staff but held off when Mr. Ickes was attacked for having had as a legal client an unsavory labor union. Judging lawyers by their clients is a particularly poor form of guilt by association. If the President needs Mr. Ickes—and he does—he should give him the job.

But in the end what will be required in this new political world will be more of the old bully pulpit of Presidential leadership. If Bill Clinton wants to cut the deficit, if he wants to reform health care, he can overcome the opposition of vested interest only by persuading us.

QUESTIONS

1. The "marketplace of ideas" concept outlined in *Abrams* has had a significant influence on the development of legal doctrine under the First Amendment. What values does that concept advance? What assumptions about access and equality in the marketplace must be made if the vision articulated in *Abrams* is to be realized?
2. According to Professor Ginsberg, how is public opinion manipulated to drive more disruptive impulses out of the public domain? What are the long-term costs to a democratic system of channeling opinion in this manner? Is the domestication of public opinion an acceptable governmental goal in a representative democracy?
3. How does opinion polling distort the very opinion it seeks to measure? What aspects of the recent move to "call-in" polls are particularly troubling? Why?
4. Advances in technology have brought closer the prospect of "direct democracy" in the near future. Can coherent policies for governing a nation of 250 million people be properly developed by direct democratic means? Would direct democracy eliminate the need for Congressional representatives? Should the legislative branch be dismantled?

CHAPTER 10

Elections

POLITICAL PARTICIPATION

See text p. 408

Most Americans are aware that they have an obligation to participate knowingly in democratic processes, particularly that they ought to be informed about major issues of public policy and that they ought to vote intelligently in light of that knowledge. As discussed in Chapter 14, studies of citizen participation reveal that this picture of an informed and effective electorate is appallingly inaccurate: most people participate only minimally in democratic processes and even then act on limited information.

In the following article, adapted from his book The Disappearing American Voter, *political scientist Ruy Teixeira discusses the myths surrounding the problem of low voter turnout. As Teixeira points out, most elections are not decided by levels of voter participation (the key factor is the intensity of support a particular candidate can generate), nor are voters significantly more involved in public policy issues than nonvoters. The simple fact may be, as Richard Harwood, a writer for the* Washington Post *pointed out in 1990, that the level of complexity in modern politics makes it virtually impossible to be informed about many issues of public moment, and different levels of participation may contribute to the smooth functioning of the democratic system as a whole.*

Ruy A. Teixeira
"Myths About Voter Turnout"*

The magnitude of nonvoting in the United States is staggering. More than 91 million voting-age Americans did not vote in 1988. And . . . the percentage of nonvoters . . . on Election Day 1992 . . . was [not much better.] . . .

This dismal record causes concern across the political spectrum. But the alarm is accompanied by a great deal of misunderstanding—sometimes bordering on hysteria—about the causes and consequences of low turnout. Much of this misunderstanding arises from well-entrenched myths.

Myth 1: Low turnout significantly helps Republicans. While low turnout has probably been of marginal assistance to some Republican candidates, there is little evidence that it has made the difference between victory and

*Ruy A. Teixeira, "Myths About Voter Turnout," *New York Times* (October 18, 1992). Copyright © 1992 by The New York Times Company. Reprinted with permission.

defeat in many races. The key for the Republicans has been relatively high support among the middle class.

Even if all eligible nonvoters had cast ballots in the last two Presidential elections, the Democrats would have lost anyway, according to data of the University of Michigan National Election Studies. Ronald Reagan and George Bush would still have won—and by a larger margin.

This suggests that Bill Clinton's strategy of reaching out to middle-class voters, instead of focusing on raising turnout among traditional Democratic constituencies like minorities and the poor, was a wise choice.

Myth 2: Low black turnout has greatly hurt the Democrats. While black support for Democrats (generally 85 percent and above) has been important to the party, the level of black turnout has not been much of a factor, positive or negative. Democratic losses have almost always been attributable to weak support among the white middle class rather than to low black turnout.

Consider the 1988 contest between Michael Dukakis and George Bush, when 45 percent of blacks voted compared with 55 percent of non-Hispanic whites. If the percentage turnout had been the same for both groups, Mr. Dukakis would have gained about 1,442,000 votes. And if black turnout had somehow been 10 percentage points higher than turnout among whites, the Democratic gain would have amounted to about 2,884,000 votes. But Mr. Dukakis lost the election by more than seven million votes.

Myth 3: A lot of elections are decided by levels of voter turnout. This statement is conventional wisdom among pundits, but it is not true. The intensity of support for a particular candidate by different groups of voters especially large blocs—is far more important than turnout in typical elections. For Democrats, for example, it is more crucial to keep the support of the overwhelming percentage of the blacks who vote than worry about those who don't. Likewise, Republican fortunes are affected more by what percentage of white middle-class Americans support G.O.P. candidates rather than by how many people go to the polls.

For example, in the 1991 contest between David Duke and Edwin Edwards for Governor of Louisiana, record numbers of blacks—64 percent—turned out to vote. But if black turnout had been as low as 16 percent, Mr. Edwards would still have been victorious, with 96 percent of the black vote and 45 percent of the white vote.

Myth 4: Turnout is going down because the poor are dropping out of politics. Voter turnout has declined more sharply among the poor, but it has been dropping steadily among all income groups. The turnout of the lowest-income Americans declined eight percentage points between 1972 and 1988 but also fell five points among the sixth of the population with the highest income.

Myth 5: Since many people see little difference between Democrats and Republicans, turnout has declined. Surveys show that the proportion of the electorate that believes important differences exist between both parties increased from 50 percent to 59 percent between 1960 and 1988. If anything, this should have increased turnout but it didn't.

Myth 6: Because Americans have become so cynical about politics, they don't see the point in going to the polls anymore. Cynicism is increasing, but it has little or nothing to do with declining turnout. Ever-larger numbers of Americans distrust their Government and believe it is controlled by special interests and wastes their tax money. But these views do not distinguish voters from nonvoters. Statistics show that, all else being equal, someone who doesn't trust the Government is no less likely to vote than someone who trusts it.

Myth 7: Nonvoters don't think their beliefs are represented in the current political system. Looking across a range of issues—the economic role of government, defense, the environment, abortion—the positions of nonvoters and voters vary only modestly. Nonvoters are slightly more liberal than voters in backing an active economic role for government and slightly more conservative on defense and social issues. But these differences are not very large and, in some cases, barely exist at all. So nonvoting cannot be attributed to nonvoters' radical beliefs.

Myth 8: Simplifying registration would be a big help to the Democrats. The political leanings of nonvoters and voters do not differ enough for the addition of even millions of formerly unregistered people to make much of a partisan impact. In fact, analysis of data reveals that an electorate expanded through registration reform would probably result in only 0.2 percent more voters with Democratic sympathies. This is hardly enough to justify the popping of champagne corks at Democratic headquarters or flying the flag at half-staff at Republican headquarters.

Myth 9: We cannot do anything to increase voter turnout, given the sorry state of American politics. In fact, a citizen's decision not to vote is very lightly held and relatively easy to change. Making it easier to register would almost certainly result in a higher turnout. Studies of registration reform efforts bear this out. My estimate is an increase of about eight percentage points, which translates into 15 million new voters. This could be accomplished through a package of reforms that included either universal motor-voter enrollment or Election Day registration.

It may even be possible to increase turnout by improving people's motivator Statistical studies, including my own, suggest that even cursory knowledge of candidates or issues, or slight attention to a campaign—perhaps reading a newspaper article or two—may be enough to turn a nonvoter into a voter. Mandated free television time for candidates to discuss issues, for example, could help here, as could other campaign reforms.

There is good reason to believe that more citizens would step forward to participate if campaigns were easier to get involved in, more informative and less subject to political manipulation. Even modest gains in voter involvement and understanding could increase civic participation on Election Day.

In the early 1970s the Constitution was amended to extend the right to vote to include individuals between the ages of 18 and 21. That amendment came on the heels of extensive civil unrest on the nation's college campuses over the government's involve-

ment in the Vietnam War, and its drafting of young men 18 and older to fight in that war. Much of the impetus for passing the amendment came from the belief that allowing Americans between 18 and 21 to participate in the electoral process could quell the protests and disruption that had divided the country in the late 1960s and early 1970s, as this excerpt from Senator Birch Bayh's statements in the Senate during debates over the Amendment indicates.

Congressional Record: March 9, 1971*

Senator Bayh:

Mr. President, today we begin an important—and historic—debate on Senate Joint Resolution 7, the proposed amendment to the Constitution which would lower the voting age to 18 for all elections, Federal, State, and local. I look forward to a thorough and spirited debate. I hope that the Senate—and the House—will pass this measure and send it to the States—because it is the right thing to do. I do not make such a recommendation casually. . . . I think our Founding Fathers were correct in requiring two-thirds of both Houses and three-fourths of the State legislatures to join in concurrence before a major change could be made in the bedrock constitutional law of the land.

No constitutional change should be proposed by this body until there has been thorough study and thought, both in the Congress and in the rest of the country. I firmly believe that there has been such study and thought, and that we have achieved a nationwide political consensus favoring such a change in the voting age.

[*The Senate Resolution had been unanimously approved by the Senate Judiciary Committee.*] . . . I plan to support this joint resolution because I believe that there is a solid series of arguments supporting an extension of the franchise to younger voters.

First, these younger citizens are fully mature enough to vote. There is no magic to the age of 21. The 21-year age of maturity is derived only from historical accident. In the 11th century 21 was the age at which most males were physically capable of carrying armor. But the physical ability to carry armor in the 11th century clearly has no relation to the intellectual and emotional qualification to vote in 20th century America. And even if physical maturity were the crucial determinant of the right to vote, 18-year olds would deserve that right: Dr. Margaret Mead and others have shown that the age of physical maturity of American youth has dropped more than 3 years since the 18th century. . . .

The simple fact is that our younger citizens today are mentally and emotionally capable of full participation in our democratic form of Government. Today more than half of the 18- to 21-year-olds are receiving some type of higher education. Today nearly 80 percent of these young people are high school graduates. It is interesting to compare these recent statistics with

**Congressional Record,* 82nd Congress, March 9, 1971, Senate Joint Resolution 7.

some from 1920, when less than 10 percent went on to college and less than 20 percent of our youngsters actually graduated from high school.

Second, our 18-year-old citizens have earned the right to vote because they bear all or most of an adult citizen's responsibilities. Of the nearly 11 million 18- to 21-year-olds today, about half are married and more than 1 million of them are responsible for raising families. Another 1,400,000 are serving their country—serving all of us—in the Armed Forces. And tens of thousands of young people have paid the supreme sacrifice in the Indochina War over the past 5 years.

. . . In 49 States, [persons at the age of 18] are treated as adults in criminal courts of law. Can we justify holding a person to be legally responsible for his or her actions in a criminal court of law when we continue to refuse to consider that same person responsible enough to take action in a polling booth? Surely a citizen's rights in our society ought to be commensurate with his responsibilities. Our younger citizens have willingly shouldered the responsibilities we have put on them, and it is morally wrong to deprive these citizens of the vote. By their actions, they clearly have earned the right to vote.

Third, these younger voters should be given the right to full participation in our political system because they will contribute a great deal to our society. Although some of the student unrest of recent years has led to deplorable violence and intolerance, much of the unrest is healthy. It reflects the interest and concern of today's youth over the important issues of our day. The deep commitment of those 18 to 21 year olds is often the idealism which Senator BARRY GOLDWATER has said:

> Is exactly what we need more of in this country . . . more citizens who are concerned enough to pose high social and moral goals for the nation.

As Prof. Paul Freund of the Harvard Law School recently wrote:

> I believe that the student movement around the world is nothing less than the herald of an intellectual and moral revolution, which can portend anew enlightenment and a wider fraternity, or if repulsed and repressed can lead to a new cynicism and even deeper cleavages. The student generation, disillusioned with absolutist slogans and utopian dogmas, has long since marked the end of ideology; wars of competing isms are as intolerable to them as wars of religion became centuries ago. Youth turned to pragmatism, to the setting of specific manageable tasks and getting them done. But that has proved altogether too uninspiring, and youth has been restless for a new vision, a new set of ideals to supplant the discarded ideologies.

We must channel these energies into our political system and give young people the real opportunity to influence our society in a peaceful and constructive manner. The President's Commission on the Causes and Prevention of Violence explored the relationships between campus unrest and the ability of our younger citizens to take a constructive part in the political process:

> The nation cannot afford to ignore lawlessness . . . It is no less permissible for our nation to ignore the legitimate needs and desires of the young . . .
>
> . . . We have seen the dedication and conviction they brought to the Civil Rights movement and the skill and enthusiasm they have infused into the political process, even though they lack the vote.

The anachronistic voting-age limitation tends to alienate them from systematic political processes and to drive them into a search for an alternative, sometimes violent, means to express their frustrations over the gap between the nation's ideals and actions. Lowering the voting age will provide them with a direct, constructive and democratic channel for making their views felt and for giving them a responsible stake in the future of the nation.

I believe that the time has come to extend the vote to 18-year-olds in all elections; because they are mature enough in every way to exercise the franchise; because they have earned the right to vote by bearing the responsibilities of citizenship; and because our society has so much to gain by bringing the force of their idealism and concern and energy into the constructive mechanism of elective government.

Debating the Issues: Opposing Views

DO ELECTIONS AND VOTING MATTER?

See text pp. 410–11

As the text notes, there is genuine concern about whether voting is simply a palliative in the American representative system, rather than a means for voters to affect policy. Before every major election, Americans are exhorted to act responsibly and vote, and yet the structure of the political system may impede real change from being realized.

The following two articles ask whether voters had a significant effect on the 1992 elections. Robin Toner, writing for the New York Times *on election eve, claims that the 1992 presidential election process was different from those that preceded it, as voters imposed "discipline" on the candidates. According to Toner, voters succeeded in getting candidates to focus on issues like the economy, rather than peripheral concerns or character-issues. Both the Republican and Democratic parties had to revamp their images, especially in light of the third party challenge mounted with relative success by Ross Perot. According to Toner, "It is a rough, new and brutally competitive world out there, and the voters seem intent on keeping it that way."*

With a few days to reflect on the election results, Midge Decter, political observer and author of Liberal Parents, Radical Children, *disagrees. While the 1992 election generated excitement and higher voter turnout than in previous years, the results were ambiguous. Although voters were concerned about the economy and forced the candidates to focus their campaigning on the issues, the vote provided only a vague agreement for change, yet offered no clear mandate about the best means to achieve this end.*

Robin Toner
"Year of Political Changes: Voters Impose Discipline on the Candidates as Perot Finds a New Way of Campaigning"*

There was a common complaint after the 1988 election, a sense that for all the maneuvering, all the nastiness, all the millions of dollars and hours of television time, surprisingly little actually happened. The campaigns rarely dealt with the big issues of the day and never carried the country very far beyond the politics of the 1980s.

This is not a complaint likely to be heard about the election of 1992. From the New Hampshire primary on, the voters provided a merciless reality check on the candidates; those who strayed from the economy for very long were quickly punished.

The parties themselves were forced to adjust to a political world remade by the collapse of Communism and the demanding new focus on domestic needs. And the process of campaigning itself was transformed, turning talk shows into primaries, allowing a Ross Perot to burst full blown on the scene while the political professionals were off analyzing caucus returns.

This was a big, sweeping, utterly serious campaign that left little in its path unchanged. It certainly changed the Democrats, who seemed rudderless and destined to lose their fourth consecutive Presidential election just 16 months ago.

Whether or not Gov. Bill Clinton wins today, his campaign represents what his party has been struggling toward for years: a more mainstream image, a reconnection with the middle class through economic issues, an attempt to lay to rest the perception that the Democrats spoke only for a collection of constituent groups, from labor to minorities.

"Clinton has gotten across the point that we are a party of growth and not redistribution," argued Representative Richard A. Gephardt, the House Majority Leader. Representative Barney Frank, the Massachusetts Democrat, added: "Bill Clinton understood the need to focus on the electorate as a whole and not our own ideological core. And he was not afraid to say to the most ideologically left of our party, I'm sorry, but you cannot have a veto over everything I say because then I will lose."

Of course, for this redefinition of the Democrats to stick, Mr. Clinton not only has to win, he has to govern the way he so often campaigned, as a "different Democrat" willing to say no and buck the orthodoxy of his party's past. This, many analysts agree, would be much harder, particularly since he would face enormous expectations from all the core Democratic constituencies that have been out of power for so long.

*Robin Toner, "Year of Political Changes: Voters Impose Discipline on the Candidates as Perot Finds a New Way of Campaigning," *New York Times* (November 3, 1992).

This was a transforming year, as well, for the Republicans, who once seemed headed for another businesslike re-election campaign complemented by heroic pictures from the war in the Persian Gulf. Instead, they were torn by the kind of divisions more typical of the Democrats.

Whether or not President Bush wins today, his party faces the formidable task of resolving the tensions between the religious right and the centrist Republicans that erupted with a vengeance this year. The cadre of Republicans who hope to follow in Mr. Bush's footsteps will have to redefine their party for an era that seems to demand a more activist Federal Government, and that seems increasingly in conflict with the party's position on such social issues as abortion.

One image seemed to capture the Republicans' stunning turnabout in this election year: Brent Scowcroft, who helped devise the foreign policy that was expected to be Bush's ticket to a second term, watching sadly from a railroad siding in a small North Carolina town while his boss struggled to defend his record on the economy and warn a group of townspeople that Mr. Clinton would do much worse.

"There's a million little groups planning to meet after the election to soul-search," said one Republican strategist close to the Administration. "And I think there needs to be one. We need fresh thinking on a variety of issues."

Few pundits (or political reporters) predicted this upheaval back in 1991, but the voters seemed to have a general shake-up in mind from the moment they entered the picture in the primaries. Former Senator Paul E. Tsongas tapped into it, and so did former Gov. Edmund G. Brown Jr.; both men gave Mr. Clinton a fight for the right to be the agent of change.

Patrick J. Buchanan's embarrassing challenge to Mr. Bush was egged on by the voters of New Hampshire, who set the tone for this campaign: they wanted to hear about the economy, and they wanted to hear it in detail. They felt that somehow the nation was unequipped for the new economic competition after the cold war, and they were very, very angry at Washington.

But it was Ross Perot who pushed the envelope.

Parallel Political Universe

Mr. Perot helped chart the existence of a parallel universe in political campaigns: Larry King, Phil Donahue, infomercials, morning talk. Other politicians had discovered those forums before, but none used them as Mr. Perot did, as an alternative to the normal round of primaries, political meetings, conventions.

Political scientists predicted that he would fade, as independent and third-party candidates usually do. His support did show signs of flagging in recent days after his remarkable accusations on the CBS News program "60 Minutes" about Republican dirty tricks. And Nelson Polsby, a political scientist at the University of California at Berkeley, argues that Mr. Perot's legacy will be far less significant than that of George Wallace and his 1968 campaign.

But Mr. Perot exposed the limits and the vulnerabilities of conventional politicians in an angry time, when the parties often seemed to be racing to keep up with the voters, when partisanship itself often seemed an outdated concept. And Kevin Phillips, the conservative analyst, said today: "I can't imagine that Ross Perot is just going to go away. And he could be a very big force in some of these states."

If the traditional parties learned anything this year, they learned not to put too much faith in predictions that the status quo would soon reassert itself. It is a rough, new and brutally competitive world out there, and the voters seem intent on keeping it that way.

Midge Decter
"Year of Living Dangerously"*

From what one heard, it was the same everywhere: the polling places were mobbed all day; no one had ever seen the like.

We had been told that an unprecedented number of new voters were being registered, but that had somehow not produced the inference that one might have to stand in line for an hour or more to reach the voting machine. The question was, *Cui bono?* For whose sake were all these people braving the considerable noise, discomfort, and disorder in places like school gymnasiums, both architecturally and acoustically uncongenial to the day's purposes?

In New York, and clearly in many other places as well, there seemed in one sense to be no mystery about the answer. That Clinton was going to carry the state handily had long been taken for granted. Yet as one waited one's turn the main impression was not of being in the presence of any serious partisan determination, let alone enthusiasm. There was in fact a good deal of enthusiasm—high cheer might be a better term—but Clinton in no way seemed to be its target. On the contrary. What all these people seemed to be simultaneously cheered, surprised, and amused by was themselves taking part in this mighty turnout.

In New York City you can always tell when crowds of strangers are sharing a moment of civic outrage or civic happiness: they begin to strike up easy conversations with one another—otherwise an uncommon experience. And what could be heard over the din in many a polling place were all sorts of stranger-to-stranger exchanges about this being democracy in action, all right, quite often followed by the observation that it was a great pity all this action had no better objects than this year's candidates for the Presidency.

*Midge Decter, "Year of Living Dangerously," *National Review* (November 30, 1992).

By the morning after the election, the sentiments expressed in New York's polling places proved (as New Yorkers' sentiments so often do, to the chagrin of many) to be nationwide. Clinton had way more than enough electoral votes, but he nevertheless had received no ringing popular mandate. Democracy in action indeed. Given the grossness of elections as a tool for measuring popular feeling, it is astonishing how close the voters can sometimes come to a nice calibration of their political sentiments.

What, then—to borrow a locution once the favorite of pundits past—were they trying to tell us? The universal shibboleth of the 1992 campaign was "change.' Every candidate spoke passionately of the need for it and claimed to be its true agent—even, comically enough, George Bush. Moreover, many of the voters questioned during post-election television interviews said either that they believed it was time for, or in some cases that they were positively yearing for, a change. "*A* change," of course, was an easy term to grasp; it simply, and circularly, meant a vote against George Bush. But the word "change," as it slipped from the tongues of all three contenders and subsequently from those of a few inarticulate voters, remained little more than a pious incantation.

In a not unrelated way the exit polls found that the overriding issue for the overwhelming majority of Clinton voters was the economy—and it goes without saying that this would have been true for the 19 percent who went for Perot as well. But again, to know that is to know less than many people might think. Clearly the economy has been making so slow a recovery from recession that a lot of people are afraid the happy old days may not come again. Then there are those who have lost their jobs, many of them probably permanently. And the President fell down badly when it came to the task of explaining to the unemployed in the North that some of the jobs Bill Clinton had "created" in Arkansas were jobs that had been moved south by employers looking for cheaper, and possibly more grateful and cooperative, labor. There's no question, in any case: left, right, and center, the President had failed to assure a lot of people that better economic days were coming, and they were pleased to punish him for it. On the other hand a not insignificant sampling of Wall Streeters, frankly professing themselves to be unsure about whether or not Clinton would do great economic harm, nevertheless were insouciant about his election; many, we may never know *how* many, voted for him. If the economy were the only issue, why would they be so pleased to be taking what they themselves freely admit is a possibly grave risk?

And as for the middle-class independents—those people only recently known as Reagan Democrats and now so important an element in the Clinton vote—where is the evidence of their faith that Bill Clinton could and would bring them better times? True, he promised to spend some money on jobs, but aren't these the very people who gravitated to Reagan in the first place out of a bitter and cynical understanding of just where in the end government spending always goes?

And above all, where in the atmosphere of those polling places were the fear, anger, frustration, outrage we had been hearing so much about? "I can't lose," said a friend while waiting for election returns. "If Clinton beats Bush, I will be pleased, and if Bush beats Clinton, I won't really mind." She was almost surely speaking for a multitude. And, she added, "Just think of the chagrin of those once taken-for-granted Democratic front-runners—Bill Bradley, Sam Nunn, and most especially Mario Cuomo—who stayed out because at the beginning Bush had such high approval ratings. How they must be gnashing their teeth! Thinking about them makes me happy, too."

Peggy Noonan came close in a *New York Times* op-ed piece when she said that, in choosing Clinton over Bush, the voters were opting for nervousness over gloom. But nervousness doesn't seem exactly right, either; the mood, while no doubt jittery, was sunnier than that. In electing Clinton the voters were—somewhat timidly, to be sure—deliberately choosing the unknown. For the first time since, let us roughly say, 1950, Americans were going to the polls with no cloud of national danger hanging over their heads. They may have been on one side of the issue or another. They may even, as the experts so tiresomely keep saying, have been "voting their pocketbooks"—though that is a just plain dumb way to talk about the subtle messages American voters have managed to convey over the years. But the cold war had been there, cautioning, sometimes threatening, always declaring limits. Now the voters were liberated. Like those Wall Streeters, people wanted knowingly to take a risk, to experience the feeling that life itself was not at stake. To be unknown and unexpected, as were both Bill Clinton and Ross Perot, was a distinct advantage—and together they took 62 percent of the vote.

And so things are for no good reason going to be very cheerful for a longer time than is normally given to presidential honeymoons. Here will finally be the celebration of the new world configuration—never call it order. And for the Bush voters, there will be the bitter amusement of knowing that, as Senator Moynihan pointed out, it's the Democrats' deficit now.

REALIGNMENT

See text p. 437

In light of the election of a Democratic administration in 1992, it is still much too early to determine whether any permanent shifts in the American electorate have occurred. No side has conceded defeat: within days of the election, conservative commentators claimed that the election represented a defeat of George Bush and his economic policies, not the end of the conservative revolution begun by Ronald Reagan. In stark contrast, in the following article from the social democratic journal, Dissent, *Harold Meyerson argues that the Clinton election signals a move away from narrowly focused traditional liberal concerns to much broader social and economic reforms that constitute a wholehearted repudiation of conservative doctrines. It will not be until after the 1996 elections that the issue of a new realignment will be resolved.*

Harold Meyerson
"The Election: Impending Realignment"*

Bill Clinton had planned some remarks for the evening of Neil Kinnock's anticipated victory in the British elections this spring—doubtless something about the global rejection of Thatcherism and Reaganism. He never delivered that speech, of course, but his private, unplanned remarks, as reported by Martin Walker, Washington bureau chief for the *Guardian,* were revealing enough. According to Walker, what Clinton said was, "I guess the Brighton program [Kinnock's attempt to recenter Labour] didn't go as far as Bad Godesberg [the German Social Democrats' very successful 1959 effort to redefine themselves]."

I cite the comment not only because a social democratic quarterly should take some notice when a presidential front-runner actually knows something about European social democracy, but also because Clinton is a bit of a Bad Godesberg Democrat himself. Like the Germans of 1959, he has repositioned his party, though not in the manner commonly surmised. The late Joseph Rauh, long-time doyen of the ADA (Americans for Democratic Action), was voicing the prevailing liberal view when he told the *New York Times* of his disappointment that "the spectrum of my party has moved so far to the right." But the Clintonization of the Democrats is anything but a simple rightward lurch. For the Democrats' rightward drift dates not from this summer but from the mid-seventies. To be sure, Bill Clinton is not a Ted Kennedy liberal or Jesse Jackson lefty—but Kennedy and Jackson never won the party's nomination. The candidates who did—Jimmy Carter, Walter Mondale and Michael Dukakis—articulated a kind of collective retreat from New Deal and Great Society liberalism. True, all three were liberal on noneconomic issues. But Carter was locked by inflation into policies of fiscal conservatism, Dukakis eschewed post-Reagan populism for the elusive appeal of Brookline technocracy, and although Mondale, by virtue of his closeness to unions, civil rights groups and other Democratic organizations, may have seemed the last living New Dealer, his battle cry—deficit reduction through higher taxes—was so conservative and glum that both Bob Dole and Paul Tsongas could happily have run on it.

The Stealth Social Democrat?

The Democrats were already a neo-liberal party long before Bill Clinton came along—and it's neo-liberal politics that Clinton has overturned. In part, that has meant repudiating some of the party's social liberalism, such as opposition to the death penalty. Even more, it's meant repudiating the party's image of social liberalism, which led to Clinton's convention-time

*Harold Meyerson, "The Election: Impending Realignment," *Dissent* (Fall, 1992). Reprinted with permission.

bashing of Jesse Jackson and Jerry Brown. (Since Clinton is the first child of the sixties to be a presidential nominee, the actual substance of his cultural politics is a good deal more complex. It's at his direction, for instance, that the Democrats have quietly but unmistakably embraced gay and lesbian rights.) But Clinton's turn away from eighties Democratic positions has also meant moving leftward on economic policy, toward the kind of universal programs that the Democrats have not espoused in decades: vastly expanded college loans, apprenticeships for non-college-bound high school graduates, a major public works program and, however fuzzy its contours, national health insurance. Clinton's affinity for Bad Godesberg, then, isn't confined to moving the Democrats away from the marginal politics of cultural liberalism and narrowly targeted (i.e., race-based) economic remedies. More than virtually any leading figure in American politics—certainly more than any other electable presidential contender—Clinton looks to the socio-economic arrangements of continental capitalism for ways to fix the U.S. economy. The Clinton stump speech is a calculated affront to American insularity—a litany of the nations we've fallen behind in wages and living standards, with side trips into comparative economic policy (lately, "We're the only nation that would throw defense workers onto the streets without any industrial policy to reemploy them"). For Clinton, the laissez-faire economics of Anglo-American capitalism has led chiefly to speculation and industrial flight. Consistently, he commends instead the policies of those nations whose economies he calls "better organized"—which means, characterized by industrial policy, an emphasis on work force skills, and a priority on manufacturing. In a word, Germany.

Which is to say, to identify Clinton simply by linking him to the Democratic Leadership Council—the corporate-funded collection of neos, con and lib, that he helped found—fails to adequately describe his politics. Yes, Clinton's embraced the DLC's attack on welfare, some of its distance from unions, and the appearance of its social conservatism. But anyone attempting to define Clinton more fully would do well to look at *Why Americans Hate Politics,* the 1991 book by *Washington Post* reporter E.J. Dionne, Jr., whose strategic conclusions both mirror and anticipate Clinton's own. (At various points along the campaign trail, Clinton has volunteered that he agreed with everything in Dionne's book.) Like Clinton (and like University of Chicago sociologist William Julius Wilson, whose defense of universal over race-based remedial programs has also had a profound effect on Clinton's thinking), Dionne has wrongly been placed in the "neo" column for urging the Democrats to refrain from refighting the cultural civil wars of the sixties with the Republicans (a fight the Democrats can't win). Less noticed has been Dionne's critique of Carter (who failed in his estimation because he didn't deliver on national health insurance and other broad-based social programs) and his recommendation of such programs to today's party.

Clinton and Dionne are stealth social democrats, applauded or reviled for backing off certain cultural/political positions, while the larger achievement to which they have contributed—ratcheting American liberalism into a new-age version of Roosevelt-Truman economics—has gone substantially unnoticed. More problematically, both espouse a social democracy without social democrats. Neither pays much heed to the decline of unions. Clinton's call for a "better organized" economy omits any reference to increasing unionization; his stump speech mantra on building "high-wage, high-skill jobs" does not acknowledge the role that unions have played in creating them in the nations to which he alludes. Who, if not unions, does Clinton think will provide the core support for industrial policy, worker retraining, the creation of upscale durable-goods manufacturing?

The contrast in these matters between Clinton's position and those of Jesse Jackson and Jerry Brown could not be greater. In their speeches to the Democratic convention, both Jackson and Brown spoke of the symbiotic role that the movements of the thirties and sixties had had with the New Deal and the Great Society; both spoke for bolstering the movements of the nineties. Though himself an activist in the antiwar movement of Vietnam days, Clinton never speaks of bolstering movements. It may be that a career spent in Arkansas inters all such thoughts; that the repositioning of the Democratic party requires silencing them; that the current weakness of labor discourages them; or that Clinton's fatal attraction to pleasing everyone precludes them. Whatever the reason, the politics that emerge seems oddly incomplete: social democracy without a base.

And yet, Clinton's summertime rise in the polls coincided with his moving steadily if discreetly leftward on economics. His economic program, released in June, favored increasing public sector investment over retiring the deficit. (One of the most heartening things about Clinton's campaign is that the deficit-reduction crew at the Brookings Institute, which did so much to paralyze Jimmy Carter, is clearly not part of his circle.) His early reaction to the Free Trade Agreement with Mexico (I write before his complete response has been delivered) suggests he's siding with those of his advisers (in particular, Ira Magaziner and Derek Shearer) who argue against an unmitigated version of free trade, maintaining that America needs not only a better trained work force but a globalization of the mixed economy.

But all of Clinton's repositioning, this entire rhumba of left and right, would be of limited use to the Democrats were it not for the long-term stagnation of the economy. At the height of sixties prosperity, the Democrats conceived a policy of taxing broadly to spend narrowly, remedially, on the Other America. Problem was, the boom years shuddered to a halt in 1973, and it took the Democrats nearly two decades to realize that the nation had regressed sharply toward a pre-New Deal distribution of wealth that enabled them to return to policies they had espoused before the postwar boom: taxing narrowly (that is, the rich) to spend broadly. For the first time since 1948, America is having an election in which prosperity is not a given, and it is that fact, and Clinton's understanding of it, that creates the possibility of realignment this November.

The Revolt of the De-Aligned

Ironically, the key to Clinton's success has been the rise, fall and mass migration of the Perot campaign into his column. Clinton, the most consummate of pols, the champion of organization, has been aided by a war against politics waged by the unorganized. The Perot campaign was strongest precisely in those sectors of American life least likely to have an organized political life. Perot support was highest in the Sunbelt, the suburbs, the West, and among independents. His campaign went boldly where no organization had gone before.

The late Lee Atwater once told political writer Thomas Edsall that the conservative ascendancy which began in 1968 had depended on the invention of a new elite. Traditional populism was arrayed against the rich, Atwater said, but the target of contemporary right-wing populist resentment was a new elite of intrusive government bureaucrats (George Wallace's pointy-heads) and the shiftless clientele it created and served (Ronald Reagan's welfare queens). But Perot's legions were arrayed against a third elite: the political class. In part, the Perot phenomenon followed reasonably enough from the under-organization of America and the corresponding professionalization of its politics. With mass mobilization largely a thing of the past, American politics has transformed itself into a system that works without popular participation. Advocacy between campaigns has been reduced to using funds raised through direct mail to pay the salaries of professional lobbyists. Here in California, elections have become so capital-intensive that some campaigns have trouble finding work for the stray volunteer who arrives on the doorstep. Like Sartre's hell, politics is other people.

The brilliance of the Perot campaign was that it needed people. After deciding at a late date to run outside the two-party system, Perot needed bodies beyond even his capacity to hire them. He needed volunteers. At its best, the Perot campaign exploited a justifiable rage at the professionalization of politics. Most of the time, though, it was fueled by a rage at politics itself. It was a rage that Perot himself stoked. His models of governance were resolutely anti-political. His administration would be staffed by "the best people"; he would seek "consensus" rather than a mere factional majority; he promised a direct line between the leader and the led that would bypass such traditional impediments as parties, interest groups, organizations. Warring on politics rather than the imbalance of power, Perot's people were heroic one moment, supine the next. Many of them rightly resisted the military martinets whom Perot set out to coordinate their efforts. But there were virtually no objections when Perot went to the mountaintop alone to formulate his platform without input from his volunteers. Input would have required organization and—well, politics.

Odd that this anti-political jihad should have aided Clinton, but that's exactly what it ended up doing. At a time when Clinton had little credibility, Perot crystallized the nation's disgust with George Bush. At a time when Clinton was extremely vulnerable to attack, it was Perot who drew Bush's fire—dragging down both target and assailant. (One Clinton aide told *Los*

Angeles Times reporter Ron Brownstein that the campaign feared "being strangled in its cradle" by Bush campaign attacks during the grim period following the New York primary. Only, the attacks were launched at Perot.) And by the time he folded his tent and noisily stole away, Perot had peeled millions of voters away from Bush. His campaign may well be seen in hindsight as a kind of halfway house for millions of Reagan Democrats, independents, even some Republicans, the midpoint of a journey into (for many, back into) Democratic ranks.

If the Democrats can deliver.

The End of the Conservative Era

I write in the summer of the Democrats' unaccustomed content—on the eve of the Republican convention, with Clinton's post-Democratic convention lead essentially undiminished, and with Congressional Democrats having opened a sizable lead over their Republican counterparts in the polls of the past two weeks. By now, it's clear that most of the conventional wisdom about 1992 no longer obtains: that the Gulf War made Bush unchallengeable, that the recovery was in the mail, that the Democrats would be incapable of getting their act together.

We may well be facing an election that will put an end to the conservative era that began in 1968. To be sure, Bush is likely to wage a campaign of sleaze and international adventurism that may take its toll on Clinton; and yes, reapportionment has given the Republicans a leg up in legislative races. But the factors that favor the Democrats are more profound. Foremost among them is the mass recognition of America's long-term economic decline. Other factors include:

- A maldistribution of wealth that has so diminished purchasing power and so increased debt for the majority of Americans that the recovery is forever delayed.
- The intellectual exhaustion not merely of the Bush administration but of conservatism generally. It's worth remembering that there never has been a Bush agenda—that just a few short weeks into office, Chief of Staff John Sununu was asking Republican legislators what they thought the administration's agenda should be. But the relative ascendancy of Jack Kemp within Republican ranks should not be mistaken for a sign of vitality. The Kemp response to the crisis of urban America, after all, amounts to misapplied Thatcherism—encouraging the very poor to take their housing projects private—or to the beggar-thy-neighbor game of enterprise zones, which Peter Dreier has characterized as robbing St. Petersburg to pay St. Paul. As I write, the party is about to go through yet one more round of the deficit-reducers against the tax-cutters. But neither camp's program will do anything to promote the necessary investments or sufficiently bolster purchasing power. By contrast, a Louis Harris poll in the August 24 issue of *Business Week* shows that by a 51 to 47 percent margin,

401 executives drawn from *Business Week*'s list of the 1,000 largest U.S. corporations believe that "After twelve years of laissez-faire economic policies, the government needs to take a more active role in stimulating jobs and investment." When the corporate elite is willing to relegate Republican economics to the realm of pure theology, the party has a relevance problem.

- The race card—after the Willie Horton saga and this year's L.A. riots—is much harder to play. All that remains of GOP divide-and-conquer politics is gay-baiting.
- The abortion issue, once a wedge to split the Democrats, now splits the Republicans deeper.
- The end of the cold war—and communism—has radically transformed American politics. It removes the one element that united all the little tents—moralists, libertarians, Brahmins, Yahoos—under one big tent.

It has also killed Republican Keynesianism. No longer can the Republicans pump up the economy through military spending, as they have for the past quarter century, particularly in their Sunbelt electoral base. The collapse of aerospace is behind such stunning developments as Clinton's lead in Orange County. It also enables the Democrats to talk about economic conversion, planning, industrial policy. Clinton and the Democrats are running hard on this issue—here in California, building the majority of his events around these themes. There are also a number of California Congressional districts designed for Republicans where Democrats are campaigning on these themes as well—and may win. It's a stunning reversal. As recently as last year, most California Democratic leaders scorned industrial policy as something for Michigan, for a fossil economy. Now, with the cold war and communism both interred, it's no longer creeping socialism to plan new industries. It's just keeping up with the Germans and the Japanese.

Finally, the end of the cold war means the end of the national project of the past forty-five years. Bush is the last of a line of presidents, going back to Truman, elected to steer America's course against Soviet communism. But with the cold war over and the nation in decline, a new national project now faces us: the reconstruction of the American economy. There's no evidence that even a significant minority of the American public thinks George Bush is up to the task. There's abundant evidence to the contrary.

Somewhere in between politics and mass psychology, there's an intuitive popular understanding, I think, that the leaders of the last war are probably not suited to be the leaders of the next. Churchill ran up against this when he was voted out of power one month after the Nazis' defeat. And I've long thought that one element of Lincoln's and Roosevelt's greatness is that both had the good fortune to die with their wars.

That's why the key line in the Democratic convention was Mario Cuomo's, when he turned from recalling the ceremonies for troops returning from the Persian Gulf to his vivid depiction of an imagined victory parade in America's next war—the war for prosperity and social solidarity.

"Step aside, Mr. Bush," Cuomo concluded. "You've had your parade!" The line dramatized the real power of the generational challenge that the Clinton-Gore ticket poses. It's not that it's the baby boomers' turn: generations don't necessarily get turns. It's that a new national project is now upon us, and that Bush is defined and limited, as Clinton and Gore are not, by his stewardship (such as it's been) of the old.

QUESTIONS

1. Should Americans be concerned about low voter turnout? In the 1992 presidential election voter turnout increased, and was attributed to anger on the part of the electorate. Does low voter turnout indicate a failure of democratic citizenship, or should it be taken as simply an indication that voters are satisfied with the status quo?
2. Advocates for the poor, whose voter participation is the lowest among the electorate, often suggest means of increasing voter participation by making registration easier. Given the ways in which the voting age was lowered during the Vietnam War in an effort to mollify public dissatisfaction, could it be argued that the poor should not seek greater access to the vote, but should be urged to register their discontent in other ways?
3. A number of the readings in this section have indicated that the primary concern of voters in the 1992 presidential election were concerned about the state of the economy, rather than more broadly reaching ideological concerns. Is the election of a new administration likely to initiate significant changes in American domestic policy? Why or why not?
4. The election of Ronald Reagan in 1980 was widely heralded as marking a shift to conservative values among the American electorate. What does the election of President Clinton indicate about the mood of the electorate? Has the Democratic Party shifted to the right, or are there profoundly different values embedded in the new administration's philosophy?

CHAPTER 11

Political Parties

WHAT ARE POLITICAL PARTIES?

See text p. 461

Political parties in America, as the text points out, have always been weaker than their counterparts in other political systems. Moreover, the parties that do exist do not take strikingly different positions on most issues, although changes in the composition of the Republican party in recent years have been interesting to watch on this account.

The absence of political parties divided along strong philosophical lines caught the attention of Alexis de Tocqueville, a young French citizen and political thinker whose observations about democracy and the American political system in the 1820s and 1830s have proved to be uncannily shrewd. In the essay that follows, de Tocqueville offered his opinion about the nature of the American party system. According to de Toqueville, the party system of the 1820s—which was strong in comparison to the contemporary party system—did not bring to the fore great issues of principle like those that had been the subject of debates between the Republicans and the Federalists only decades earlier. To de Tocqueville's eyes, American parties dallied on small issues; they took their direction not from principles, but from material interests. Parties, according to de Tocqueville, are not formed to contest the basic foundations of government, although "aristocratic or democratic passions can easily be found at the bottom of all parties . . . though they may slip out of sight there. . . ." Parties, instead, provide the means for advancing one's own interests. "[A]ll the skill of politicians consists in forming parties; . . . a politician first tries to see what his own interest is and who have analogous interests which can be grouped around his own. . . ."

Alexis de Tocqueville
"Parties in the United States"*

. . . When there are differences between the citizens concerning matters of equal importance to all parts of the country, such for instance as the general principles of government, then what I really call parties take shape.

Parties are an evil inherent in free governments, but they do not always have the same character and the same instincts.

There are times when nations are tormented by such great ills that the

*Alexis de Tocqueville, "Parties in the United States," from *Democracy in America,* ed. J. P. Mayer and Max Lerner, tr. G. Lawrence.

idea of a total change in their political constitution comes into their minds. There are other times when the disease is deeper still and the whole social fabric is compromised. That is the time of great revolutions and of great parties.

Between these centuries of disorder and of misery there are others in which societies rest and the human race seems to take breath. That is in truth only apparently so: time does not halt its progress for peoples any more than for men. . . .

[T]here are times when the changes taking place in the political constitution and social structure of peoples are so slow and imperceptible that men think they have reached a final state; then the human spirit believes itself firmly settled on certain fundamentals and does not seek to look beyond a fixed horizon.

That is the time for intrigues and small parties.

What I call great political parties are those more attached to principles than to consequences, to generalities rather than to particular cases, to ideas rather than to personalities. Such parties generally have nobler features, more generous passions, more real convictions, and a bolder and more open look than others. Private interest, which always plays the greatest part in political passions, is there more skillfully concealed beneath the veil of public interest; sometimes it even passes unobserved by those whom it prompts and stirs to action.

On the other hand, small parties are generally without political faith. As they are not elevated and sustained by lofty purposes, the selfishness of their character is openly displayed in all their actions. They glow with a factitious zeal; their language is violent, but their progress is timid and uncertain. The means they employ are as disreputable as the aim sought. That is why, when a time of calm succeeds a great revolution, great men seem to disappear suddenly and minds withdraw into themselves.

Great parties convulse society; small ones agitate it; the former rend and the latter corrupt it; the first may sometimes save it by overthrowing it, but the second always create unprofitable trouble.

America has had great parties; now they no longer exist. This has been a great gain in happiness but not in morality.

When the War of Independence came to an end and a new government had to be established, the nation was divided between two opinions. Those opinions were as old as the world itself and are found under different forms and with various names in all free societies. One party wanted to restrict popular power and the other to extend it indefinitely.

With the Americans the struggle between these two opinions never took on the violent character that has often marked it elsewhere. In America the two parties agreed on the most essential points. Neither of the two had, to succeed, to destroy an ancient order or to overthrow the whole of a social structure. Consequently, in neither case did the private existence of a great number of people depend on the triumph of its principles. But immaterial interests of the first importance, such as love of equality and of independence, were affected. That was enough to rouse violent passions.

The party which wished to restrict popular power sought especially to have its ideas applied in the federal Constitution, from which it gained the name of Federal.

The other, which claimed to be the exclusive lover of liberty, called itself Republican.

America is the land of democracy. Consequently, the Federalists were always in a minority, but they included almost all the great men thrown up by the War of Independence, and their moral authority was very far-reaching. Moreover, circumstances favored them. The ruin of the first Confederation made the people afraid of falling into anarchy, and the Federalists profited from this passing tendency. For ten or twelve years they directed affairs and were able to apply some but not all of their principles, for the current running in the opposite direction became daily stronger and they could not fight against it. . . .

There had always been something artificial in the means and temporary in the resources which maintained the Federalists; it was the virtues and talents of their leaders, combined with lucky circumstances, which had brought them to power. When the Republicans came in turn to power, the opposing party seemed to be engulfed by a sudden flood. A huge majority declared against it, and suddenly finding itself so small a minority, it at once fell into despair. Thenceforth the Republican, or Democratic, party has gone on from strength to strength and taken possession of the whole of society.

The Federalists, feeling themselves defeated, without resources, and isolated within the nation, divided up; some of them joined the victors; the others lowered their flag and changed their name. For many years now they have entirely ceased to exist as a party.

The period of Federalist power was, in my view, one of the luckiest circumstances attending the birth of the great American Union. The Federalists struggled against the irresistible tendency of their age and country. Whatever the virtues or defects of their theories, they had the disadvantage of being inapplicable in their entirety to the society they wished to control, so what happened under Jefferson would have come about sooner or later. But their rule at least gave the new republic time to settle down and afterwards to face without ill consequences the rapid development of the very doctrines they had opposed. Moreover, in the end many of their principles were introduced under their adversaries' slogans, and the still-extant federal Constitution is a lasting memorial to their patriotism and wisdom.

Thus today there is no sign of great political parties in the United States. There are many parties threatening the future of the Union, but none which seem to attack the actual form of government and the general course of society. The parties that threaten the Union rely not on principles but on material interests. In so vast a land these interests make the provinces into rival nations rather than parties. Thus recently we have seen the North contending for tariffs and the South taking up arms for free trade, simply because the North is industrial and the South agricultural, so that restrictions would profit the former and harm the latter.

Debating the Issues: Opposing Views

PARTY POLITICS IN AMERICA: ARE THREE PARTIES BETTER THAN TWO?

See text pp. 496–97

As the text discusses, the traditional two-party system in America has been in the process of steady decline for a number of years. The 1992 presidential election saw the surprisingly strong performance of Ross Perot as a third-party candidate.

The following two pieces take up the question of whether the two-party system should be salvaged, or whether it is time to move to a three- or more party system. The first piece, written shortly before the 1992 presidential elections by two Harvard law professors, Alan Dershowitz, a Clinton supporter, and Charles Fried, a supporter of George Bush, urges voters not to waste their votes on Ross Perot. "[T]he structure of our democracy will be diminished," they argue, if a third-party candidate makes a strong showing. The two-party system, they contend, stabilizes American politics and provides the necessary consensus for effective governance.

Theodore Lowi, a political scientist from Cornell University, disagrees. A third party is required to break the "institutional gridlock" that has beset American politics for two decades. According to Lowi, "the two-party system has long been brain dead"—unresponsive to change, unable to act even if the need for change is perceived, and increasingly corrupt. A third party would refocus politics on issues, and "the President's opportunities for bargaining for majority support [consensus building] would be more fluid and frequent."

Alan M. Dershowitz and Charles Fried
"Don't Waste Your Vote on Perot"*

One of us is a supporter of George Bush, the other a supporter of Bill Clinton. But we share a common belief in the importance of the two-party system as a vehicle of majority rule in America. We urge everyone to vote for either Bush or Clinton; don't endanger our valued traditions by casting a disruptive "protest" vote for Ross Perot.

Despite his spirited debate performance, Perot cannot win this election—and he should not. Indeed, he cannot carry a single state or win a single electoral vote. But it is possible, though unlikely, that even a few thousand votes for him in several closely contested states could change the outcome of the presidential election. In some states, President Bush may benefit if Perot siphons off votes that would otherwise have gone to Gov. Clinton. In other states, Clinton may benefit if Perot siphons off votes from President Bush. In any state that is turned around by Perot voters, the winner will necessarily have less than a majority of the votes cast.

*Alan M. Dershowitz and Charles Fried, "Don't Waste Your Vote on Perot," *Los Angeles Times* (October 8, 1992). Reprinted with permission.

Neither of us is trying to gain any tactical advantage for our candidate by urging citizens not to vote for Perot. Our purpose in writing this is to warn voters that if Perot becomes a factor in this election, regardless of which candidate is helped or harmed the structure of our democracy will be seriously diminished.

The two-party and winner-take-all majority rule system has had a stabilizing effect in American politics. To win an election in this country, a candidate must generally appeal to a majority of the voters. In other democracies with multi-party traditions and proportional representation, plurality candidates have emerged as victors with as little as 30% of the vote. In our country, candidates who might win 20% or 30%—for example, Jesse Jackson, Pat Robertson and Pat Buchanan—are regarded as "fringe" candidates.

Consensus-building is required for electoral success. This pull toward the mainstream may sometimes create a Tweedledum-and-Tweedledee appearance of similarity between the two parties and the candidates, but that merely reflects the reality that the vast majority of American voters share many basic values. Extremism of the left and right has never had much popular appeal in this nation of centrists, and that is all to the good.

Another important democratic structure that would be disserved if votes for Perot were to prove decisive is the primary system under which candidates must earn the right to be nominated for President. Perot did not run in any primaries; he simply used his enormous fortune to elicit the support of an unknown number of "volunteers" who he says "nominated" him by putting his name on the ballot in every state.

Related to this is the danger of a candidacy for our highest office by a relative unknown—two unknowns, really, considering Perot's choice of running-mate. Perot has not been tried by the fire of holding public office. He may well be a decent and honorable man, but the precedent that would be established by taking his candidacy seriously would encourage others to take short cuts to high office. And these others may have serious character flaws that would be exposed only by the scrutiny we apply to those in public life.

There have been candidates from outside the political system before, though none has used enormous personal fortune to parachute into the political process just short of the finish line. There have also been third-party candidacies before, and the Republic has survived. And it will survive if Ross Perot garners enough votes to change the outcome of next month's election. But such a result, whoever is the beneficiary, would weaken our system and endanger our future.

We urge you to choose between President Bush and Gov. Clinton, even if you regard the choice as between the lesser of two evils. If you cannot vote for the better candidate of the two, then vote against the second-best, for a vote for Perot is likely to help the candidate you least prefer. Remember, a voter discharges his or her duty as a participant in a democratic republic not by making a vindictive gesture or hoping to effect some far-fetched strategy, but by voting as if the outcome depended on his or her vote alone.

Theodore J. Lowi
"The Party Crasher"*

Whatever the outcome of this year's Presidential race, historians will undoubtedly focus on 1992 as the beginning of the end of America's two-party system. The extraordinary rise of Ross Perot and the remarkable outburst of enthusiasm for his ill-defined alternative to the established parties removed all doubt about the viability of a broad-based third party. Republicans, Democrats and independents alike have grasped the essential point that the current incumbents will not, and cannot, reform a system that drastically needs overhauling.

A third party would do more than shock the powers that be into a few reforms. Its very existence—never mind its specific policies—would break the institutional gridlock that has paralyzed Washington for most of the past 20 years. Ultimately, it would give us a more parliamentary style of government, in keeping, it seems to me, with what the Founding Fathers had in mind. Perot demonstrated the possibility. It now falls to the rest of us to make the breakthrough to a three-party system. The New Party, self-defined as "broadly Social Democratic," which has been gathering strength over the past couple of months; the John Anderson crowd from the 1980s, of which I am one; the perennial Libertarian Party—we are going to have to get together.

One of the best-kept secrets in American politics is that the two-party system has long been brain dead—kept alive by support systems like state electoral laws that protect the established parties from rivals and by Federal subsidies and so-called campaign reform. The two-party system would collapse in an instant if the tubes were pulled and the IVs were cut.

Back when the Federal Government was smaller and less important, the two parties could be umbrella parties—organizing campaigns, running elections and getting the vote out—without much regard to ideology or policy. But with the New Deal and the rise of the welfare state, the Federal Government became increasingly vulnerable to ideological battles over policy. None of this was particularly noticeable while the Government and the economy were expanding, but in the early 1970s class and ideological conflicts began to emerge more starkly.

Thus were born the familiar "wedge" issues—crime, welfare, prayer, economic regulation, social regulation, taxes, deficits and anti-Communism. No matter what position party leaders took on such issues, they were bound to alienate a substantial segment of their constituency. While the Democrats were the first to feel the cut of wedge issues, particularly concerning race, Republicans are now having their own agonies over abortion, foreign policy and budget deficits. Wedge issues immobilize party leader-

*Theodore J. Lowi, "The Party Crasher," *New York Times Magazine* (August 23, 1992).

ship, and once parties are immobilized the Government is itself immobilized.

The parties have also atrophied because both have been in power too long. In theory, a defeated party becomes vulnerable to new interests because it is both weaker and more willing to take risks. But for nearly 40 years, both parties have in effect been majority parties. Since each party has controlled a branch of Government for much of that time, neither is eager to settle major policy issues in the voting booth. A very important aspect of the corruption of leadership is the tacit contract between the two parties to avoid taking important issues to the voters and in general to avoid taking risks.

Party leaders have responded to gridlock not with renewed efforts to mobilize the electorate but with the strategy of scandal. An occasional exposure of genuine corruption is a healthy thing for a democracy, but when scandal becomes an alternative to issues, leaving the status quo basically unaltered, it is almost certain that all the lights at the crossroads are stuck on red. In fact, the use of scandal as a political strategy has been so effective that politicians have undermined themselves by demonstrating to the American people that the system itself is corrupt.

The Perot candidacy differed fundamentally from past independent Presidential candidacies, which were basically single-issue appeals. Perot tapped into a genuinely unprecedented constituency—moderates disgusted with the two major parties, regardless of the nominees. Two major polls completed in May and June found that about 60 percent of Americans favored the establishment of a new political party.

Predictably, the two-party system defenders have devoted considerable energy to shooting down any suggestion that the status quo can be improved upon. They have produced all sorts of scenarios about how a third party could throw Presidential elections into the Congress, with the House of Representatives choosing the President and the Senate choosing the Vice President—not only delaying the outcome but producing a Bush-Gore, a Clinton-Quayle or, God forbid, a Quayle-Who-Knows administration. Worse yet, if it survived to future elections, a third party would hold the balance of power and, as a result, wield an influence far out of proportion to its electoral size. It might, by its example, produce a fourth or a fifth party. And if it elected members to Congress, it might even inconvenience Congressional leaders in their allocation of committee assignments.

In fact, genuine third parties have been infrequent in the United States, but wherever they have organized they have had significant, generally positive effects. One of these is providing a halfway house for groups wedged out of the two larger parties. In 1924, the progressive movement succeeded in forming the Progressive Party in Wisconsin and other Midwestern states, which nominated Robert M. La Follette for President. In the 1930s, the Farmer-Labor Party flourished in Minnesota, where it eventually fused with an invigorated Democratic Party. In the process, both of these third parties provided the channel through which many dissident and alienated groups found their way back into politics, and their influence lingered long after the parties themselves. Similarly, wherever the Dixiecrats organized as a party, that state was later transformed to a genuinely competitive two-party state.

With three parties, no party needs to seek a majority or pretend that it is a majority. What a liberating effect this would have on party leaders and candidates, to go after constituencies composed of 35 percent rather than 51 percent of the voters. A three-party system would be driven more by issues, precisely because parties fighting for pluralities can be clearer in their positions. Third parties have often presented constructive and imaginative programs, which have then been ridiculed by leaders of the two major parties, who point out that third-party candidates can afford to be intelligent and bold since they can't possible win. In a three-party system, even the two major parties would have stronger incentives to be more clearly programmatic, because their goal is more realistic and their constituency base is simpler.

Flowing directly from this, voting would increase, as would other forms of participation. Virtually our entire political experience tells us that more organized party competition produces more participation. And we already know that genuine three-party competition draws people into politics—not merely as voters but as petition gatherers, door knockers, envelope lickers and $5 contributors—making the three-party system an antidote to the mass politics that virtually everybody complains about nowadays.

Even defenders of the two-party system criticize the reliance of candidates on television, computerized voter lists, mass mailings and phone banks—which dehumanize politics, discourage participation, replace discourse with 15-second sound bites and reduce substantive alternatives to subliminal imagery and pictorial allusion. And the inordinate expense of this mass politics has led to a reliance on corporate money, particularly through the political action committees, destroying any hope of collective party responsibility.

These practices and their consequences cannot be eliminated by new laws—even if the laws didn't violate the First Amendment. A multiparty system would not immediately wipe out capital-intensive mass politics, but it would eliminate many of the pressures and incentives that produce its extremes, because of the tendency of third parties to rely on labor-intensive politics. Third parties simply do not have access to the kind of financing that capital-intensive politics requires. But more than that, there is an enthusiasm about an emerging party that inspires people to come out from their private lives and convert their civic activity to political activity.

Finally, a genuine three-party system would parliamentarize the Presidency. Once a third party proves that it has staying power, it would increase the probability of Presidential elections being settled in the House of Representatives, immediately making Congress the primary constituency of the Presidency. Congress would not suddenly "have power over" the Presidency. It has such power already, in that the Constitution allows it complete discretion in choosing from among the top three candidates. But if Congress were the constituency of the President, the President would have to engage Congress in constant discourse. The President might under those circumstances have even more power than now, but he would have far less incentive to go over the head of Congress to build a mass following.

Even now, with two parties based loosely on mythical majorities, a President cannot depend on his party to provide a consistent Congressional majority. The whole idea of a mandate is something a victorious President claims but few members of Congress accept, even for the length of the reputed honeymoon. Thus, current reality already involves the President in bargains with members of the opposition party.

Confronting three parties in Congress, each of whose members is elected on the basis of clear policy positions, the President's opportunities for bargaining for majority support would be more fluid and frequent. In our two-party environment, issues are bargained out within the ranks of each party and often never see the light of day, particularly during the session prior to a Presidential election. A third party with a small contingent of members of Congress would insure a more open and substantive atmosphere for bargaining to take place—*after* the election.

A third party would play the role of honest broker and policy manager, because it would hold a balance of power in many important and divisive issues. There would be little fear of the tail wagging the dog, because, unlike European parties, Democrats and Republicans are not ideologically very far apart—they have simply not been cooperating with each other. The presence of a third-party delegation gives the President an alternative for bargaining, but if the new party raised its price too high, it would simply give the President a greater incentive to bargain with the other major party.

The point here is that the third party is a liberating rather than a confining force, a force for open debate on policies. Another important myth in the United States is that policy making is a matter of debate between the affirmative and the negative. But simple yea versus nay on clearly defined alternatives is a very late stage in any policy-making process. In sum, just as the rise of the two-party system fundamentally altered the constitutional structure of our Government appropriately for the 19th century, so a three-party system would alter the structure appropriately for the 21st century.

Immediately, one must add an important proviso: A genuine third party must be built from the bottom up. It must be an opportunistic party, oriented toward the winning of elections. It must nominate and campaign for its own candidates at all levels and not simply run somebody for President. And it must attract regular Democrats and Republicans by nominating some of them to run as candidates with the third-party nomination as well as that of their own party. Joint sponsorship has been practiced by the Liberal and Conservative Parties in New York for decades. Being listed on two lines on the ballot is a powerful incentive for regular Democrats and Republicans to cooperate with a new party, if not to switch over. About 40 states have laws preventing or discouraging this practice, but their provisions will probably not stand up to serious litigation.

By whatever means, the new party must have enough organizational integrity to last beyond one election. Running candidates for office in every election is the only way to secure organizational integrity. And a new, third political party is the best moderate means of breaking the institutional impasse in American politics.

Ross Perot was never the issue. The issue is a third party, and this is a call to arms, not a dispassionate academic analysis. A third party could, it just could, turn the switches at the crossroads from red to green.

THE FUNCTIONS OF THE PARTIES

See text p. 473

As the text notes, the importance of the mechanical functions of the parties—nominating candidates and getting out the vote—can be easily overlooked. Party influence builds from the ground up, as members of the Christian Coalition have discovered in their efforts to gain a foothold in the Republican Party over the last several years. Scrupulous attention to grass roots organizing has allowed the Christian Coalition to become, as the following article notes, one of the "most powerful political organization[s] in America." Christian conservatives are operating at the very heart of the political process, organizing in malls and neighborhoods to gain ascendancy in state and national politics and to dominate those political conventions.

Robert Sullivan
"Army of the Faithful"*

Usually, Christie Adkisson stays home when it snows. But on this particular snowy day, a Saturday at the beginning of January, she and her husband, Jim—founding members of the Oregon Christian Coalition—jump in the car for the 45-minute trip into Portland. They pass a few lonely cars along the way, but when they arrive at the downtown Red Lion Hotel they are more pleased than surprised to see the parking lot stuffed with the cars of Oregon's most prominent Republicans. After all, the day is being billed by all concerned as the battle for the soul of Oregon's Republican Party.

Within minutes of the vote for state party chairman—a contest between two local businessmen—Bill Witt, a conservative, and Randy Miller, who is only slightly more moderate—the political skirmishing begins, and the delegates find themselves wrangling over obscure rules and complex voting regulations. "They disenfranchised us twice before," Jim Adkisson says of the party regulars, "but now the shoe's on the other foot." Still, like every other conservative in the room, he is worried about 10 crucial swing votes. "It's going to be close," Adkisson says, pacing past urns of coffee in the back of the Red Lion conference room.

Christie Adkisson, sitting up front, is much cooler, for she figures her

*Robert Sullivan, "Army of the Faithful," *New York Times Magazine* (April 25, 1993).

side will eventually win no matter what the outcome of this contest. After years of tedious legwork, networking through the less glitzy channels of politics—in malls, at kitchen tables and in the sticky plastic chairs of local churches and schools—she and her husband and their friends have moved the mountain of political debate in Oregon miles to the right. "This has been a great education," she is saying to the people around her, "and the greatest thing I've learned is that the power of the individual precinct person is tremendous. This is where the rubber meets the road."

If there was one thing the conservative wing of the party didn't want that day, however, it was the coverage the local press was splashing on Bill Witt, their man at the top of the ticket. Witt had helped found the Oregon Christian Coalition the previous fall; yet, when he announced his candidacy for the chairmanship, he also withdrew from the coalition, calling himself "a consensus candidate." To the Oregon press, as well as to frightened Republican moderates and liberals, this sounded ominously like the "stealth tactics" employed by many Christian Coalition members running for school boards, state Republican parties and city council seats around the country last year. ("You should never mention the name Christian Coalition in Republican circles," reads an organizational manual of the Pennsylvania Christian Coalition.)

Employing another well-established tactic, Witt counterattacked by questioning the motives of his critics and the press. "I find it curious that when Christians want to get politically involved, people start asking questions," he says. "There seems to be some special scrutiny."

But this whole issue, as Christie Adkisson already knew, was almost beside the point. Randy Miller, the ostensibly moderate candidate, was anti-abortion and was even opposed by many gay activists. For once, the Christian conservatives felt, the battle was being fought on their terms; that groups like the Christian Coalition could finally force a halt to what they see as a militant homosexual agenda and the decline of traditional morality.

"People are concerned," Christie Adkisson says. "They care. They recognize the importance of their involvement now."

The Christian Coalition was spawned in 1989 from the mailing lists of Pat Robertson's failed 1988 presidential campaign. Since then, under its director, Ralph Reed, 31, it has grown into a group with 350,000 members, 750 local chapters across the United States, full-time staff in 15 states, a lobbyist in Washington and an annual budget of $8 million to $10 million.

Though it claims tax-exempt status as a religious-education organization (an exemption that is currently under review by the Internal Revenue Service), its critics argue that its political-training seminars, its fund-raising techniques and its support of causes that are apolitical only on their face (the battle against homosexuals in the military, for example) prove it to be nothing less than a miniature political party—and one with large ambitions, to boot. "We at the Christian Coalition are raising an army who cares," Pat Robertson wrote in a 1991 fund-raising letter. "We are training people to be effective—to be elected to school boards, to city councils, to state legislatures and to key positions in political parties." Later in the letter, he added, "By the end of this decade, if we work and give and organize and train, THE

CHRISTIAN COALITION WILL BE THE MOST POWERFUL POLITICAL ORGANIZATION IN AMERICA."

A lot of Republicans insist the strength of the coalition is greatly overrated. "Never has so much been conjured about something with such little political impact," says Stuart Stevens, a Republican political consultant. "I mean, I think the Vietnamese have more influence."

But as the best-run organization within what has been called the New Religious Right, the Christian Coalition is a growing force, intent on quietly winning the least visible and vied-for of America's political offices. Under the savvy direction of Reed, a former political consultant, the coalition has managed, in just four years, to prove the potency of a relatively small, highly committed group, in this case a mixture of the evangelical, fundamentalist and charismatic Christians.

For the religious right, the Christian Coalition is the second grass-roots try at modern politics. The first, with groups organized in the style of the personality-driven Moral Majority of Jerry Falwell, dissolved in the 80s when many of the leaders (but not Falwell) fell in a wave of scandals.

This time around, the emphasis is on the rank and file and political nuts and bolts, rather than on personality cults. Those who track its activities claim the Christian Coalition had about 20 members and 8 allies on the 165-member platform committee at the Republican National Committee and controlled seven state delegations at the convention—including 42 of the 46 Iowa delegates, three-fourths of the Oregon delegation, the majority of South Carolina's and Alaska's delegates and one-third of California's. According to a study by the Institute for First Amendment Studies, a group that monitors the activities of the religious right, seven winners of 1991 congressional races had direct connections to the coalition and 64 others were given 100 percent ratings in voter-education guides distributed by the group.

Taking advantage of low voter turnout and a national decline in party identification, the Christian Coalition has managed to win, by one estimate, 40 percent of the races it has targeted, all with the old-fashioned legwork that had until now been supplanted by mailing lists, computers and media consultants. Says Skipp Porteous, president of the Institute for First Amendment Studies: "People look at TV evangelists and think that's the religious right but it actually has little or nothing to do with it. It's like they have a union hall in every town."

For national Republicans, the emergence of the Christian Coalition represents the latest flare-up in the chronic struggle between the party's conservative and moderate wings. In this latest episode, moderate Republicans charge that the seeds of George Bush's defeat were sown at the Republican National Convention in Houston, with its emphasis on abortion and Pat Buchanan's right-wing rhetoric. In response, members of the Christian Coalition point out that its members provided the former President's only solid electoral support. Says one activist, "Ralph Reed said it best when he said that blaming the Christians for losing the election is like blaming the guys who were shoveling coal on the Titanic."

Nevertheless, recent surveys show that the public now associates phrases like "rigid," "right wing" and "restrictive" with the Republicans. And with Republican voter identification in decline, new groups of moderate Republicans are popping up nearly as quickly as Christian Coalition chapters, each trying to keep a particular segment of the Republican middle from running off with the Democrats or Ross Perot.

At the moment, though, it's not at all clear that any of these new groups will succeed. "The moderates who had stayed with the Republican Party stayed mostly for economic reasons, and put up with the right-wing social agenda, found that in 1992 the economic issues weren't there anymore, so they left," says William Schneider, a political analyst for the American Enterprise Institute. "Now the question is, Is there going to be a civil war in the Republican Party?"

If there is a civil war, and families like the Adkissons are the infantry, then Darrell Fuller, 27, will be one of the lieutenants. In a double-breasted suit on the floor of the Republican-controlled House, the executive director of the Oregon Christian Coalition looks like another state senator debating health care, a representative talking deals in the house. On weekends, with his wife, he looks for antiques for their apartment in Salem, or drives up to Portland to take in some classical music or, say, the latest traveling Andrew Lloyd Webber play. At the Hi-Ho Diner, wearing polo shirt and khakis, discussing modern politics and natural law, he orders ice cream on his berry pie. He stands as the opposite of the Northwest's well-publicized tendency toward grunge.

Fuller became involved in politics as a student at Willamette University in Oregon, where he worked on local campaigns; when he graduated, he began his own political consulting business. For a while he was a field coordinator with the Oregon Citizens Alliance, the group that sponsored the notorious anti-gay No Special Rights Initiative. The measure, which was defeated last November, would have amended the state constitution to label homosexuality as "abnormal, wrong, unnatural and perverse . . . to be discouraged and avoided."

Now, since the organizational merger of the alliance and the Christian Coalition (the director of the alliance, Lon Mabon, heads the Oregon Christian Coalition's board). Fuller is the coalition's full-time executive director. Because of the merger, critics say, the coalition is strong-arming its way into the political process, capitalizing on ignorance and fear, and equating equal rights for gay men and women with equal rights for pedophiles. But Fuller says he simply wants to give Christians a political voice. "If you're an African-American you have the N.A.A.C.P.," he says. "If you're a small business you have the National Federation of Independent Business and if you work for the government you have the public employees union. Practically all the groups have their lobbyists, except evangelical Christians."

Like many Christian Coalition members, Fuller talks most about what he calls "the militant homosexual agenda," the point of battle in what conservatives call the great cultural war. "I don't care if you believe in evolution or creationism." Fuller says, "Either way, homosexuality is unnatural for government to be sanctioning."

Fear that gay people are becoming the predominant political force in the country is only one concern of Fuller and his members; they also see an overall national decline. "It's a moral degeneration," Fuller says. "The existing values that founded this country aren't represented anymore. And the symptoms of this degeneration are all over the place. Forty years ago in schools the biggest problems were spitballs and bubble gum. Now, it's pregnancy and teen suicide, and we have metal detectors."

Fuller's is a world filled with the social, economic and political problems described in Pat Robertson's books—a world where the United Nations is on its way to constructing a one-world, godless government, a socialist state, crippled by political correctness, with no place in it for the traditional family. In this light, Fuller and his members see themselves as the last hope, as taking a desperate final stand to keep God as the linchpin of their country. "Everyone's talking about conservatives pushing these issues but conservatives are reacting to the issues," Fuller says.

In fact, like Fuller, most Christian Coalition members around the country became involved in politics for fear of all the more terrible things that might happen if they didn't. As Fuller sees it, it is his task to provide his people with the tools to reverse the decline—tools like political training seminars, instruction in public relations techniques, voter education guides or whatever else his expertise as a political consultant can offer. "We provide the quote unquote little people with good information," he says, "and we find that when you give good people good information, they make good decisions."

"The political party apparatus is organized in such a manner that it makes it very easy for it to be taken over by zealots because they have a cause," says Craig Berkman.

Berkman, a successful Portland entrepreneur, left his chairmanship of the Oregon Republican Party ostensibly to run for the national Republican Party chairmanship, won eventually by a Mississippian, Haley Barbour. Many people in his state, however, believe that Berkman ran for national office because conservatives had enough power in the Oregon Republican Party to prevent him from winning re-election, a charge that Berkman dismisses. Whatever his reason, Berkman, seen as a liberal city slicker by the Christian Coalition and its mostly out-of-Portland kind, is not too friendly toward his party's most conservative wing. "The scripture, as I read it, says that you should be truthful and these people try to tell untruths and disinformation," he says, "and this is the opposite of being Christian to me."

During his four-year tenure, Berkman brought the party out of bankruptcy. But, while the liberal and moderate Republicans were out fundraising, the conservatives were out winning the precinct seats. Now, like moderate Republicans elsewhere, Berkman has begun to consider ways to counterattack. He is campaigning to have the party organization changed to include its elected representatives and financial donors, so that party activists—in this case, religious conservatives—aren't the only ones with a say. He also hopes to require runoffs in state elections that include more than two candidates when no candidate has 51 percent. Unconcerned by his adversaries' charges of elitism, Berkman says simply: "Somebody has to step up and stop this."

Berkman's concerns are shared by moderate Republicans in Iowa, Kansas, Minnesota and especially Texas. There, Steven Hotze, a proponent of the death penalty for homosexuals (based on a narrow and literal reading of the Bible) is the de facto chairman of the Harris County Republican Party, the third-largest county Republican Party in the country and the home Republican Party to President Bush.

Berkman's concerns are also shared by moderate Republicans watching things like teachers' organizations in Pennsylvania fighting to introduce a state curriculum that the religious right says is anti-God; or a woman running for county sheriff in Louisville, Kent., who the local Pro-Family Coalition says is insufficiently pro-family and who, in any event, "ought to be a man." In New York City, the symbolic heart of godless liberalism, the coalition is backing scores of school-board candidates and has enlisted the Roman Catholic Archdiocese to distribute voter guides in its 213 parishes.

Using the motto "Winning Elections by Inclusion," Burt Day, a moderate Republican from Iowa, has begun Pro Party, a group of Republicans who feel the religious right is involved in politics more for the sake of their key issues (abortion, gay rights) than for the sake of the Republican Party. Having watched the coalition seize control of the Iowa central committee's seats in 1992, Day sees an unremitting political threat. "Republicans in other states say to us, 'Oh, you've got to get along with these people because you can't win elections without them,' " he says. "But they don't understand that these people are very well organized and that their 51 percent becomes 100 percent. They're in it for the long run. They're not going to go away."

Much of what people like Berkman and Day are proposing is being proposed on the national level as well. As is often the case after they lose the White House, Republicans want to make their "Big Tent" big again, which would mean a compromise on abortion. "What the party's got to do is broaden its focus," says Tommy G. Thompson, the moderate Republican Governor of Wisconsin. "People who have certain morals and ethics are welcome as they always have been, but we also have to be more tolerant. We have to take in people who vote with us only 60 percent of the time."

But such appeals, commonplace in Republican circles, go nowhere among social conservatives, for whom there is no compromising on abortion. If moderate Republicans succeed in ripping the anti-abortion plank from the platform, the conservative Christians could leave in force. And that, as moderates well know, could inflict deep wounds on election day.

"The voice of the religious right is a voice that you can't ignore," says Senator Nancy Kassebaum who, with two former legislators, Senator Warren Rudman of New Hampshire and Tom Campbell of California, has set up the Republican Majority Coalition. "It's a voice that in many ways comes from people who feel they've never been part of the political process, and they've won their precinct positions fair and square. If we want them back then we've got to go back in there and win them. I don't think that you can just stand back and wring your hands and say, 'Look what's happened!' "

In a recent Wall Street Journal article titled "The Coming 'Conservative

Century,' " Irving Kristol, editor of The Public Interest, argues that the key to the future of the Republican Party lies in appealing to the religious voter in the same way the Democrats appealed to European immigrants at the turn of the century. "The Democrats are never going to be able to welcome the religious, but if the Republicans keep them at arm's length instead of embracing them, and shaping their political thinking, a third party and a restructuring of American politics are certain," he warns. The problem is, embracing the religious right—and its anti-abortion position—also risks creating a third party, or perhaps a new Democratic majority.

Aware of all this, Craig Berkman has lately made frequent overtures to his party's right wing. Last year, he made a pilgrimage to Ralph Reed's office, where they both promised to work together; and on his final day in office, Berkman called for reconciliation for the sake of winning. For the moment, power in the Oregon Republican Party is in the hands of the conservatives. But the moderates think conciliation on both sides is necessary for the party to survive. "We have to take the steps to be the party of the open door," Berkman said at the Red Lion, in his final speech as party chairman, "not of exclusion and division."

The Adkissons' home outside Portland is something of a Christian conservative's dream world. It is a big patch of rolling land with a cute red farmhouse and a quiet little creek. Their two girls play with the three dogs outside; the new Christian American newspaper is in the den, and family publications are arranged neatly on tables around the house.

Sitting down to reminisce about the past few months of electioneering and grassroots work, the Adkissons are as proud of their quick and fruitful entry into politics as they are fearful of America's future. For them, the election of the county officers at the Red Lion was the high point of a political involvement that began slowly, if not reluctantly, about five years ago when they helped oppose a state executive order that sought to protect gay rights. Around that time, they'd begun to realize that their way of life was in jeopardy.

"I finally understood that I was in someone's cross hairs," Jim says, sitting in his big-backed comfortable chair. "The things that I believe in and that are important to me, I felt were being targeted. It's like when I was in Vietnam. When someone was targeting you, you knew."

"Obviously," says Christie, speaking of homosexuals, "in the last 20 years since they wrote their homosexual agenda, they have had a methodical plan. That's why we've had to wake up."

Since the Adkissons have begun their political involvement, almost everything they have seen has convinced them of their work's inherent worthiness. Early on, Christie says, she watched Act Up members throw condoms at her and her friends' small children, who then picked them up thinking the condoms were gum. ("A baptism by fire," she calls the experience.) They have been shouted at while collecting signatures in malls; people once came to protest in their own driveway but were scared away when the two Adkisson girls came running from around the house with their BB guns, innocently checking to see what was going on.

Christie's trip to a training seminar for teachers has confirmed her worst fears: that the seminars are designed to advance the gay agenda among children. Likewise, her experience in counseling sessions for homosexuals (she believes homosexuality is an illness that can be treated) has given her hope that, with more work, things can be changed. She believes she is simply doing what any good Christian would do. "This is one of the greatest gifts that I can give my children," she says. "To be what I say I am."

In the meantime, the Adkissons marvel at how they are stereotyped. Jim Adkisson is the president of a software and database company, with a degree in international business. Christie has a B.A. in education and has taken courses in international business. They both hear all the talk about the poor, undereducated Christian voter and laugh.

"I think it's impressive to see," says Christie, in telling about Jim's background and her own, "so that people don't think we're dumb hicks."

Jim says: "In the press the slant is that we're the radicals, we're the crazies. I guess the untold story is that it's not so much that the so-called religious right or social conservatives or whatever brand you want to put on them, it isn't that they're trying to change anything; the untold story is that they're running around trying to put their fingers in the dikes."

The Adkissons are taking a little time to rest these days, feeling worn down by the rigors of the past election. But they remain involved with the coalition, in which they have a great moral investment. "The thing about the coalition," Jim says, "is that it is telling people to stop talking about it and get involved." Sometimes Jim seems to get a little depressed considering the stakes. "The reason I get so emotional," he says, "is that the things I held dear are just not what they were—our court system, our schools. I don't have the same patriotic allegiance because it's been destroyed by the reality of what these lofty institutions have turned into."

Christie, on the other hand, appears to remain strong and always assured, whether at home or speaking to an audience, moving herself to tears in a small church. Her talks on the infiltration of the gay agenda in the schools are beginning to be recorded and passed around the state. She takes consolation in such things as the fall of Joseph Fernandez, the outgoing chancellor of the New York City Schools, who fought for condom distribution and a controversial Rainbow curriculum. The Adkissons regularly pray that homosexuality will one day be considered wrong in the eyes of the law. To them it is just a matter of realigning man's law with the laws of nature and God.

"Any Christian that tells you that on some of these issues it's all a matter of perspective just doesn't read the Bible," Jim says.

By midmorning on that snowy winter day in the Red Lion conference room, it was clear to all the party's conservatives that their candidate was going to lose. When the vote finally was taken, Randy Miller beat the conservative candidate, Bill Witt, by just seven votes. "This is a victory for the Republican Party," Craig Berkman said. Then, relinquishing his chairmanship to the barely masked joy of the conservatives, Berkman got into his car and drove away.

The remainder of the election was something of a duck shoot for the

Christian Coalition, whose candidates won the remaining seats. To some extent, this was because of the inclement weather: in many cases, the conservatives had managed to outwait the moderates who had to drive—and, in some instances, fly—back across the icy state before dark. But it also seemed to have to do with political trickery.

The moderate candidate running for treasurer, for instance, assured by Bill Witt he would have no opposition, discovered a slate backed by the Oregon Citizens Alliance too late in the game for him to start campaigning. It wasn't typical political sour grapes that brought on accusations of lies when Monday morning quarterbacking time came around. All through his campaign Bill Witt was fooling the people who believed he had only incidental connections to the Christian Coalition and the alliance.

Even Witt's loss of the chairmanship felt a little like a win to the conservatives. Lon Mabon, the head of the Oregon Citizens Alliance and the key conservative power broker, announced that he would be able to work with Randy Miller, in light of Miller's anti-abortion stance; he said Miller was nearly a conservative. Jimm Adkisson, for one, was pacing a little less now. "The irony is seeing these liberals support Randy Miller when they wouldn't have sat at the same table with him two months ago," he said when it was all over.

Similarly, Darrell Fuller left the hotel thinking to himself that the Oregon Republican Party was now being run by a man who shared many of the key tenets of the Christian Coalition, a fact that would make his life as the coalition's local representative a little easier: in addition to telling people of the cultural havoc being wrought by the Clinton Administration, Fuller could now point to actual political inroads made by the coalition. In fact, minutes after the chairmanship had been lost, quite a few coalition members and other conservatives were beginning to say that Bill Witt could have won by avoiding the fatal stealth label and *embracing* his membership in the Christian Coalition.

It was getting dark by the time the conservatives were pulling out of the Red Lion's parking lot, and the political fires were dying out; the slush, long ago pushed to the sides of the road, was beginning to creep back and freeze to ice. The Adkissons were two of the last people to leave the Red Lion conference room. Now, finally, after a long and tedious day, Christie could drive home in the car alongside her husband, pull into her driveway, kiss her two daughters hello and know that she had rolled up her political sleeves, stood up for what she believes in and made the world more like the kind of place that she had grown up in—more the kind of place that she wants her two girls to grow up in, too.

WEAKENING OF PARTY ORGANIZATION

See text p. 485

Political parties are the focal point for assigning responsibility for various governmental actions; as party organization has weakened, according to political scientist Morris Fiorina, so has political accountability.

Morris P. Fiorina
"The Decline of Collective Responsibility in American Politics"*

Though the Founding Fathers believed in the necessity of establishing a genuinely national government, they took great pains to design one that could not lightly do things *to* its citizens; what government might do *for* its citizens was to be limited to the functions of what we know now as the "watchman state." . . .

Given the historical record faced by the Founders, their emphasis on constraining government is understandable. But we face a later historical record, one that shows two hundred years of increasing demands for government to act positively. Moreover, developments unforeseen by the Founders increasingly raise the likelihood that the uncoordinated actions of individuals and groups will inflict serious damage on the nation as a whole. The by-products of the industrial and technological revolutions impose physical risks not only on us, but on future generations as well. Resource shortages and international cartels raise the spectre of economic ruin. And the simple proliferation of special interests with their intense, particularistic demands threatens to render us politically incapable of taking actions that might either advance the state of society or prevent foreseeable deteriorations in that state. None of this is to suggest that we should forget about what government can do *to* us—the contemporary concern with the proper scope and methods of government intervention in the social and economic orders is long overdue. But the modern age demands as well that we worry about our ability to make government work *for* us. The problem is that we are gradually losing that ability, and a principal reason for this loss is the steady erosion of *responsibility* in American politics. . . .

Unfortunately, the importance of responsibility in a democracy is matched by the difficulty of attaining it. In an autocracy, individual responsibility suffices; the location of power in a single individual locates responsibility in that individual as well. But individual responsibility is insufficient whenever more than one person shares governmental authority. We can hold a particular congressman individually responsible for a personal trans-

*Morris P. Fiorina, "The Decline of Collective Responsibility in American Politics," reprinted by permission of *Daedalus,* Journal of the American Academy of Arts and Sciences, from the issue entitled, "The End of Consensus?" Summer 1980, Vol. 109/3.

gression such as bribe-taking. We can even hold a president individually responsible for military moves where he presents Congress and the citizenry with a *fait accompli.* But on most national issues individual responsibility is difficult to assess. If one were to go to Washington, randomly accost a Democratic congressman, and berate him about a 20-percent rate of inflation, imagine the response. More than likely it would run, "Don't blame me. If 'they' had done what I've advocated for *x* years, things would be fine today." . . .

American institutional structure makes this kind of game-playing all too easy. In order to overcome it we must lay the credit or blame for national conditions on all those who had any hand in bringing them about: some form of *collective responsibility* is essential.

The only way collective responsibility has ever existed, and can exist given our institutions, is through the agency of the political party; in American politics, responsibility requires cohesive parties. This is an old claim to be sure, but its age does not detract from its present relevance. In fact, the continuing decline in public esteem for the parties and continuing efforts to "reform" them out of the political process suggest that old arguments for party responsibility have not been made often enough or, at least, convincingly enough, so I will make these arguments once again in this essay.

A strong political party can generate collective responsibility by creating incentive for leaders, followers, and popular supporters to think and act in collective terms. First, by providing party leaders with the capability (e.g., control of institutional patronage, nominations, and so on) to discipline party members, genuine leadership becomes possible. Legislative output is less likely to be a least common denominator—a residue of myriad conflicting proposals—and more likely to consist of a program actually intended to solve a problem or move the nation in a particular direction. Second, the subordination of individual officeholders to the party lessens their ability to separate themselves from party actions. Like it or not, their performance becomes identified with the performance of the collectivity to which they belong. Third, with individual candidate variation greatly reduced, voters have less incentive to support individuals and more incentive to support or oppose the party as a whole. And fourth, the circle closes as party-line voting in the electorate provides party leaders with the incentive to propose policies that will earn the support of a national majority, and party back-benchers with the personal incentive to cooperate with leaders in the attempt to compile a good record for the party as a whole.

In the American context, strong parties have traditionally clarified politics in two ways. First, they allow citizens to assess responsibility easily, at least when the government is unified, which it more often was in earlier eras when party meant more than it does today. Citizens need only evaluate the social, economic, and international conditions they observe and make a simple decision for or against change. They do not need to decide whether the energy, inflation, urban, and defense policies advocated by their congressman would be superior to those advocated by [the president]—were any of them to be enacted!

The second way in which strong parties clarify American politics follows from the first. When citizens assess responsibility on the party as a whole, party members have personal incentives to see the party evaluated favorably. They have little to gain from gutting their president's program one day and attacking him for lack of leadership the next, since they share in the president's fate when voters do not differentiate within the party. Put simply, party responsibility provides party members with a personal stake in their collective performance.

Admittedly, party responsibility is a blunt instrument. The objection immediately arises that party responsibility condemns junior Democratic representatives to suffer electorally for an inflation they could do little to affect. An unhappy situation, true, but unless we accept it, Congress as a whole escapes electoral retribution for an inflation they *could* have done something to affect. Responsibility requires acceptance of both conditions. The choice is between a blunt instrument or none at all. . . .

In earlier times, when citizens voted for the party, not the person, parties had incentives to nominate good candidates, because poor ones could have harmful fallout on the ticket as a whole. In particular, the existence of presidential coattails (positive and negative) provided an inducement to avoid the nomination of narrowly based candidates, no matter how committed their supporters. And, once in office, the existence of party voting in the electorate provided party members with the incentive to compile a good *party* record. In particular, the tendency of national midterm elections to serve as referenda on the performance of the president provided a clear inducement for congressmen to do what they could to see that their president was perceived as a solid performer. By stimulating electoral phenomena such as coattail effects and mid-term referenda, party transformed some degree of personal ambition into concern with collective performance. . . .

The Continuing Decline of Party in the United States

Party Organizations

In the United States, party organization has traditionally meant state and local party organization. The national party generally has been a loose confederacy of subnational units that swings into action for a brief period every four years. This characterization remains true today, despite the somewhat greater influence and augmented functions of the national organizations. Though such things are difficult to measure precisely, there is general agreement that the formal party organizations have undergone a secular decline since their peak at the end of the nineteenth century. The prototype of the old-style organization was the urban machine, a form approximated today only in Chicago. . . .

[Fiorina discusses the reforms of the late nineteenth and early twentieth century discussed in the text.]

In the 1970s two series of reforms further weakened the influence of organized parties in American national politics. The first was a series of legal changes deliberately intended to lessen organized party influence in the presidential nominating process. In the Democratic party, "New Politics" activists captured the national party apparatus and imposed a series of rules changes designed to "open up" the politics of presidential nominations. The Republican party—long more amateur and open than the Democratic party—adopted weaker versions of the Democratic rules changes. In addition, modifications of state electoral laws to conform to the Democratic rules changes (enforced by the federal courts) stimulated Republican rules changes as well. . . .

A second series of 1970s reforms lessened the role of formal party organizations in the conduct of political campaigns. These are financing regulations growing out of the Federal Election Campaign Act of 1971 as amended in 1974 and 1976. In this case the reforms were aimed at cleaning up corruption in the financing of campaigns; their effects on the parties were a by-product, though many individuals accurately predicted its nature. Serious presidential candidates are now publicly financed. Though the law permits the national party to spend two cents per eligible voter on behalf of the nominee, it also obliges the candidate to set up a finance committee separate from the national party. Between this legally mandated separation and fear of violating spending limits or accounting regulations, for example, the law has the effect of encouraging the candidate to keep his party at arm's length. . . .

The ultimate results of such reforms are easy to predict. A lesser party role in the nominating and financing of candidates encourages candidates to organize and conduct independent campaigns, which further weakens the role of parties. . . . [I]f parties do not grant nominations, fund their choices, and work for them, why should those choices feel any commitment to their party?

Party in the Electorate

In the citizenry at large, party takes the form of a psychological attachment. The typical American traditionally has been likely to identify with one or the other of the two major parties. Such identifications are transmitted across generations to some degree, and within the individual they tend to be fairly stable. But there is mounting evidence that the basis of identification lies in the individual's experiences (direct and vicarious, through family and social groups) with the parties in the past. Our current party system, of course, is based on the dislocations of the Depression period and the New Deal attempts to alleviate them. Though only a small proportion of those who experienced the Depression directly are active voters today, the general outlines of citizen party identifications much resemble those established at that time.

Again, there is reason to believe that the extent of citizen attachments to parties has undergone a long-term decline from a nineteenth-century high. And again, the New Deal appears to have been a period during which the decline was arrested, even temporarily reversed. But again, the decline of party has reasserted itself in the 1970s. . . .

As the 1960s wore on, the heretofore stable distribution of citizen party identifications began to change in the general direction of weakened attachments to the parties. Between 1960 and 1976, independents, broadly defined, increased from less than a quarter to more than a third of the voting-age population. Strong identifiers declined from slightly more than a third to about a quarter of the population. . . .

Indisputably, party in the electorate has declined in recent years. Why? To some extent the electoral decline results from the organizational decline. Few party organizations any longer have the tangible incentives to turn out the faithful and assure their loyalty. Candidates run independent campaigns and deemphasize their partisan ties whenever they see any short-term electoral gain in doing so. If party is increasingly less important in the nomination and election of candidates, it is not surprising that such diminished importance is reflected in the attitudes and behavior of the voter.

Certain long-term sociological and technological trends also appear to work against party in the electorate. The population is younger, and younger citizens traditionally are less attached to the parties than their elders. The population is more highly educated; fewer voters need some means of simplifying the choices they face in the political arena, and party, of course, has been the principal means of simplification. And the media revolution has vastly expanded the amount of information easily available to the citizenry. Candidates would have little incentive to operate campaigns independent of the parties if there were no means to apprise the citizenry of their independence. The media provide the means.

Finally, our present party system is an old one. For increasing numbers of citizens, party attachments based on the Great Depression seem lacking in relevance to the problems of the late twentieth century. Beginning with the racial issue in the 1960s, proceeding to the social issue of the 1970s, and to the energy, environment, and inflation issues of today, the parties have been rent by internal dissension. Sometimes they failed to take stands, at other times they took the wrong ones from the standpoint of the rank and file, and at most times they have failed to solve the new problems in any genuine sense. Since 1965 the parties have done little or nothing to earn the loyalties of modern Americans.

Party in Government

If the organizational capabilities of the parties have weakened, and their psychological ties to the voters have loosened, one would expect predictable consequences for the party in government. In particular, one would expect to see an increasing degree of split party control within and across the levels of American government. The evidence on this point is overwhelming. . . .

The increased fragmentation of the party in government makes it more difficult for government officeholders to work together than in times past (not that it has ever been terribly easy). Voters meanwhile have a more difficult time attributing responsibility for government performance, and this only further fragments party control. The result is lessened collective responsibility in the system.

What has taken up the slack left by the weakening of the traditional [party] determinants of congressional voting? It appears that a variety of personal and local influences now play a major role in citizen evaluations of their representatives. Along with the expansion of the federal presence in American life, the traditional role of the congressman as an all-purpose ombudsman has greatly expanded. Tens of millions of citizens now are directly affected by federal decisions. Myriad programs provide opportunities to profit from government largesse, and myriad regulations impose costs and/or constraints on citizen activities. And, whether seeking to gain profit or avoid costs, citizens seek the aid of their congressmen. When a court imposes a desegregation plan on an urban school board, the congressional offices immediately are contacted for aid in safeguarding existing sources of funding and in determining eligibility for new ones. When a major employer announces plans to quit an area, the congressional offices immediately are contacted to explore possibilities for using federal programs to persuade the employer to reconsider. Contractors appreciate a good congressional word with DOD procurement officers. Local artistic groups cannot survive without NEA funding. And, of course, there are the major individual programs such as social security and veterans' benefits that create a steady demand for congressional information and aid services. Such activities are nonpartisan, nonideological, and, most important, noncontroversial. Moreover, the contribution of the congressman in the realm of district service appears considerably greater than the impact of his or her single vote on major national issues. Constituents respond rationally to this modern state of affairs by weighing nonprogrammatic constituency service heavily when casting their congressional votes. And this emphasis on the part of constituents provides the means for incumbents to solidify their hold on the office. Even if elected by a narrow margin, diligent service activities enable a congressman to neutralize or even convert a portion of those who would otherwise oppose him on policy or ideological grounds. Emphasis on local, nonpartisan factors in congressional voting enables the modern congressman to withstand national swings, whereas yesteryear's uninsulated congressmen were more dependent on preventing the occurrence of the swings. . . .

[The result is the insulation of the modern congressional member from national forces altogether.]

The withering away of the party organizations and the weakening of party in the electorate have begun to show up as disarray in the party in government. As the electoral fates of congressmen and the president have diverged, their incentives to cooperate have diverged as well. Congressmen have little personal incentive to bear any risk in their president's behalf, since they no longer expect to gain much from his successes or suffer much from his failures. Only those who personally agree with the president's program and/or those who find that program well suited for their particular district support the president. And there are not enough of these to construct the coalitions necessary for action on the major issues now facing the country. By holding only the president responsible for national conditions, the electorate enables officialdom as a whole to escape responsibility. This situation lies at the root of many of the problems that now plague American public life.

Some Consequences of the Decline of Collective Responsibility

The weakening of party has contributed directly to the severity of several of the important problems the nation faces. For some of these, such as the government's inability to deal with inflation and energy, the connections are obvious. But for other problems, such as the growing importance of single-issue politics and the growing alienation of the American citizenry, the connections are more subtle.

Immobilism

As the electoral interdependence of the party in government declines, its ability to act also declines. If responsibility can be shifted to another level or to another officeholder, there is less incentive to stick one's neck out in an attempt to solve a given problem. Leadership becomes more difficult, the ever-present bias toward the short-term solution becomes more pronounced, and the possibility of solving any given problem lessens.

... [P]olitical inability to take actions that entail short-run costs ordinarily will result in much higher costs in the long run—we cannot continually depend on the technological fix. So the present American immobilism cannot be dismissed lightly. The sad thing is that the American people appear to understand the depth of our present problems and, at least in principle, appear prepared to sacrifice in furtherance of the long-run good. But they will not have an opportunity to choose between two or more such long-term plans. Although both parties promise tough, equitable policies, in the present state of our politics, neither can deliver.

Single-Issue Politics

In recent years both political analysts and politicians have decried the increased importance of single-issue groups in American politics. Some in fact would claim that the present immobilism in our politics owes more to the rise of single-issue groups than to the decline of party. A little thought, however, should reveal that the two trends are connected. Is single-issue politics a recent phenomenon? The contention is doubtful; such groups have always been active participants in American politics. The gun lobby already was a classic example at the time of President Kennedy's assassination. And however impressive the antiabortionists appear today, remember the temperance movement, which succeeded in getting its constitutional amendment. American history contains numerous forerunners of today's groups, from anit-Masons to abolitionists to the Klan—singularity of purpose is by no means a modern phenomenon. Why, then, do we hear all the contemporary hoopla about single-issue groups? Probably because politicians fear them now more than before and thus allow them to play a larger role in our politics. Why should this be so? Simply because the parties are too weak to protect their members and thus to contain single-issue politics.

In earlier times single-issue groups were under greater pressures to reach accommodations with the parties. After all, the parties nominated candidates, financed candidates, worked for candidates, and, perhaps most important, party voting protected candidates. When a contemporary single-issue group threatens to "get" an officeholder, the threat must be taken seriously. . . .

Not only did the party organization have greater ability to resist single-issue pressures at the electoral level, but the party in government had greater ability to control the agenda, and thereby contain single-issue pressures at the policy-making level. Today we seem condemned to go through an annual agony over federal abortion funding. There is little doubt that politicians on both sides would prefer to reach some reasonable compromise at the committee level and settle the issue. But in today's decentralized Congress there is no way to put the lid on. In contrast, historians tell us that in the late nineteenth century a large portion of the Republican constituency was far less interested in the tariff and other questions of national economic development than in whether German immigrants should be permitted to teach their native language in their local schools, and whether Catholics and "liturgical Protestants" should be permitted to consume alcohol. Interestingly, however, the national agenda of the period is devoid of such issues. And when they do show up on the state level, the exceptions prove the rule; they produce party splits and striking defeats for the party that allowed them to surface.

In sum, a strong party that is held accountable for the government of a nation-state has both the ability and the incentive to contain particularistic pressures. It controls nominations, elections, and the agenda, and it collectively realizes that small minorities are small minorities no matter how intense they are. But as the parties decline they lose control over nominations and campaigns, they lose the loyalty of the voters, and they lose control of the agenda. Party officeholders cease to be held collectively accountable for party performance, but they become individually exposed to the political pressure of myriad interest groups. The decline of party permits interest groups to wield greater influence, their success encourages the formation of still more interest groups, politics becomes increasingly fragmented, and collective responsibility becomes still more elusive.

Popular Alienation from Government

For at least a decade political analysts have pondered the significance of survey data indicative of a steady increase in the alienation of the American public from the political process . . . The American public is in a nasty mood, a cynical, distrusting, and resentful mood. The question is, Why?

If the same national problems not only persist but worsen while ever-greater amounts of revenue are directed at them, why shouldn't the typical citizen conclude that most of the money must be wasted by incompetent officials? If narrowly based interest groups increasingly affect our politics, why shouldn't citizens increasingly conclude that the interests run the government? For fifteen years the citizenry has listened to a steady stream of promises but has seen very little in the way of follow-through. An increasing proportion of the electorate does not believe that elections make a difference, a fact that largely explains the much-discussed post-1960 decline in voting turnout.

Continued public disillusionment with the political process poses several real dangers. For one thing, disillusionment begets further disillusionment. Leadership becomes more difficult if citizens do not trust their leaders and will not give them the benefit of a doubt. Policy failure becomes more likely if citizens expect the policy to fail. Waste increases and government competence decreases as citizens disrespect for politics encourages a lesser breed of person to make careers in government. And "government by a few big interests" becomes more than a cliché if citizens increasingly decide the cliché is true and cease participating for that reason.

Finally, there is the real danger that continued disappointment with particular government officials ultimately metamorphoses into disillusionment with government per se. Increasing numbers of citizens believe that government is not simply overextended but perhaps incapable of any further bettering of the world. Yes, government is overextended, inefficiency is pervasive, and ineffectiveness is all too common. But government is one of the few instruments of collective action we have, and even those committed to selective pruning of government programs cannot blithely allow the concept of an activist government to fall into disrepute.

Of late, however, some political commentators have begun to wonder whether contemporary thought places sufficient emphasis on government *for* the people. In stressing participation have we lost sight of *accountability?* Surely, we should be as concerned with what government produces as with how many participate. What good is participation if the citizenry is unable to determine who merits their support?

Participation and responsibility are not logically incompatible, but there is a degree of tension between the two, and the quest for either may be carried to extremes. Participation maximizers find themselves involved with quotas and virtual representation schemes, while responsibility maximizers can find themselves with a closed shop under boss rule. Moreover, both qualities can weaken the democracy they supposedly underpin. Unfettered participation produces Hyde Amendments and immobilism.

QUESTIONS

1. Do parties represent broad political philosophies or are they more narrowly focused upon advancing limited material interests, as Alexis de Tocqueville claimed? What are the major differences between the Republican and Democratic parties in the United States? Should a democracy encourage the formation of parties with widely divergent views of social, political, and economic justice?
2. Numerous observers of American political life have bemoaned the weakening of the party system, but the solution is unclear. Is the two-party system incapable of representing the variety of interests that compose a large and diverse national community? Does the argument that a two-party system provides a means of achieving consensus adequately account for the fact that a number of interests may never get articulated?
3. In what ways might a three-party system force a focus on issues and consensus building, as Lowi suggests? Would a four-, five-, or six-party system be even more effective at focusing politics around substantive issues?
4. Parties operate most effectively when they mobilize large numbers of people at the grass roots level. Given that structure, however, is there a danger that parties will be too easily dominated by a narrow group of interests? How can such a capture be countered?
5. In what ways do parties increase political accountability, according to Morris Fiorina? Has the weakening of traditional party structures led to an ennervated and ineffectual political system?

CHAPTER 12

Groups and Interests

THE CHARACTER OF INTEREST GROUPS: WHO IS REPRESENTED?

See text p. 505

In the United States the right to associate freely with others—and particularly to pursue political ends—has long been viewed as the cornerstone of American democracy. Respect for that right, in fact, stood in marked contrast to political systems in Europe at the time the Constitution was granted, which often suppressed political associations that were perceived as posing threats to the existing regime.

Alexis de Tocqueville argued that the right to associate provides an important check on the power of majorities in democratic regimes, where that power places minority interests in constant jeopardy. Tocqueville pointed out that allowing citizens to associate in a variety of groups with a variety of crosscutting interests enables compromises to be reached, as each interested group attempts to build support among shifting coalitions.

Alexis de Tocqueville "Political Association in the United States"*

Better use has been made of association and this powerful instrument of action has been applied to more varied aims in America than anywhere else in the world. . . .

The inhabitant of the United States learns from birth that he must rely on himself to combat the ills and trials of life; he is restless and defiant in his outlook toward the authority of society and appeals to its power only when he cannot do without it. The beginnings of this attitude first appear at school, where the children, even in their games, submit to rules settled by themselves and punish offenses which they have defined themselves. The same attitude turns up again in all the affairs of social life. If some obstacle blocks the public road halting the circulation of traffic, the neighbors at once form a deliberative body; this improvised assembly produces an executive authority which remedies the trouble before anyone has thought of the possibility of some previously constituted authority beyond that of those concerned. Where enjoyment is concerned, people associate to make festivities grander and more orderly. Finally, associations

*Alexis de Tocqueville, "Political Associations in the United States," in *Democracy in America,* ed. J.P. Mayer and Max Lerner, tr. G. Lawrence.

are formed to combat exclusively moral troubles: intemperance is fought in common. Public security, trade and industry, and morals and religion all provide the aims for associations in the United States. There is no end which the human will despairs of attaining by the free action of the collective power of individuals. . . .

The right of association being recognized, citizens can use it in different ways. An association simply consists in the public and formal support of specific doctrines by a certain number of individuals who have undertaken to cooperate in a stated way in order to make these doctrines prevail. Thus the right of association can almost be identified with freedom to write, but already associations are more powerful than the press. When some view is represented by an association, it must take clearer and more precise shape. It counts its supporters and involves them in its cause; these supporters get to know one another, and numbers increase zeal. An association unites the energies of divergent minds and vigorously directs them toward a clearly indicated goal.

Freedom of assembly marks the second stage in the use made of the right of association. When a political association is allowed to form centers of action at certain important places in the country, its activity becomes greater and its influence more widespread. There men meet, active measures are planned, and opinions are expressed with that strength and warmth which the written word can never attain.

But the final stage is the use of association in the sphere of politics. The supporters of an agreed view may meet in electoral colleges and appoint mandatories to represent them in a central assembly. That is, properly speaking, the application of the representative system to one party. . . .

In our own day freedom of association has become a necessary guarantee against the tyranny of the majority. In the United States, once a party has become predominant, all public power passes into its hands; its close supporters occupy all offices and have control of all organized forces. The most distinguished men of the opposite party, unable to cross the barrier keeping them from power, must be able to establish themselves outside it; the minority must use the whole of its moral authority to oppose the physical power oppressing it. Thus the one danger has to be balanced against a more formidable one.

The omnipotence of the majority seems to me such a danger to the American republics that the dangerous expedient used to curb it is actually something good.

Here I would repeat something which I have put in other words when speaking of municipal freedom: no countries need associations more—to prevent either despotism of parties or the arbitrary rule of a prince—than those with a democratic social state. In aristocratic nations secondary bodies form natural associations which hold abuses of power in check. In countries where such associations do not exist, if private people did not artificially and temporarily create something like them, I see no other dike to hold back tyranny of whatever sort, and a great nation might with impunity be oppressed by some tiny faction or by a single man. . . .

In America the citizens who form the minority associate in the first place to show their numbers and to lessen the moral authority of the majority, and secondly, by stimulating competition, to discover the arguments most likely to make an impression on the majority, for they always hope to draw the majority over to their side and then to exercise power in its name.

Political associations in the United States are therefore peaceful in their objects and legal in the means used; and when they say that they only wish to prevail legally, in general they are telling the truth. . . .

The Americans . . . have provided a form of government within their associations, but it is, if I may put it so, a civil government. There is a place for individual independence there; as in society, all the members are advancing at the same time toward the same goal, but they are not obliged to follow exactly the same path. There has been no sacrifice of will or of reason, but rather will and reason are applied to bring success to a common enterprise.

THE PROLIFERATION OF GROUPS

See text p. 510

This section of the text and the one following it explore a variety of issues relating to the creation and maintenance of interest groups. As the text notes on page 512, individuals at the bottom of the socioeconomic ladder have traditionally lacked the power and resources to advance their interests in the political arena; effective articulation of those interests requires mobilization on a far larger scale than that required for wealthier and more limited interest groups.

Coalitions of large numbers of people are, of course, far more difficult to maintain over the long term. Different interest groups within the coalition will inevitably perceive problems differently, and political solutions acceptable to one element of the coalition may be unacceptable to another. The coalition may splinter as political solutions affect members of the coalition at disparate rates and with disparate degrees of success.

Holding together an effective coalition has at times been a problem for public interest groups representing people of color. While an interest in fighting against racism may provide common ground for organizing among Latinos, Asian-Americans, and African-Americans, the problems play out differently in each of the communities. The concerns the groups hold in common may be eclipsed by problems of concern to only part of the group, such as discrimination on the basis of immigrant status; as noted below, African-Americans may see their opportunities increased by supporting restrictive immigration programs, while Latinos and Asian-Americans have a vested interest in eliminating discriminatory immigration laws. As the following article discusses, the Leadership Conference on Civil Rights, which began with a focus on the interests of African-Americans but has expanded to embrace a broader community, finds itself engaged in a constant struggle to keep its membership in some kind of equilibrium.

Dick Kirschten
"Not Black-And-White"*

When not in combat against Republican Presidents and others they regard as champions of "the right wing and the privileged," the field marshals of the civil rights lobbying community sometimes keep in shape by fighting among themselves.

The top legislative strategists of the rights movement tend to be a close-knit group united by the tears and triumphs that have come with decades of trench warfare on behalf of liberal causes. But shared values do not always translate into identical agendas: Even the social justice crowd is vulnerable to the pulls and tugs of competing constituencies.

The Leadership Conference on Civil Rights (LCCR), the Washington command post for antidiscrimination advocacy, has been the scene of plenty of intramural disagreement during its 40-year lifetime. The sparsely staffed LCCR functions as a switchboard operation that tries to keep a sprawling network of member organizations from getting their wires crossed.

Maintaining peace within the coalition hasn't been easy. The conference has endured heated debates over affirmative action, has prudently skirted the tricky issue of abortion and . . . appears to have averted a major rupture caused by a disagreement between its members from organized labor and its Hispanics.

Born of the crusade to end segregation of blacks, the LCCR attracted new members as it chalked up victories, coming under pressure to broaden its agenda as it did so.

Demographic shifts have dramatically altered the politics of minority-group advocacy. The nation's Hispanic population is growing more than twice as fast as the black population. Asians, though less numerous, are increasing even faster. The 1990 census is expected to show that Hispanics and Asians, taken together, are now almost as numerous as blacks.

With blacks competing against other minorities for jobs, frequently on the lower rungs of the economic ladder, the potential for political division between the groups is intensifying. That tension is also being felt at the highest level of the civil rights leadership structure.

NAACP executive director Benjamin L. Hooks, who chairs the LCCR, said he fears a major setback for the civil rights effort if minority groups permit themselves to be played off against one another. "The Establishment thinks that it is to its advantage to keep people at the bottom fighting among themselves over low-wage jobs with poor working conditions," Hooks said. "I think our strength is having women, Hispanics and blacks working together."

But the relationship between Hispanics and Washington's civil rights establishment has never been smooth. Last May, Raoul Yzaguirre, president

*Dick Kirschten, "Not Black-And-White," *National Journal* (March 2, 1991).

of the National Council of La Raza and a member of the LCCR executive committee, came within an hour of leading a Hispanic walkout from the leadership conference. Thanks to quick intervention by Hooks, Yzaguirre was persuaded to retract an already distributed press release that denounced the LCCR as "a coalition which neither respects nor supports the civil rights of the Hispanic community."

LCCR vice chairwoman Antonia Hernandez, the president and general counsel of the Mexican American Legal Defense and Education Fund (MALDEF), said Hispanics are restive because they perceive a lack of sensitivity to their problems and their history. "Washington, D.C., and the East Coast still see civil rights as a black-white issue," she said. "It is the invisible wall that we Hispanics face; the idea that nothing important happens beyond the Potomac River."

For Hernandez, who is based in Los Angeles, the realities of the civil rights struggle are hardly black-and-white. In California, Hispanics are by far the dominant minority group. They outnumber blacks 3-1. When Asians—a 10th of the state's population—are added in, the two groups make up more than a third of Californians.

Although the nation's civil rights laws bar discrimination on the basis of national origin, Latins and Asians face what their advocates regard as a serious new threat of discrimination: the denial of jobs by employers who harbor doubts about their immigration status. The concern stems from a legislative deal struck five years ago to tighten control of the nation's borders by imposing penalties against those who hire illegal aliens.

Those penalties, legalistically referred to as "employer sanctions," have since then emerged as a cause célèbre for Hispanic interest groups who want them repealed. But organized labor, the financial and institutional cornerstone of the leadership conference, differs strenuously with Hispanic leaders over the fairest way to rid the U.S. workplace of unauthorized foreigners.

Labor is worried that illegal immigration, if allowed to continue unchecked by employer sanctions, will adversely affect the wages and working conditions of U.S. citizens and legal aliens. "We feel so strongly that if an employer can knowingly hire undocumented workers, there is going to be tremendous discrimination not only against Hispanics but against other folks who are entitled to jobs or are already on payrolls," explained Kenneth Young, the AFL-CIO's representative on the LCCR executive committee.

Labor's adamance initially was met with militance on the part of Latino activists, creating a major migraine for the consensus-minded LCCR leadership. It took nine months to work out a solution satisfactory to both groups. The story of those peace negotiations reveals much about the potential divisions within the civil rights community and what it has taken to keep the coalition intact over four decades of historic social change.

Growing Pains

. . . The LCCR "started out with a black focus; it was to do something for the blacks," recalled Washington attorney Joseph L. Rauh Jr., who has been the organization's counsel since its inception. But Rauh, whose passion for advocacy remains undimmed at the age of 80, quickly added that "what's happened in this country is that the black fight has become much broader than black."

Former LCCR executive director Marvin Caplan stressed the same point in a review of the conference's history on its 40th anniversary. "The success of the movement for civil rights of black people in the Congress and in the courts provided a model for other groups fighting discrimination," Caplan wrote.

The original band of 58 groups that agitated on behalf of Negro Americans in 1950 has since more than tripled. The 185 organizations that now belong to the conference cover the waterfront of antibias issues from racial and ethnic concerns to those of feminists, gays and lesbians and the disabled.

With the broadening of its grass-roots political base, the LCCR has become tougher to manage. . . .

The glue used to hold the coalition together is the requirement that consensus be reached among its disparate interests before a formal leadership conference position is taken. Individual organizations do not have veto power, but basic constituency blocs do.

The LCCR's stands in favor of affirmative action programs to remedy past discrimination, for example, were taken only after the bulk of the Jewish organizations within its membership agreed that such steps did not constitute establishment of ethnic and racial preferences or quotas. Debate within the conference raged hot and heavy over that issue. . . .

. . . If past debates strained relations between Jews and other members of the coalition, particularly blacks, they nonetheless helped to forge agreement on affirmative action remedies for society's past discriminatory practices. . . .

. . . Rubin stressed that debate over preferential treatment of minorities is not just a "Jewish-black" issue. "Various opinions on quotas" are to be found among women's groups and Hispanic and Asian organizations within the LCCR, he said. The AJC official also pointed out that the Jewish community and several church groups are currently prodding the leadership conference to "expand its definition of civil rights to include discrimination on the basis of religious practices," an area in which, he said, protections have been eroded by recent court decisions.

Although many of the women's organizations that belong to the conference have a strong abortion-rights orientation, the LCCR has never reached a consensus on the question of legal abortion. "My wife asks how can I be counsel for a civil rights organization that has no position on abortion," remarked Rauh, who answered his own question by stressing the importance of keeping abortion opponents, such as the U.S. Catholic Conference, and other groups (including the NAACP) that take no stand on abortion within the fold.

Judith L. Lichtman, president of the Women's Legal Defense Fund and a vice chairwoman of the LCCR, said, "You don't expect of a coalition more than a coalition can deliver." The leadership conference, she said, derives its "energy and strength" from the size and diversity of its membership. "The name of the game over 40 years has been to maximize the areas of agreement and sidestep the areas of conflict." . . .

The Hispanic View

La Raza president Yzaguirre likes to remind visitors that the Supreme Court's watershed 1954 school desegregation decision, *Brown v. Board of Education,* was preceded by a Texas state court decision six years earlier barring bias against Hispanic students. It's his way of pointing out that his people are not exactly newcomers to the civil rights battle.

It was not until 1963, however, that a Hispanic lobbying presence was established in Washington. It took the form of a group called the National Organization for Mexican-American Services (NOMAS), which later was folded into La Raza. NO MAS, Spanish for "no more," was quickly welcomed into the LCCR, just in time to take part in "the big push" for the 1964 Civil Rights Act, Yzaguirre recalled.

But the relationship has been slow to bear fruit, from the Hispanics' perspective. There still are bitter memories of the clash that occurred in 1975, when the late Clarence Mitchell Jr., then the lobbyist for the NAACP and the leader of the LCCR, refused to back provisions, including one to allow foreign language ballots, that Hispanics sought to include in the renewal of the 1965 Voting Rights Act.

With the support of many of the leadership conference's members, acting as a separate coalition, the Hispanic-backed provisions were enacted. Mitchell, who felt strongly that the law should pertain solely to black voting rights, was furious. In his book about Mitchell, *Lion in the Lobby,* . . . author Denton L. Watson reports that "afterward in a meeting between representatives of the leadership conference and Hispanic groups, everyone sat dumbfounded as Mitchell lost his temper [and asserted that] 'blacks were dying for the right to vote when you people couldn't decide whether you were Caucasians.' "

. . . He added that "the reality is that the Hispanic civil rights struggle never made it to the front pages of *The Washington Post* or *The New York Times,* so therefore, in the mind of Clarence Mitchell it didn't exist." . . .

. . . As Yzaguirre sees it, there has been a reluctance on the part of black civil rights leaders to do political work with Hispanics. In joining the LCCR, which always has been headed by a top official of the NAACP, "Hispanics were adding credibility to a coalition, and continually supporting it on a lot of issues that didn't have any particular relevance to us. But when we asked for help on our issues, the door was closed."

When the voting rights law again came up for renewal in 1982, blacks and Hispanics worked in concert to resist Reagan Administration attempts to weaken the measure. But fissures were reopened with the passage in 1986 of the Immigration Reform and Control Act. Hispanic efforts to get the LCCR to oppose the employer sanctions came to naught because both the AFL-CIO and the NAACP supported the controversial provision.

The employer sanctions issue boiled over again last March when a study by the General Accounting Office (GAO) determined that employer sanctions had caused "a widespread pattern of discrimination" against Hispanics and other persons who appear to be foreign. When it became apparent that the LCCR would still be unable to achieve a consensus in favor of repealing the sanctions, Hispanic groups picketed a leadership conference banquet and threatened to resign from the coalition.

In calling public attention to their cause, Latino leaders also exposed themselves to renewed criticism from conservatives who questioned whether Hispanics are entitled to the full panoply of civil rights protections that have been accorded to blacks.

Peter Skerry, a scholar with the Washington-based Center for American Politics and Public Policy of the University of California (Los Angeles), challenged both the methodology and the conclusions of the GAO study in an article published in *The Wall Street Journal.* Skerry wrote: "To be sure, at various times and places, Hispanics have been subjected to something quite close to racial discrimination. But the evidence on the integration of Hispanics into American society indicates that they generally do not face the same problems as blacks."

Skerry, who has written extensively about Hispanic groups while at the Brookings Institution and the American Enterprise Institute for Public Policy Research, said in an interview: "It is not very smart strategically for Hispanics to define their problems in the racial discrimination terms that blacks do. I think it ultimately stigmatizes Hispanics and sets off alarms in the rest of society that here is another group that is going to come in and claim that the rest of us are being unfair." . . .

Repairing the Rift

As head of the LCCR, the NAACP's Hooks shows little interest in a divisive debate over the civil rights entitlements of blacks and Hispanics. "I may have personal feelings about who suffered most, but they aren't worth a damn," he said. "We've been lumped together by those above, so we better work amicably together. It will enhance the nation." . . .

Debating the Issues: Opposing Views

PACS AND POLITICS

See text pp. 532–33

Every group that hopes to make its interests known must lobby members of Congress. Lobbying may take many forms: it may be as benign as urging group members to send letters or telegrams, or it may involve hiring professionals whose actions are planned as carefully as a major military campaign. Whatever form it takes, lobbying generates concerns because of the potential for undue influence.

Over the last several years, a variety of reform efforts have been proposed. Most of those efforts have been directed at imposing disclosure requirements in order to bring to light facts about how much money is being spent, on whose behalf lobbyists are working, and whether the efforts cross ethical boundaries.

The following two articles look at the issue of professional lobbying. In the first piece, lobbyist Thomas Hale Boggs, Jr., argues that lobbyists are essential to the successful functioning of the American democratic system. According to Boggs, lobbyists "fill the information vacuum": they garner facts and information that legislators need in order to make informed decisions. Lobbyists also "help to identify and mobilize grass-roots constituents who agree with [a] client's position . . . [and] build coalitions among . . . diverse groups." Boggs agrees that lobbyists may be too influential in raising money for candidates, but argues that the answer to that problem lies in reforming campaign finance altogether and not in limiting the influence of lobbyists.

The second article discusses the influence of lobbyists, arguing that many lobbyists have "virtual veto power over legislation in their fields." The result is that politicians may find themselves hamstrung by a number of different lobbying interests and unable to "forge enough of a consensus to make bold decisions of any kind," which ultimately undercuts the democratic process.

Thomas Hale Boggs, Jr.
"All Interests Are Special"*

Shakespeare's "kill all the lawyers" has been replaced with "kill all the lobbyists." Journalists at most major publications have joined the chorus. In a recent editorial, for example, [the *New York Times*] described the "threat that corporate influence and big-time lobbying represent to enlightened populism."

I agree that the system needs to be changed. Campaign finance reform, stricter lobbying disclosure rules and post-employment restrictions for Government officials and employees would serve the democracy well. But few

*Thomas Hale Boggs, "All Interests Are Special," *New York Times* (February 16, 1993).

commentators ever stop to consider the legitimate role lobbyists play in policy-making.

Critics charge that the use of lobbyists by special interests is unfair, that if members of Congress respond to the influence of special interests, they are somehow acting contrary to the benefit of their constituents as a whole.

All interests are special and every individual and organization seeks to advance its own special interests. In the last quarter of 1992 alone, the House Clerk listed more than 6,000 registered lobbyists, who were supported by tens of thousands of additional personnel. These individuals fight for the interests of 40,000 registered clients, including religious organizations, foreign governments, the Boy Scouts, doctors, gambling organizations, trial lawyers, consumers, environmental protectionists, baseball players—the list goes on and on.

To cite a few of my firm's activities, is it unfair to: Lobby for Federal assistance to Chrysler to save thousands of jobs? Seek a regulatory structure to keep newspaper publishers from being forced out of business by legal monopolies? Help defeat a constitutional amendment on flag burning? Seek legislation making it easier for homeless people to vote?

Lawyer-lobbyists advocate the position of their clients. Our first role is to determine the proper forum—the courts, Congress or a regulatory agency—in which the client can seek to achieve its goals.

When the issue involves Congress, we prepare substantive materials explaining the issue and the likely impact on the member's district: How many jobs are at stake? What's the likely impact on the local economy? We help to identify and mobilize grass roots constituents who agree with our client's position. We build coalitions among these diverse groups.

Facts are the first source of a lobbyist's power. Forty-three percent of House members have served less than five years. Newspapers cannot give them the substantive detail they need. Congressional staffs are overworked and underpaid. Lobbyists help fill the information vacuum.

The second source of the lobbyist's power is money. In 1992 House races, including uncontested seats, major party candidates spent $369,000 on average. That's less than $1 per voter. Citizens see more advertising for hamburgers and beer than for political candidates. The problem with the campaign finance system lies not in the amount spent but in the incursion on a member's time that fund-raising entails. In a $500,000 campaign, the member may have to make 4,000 phone calls at two calls per contribution to get an average contribution of $250.

Lobbyists help by raising money from clients, colleagues and allies. And the help brings influence, connections and returned phone calls. But anyone can give or raise money. A lawyer cannot become a truly effective lobbyist without strategic skills and information, which can be shared with the member of Congress.

The first source of power—facts—is essential to the democratic process. The second—fund-raising—we all could do without. Meaningful campaign finance reform would reduce this source of power.

To take the fund-raising burden away from the candidate, and with it the need to rely on lobbyists' assistance, we should strengthen the parties and make them the primary recipients and distributors of campaign funds. We could begin with a transition period when candidates could raise a fixed amount, which would be matched by the party. As the parties grew stronger, candidate fund-raising could be phased out.

Many observers advocate public financing and permanent campaign-spending limits—ill-advised proposals, in my opinion. Public financing requires spending limits, and such limits would protect incumbents blessed with name recognition, franking privileges and free media time. Voters need more information, not less. Candidates, particularly challengers, spend money to get their message to the people.

Other reforms are needed. Lobbying disclosure rules only require the reporting of meetings with a member of Congress to influence him or her about pending legislation, along with very limited information about the legislation involved. The rules should be amended to include contacts with executive branch officials. A central repository should be maintained with uniform reporting requirements for all types of contacts. More detail should be required on the subject involved.

Some limitation on post-government employment lobbying should be maintained. But the restriction cannot be so Draconian as to limit the talent available to the legislative and executive branches.

A third source of lobbying power has waned with time. In the 1980s, lobbyists were needed to bridge the gap of divided government. On occasions when gridlock was overcome, lobbyists usually played a significant role in bringing factions of the two parties together. Conversely, lobbyists in the 80s could use gridlock by championing partisanship in order to obtain the opposition of the White House or Congress to the proposals of the other branch.

But the American people spoke clearly in November [1992]: no more gridlock. Public officials and lobbyists alike should get that message.

The system has some problems. Too much time is spent raising money, and lobbyists play too important a function in that regard. But the democratic process works best when all "special interests" are heard and all information is available to policymakers. Lobbyists serve an important role in the process.

Christopher Drew and Michael Tackett "More and More, Lobbyists Call Shots in D.C."*

Soon after the U.S. Senate passed an amendment last year that would have forced banks to lower the interest rate on credit cards, Jack Bonner's phone was ringing.

Banking industry officials, fearful of losing billions in profits, urgently needed Bonner's help. They wanted his "grass roots" lobbying firm to create the appearance of a spontaneous uprising against the measure.

The amendment had enormous appeal. What consumer wouldn't want to pay less interest? And why should banks be able to charge 19 percent interest on credit card purchases, more than 10 percentage points above the prime lending rate?

The Senate had approved the amendment by an overwhelming vote, 79–14. Sen. Alfonse D'Amato (R-N.Y.), the amendment's sponsor, bounced all over television, delighting in the role of the little guy's champion. House Speaker Tom Foley (D-Wash.) voiced initial support. And President Bush had started the push by calling for lower rates in a speech.

The issue had gale-force Washington wind behind it.

"It came out of the blue," said Philip Corwin, a lobbyist for the American Bankers Association. "Everybody concerned was panicked."

The banking industry wanted Bonner to fan opposition among influential people in the congressional districts of 10 carefully selected members of the House Banking Committee. With the support of these members, along with those considered reliable allies, the bankers believed they could kill the amendment to a broader banking bill.

Bonner sells instant democracy. He offers clients help in winning a legislative fight "predicated on the belief" that the best way to sway elected officials to vote in a particular way is to prove "that a broad cross section of their constituency understands the issue and supports a certain legislative outcome." . . .

. . . To fight the credit card amendment, hundreds of Bonner's people, schooled in guerrilla tactics of persuasion, made more than 10,000 phone calls over a four-day period, including a weekend, urging voters to call or write their lawmakers.

His people are not standard telemarketers who speak in monotones. He calls them "unemployed policy junkies," available only in Washington's unique labor pool. Many had worked in politics and government; they knew how to construct an argument and fervently pitched the banking industry position.

The callers' argument was that if the amendment became law, millions of people might have to give up their credit cards. (The bankers association now concedes it had no firm evidence to support the claim.) They also

*Christopher Drew and Michael Tackett, "More and More, Lobbyists Call Shots in D.C.," *Chicago Tribune* (December 6, 1992). Reprinted with permission.

argued that small businesses would suffer because the number of credit buyers would drop.

"They want to scare the hell out of people," said a staff member of the House Banking Committee. "There's no hard evidence."

If the telephone pitch worked, Bonner's people immediately patched the voters through to their representative's office or persuaded them to write a personalized letter. . . .

. . . Collectively, Bonner and other bank lobbyists created a fog so thick that Congress did what it usually does when faced with enormous pressure: preserve the status quo. The amendment died in a House-Senate conference committee.

Curtis Prins, staff director of a House banking subcommittee, said an operation like Bonner's "prostitutes the legislative process" by spreading questionable information.

Bonner disagrees, saying, "We are in a democracy, in case anybody has forgotten. A democracy is a symphony of noise, oboes to kettle drums. The more competition there is from the Right, the Left, the center, the healthier democracy is."

"Everyone spins," he said, "Civil rights groups, environmentalists, the business groups, every group on God's green acre spins." . . .

. . . "Creating a situation," "creating an environment" and "allowing the other side to be heard" are catch phrases of Washington's fog merchants, those who take facts, craft them into a politically salable message and attempt to influence government policy. . . .

. . . This vast army of lobbyists, consultant groups, political law firms, public relations wizards and special interest groups has become a virtual fourth branch of government—one that remains powerful no matter which party is in the White House.

Many in public affairs believe the industry's spectacular growth also is tilting the balance of power in America and corrupting the basic character of its democracy. . . .

. . . And [the industry's] hold over public policy has become so tight that it practically takes a political or economic crisis for leaders to break through it. . . .

. . . Many [special interest groups and their representatives] have a virtual veto over legislation in their fields and can rip apart proposals they dislike. When their interests diverge, they often clash so ferociously that political leaders are unable to forge enough of a consensus to make bold decisions of any kind. . . .

. . . "The bottom line is that we have to change the way business is done in Washington if we are going to achieve change in the country," said Fred Wertheimer, president of Common Cause, the citizens lobby that has long pressed for reform of the campaign-finance system. . . .

. . . The influence consultants don't spend tax dollars, at least not directly. Yet their actions affect nearly every aspect of citizens' lives, from the price of medicine to the quality of food, the safety of a car and the very security of American jobs. . . .

. . . Some say the actions of lobbyists . . . have damaged the United States' competitive standing in the world economy. As international trade expands, well-connected American lobbyists often represent Japanese and other foreign corporations in their battles with Washington, sometimes at a direct cost in American jobs. . . .

. . . To be sure, no one disputes the right of any group to petition the government or to seek a guide through its bureaucratic maze. And everyone knows that a well-placed bit of pressure long has been a part of life in Washington. . . .

. . . But the lobbying community generally operated on the fringe of Washington power until the late 1960s and the early 1970s, when an explosion of federal regulations greatly extended the reach of government and convinced many corporations that they should be represented in the nation's capital.

Post-Watergate reforms in campaign financing made the under-the-table cash payment nearly extinct but created a whole gamut of legal devices, such as political action committees, to pay for influence. The 1970s also brought changes to reduce the power of the congressional leadership, fragmenting discipline in Congress and giving lobbyists more levers of appeal.

During the Reagan and Bush administrations, the demand for lobbyists soared even more, as the tension between regulation and deregulation made the executive branch [and critical agencies] an increasingly important place to do business. . . .

. . . In many ways, lobbying, like politics, is the most human of endeavors. The lobbyist's job is to get in to see the chief decision-maker and win him or her over—through friendship, blandishments or political ties. But in other ways, the influence business has become as complex and arcane as science and as nasty as political campaigning. . . .

. . . Every day, lobbyists and government officials share lunch tables at expensive Washington restaurants, such as 21 Federal and the Jockey Club at the Ritz-Carlton Hotel. Lobbyists buy up blocks of tickets to Washington Redskins games and Kennedy Center shows to entertain officials. They play host to the most lavish parties in town. They put together golf outings, Potomac River cruises and duck shoots on nearby Chesapeake Bay. Some are said to be willing losers in poker games with somebody they want to influence.

All of this has created a cocoon-like atmosphere in Washington. Indeed, the governing circles have become so inbred that harried members of Congress often turn to friendly lobbyists for advice on how to vote—or even let them draft bills.

But if quiet persuasion fails, today's lobbyists do not hesitate to launch high-tech "grass roots" campaigns—using advertisements, phone banks, a flood of computer-generated letters and hastily formed coalitions of citizen groups—to place their own spin on an issue and create the appearance of enormous public pressure. . . .

In many ways, information has become as important a form of political currency as campaign contributions.

. . . Essential Information, a self-described public interest research group, studied front groups and concluded, "Every day, groups with deceptive-sounding names, groups that represent major American corporate powers, are seeking to convince journalists and the American people that the groups represent something more than the usual corporate interests. . . .

. . . Lobbying has "stalled a lot of what the ordinary American would care about and facilitated a lot of what the average American wouldn't like," said Kevin Phillips, a Republican political strategist.

Phillips said that on a wide range of little-publicized issues, lobbyists routinely "take advantage of the process. They can preempt it, tailor it sometimes with a little amendment that doesn't affect very many people, just the Glotz Corp."

But on the bigger issues, where there is a wide public interest and greater scrutiny, Phillips said that often the net effect of all the lobbying is to "paralyze the process. Sometimes it means you wind up with the status quo. Often what it means is it is impossible to achieve any innovative breakthrough."

The revolving door between the government and the private sector is spinning faster than ever, and people who enter government often must confront lobbyists who once held their jobs and who know the rivalries and minefields within their agencies better than they do.

Indeed, some critics say government positions have become little more than a training camp for high-paying jobs in the influence industry. . . .

. . . The critics also are concerned about the lengths to which many special interests will go to try to overwhelm officials who disagree with them. . . .

. . . Some lobbyists also recognize this. Many enter the business with enthusiasm, then burn out and quit in disgust.

"I think the whole system should be stood on its head right now," said Stephen Gabbert, who was the top lobbyist for the nation's rice millers for 17 years before shifting to business consulting. "It's the way, the mindset, the attitude of the hidden government that has operated for a period of time.

"And we've reached the point where it's unable to deliver to the needs of the country," he said. "So all of these people who have been sucking their livelihoods off it, there's going to have to be some changes made."

See text p. 529

Public interest groups have often turned to the courts to gain influence, as the text notes. Access to the courts has not been unlimited, however; courts utilize rules of standing and justiciability to limit the number and kinds of cases that they hear. When public interest groups first began using the courts heavily, in the late 1960s and early 1970s, they had to establish their right to use the courts by convincing the courts that they had sufficiently specific interests and had suffered sufficiently specific harms that made it appropriate for the courts to hear their claims. At that time, the Supreme Court construed many of the requirements broadly in ways that encouraged public interest groups to initiate litigation. In recent years, however, the more conservate Reagan/Bush Court has begun to read the rules more restrictively.

In Lujan v. Defenders of Wildlife, *printed below, the Supreme Court considered whether the president and another member of the Defenders of Wildlife had standing to sue the Department of Interior over its interpretation of the requirements of the Endangered Species Act. That Act requires all federal agencies to consult with the Department of Interior to insure that their policies and programs will not jeopardize threatened or endangered species or their habitats, and to take appropriate mitigating measures to lessen the negative impact of their actions on such endangered or threatened species. In some cases, the Endangered Species Act permits the Department of Interior to derail projects altogether if their impacts cannot be diminished.*

The case below began when the Department of Interior revised its regulations to eliminate the consulting requirements for overseas projects carried out by other agencies. The Defenders of Wildlife feared that the reinterpretation gutted the central provisions of the Endangered Species Act. The group therefore sued to force the Agency for International Development and other agencies to consult with the Interior Department about an irrigation project in Sri Lanka and a redevelopment project in Egypt, claiming that those projects threatened the continued viability of elephants and leopards in the former country and crocodiles in the latter. The president and another member of Defenders of Wildlife claimed they had standing because of their interests in protecting those species. The question before the Supreme Court was whether the president and her associate met the standing requirements. To bring a suit, a plaintiff must suffer a concrete and particular injury to a legally protected right; there must be a direct causal connection between the injury and the agency's action; and it must be likely that a court decision will be effective in redressing the injury. The Court held that the plaintiffs had not met their burden, and dismissed the case.

Lujan v. *Defenders of Wildlife* (1992)*

III

. . . Respondents [have] not made the requisite demonstration of (at least) injury and redressability.

A Respondents' claim to injury is that the lack of consultation with respect to certain funded activities abroad "increases the rate of extinction of endangered and threatened species." Of course, the desire to use or observe an animal species, even for purely aesthetic purposes, is undeniably a cognizable interst for purpose of standing. "But the 'injury in fact' test requires more than an injury to a cognizable interest. It requires that the party seeking review be himself among the injured." . . . [R]espondents had to submit affidavits or other evidence showing, through specific facts, not only that listed species were in fact being threatened by funded activities abroad, but also that one or more of respondents' members

*Lujan v. Defenders of Wildlife, U.S. 112 S.Ct. 2130, 1992.

would thereby be "directly" affected apart from their " 'special interest' in the subject." . . .

We shall assume for the sake of argument that these affidavits contain facts showing that certain agency-funded projects threaten listed species—though that is questionable. They plainly contain no facts, however, showing how damage to the species will produce "imminent" injury to Mss. Kelly and Skilbred. That the women "had visited" the areas of the projects before the projects commenced proves nothing. . . .

Besides relying upon the Kelly and Skilbred affidavits, respondents propose a series of novel standing theories. The first, inelegantly styled "ecosystem nexus," proposes that any person who uses any part of a "contiguous ecosystem" adversely affected by a funded activity has standing even if the activity is located a great distance away. . . . [But to] say that the Act protects ecosystem is not to say that the Act creates (if it were possible) rights of action in persons who have not been injured in fact, that is, persons who use portions of an ecosystem not perceptibly affected by the unlawful action in question.

Respondents' other theories are called, alas, the "animal nexus" approach, whereby anyone who has an interest in studying or seeing the endangered animals anywhere on the globe has standing; and the "vocational nexus" approach, under which anyone with a professional interest in such animals can sue. Under these theories, anyone who goes to see Asian elephants in the Bronx Zoo, and anyone who is a keeper of Asian elephants in the Bronx Zoo, has standing to sue because the Director of AID did not consult with the Secretary regarding the AID-funded project in Sri Lanka. This is beyond all reason. . . . It goes beyond the limit, however, and into pure speculation and fantasy, to say that anyone who observes or works with an endangered species, anywhere in the world, is appreciably harmed by a single project affecting some portion of that species with which he has no more specific connection.

B The most obvious problem in the present case is redressability. Since the agencies funding the projects were not parties to the case, the District Court could accord relief only against the Secretary: He could be ordered to revise his regulation to require consultation for foreign projects. But this would not remedy respondents' alleged injury unless the funding agencies were bound by the Secretary's regulation, which is very much an open question. . . . [The other agencies] were not parties to the suit, and there is no reason they should be obliged to honor an incidental legal determination the suit produced. . . .

A further impediment to redressability is the fact that the agencies generally supply only a fraction of the funding for a foreign project. AID, for example, has provided less than 10% of the funding for the Mahaweli Project. Respondents have produced nothing to indicate that the projects they have named will either be suspended, or do less harm to listed species, if that fraction is eliminated. . . .

IV

The Court of Appeals found that respondents had standing for an additional reason: because they had suffered a "procedural injury." The so-called "citizen-suit" provision of the ESA provides, in pertinent part, that "any person may commence a civil suit on his own behalf (A) to enjoin any person, including the United States and any other governmental instrumentality or agency . . . who is alleged to be in violation of any provision of this chapter." . . . [T]he court held that the injury-in-fact requirement had been satisfied by congressional conferral upon all persons of an abstract, self-contained, noninstrumental "right" to have the Executive observe the procedures required by law. We reject this view. . . .

. . . The question presented here is whether the public interest in proper administration of the laws (specifically, in agencies' observance of a particular, statutorily prescribed procedure) can be converted into an individual right by a statute that denominates it as such, and that permits all citizens (or, for that matter, a subclass of citizens who suffer no distinctive concrete harm) to sue. If the concrete injury requirement has the separation-of-powers significance we have always said, the answer must be obvious: To permit Congress to convert the undifferentiated public interest in executive officers' compliance with the law into an "individual right" vindicable in the courts is to permit Congress to transfer from the President to the courts the Chief Executive's most important constitutional duty, to "take Care that the Laws be faithfully executed," Art. II, Sec. 3. It would enable the courts, with the permission of Congress, "to assume a position of authority over the governmental acts of another and coequal department," and to become "virtually continuing monitors of the wisdom and soundness of Executive action.' " We have always rejected that vision of our role. . . . We hold that respondents lack standing to bring this action.

JUSTICE STEVENS concurring in the judgment.

Because I am not persuaded that Congress intended the consultation requirement in Sec. 7(a)(2) of the Endangered Species Act of 1973 (ESA) to apply to activities in foreign countries, I concur in the judgment of reversal. I do not, however, agree with the Court's conclusion that respondents lack standing because the threatened injury to their interest in protecting the environment and studying endangered species is not "imminent." Nor do I agree with the plurality's additional conclusion that respondents' injury is not "redressable" in this litigation.

JUSTICE BLACKMUN, with whom JUSTICE O'CONNOR joins, dissenting.

I part company with the Court in this case in two respects. First, I believe that respondents have raised genuine issues of fact—sufficient to survive summary judgment—both as to injury and as to redressability. Second, I question the Court's breadth of language in rejecting standing for "procedural" injuries. I fear the Court seeks to impose fresh limitations on the constitutional authority of Congress to allow citizen-suits in the federal courts for injuries deemed "procedural" in nature. I dissent.

. . . In conclusion, I cannot join the Court on what amounts to a slash-and-burn expedition through the law of environmental standing. In my view, "the very essence of civil liberty certainly consists in the right of every individual to claim the protection of the laws, whenever he receives an injury." *Marbury v. Madison,* 1 Cranch 137 (1803).

QUESTIONS

1. With what different interest groups do you identify? Where are the points of intersection between the different groups? In what ways does belonging to a variety of groups with crosscutting interests promote compromise and consensus among those groups, as Tocqueville claims? Could it also be argued that the proliferation of interest groups with different aims paralyzes the policy process?
2. As the article discussing the Leadership Conference on Civil Rights points out, even organizations dedicated to broad common goals such as the elimination of racial bias may find it difficult to present a united front. If lobbying groups themselves cannot agree on central aims, is it reasonable to believe that Congress can make rational policy decisions that advance even wider public interests? What considerations about public welfare should be important when Congress makes policy that lobbying groups may ignore?
3. Many critics argue that lobbyists have far too much power over policy formulation in state and national governments, while lobbyists themselves argue that they are simply performing a form of public service by "filling the information vacuum." What kinds of reforms should Congress consider to lessen the power of lobbyists and political action committees? Would limits of that nature fly in the face of constitutional understandings about the rights of people to organize for political action?
4. As the text notes, litigation has increasingly become a tool that interest groups rely upon to motivate legislative action. In what ways do litigation by interest groups make agencies and Congress accountable for their actions? Alternately, does the potential for litigation simply make it possible for interest groups to push their political agendas in a different and less democratically responsible forum?

CHAPTER 13

The Media

ORGANIZATION OF THE MEDIA

See text p. 547

Few of the provisions of the Bill of Rights are as direct as the First Amendment's declaration that "Congress shall make no law . . . abridging the freedom of speech, or of the press. . . ." For this reason, and because the "marketplace of ideas" concept (discussed in Chapter 9 of the text) is so firmly a part of American political ideology, the Supreme Court has been quite reluctant to allow the states or the federal government to regulate the news industry, and attempts to censor the dissemination of material in this century have been regarded with deep suspicion.

Broad readings of the First Amendment's protection of the press also have been supported by the assertion that only a free and independent press can be the watchdog of the state.

The broadest possible readings of the First Amendment have always been supported by the claim that only a free and independent press can be the watchdog of the state. Accordingly, attempts of the government to censor the dissemination of information have always been regarded with deep suspicion, and have virtually never withstood constitutional scrutiny. The Supreme Court made this point explicitly in its decision in New York Times v. U.S. *(1971). The case involved the efforts of the* New York Times *and the* Washington Post *to publish the contents of a several-volume classified study (known as* The Pentagon Papers*) detailing the history of U.S. policy decisions during the Vietnam War, which was ongoing at the time. The United States government tried to enjoin the publication of the materials in the interests of national security. While at least two of the justices argued that the materials, if disclosed, would do "substantial damage to public interests," the Court nonetheless refused to limit the disclosure of the information. The decision denying the government's request was a very short* per curiam *opinion, meaning that the opinion was not authored by a single justice. What follows are separate concurring and dissenting opinions, reflecting the extent to which the Court was struggling with the issue of censorship of materials claimed to directly affect national security.*

New York Times Company v. *U.S.* (1971)*

JUSTICE BLACK, with whom JUSTICE DOUGLAS joins, concurring.

[Justice Black first asserts that he fears his breathren have suggested that "the publication of news may sometimes be enjoined."]

In the First Amendment the Founding Fathers gave the free press the protection it must have to fulfill its essential role in our democracy. The press was to serve the governed, not the governors. . . . The press was protected so that it could bare the secrets of government and inform the people. Only a free and unrestrained press can effectively expose deception in government. And paramount among the responsibilities of a free press is the duty to prevent any part of the government from deceiving the people and sending them off to distant lands to die of foreign fevers and foreign shot and shell. In my view, far from deserving condemnation for their courageous reporting, the New York Times, the Washington Post, and other newspapers should be commended for serving the purpose that the Founding Fathers saw so clearly. In revealing the workings of government that led to the Vietnam war, the newspapers nobly did precisely that which the Founders hoped and trusted they would do.

[W]e are asked to hold that despite the First Amendment's emphatic command, the Executive Branch, the Congress, and the Judiciary can make laws enjoining publication of current news and abridging freedom of the press in the name of "national security." The Government . . . makes the bold and dangerously far-reaching contention that the courts should take it upon themselves to "make" a law abridging freedom of the press i the name of equity, presidential power and national security, even when the representatives of the people in Congress have adhered to the command of the First Amendment and refused to make such a law. To find that the President has "inherent power" to halt the publication of news by resort to the courts would wipe out the First Amendment and destroy the fundamental liberty and security of the very people the Government hopes to make "secure." No one can read the history of the adoption of the First Amendment without being convinced beyond any doubt that it was injunctions like those sought here that Madison and his collaborators intended to outlaw in this Nation for all time.

The word "security" is a broad, vague generality whose contours should not be invoked to abrogate the fundamental law embodied in the First Amendment. The guarding of military and diplomatic secrets at the expense of informed representative government provides on real security for our Republic. The Framers of the First Amendment, fully aware of

*New York Times Company v. United States., 403 713, 1971.

both the need to defend a new nation and the abuses of the English and Colonial governments, sought to give this new society strength and security by providing that freedom of speech, press, religion, and assembly should not be abridged. . . .

JUSTICE STEWART, with whom JUSTICE WHITE joins, concurring.

. . . [T]he Executive Branch insists [that some of the materials in question] should not, in the national interest, be published. I am convinced that the Executive is correct with respect to some of the documents involved. But I cannot say that disclosure of any of them will surely result in direct, immediate, and irreparable damage to our Nation or its people. That being so, there can under the First Amendment be but one judicial resolution of the issues before us. I join the judgments of the Court.

JUSTICE WHITE, with whom MR. JUSTICE STEWART joins, concurring.

I concur in today's judgments, but only because of the concededly extraordinary protection against prior restraints enjoyed by the press under our constitutional system. I do not say that in no circumstances would the First Amendment permit an injunction against publishing information about government plans or operations.

The Government's position is simply stated: The responsibility of the Executive for the conduct of the foreign affairs and for the security of the Nation is so basic that the President is entitled to an injunction against publication of a newspaper story whenever he can convince a court that the information to be revealed threatens "grave and irreparable" injury to the public interest; and the injunction should issue whether or not the material to be published is classified, whether or not publication would be lawful under relevant criminal statutes enacted by Congress, and regardless of the circumstances by which the newspaper came into possession of the information.

. . . If the United States were to have judgment under such a standard in these cases, our decision would be of little guidance to other courts in other cases, for the material at issue here would not be available from the Court's opinion or from public records, nor would it be published by the press. Indeed, even today where we hold that the United States has not met its burden, the material remains sealed in court records and it is properly not discussed in today's opinions. Moreover, because the material poses substantial dangers to national interests and because of the hazards of criminal sanctions, a responsible press may choose never to publish the more sensitive materials. To sustain the Government in these cases would start the courts down a long and hazardous road that I am not willing to travel, at least without congressional guidance and direction.

Justice Marshall, concurring.

. . . The Constitution provides that Congress shall make laws, the President execute laws, and courts interpret laws. It did not provide for government by injunction in which the courts and the Executive Branch can "make law" without regard to the action of Congress. . . .

On at least two occasions Congress has refused to enact legislation that would have made the conduct engaged in here unlawful and given the President the power that he seeks in this case.

It would, however, be utterly inconsistent with the concept of separation of power for this Court to use its power of contempt to prevent behavior that Congress has specifically declined to prohibit.

Chief Justice Burger, dissenting.

. . . An issue of this importance should be tried and heard in a judicial atmosphere conducive to thoughtful, reflective deliberation. . . .

Would it have been unreasonable, since the newspaper could anticipate the Government's objections to release of secret material, to give the Government an opportunity to review the entire collection and determine whether agreement could be reached on publication? Stolen or not, if security was not in fact jeopardized, much of the material could no doubt have been declassified, since it spans a period ending in 1968. [T]he newspapers and Government might well have narrowed the area of disagreement as to what was and was not publishable, leaving the remainder to be resolved in orderly litigation, if necessary. To me it is hardly believable that a newspaper long regarded as a great institution in American life would fail to perform one of the basic and simple duties of every citizen with respect to the discovery or possession of stolen property or secret government documents. That duty, I had thought—perhaps naively—was to report forthwith, to responsible public officers. This duty rests on taxi drivers, Justices, and the New York Times. The course followed by the Times, whether so calculated or not, removed any possibility of orderly litigation of the issues. If the action of the judges up to now has been correct, that result is sheer happenstance. . . .

Justice Harlan, with whom Chief Justice [Burger] and Justice Blackmun join, dissenting.

. . . With all respect, I consider that the Court has been almost irresponsibly feverish in dealing with these cases.

. . . Due regard for the extraordinarily important and difficult questions involved in these litigations should have led the Court to shun such a precipitate timetable. In order to decide the merits of these cases properly, some or all of the following questions should have been faced:

—Whether the First Amendment permits the federal courts to enjoin publication of stories which would present a serious threat to national security.

—Whether the threat to publish highly secret documents is of itself a sufficient implication of national security to justify an injunction on the theory that regardless of the contents of the documents harm enough results simply from the demonstration of such a breach of secrecy.

—Whether the unauthorized disclosure of any of these particular documents would seriously impair the national security.

—What weight should be given to the opinion of high officers in the Executive Branch of the Government with respect to [earlier questions.]

—Whether the threatened harm to the national security or the Government's possessory interest in the documents justifies the issuance of an injunction against publication in light of . . . the strong First Amendment policy against prior restraints on publication . . .

These are difficult questions of fact, of law, and of judgment; the potential consequences of erroneous decision are enormous. The time which has been available to us, to the lower courts, and to the parties has been wholly inadequate for giving these cases the kind of consideration they deserve. . . .

Forced as I am to reach the merits of these cases, I dissent from the opinion and judgments of the Court. . . . Even if there is some room for the judiciary to override the executive determination, it is plain that the scope of review must be exceedingly narrow. I can see no indication in the opinions of either the District Court or the Court of Appeals in [related] litigation that the conclusions of the Executive were given even the deference owing to an administrative agency, much less that owing to a co-equal branch of the Government operating within the field of its constitutional prerogative. . . .

JUSTICE BLACKMUN, dissenting.

. . . Judge Wilkey, dissenting in the District of Columbia case, . . . concluded that there were a number of examples of documents that, if in the possession of the Post, and if published, "could clearly result in great harm to the nation," and he defined "harm" to mean "the death of soldiers, the destruction of alliances, the greatly increased difficulty of negotiation with our enemies, the inability of our diplomats to negotiate. . . ." I, for one, have now been able to give at least some cursory study . . . to the material itself. I regret to say that from this examination I fear that Judge Wilkey's statements have possible foundation. I therefore share his concern. I hope that damage has not already been done. If, however, damage has been done, and if, with the Court's action today, these newspapers proceed to publish the critical documents and there results therefrom "the death of soldiers, the destruction of alliances, the greatly increased difficulty of negotiation with our enemies, the inability of our diplomats to negotiate," to which list I might add the factors of prolongation of the war and of further delay in the freeing of

United States prisoners, then the Nation's people will know where the responsibility for these sad consequences rests.

See text p. 550

While the press is expected to act responsibly when it disseminates the news, lapses in accuracy are bound to occur. The extent of the press's obligation to verify every fact it reports is a troubling question. Traditionally, the press was responsible for compensating individuals who were defamed by false or malicious press accounts. In the last thirty years, however, media liability for damaging reputations has narrowed significantly.

The fundamental case granting greater protection to the media is New York Times v. Sullivan *(1964). L. B. Sullivan, a city commissioner in Montgomery, Alabama, whose duties included supervising the police and fire departments of that city, claimed that he had been libeled by a newspaper advertisement carried in the* New York Times. *The advertisement criticized the actions of the Montgomery police in connection with a variety of civil rights protests. There was no question that some of the violent actions ascribed to the Montgomery police force occurred, nor was there any question that some of the facts reported were inaccurate, although the materiality of those misrepresentations was questionable. The Alabama courts entered a judgement for damages against the* New York Times. *The U.S. Supreme Court reversed, holding that the newspaper would be responsible for damages resulting from inaccuracies only when the inaccuracies were reported with "actual malice." In other words, the* New York Times *was protected from liability for inadvertent falsehoods.*

New York Times Company v. *Sullivan* (1964)*

JUSTICE BRENNAN delivered the opinion of the Court.

[W]e consider this case against the background of a profound national commitment to the principle that debate on public issues should be uninhibited, robust, and wide-open, and that it may well include vehement, caustic, and sometimes unpleasantly sharp attacks on government and public officials. The present advertisement, as an expression of grievance and protest on one of the major public issues of our time, would seem clearly to qualify for the constitutional protection. The question is whether it forfeits that protection by the falsity of some of its factual statements and by its alleged defamation of respondent.

Authoritative interpretations of the First Amendment guarantees have consistently refused to recognize an exception for any test of truth, whether administered by judges, juries, or administrative officials—and especially not one that puts the burden of proving truth on the speaker. That erro-

*New York Times Company v. Sullivan, 376 U.S. 254, 1964.

neous statement is inevitable in free debate, and that it must be protected if the freedoms of expression are to have the "breathing space" that they "need to survive," [has been previously recognized].

Injury to official reputation affords no more warrant for repressing speech that would otherwise be free than does factual error, . . . even though the utterance contains "half truths" and "misinformation." Such repression can be justified, if at all, only by a clear and present danger of the obstruction of justice. [Public officials must be] treated as "men of fortitude, able to thrive in a hardy climate." Criticism of their official conduct does not lose its constitutional protection merely because it is effective criticism and hence diminishes their official reputations.

If neither factual error nor defamatory content suffices to remove the constitutional shield from criticism of official conduct, the combination of the two elements is no less inadequate. This is the lesson to be drawn from the great controversy over the Sedition Act of 1798, which first crystallized a national awareness of the central meaning of the First Amendment. Although the Sedition Act was never tested in this Court, the attack upon its validity has carried the day in the court of history. . . .

A rule compelling the critic of official conduct to guarantee the truth of all his factual assertions—and to do so on pain of libel judgments virtually unlimited in amount—leads to a comparable "self-censorship." Allowance of the defense of truth, with the burden of proving it on the defendant, does not mean that only false speech will be deterred. Even courts accepting this defense as an adequate safeguard have recognized the difficulties of adducing legal proofs that the alleged libel was true in all its factual particulars. Under such a rule, would-be critics of official conduct may be deterred from voicing their criticism, even though it is believed to be true and even though it is in fact true, because of doubt whether it can be proved in court or fear of the expense of having to do so. They tend to make only statements which "steer far wider of the unlawful zone." The rule thus dampens the vigor and limits the variety of public debate. It is inconsistent with the First and Fourteenth Amendments.

The constitutional guarantees require, we think, a federal rule that prohibits a public official from recovering damages for a defamatory falsehood relating to his official conduct unless he proves that the statement was made with "actual malice"—this is, with knowledge that it was false or with reckless disregard of whether it was false or not. . . .

We conclude that such a privilege is required by the First and Fourteenth Amendments. We hold today that the Constitution delimits a State's power to award damages for libel in actions brought by public officials against critics of their official conduct. Since this is such an action, the rule requiring proof of actual malice is applicable. . . .

[The Alabama court's ruling would result in] transmuting criticism of government, however impersonal it may seem on its face, into personal criticism, and hence potential libel, of the officials of whom the government is composed. Raising as it does the possibility that a good-faith critic of government will be penalized for his criticism, the proposition relied on by the Alabama courts strikes at the very center of the constitutionally protected area of free expression. We hold that such a proposition may not constitutionally be utilized to establish that an otherwise impersonal attack on governmental operations was a libel of an official responsible for those operations.

The judgment of the Supreme Court of Alabama is reversed and the case is remanded to that court for further proceedings not inconsistent with this opinion.

Reversed and remanded.

JUSTICE BLACK, with whom JUSTICE DOUGLAS joins, concurring.

I base my vote to reverse on the belief that the First and Fourteenth Amendments not merely "delimit" a State's power to award damages to "a public official against critics of his official conduct" but completely prohibit a State from exercising such a power. The Court goes on to hold that a State can subject such critics to damages if "actual malice" can be proved against them. "Malice," even as defined by the Court, is an elusive, abstract concept, hard to prove and hard to disprove. The requirement that malice be proved provides at best an evanescent protection for the right critically to discuss public affairs and certainly does not measure up to the sturdy safeguard embodied in the First Amendment. Unlike the Court, therefore, I vote to reverse exclusively on the ground that the Times and the individual defendants had an absolute, unconditional constitutional right to publish in the Times advertisment their critisms of the Montgomery agencies and officials.

NEWS COVERAGE

See text p. 551

As the text notes, a variety of factors—journalists, sources, and audience—affect the nature of the news that is reported. While journalists have long been subject to criticism for their "liberal bias," hostility toward the media and distrust of the news it is reporting has increased substantially in the last several years. Investigative reporter David Shaw of the Los Angeles Times *explores this phenomenon in the following article. Increased coverage of all kinds has exposed the process of newsmaking itself, he argues, which provides greater opportunities for criticism. Moreover, journalists have become increasingly a part of the elite about whom they report, and hostility increases along with the distance the press creates from ordinary people.*

David Shaw
"Distrustful Public Views Media as 'Them—Not Us' "*

By almost any reasonable measure, the mainstream news media in this country are more responsible and more ethical today than at any time in their history.

Gone—for the most part—are the days when editors and reporters accepted extravagant gifts and free meals from news sources, when reporters routinely masqueraded as police officers, doctors and others in pursuit of a story, when stories were featured or killed almost daily to accommodate the financial, political or social interests of the publisher—or his wife.

And yet public confidence in the news media is in steady decline. In a *Times* poll conducted last month, only 17% said the media, overall, are doing a "very good" job—down from 30% in 1985. Almost 70% agreed with the statement: "The news media give more coverage to stories that support their own point of view than to those that don't." Forty percent said they have less confidence in the news media today than they did when they first began paying attention to news and current events.

Why?

One explanation may be that many members of the public feel a growing disenfranchisement from the news media, as they do from the government. Increasingly, they think, the people who report, edit and broadcast the news are elitist—well-paid, well-educated sophisticates who are more interested in (and have more in common with) the movers and shakers they cover than in the everyday concerns of the average reader and viewer.

Many in the responsible, mainstream news media—especially the print media—say there's another problem. They're paying, they say, for the sins of their less responsible, sensation-minded brethren, many of them in television.

Fact-based docudramas, tabloid TV shows such as "Hard Copy," "Inside Edition" and "A Current Affair," and local TV news shows that emphasize murder and mayhem—flash, crash and trash—have blurred the lines between substance and fluff, between journalism and hype, between news and entertainment. . . .

. . . [F]or many people the programs, "all have fundamentally the same perceived value."

As David Paletz, a professor at Duke University who writes about media and politics, puts it: "All the stuff on TV which is not news but is in some way close to news amplifies the diversity of what can be considered news, and people . . . ultimately equate them with regular news."

The result, Paletz says, is a kind of "news miasma."

*David Shaw, "Distrustful Public Views Media As 'Them—Not Us,' " *Los Angeles Times* (April 1, 1993). Reprinted with permission.

But readers and viewers are not the only victims of this miasma. Reporters, editors and television news directors also seem at times to give news organizations with widely varying standards "fundamentally the same perceived value."

Jose Rios, news director at KTTV Channel 11, a Fox station, says the success of the tabloid TV programs has influenced the way traditional television newsrooms operate. "You look at what's on the air on some stations, just in terms of production, it would have been absolutely *verboten* five years ago," he says.

Mainstream newspapers have been similarly influenced by both tabloid television and the tabloid newspapers sold in supermarkets. . . .

. . . [A] supermarket tabloid, the *Globe,* was the first U.S. publication to name the Florida woman who accused William Kennedy Smith of raping her two years ago. (Smith was acquitted.) Despite policies against using the names of rape victims, NBC used the tabloid's story to justify its own broadcast of the woman's name—and the *New York Times* decided that if NBC News could do so, the *Times* should too. . . .

. . . Since the public tends to lump much of the news media together, it may not matter much which medium or which news organization is the silliest or most irresponsible. As Dan Rather says, "I don't think it helps anybody in journalism to point fingers and make accusations along the lines of, 'Your end of the boat is sinking.' There's no such thing as 'Your end of the boat is sinking.' If the boat is sinking, then we're all sinking—the boat in this case being our reputation, our credibility with the public."

Media credibility is not all that's sinking in contemporary society, though. Public opinion polls reveal a growing disenchantment with all social institutions. The number of people saying they have a "great deal" or "a lot" of confidence in Congress, organized religion, the Supreme Court, public schools, big business and organized labor have all declined in those polls over the last 20 or 25 years. . . .

. . . "The gnawing contrast between what life should be, according to [the commercial] blandishments we see, and what it is increasingly . . . has contributed to a pervasive hostility between the races, between men and women, between people and their institutions, including the media," says Mark Crispin Miller, a professor of media studies at Johns Hopkins University. . . .

In the case of the news media, the hostility may be especially virulent because the role and visibility of the media have probably changed more in recent years than have the role and visibility of any other major social institution.

Historically, most of the news that people read and saw was prepackaged; reporters asked questions and wrote stories and when newspaper and magazine editors and television news directors deemed them ready for the public, they were published and broadcast. The journalistic process itself was invisible—concealed.

Now CNN, C-SPAN and the major networks bring live news—press conferences, troop landings, presidential debates—into the nation's living rooms as they're happening; viewers often get to see reporters asking rude, stupid, arrogant, insensitive questions, whether shouted at President Ronald Reagan in the Rose Garden or directed at military leaders in press briefings during the Persian Gulf War.

The actual process of journalism, like that of making sausage, is not very attractive. Many people wouldn't eat sausage if they had to watch it being made; it shouldn't be surprising that they often feel like throwing up when they watch reporters at work. . . .

. . . Not only have the media become visible and ubiquitous but—perhaps most important—they have become substantially more powerful. Mergers and monopolies have given individual news organizations more power, and the decline of political parties and several other institutions have given the news media overall more power.

Americans have traditionally been skeptical of powerful individuals and institutions, and as the media have become more powerful—in effect, replacing the political parties as kingmakers (and kingbreakers) on the campaign trail, for example—growing public hostility was probably inevitable. The media, collectively, have simply become a bigger and more inviting target.

Along with increased power, however, has come a growing elitism in the media and a concomitant sense in the public that the media no longer represents the average person.

Alexis de Tocqueville, the French author and statesman, wrote in the late 1830s that American journalists, while "not great writers," nonetheless were the only American writers he would acknowledge because, "generally in a very humble position, with a scanty education . . . they speak the language of their country."

Most journalists remained—until relatively recently—"of the people, not above the people" and as a result, they were generally portrayed in popular culture as good men with "good values; they represented the common American," in the words of Roy Peter Clark of the Poynter Institute for Media Studies.

Real-life journalists were typically underpaid, unsophisticated, chain-smoking, hard-drinking "blue-collar, salt-of-the-earth types . . . [who] stood up for the little guy" and they were depicted accordingly on the silver screen, says Glenn Garelik, a longtime magazine journalist who teaches courses in "the media and society in the 1990s" at Georgetown University. . . .

. . . No more.

Over the past dozen years, in movies such as "Absence of Malice," "Die Hard," "Bob Roberts" and "The Bonfire of the Vanities"—and in such television series as "Hearts Afire" and "Love & War"—journalists have been variously depicted as superficial, callous, exploitative and possessed of overweening ambition and "values that much of their audience find inimical," as Garelik wrote in the *New York Times* early this year.

Back when reporters were "paid $9 a week and had just a high school education . . . [they] knew the streets . . . they could go where the rats could go," Garelik said in an interview.

Now, to many, the media are the rats. . . .

. . . It could be argued, of course, that this pop culture depiction of the journalist doesn't mirror reality so . . . much as it creates (or at least influences) reality—that people think ill of journalists because they're responding to recent movie and television portrayals that have made journalists look bad.

Which came first—the image or the reality? Do the two reinforce each other? Or do the images created by movies and television have such resonance with the public largely because they confirm what the public already thinks?

To be sure, today's better-educated, more sophisticated journalists bring a quality and range of knowledge and expertise to the job that makes today's newspapers, on balance, better and more comprehensive than they were 30 years ago, says Shelby Coffey, editor of the *Los Angeles Times.* But those improvements have come at a price—a growing gap between the news media and the people for whom they write and broadcast.

There's "a sense that we're elite," says Fancher of the *Seattle Times.* "We come off as thinking we're a whole helluva lot smarter than the people we [write] . . . for, and they don't like that."

[Van Gordon] Sauter, the Fox News president, worries that many in the media have become so "arrogant . . . so damned stuffy and self-important and self-righteous and, in effect, sort of removed from the daily concerns of people that it was easy for people to go to other sources [of news] that just seem a bit more real."

Too many traditional journalists these days, Sauter says, "think that they somehow have been anointed by some higher power to bring 'The Truth' to the peasantry—and the peasantry is saying, 'Up yours.' "

It's no wonder that during several controversies in recent years—the congressional pay raise in 1988, the House banking scandal in 1991–92, the nomination of Zoe Baird as U.S. attorney general this year—it was radio and TV talk shows, not the mainstream news media, that first connected with the anger and resentment many Americans felt.

The news media are "just not making the connections to the audience" that they once did, says Maxwell McCombs, a professor of communications at the University of Texas. "People simply aren't interested in what we have to say. . . . What's in newspapers, what's on television, just doesn't have much relevance to their daily lives."

Newspaper editors have been talking more in recent years about the need for "diversity" in the newsroom, in part to make their publications more relevant to many readers in our increasingly multicultural society. That's obviously an urgent need; for all the talk newspaper newsrooms remain 90% white—and 66% male. One reason there is growing public disenchantment with the news media is that there are growing numbers of ethnic minorities in our society—and growing numbers of very vocal critics among minorities and women—who do not see the reality of their daily lives reflected in news coverage.

But newsroom diversity must also include white ethnics and others from middle-class, non-Ivy League homes, people who drive Fords, not BMWs, people who—like their predecessors—can relate to the people they write for.

More than 80% of all U.S. journalists hold bachelor's degrees, compared with 21% in the general population. The median salary for a journalist is $31,000—compared with an average per capita income in this country of $19,000—and many top journalists in big cities make six-figure salaries; some of the most influential, especially in television, make more than $1 million a year.

Increasingly, these journalists-cum-entrepreneurs frequent fancy French restaurants, write books and go on lucrative lecture tours. Like the politicians, entertainers, athletes, Wall Street lawyers and titans of industry they write about, they've become celebrities in their own right.

A *Los Angeles Times* story listing celebrities who attended President Clinton's inaugural ball listed "media celebrities" Bob Woodward, Carl Bernstein and Peter Jennings *before* mentioning either the "Hollywood celebrities"—Warren Beatty, Jack Nicholson, Sigourney Weaver and Shirley MacLaine—or the "political celebrities"—George Stephanopoulos, the White House press secretary; Gov. Ann Richards of Texas, and Ron Brown, then Commerce secretary-designate.

Media celebrities routinely party and vacation with top government officials and other famous people; they also grace the covers of national magazines and appear regularly on the Sunday morning television talk shows, where they chat up—on a first-name basis—the very politicians the public has become disillusioned with.

In the recent *Times* poll, 65% of the people agreed with the statement, "The press looks out mainly for powerful people," 60% said people who work in the news media have little in common with people like them; 50% said they only "infrequently" see things that are relevant to their own lives reported in the news media.

"The top journalists move in packs with the affluent and powerful in Washington," says Hodding Carter, the columnist and television commentator. "They swarm with them in the summer to every agreeable spot on the Eastern Seaboard. When any three or four of them sit down together on a television talk show, it is not difficult to remember that the least well paid of these pontificators make at least six times more each year than the average American family."

Many journalists, it seems, have lost not only their traditional connection to the common man but their sense of being outsiders, their perspective, even, at times, their independence. They may still talk about the underdog, but their friends are often the "overdogs"; many journalist now have more in common, socially and financially, with the ruling class than the underclass. In a time of unprecedented public skepticism toward those in government, the most prestigious news media have virtually become part of government—the Fourth Estate in word and deed.

"The power structure has co-opted us, and . . . our egos were such that we allowed it to happen," says Dennis Britton, editor of the *Chicago Sun-Times*.

When Bill and Hillary Rodham Clinton decided to enroll their daughter, Chelsea, in the private Sidwell Friends school in Washington, a *New York Times* story on the school was headlined "Sidwell Is Often Chosen by Capital's Elite;" the first "elite" parents named in the story were Donald E. Graham, publisher of the Washington Post; Judy Woodruff, the PBS reporter, and Albert R. Hunt, Washington bureau chief of the Wall Street Journal. After these Washington elite came three U.S. senators. Then: David Brinkley of ABC News and Leslie Stahl of CBS News.

As Charles Peters, editor of the *Washington Monthly,* said in his March column, "This helps explain the lack of criticism from the Washington press about the Clintons' decision to send Chelsea to a private school."

Peters says these shared attitudes also help explain why the news media were "so slow to see the problem" presented by "another common practice among the elite"—hiring an illegal immigrant housekeeper and not paying Social Security taxes.

When it was disclosed that Baird, President Clinton's first choice for attorney general, had done just that, the Washington Post headlined a story, "Baird's Hiring Not Seen as a Major Block."

But the public was outraged, and a week later, the nomination was withdrawn.

It's not surprising that many in the public see the news media as part of "them" in the increasing "us" vs. "them" polarization of American society.

"I think we are elitist in that the people who are in my [newsroom] . . . and in . . . your newsroom aren't representative of the broader society that they cover," says William Woo, editor of the *St. Louis Post-Dispatch.* "I think we are out of touch in terms of associations.

"How many members of the *Los Angeles Times* and the *Post-Dispatch* belong to the American Legion, belong to Kiwanis, go to prayer breakfast? I can tell you that a helluva lot of people that we like to sell the paper to go to those things. . . . I think we are disconnected," he says.

With that disconnect comes, inevitably, a certain insensitivity, even callousness. As a result, many members of the public say, the news media too often intrude into the private lives and private moments of non-public figures, people very much like themselves.

"They stick a microphone in front of accident victim and say, 'Hi, I'm from the news. How do you feel now that you're dying?' " Marian Dolan, 56, of Folkston, Ga., told a *Times* reporter in a follow-up interview to the *Times* poll.

"How do they think someone feels? Don't they know? Don't they care?" . . .

. . . This public disenchantment has given rise to a whole range of media critics as well as to several media watchdog groups. Accuracy in Media. Fairness and Accuracy in Reporting. The Media Research Center. The Center for Media and Public Affairs.

The very existence—and virulence—of their criticism has helped contribute to the perception that the media are more flawed than ever.

In an attempt to analyze this perception—and the underlying realities—news media executives in their annual meetings routinely feature speeches and panel discussions on what the press is doing wrong and how performance can be improved. Newspapers, magazines and, less often, television also carry occasional stories that examine media misconduct. Media companies like *Times Mirror*—and its subsidiary the *Los Angeles Times*—conduct polls on public attitudes toward the media. . . .

. . . But these remain the exceptions. There is little systematic examination in the media of how the media do their job, what their decision-making processes are, what their traditions, limitations, objectives and profit margins are.

"We pride ourselves on doing superficial looks at whether we wrote a story for the right reasons or not," says Geneva Overholser, editor of the *Des Moines Register*. "But we don't let it all hang out about whether the corporatization of American journalism is terrible for American democracy." . . .

. . . If the news media want to reverse their decline in public esteem, "We better start explaining ourselves more," Rather says. "I do not except myself from the criticism that we haven't done a very good job of it."

Debating the Issues: Opposing Views

THE MEDIA: HOW INFLUENTIAL ARE THEY?

See text pp. 566–67

The text points out that the members of the media have significant potential for shaping public perceptions of issues and public opinion generally. The extent of that power is taken up in the next two pieces.

In the first piece, David Shaw (whose article on media elitism is reprinted on page 000) takes a look at how the media sets the agenda for generating news. He argues that the process is more haphazard than may be presumed; he also argues that the newsworthiness of an item may have less to do with journalistic preferences than with how easily the item translates into a real "story"—with believable characters, a narrative flow, and a plot line. This need to create a story makes it difficult to generate attention for some stories, because of the lack of simplicity of some issues and the lack of persistence by journalists. Nonetheless, Shaw agrees that "it's clear that the media [does] play a major role in determining what impact a given story will have on the public—on the political-governmental process."

The shorter editorial piece that follows, written shortly before the 1992 presidential election by Richard Harwood of the Washington Post, *suggests that journalists wield less power than they think. He argues that journalists have tried to usurp the power to create the news, and that candidates like Ross Perot and then-candidate Bill Clinton were effective in bypassing the traditional media. Harwood asserts that journalists have tried to capture too much attention themselves, and that the real problem is getting journalists "off the stage and back into the audience where they belong."*

David Shaw
"Media Set Agenda But Often Misjudge Public's Interest"*

That's one reason the media devoted so much time and space in the last two presidential campaigns to stories on the alleged infidelities of Sen. Gary Hart and Gov. Bill Clinton.

But public opinion surveys show that people think the media went overboard; 70% said Hart's sex life received too much media coverage in 1988, and in one poll, 69% said the same about Clinton this year. More than 60% also said the press has paid too much attention to another big story in the 1992 campaign—Clinton's problems with the draft during the Vietnam War.

Does this mean that editors and television news executives do not know what the public's really interested in—what stories will (or won't) have genuine impact?

In a sense, that's exactly what it means.

Newspapers, magazines and television stations periodically conduct readership surveys and focus groups, but journalism is not an exact science; it's an art—a craft.

"In a given news meeting, there may be 10 different editors sitting around, all very smart, each with a different idea of what the reader wants," says Bob McGruder, managing editor for news at the *Detroit Free Press.* "All around the country, declining newspaper circulation suggests that a whole bunch of us may not be right."

Respondents to public opinion polls may be embarrassed to say they are interested in stories on sex and other gossip, but it is clear that reporters and editors simply have "no real measure of public interest," says Herbert J. Gans, a sociologist at Columbia University and the author of "Deciding What's News."

Perhaps that is why editors are so often surprised when one story has an enormous public impact and another, which they think will have an impact, vanishes without a trace.

Robert Kaiser, managing editor of the *Washington Post,* expected that the presidential campaign of former California Gov. Edmund G. (Jerry) Brown would be "wiped out" last March by a "fabulous . . . splendidly done" page 1 story in the *Post* alleging that he had plagiarized the speech announcing his candidacy. But Brown went on to win the Vermont presidential primary the day after the *Post* story and he finished a strong second in Minnesota a week later before his campaign ran out of gas—without either the public or other media ever paying much attention to the *Post* story.

Virtually every other editor in the country can tell a similar tale. But

*David Shaw, "Media Set Agenda But Often Misjudge Public's Interest," *Los Angeles Times* (October 26, 1992). Reprinted with permission.

many editors—and many reporters and television news directors—say that does not really bother them. They're just messengers, they say; they don't try to create impact—they merely report the news. They do place some stories on page 1 because they think readers should know—and care—about them, and if the story ultimately has impact, that's fine; but if it doesn't, that's fine, too.

McGruder thinks that's disingenuous.

"When editors put a story at the top of page 1, they want it to have impact," he says. "That's why they put it there."

Intentional or not, it's clear that the media do play a major role in determining what impact a given story will have on the public—and on the political-governmental process.

Given the decline of political parties in the United States in recent years, the media have become "the principal gatekeepers for the dialogues of political debate," William Greider writes in his book "Who Will Tell the People?"

"What matters to the press matters perforce to politicians," Greider says. "What the press ignores, the politicians may safely ignore too. What the newspapers tell people, whether it is true or false or cockeyed, is what everyone else must react to."

Hence, Greider argues, no media coverage means no public reaction, which means no government action.

And when the media *do* devote attention to an issue?

Just by reporting it, how they report it and how they play it—emphasizing one angle over another, using it at the top of page 1 or as the lead story on the evening newscast—the media can help shape or crystallize or accelerate public response to a story.

The "dominant interpretation" of the Los Angeles riots by the local media was that the riots were "triggered by economic deprivation, by years of neglect [on] . . . housing, jobs and education," says Shanto Iyengar, a UCLA professor of political science and the author of "News That Matters: Television and American Opinion."

The media carried far more references to these issues than to "hoodlums and thugs and vandalism," Iyengar says, and that helped determine how the public, locally and nationally, interpreted and responded to the riots.

To many in the media and community, that's exactly how the riots should be interpreted. But from "a conservative point of view," Iyengar says, it could be argued that "this was distorted by the media."

Many Republicans felt that media coverage was similarly distorted in the case of President Gerald Ford's comment during a 1976 presidential debate that "there is no Soviet domination of Eastern Europe."

Focus groups interviewed immediately after the presidential debate in which Ford made the remark thought his comment of so little importance that no one mentioned it. Polls taken at the same time showed that viewers, by a 44% to 33% margin, thought Ford had done a "better job" in the debate than Jimmy Carter.

But as University of Virginia political science professor Larry Sabato writes in his book "Feeding Frenzy," the news media judged Ford the loser "almost entirely on the strength—or weakness—of the 'free Poland' remark."

"All three networks focused on the costly mistake in their post-debate commentary. . . . Most of the major newspapers reinforced this message the following morning; so did the next evening's television coverage.

"The drumbeat of negative coverage took a heavy and steady toll on Ford's standing," Sabato writes, and within 24 hours, his 44% to 33% "victory" disappeared; suddenly, people said Carter had won the debate—and they said so by the astonishing margin of 62% to 17%.

Ford's campaign never recovered.

Many critics saw that as a "typical case of the media's liberal bias." Indeed, to these critics, a given story has impact (or not) simply because The Media want it to have impact (or not). As Ross Perot said in a recent NBC interview with Bryant Gumbel: "Y'all decide what's going to happen, then make it happen."

Critics on the left advance a similar theory. Just as conservatives say the media is biased because most reporters and editors are liberal, so liberals say the media is biased because most media owners have financial interests and social and political ties that give them a vested interest in protecting the Establishment, preserving the status quo.

Thus, Bruce Brugman, editor and publisher of the *Bay Guardian,* offers this explanation—denied by all concerned—for why the *Miami Herald* exposed Hart's evening with Donna Rice in 1988:

Vice President George Bush saw Hart as his most formidable potential foe. The *Herald* belongs to the Knight-Ridder newspaper chain. Knight-Ridder at that time "needed two . . . billion-dollar favors from the Reagan/Bush administrations"—approval of a money-saving Joint Operating Agreement (JOA) for its paper in Detroit and agreement not to interfere with the planned shutdown of its JOA partner/competitor in Miami, the *Miami News. Viola*—the *Herald* staked out Hart's townhouse and destroyed his campaign. Bush was reelected in a landslide and Knight-Ridder got what it wanted in Miami and Detroit.

Similarly, critics on the left point to many other stories that have had no impact simply because the media ignored them. Many women and ethnic minorities say this is because decisions on media coverage and play are usually made by white male editors. But other stories are also ignored or given minimal attention.

Carl Jensen, a professor of communications at Sonoma State University, runs "Project Censored," which for the last 16 years has compiled and disseminated a list of "The 10 Best Censored Stories" of each year—meaning stories that were either largely ignored or not covered as widely and intensely by the national media as Jensen's jury thinks they should have been. Although Jensen insists he has no ideological ax to grind, a significant majority of the stories cited each year do conform to what might be called a "liberal agenda."

In recent years, Jensen's "censored" stories have included "corporate America's anti-environmental campaign," the Bush family's financial "conflicts of interest," the Pentagon's "secret black budget," Bush Administration policies in Guatemala, and stories on toxic waste, radioactive waste and how NASA space shuttles "destroy" the ozone layer. . . .

[Sometimes a newsworthy story gets buried because no public figure stands to gain from its revelations.]

. . . [F]ew reporters covering [the S&L scandal] in its early stages could find no one with sufficient standing who was willing to make serious charges of wrongdoing.

Unlike the House banking scandal—which had partisan protagonists—the savings and loan crisis was a thoroughly bipartisan disaster, with enough blame to embarrass Democrats and Republicans alike at all levels of government.

As the chief lobbyist for the American Bankers Assn. says in Greider's "Who Will Tell the People?" neither Republicans nor Democrats originally wanted to make a political issue of the S&L crisis because that would have claimed "more bodies on both sides than anyone wants to lose."

With no partisan protagonist to point the finger of blame—no one to, in effect, do the early dirty work for the media—the S&L story long languished in the political and journalistic backwaters. . . .

. . . "Not one paper covered it thoroughly from beginning to end," says Gregory Hill, San Francisco bureau chief for the *Journal.*

Hill says there are three reasons for this:

- Federal regulators "felt it was their duty to lie to preserve the soundness and safety of the financial system . . . [and] to help the Bush election campaign."
- "The main operators of the worst S&Ls were also lying, cooking their books, with the help of various accountants and lawyers. . . . We had no access to the examiners' financial reports of most S&Ls. . . . They were secret."
- "We as reporters simply dropped the ball. The people covering the financial institutions didn't do the job" they should have. . . .

. . . Unlike the House banking scandal, the S&L crisis was neither easy nor sexy. Despite its long-term implications for every American, it had no immediately apparent personal resonance.

"If Bush had gone on television and said: 'I am adding $100 to each . . . family's tax bill this year to pay for the S&L scandal,' then people would've reacted to it a little more," says Narda Zacchino, associate editor of the *Los Angeles Times.* But the President made no such announcement.

Nor did the early S&L stories have any villains as instantly identifiable as your local congressman.

Doug Ramsey, senior vice president of the Los Angeles-based Foundation for American Communications, says the tendency of the media to go looking for "good guys and bad guys" often prevents them from looking seriously at "systems and structures," and the S&L story is definitely a "systems and structures" story.

It is a complex, convoluted story, with roots in federal monetary policy decisions made a decade earlier and dollar figures that boggled the mind. Most people can grasp the concept of one person "bouncing" a check for $300; not many can identify with a $1-billion swindle involving an alphabet soup of little-known federal agencies.

That applies to journalists as well as to readers and viewers.

"Lack of intellectual sophistication . . . really understanding complex issues, from Soviet politics to the banking system to global warming . . . is a big problem in the news business," says Robert Kaiser of the *Washington Post.* "This is where we let our readers and our country down most often. We fail ourselves to grasp the real meaning, the real significance of something that's happening around us." . . .

. . . "Stories that are hard to grasp, that aren't black and white from the beginning, require a lot of persistence," says Jennie Buckner, vice president for news at Knight-Ridder newspapers. Some stories don't have the impact they should, she says, because the media "don't stick with it."

What social psychologists call our "media-dense environment" may also be a significant factor, especially with a story like the savings and loan crisis. . . .

Only certain messages are likely to penetrate our consciousness when we're buried in . . . an avalanche [of news and advertising]. As Aronson and Pratkanis say: "Most people are more deeply influenced by one clear, vivid, personal example than by an abundance of statistics," and the S&L story, especially as it was first told by the media, was a blizzard of statistics; what clear, vivid, personal examples there were clearly didn't resonate with the American public. . . .

. . . Lengthy, complex stories can be made interesting—compelling—as Donald Barlett and James Steele proved last year with their nine-part series in the *Philadelphia Inquirer* on the decline of the American economy. The series—titled "America: What Went Wrong?"—was filled with statistics and personal stories. Although some critics found the series oversimplified and biased, others praised its thoroughness and readability, and it clearly struck a chord with readers, triggering more than 20,000 letters and calls. The *Inquirer* sent out 400,000 reprints of the series, and the series has been expanded into a book—which has another 400,000 copies in print.

"That series proved that if you . . . speak clearly, in human terms, about what some of these complex things mean . . . people are really hungry for it," says Buckner of Knight-Ridder, which publishes the *Inquirer.*

Indeed, when Clinton appeared on Phil Donahue's syndicated television show in April and Donahue grilled him for 25 minutes about infidelity, marijuana use and other, similar matters, a woman in the audience—a Republican—demonstrated this hunger for a substantive discussion of the issues by lashing out at Donahue.

"I think . . . given the pathetic state of most of the United States at this point—Medicare, education, everything else—I can't believe you spent half an hour of air time attacking this man's character. I'm not even a Bill Clinton supporter, but I think this is ridiculous." . . .

. . . But many in the media find it easier to focus on infidelity and inhalation than on Medicare, education or—especially—high (and low) finance. Difficult stories—including most on the S&L crisis—have not often met Buckner's standards of clarity, comprehension and personal resonance. . . .

. . . To connect with readers, a story generally must be a "story" in the traditional sense—a good narrative, with a beginning, a middle and an end; dramatic examples, vivid images, recognizable characters, heroes and villains and some sense of change or development. This is especially true in the era of television, but these elements are crucial to all successful storytelling, whether on the screen, in print, over a drink or by a campfire.

That's one reason that political stories of all kinds often have an impact far beyond their substance; they have recognizable characters, plot lines and—like sports events—competition, conflict, a clear resolution, a winner and a loser. . . .

[Finally, it is difficult to generate stories outside of the "New York-Washington axis."]

Sometimes, a respected news organization from Out There can awaken national interest in a given story, but the *Houston Post*—like the *San Diego Union-Tribune*—isn't even a blip on the radar screen of the media that matter in this country. . . .

Richard Harwood
"Media Wilt: The Waning Power of the Press"*

It seems like only yesterday that the "power of the press" was a perfectly respectable topic for doctoral dissertations and serious cocktail party conversation.

The political scientists, you will recall, had constructed in the late '60s and early '70s a provocative new theory of electoral politics in America. It was premised on the notion that the political parties were functionally dead. They had been replaced by The Media. The media had no patronage or other spoils of office to dispense. They hawked no original or stirring ideology to discontented masses. But they possessed, it seemed, the awesome

*Richard Harwood, "Media Wilt: The Waning Power of the Press," *Washington Post* (June 26, 1992). Copyright 1992 by The Washington Post. Reprinted with permission.

capacity to shape the minds of the people and set the national agenda. By defining and casting judgment on the "character" of candidates, they controlled the presidential nominating process, sorting out good people from the bad.

The exiled Russian novelist, Alexander Solzhenitsyn, not only accepted that analysis but declared—though the idea appalled him—that the press had become the greatest force in Western civilization. Our presumed power and hostility became one of Richard Nixon's wretched obsessions, a major source of his paranoia, a major factor in his public disgrace.

The snuffing out in 1987 of Gary Hart's political career by a peeping Tom squad from the *Miami Herald* added to the press mystique. Bill Clinton, earlier this year, seemed condemned by us to share Hart's fate. His "character" was pounded like a cheap steak by both feral and civilized elements of the press. If he had suffered a premature political death, our role as the Attila of public life would have been affirmed yet again.

But Clinton survived, easily won the race for the Democratic nomination and pricked the popular image of the press as kingmaker. He wore his media scars as a badge of honor and, quite possibly, influenced the media strategy of the maverick candidate, Ross Perot. Rather than grovel or show deference to the press, the Perot camp has assumed from the beginning a confrontational posture: You need us; we don't need you. It hired as its public relations chief Jim Squires, a combative ex-newspaperman whose contempt for his erstwhile colleagues in journalism is unconcealed. As for the candidate, Mr. Perot, he chose to arrange his own nomination without prior reconnaissance or consultation with either the political establishment or such pillars of the media establishment as the *Washington Post,* the *New York Times* and the networks.

QUESTIONS

1. As the Supreme Court's decision in *New York Times v. United States,* points out, the circumstances under which prior restraints may be imposed upon the media are very limited indeed. How does the Court characterize the values served by the doctrine enunciated in *New York Times v. United States,* and how are those values related to broader concerns about the operations of a representative democracy?
2. Since the Supreme Court's decision in *New York Times v. Sullivan,* successful suits for libel or slander against the media have virtually disappeared. What is the extent of the media's obligation to determine the accuracy of the facts it reports? In real terms, how likely is it that a plaintiff could prove that the media acted with "actual malice" when its reports contain inaccuracies?
3. The media have long been assumed to have a liberal bias. What is meant by that term? Does a liberal bias, if one exists, serve any function, such

as offsetting the tendency of politics to reinforce the status quo? What is the difference between a liberal bias and the elite bias that is reported by David Shaw in the article reprinted above? Is an elite bias preferable to a liberal bias?

4. While the media can undoubtedly shape the news, David Shaw argues that the impact of a given story is more a function of its adaptability to a story format than to a conscious decision on the media to push one set of issues over another. Do you agree? Would the media be acting responsibly if they simply decided not to report some categories of stories, like those dealing with embarrassing revelations about a public figure's personal life? Does the media's unwillingness to devote time to reporting complex stories, like the S&L scandal discussed in the Shaw piece, reflect a failing on the part of the media or on the part of consumers of the news?
5. After reading the article by Richard Harwood, do you think the media spend too much time focused upon their own commentary on the news? In what ways might the media be encouraged to engage in more extensive investigative reporting?

CHAPTER 14

Politics and Government: The Problem with the Process

CAN THE GOVERNMENT GOVERN?

See text p. 579

As the text points out, America heads into the 21st century with a number of problems. Our government often seems impotent; the task of governing a large population with complex and rapidly changing problems seems impossible. Voters are apathetic and disconnected, the gap between the rich and the poor is increasing, and Congress and the President seem unable to agree on anything except their own re-elections.

The problems of governing in a republican democracy, however, have always been with us. In a letter to James Madison written from Paris on January 30, 1787, Thomas Jefferson spoke about the difficulties of life in such a governmental system. Referring to political unrest in the new republic, Jefferson suggested to Madison that "I hope [that the acts of rebellion among the Eastern States, while not justifiable] will provoke no severities from their governments." Political systems, he warned, especially those where "the will of everyone has a just influence," are subject to turbulence. He concluded that "a little rebellion, now and then, is a good thing, and as necessary in the political world as storms in the physical." It should not be inferred from this language that Jefferson was espousing armed rebellion at every turn. In other writings, he suggests that revolutions should occur approximately every ten years. A revolution refers to both rebellion and cycles; every decade, perhaps, the people of a nation ought to return to first principles.

Thomas Jefferson
*A Letter to James Madison**

To James Madison.

Paris, January 30, 1787.

Dear Sir,

My last to you was of the 16th of December; since which, I have received

*From "The Writings of Thomas Jefferson," in Boyd, Julian P., ed. *The Papers of Thomas Jefferson* (Princeton: Princeton University Press, 1955). Reprinted with permission.

yours of November the 25th, and December the 4th, which afforded me, as your letters always do, a treat on matters public, individual and economical. I am impatient to learn your sentiments on the late troubles in the Eastern States. So far as I have yet seen, they do not appear to threaten serious consequences. Those States have suffered by the stoppage of the channels of their commerce, which have not yet found other issues. This must render money scarce, and make the people uneasy. This uneasiness has produced acts absolutely unjustifiable; but I hope they will provoke no severities from their governments. A consciousness of those in power that their administration of the public affairs has been honest, may, perhaps, produce too great a degree of indignation; and those characters, wherein fear predominates over hope, may apprehend too much from these instances of irregularity. They may conclude too hastily, that nature has formed man insusceptible of any other government than that of force, a conclusion not founded in truth nor experience. Societies exist under three forms, sufficiently distinguishable. 1. Without government, as among our Indians. 2. Under governments, wherein the will of every one has a just influence; as is the case in England, in a slight degree, and in our States, in a great one. 3. Under governments of force; as is the case in all other monarchies, and in most of the other republics. To have an idea of the curse of existence under these last, they must be seen. It is a government of wolves over sheep. It is a problem, not clear in my mind, that the first condition is not the best. But I believe it to be inconsistent with any great degree of population. The second state has a great deal of good in it. The mass of mankind under that, enjoys a precious degree of liberty and happiness. It has its evils, too; the principal of which is the turbulence to which it is subject. But weigh this against the oppressions of monarchy, and it becomes nothing. *Malo periculosam libertatem quam quietam servitutem.* Even this evil is productive of good. It prevents the degeneracy of government, and nourishes a general attention to the public affairs. I hold it, that a little rebellion, now and then, is a good thing, and as necessary in the political world as storms in the physical. Unsuccessful rebellions, indeed, generally establish the encroachments on the rights of the people, which have produced them. An observation of this truth should render honest republican governors so mild in their punishment of rebellions, as not to discourage them too much. It is a medicine necessary for the sound health of government. . . .

[Jefferson continues with a discussion of unrelated political affairs.]

I am, dear Sir, with sincere esteem and affection, your most obedient humble servant.

THE DECLINE OF VOTING AND THE RISE OF POLITICS BY OTHER MEANS

See text p. 581

The RIP process discussed in the text was used with efficiency by conservatives who opposed the nomination of law school professor Lani Guinier, who was nominated by President Clinton in April 1993 to head the Civil Rights Division of the Department of Justice. In the initial volley, Clint Bolick, a conservative political commentator, published an article entitled "Clinton's Quota Queens" in the April 25, 1993, edition of the Wall Street Journal. *That article, reprinted below, raised questions about Guinier's fitness to serve based upon her suggestions for increasing the voting power of minorities in a number of law review articles. Guinier's statements in the articles were often provocative, arguing that politics as usual would not give minorities effective voting power. She proposed a number of alternatives, including systems of "cumulative voting," which critics viewed as contrary to a time-honored principle of "one person, one vote." The initial article was followed by a series of articles excerpting the law review materials; at one point, Bolick lampooned the Critical Race Theory school of jurisprudence as a radical movement attempting to undermine the entire American political process.*

Guinier's nomination was withdrawn within two weeks. Guinier herself expressed disappointment at the degree to which she had been personally attacked. Liberals cried, "Unfair!" claiming that Guinier's ideas were taken out of context and distorted, especially since academics are rewarded for proposing innovative and contentious ideas. Liberals also criticized President Clinton for failing to act on principle. The uproar was somewhat disingenuous, since liberals had used exactly the same process to unseat Supreme Court nominee Robert Bork only a few years earlier. Indeed, Lani Guinier was efficiently and effectively "borked."

Clint Bolick
"Clinton's Quota Queens"*

"New Democrat" Bill Clinton has taken a sharp left turn by appointing two civil rights ideologues to major posts. Yesterday he named University of Pennsylvania law professor Lani Guinier, a Carter civil rights alumna and for nine years a lawyer with the NAACP Legal Defense and Education Fund, to the top post as assistant attorney general for civil rights. Previously he nominated Norma Cantu, the Southwestern Regional Counsel for the Mexican American Legal Defense and Educational Fund (MALDEF), as assistant secretary for civil rights in the Department of Education.

Ms. Guinier and Ms. Cantu are far from household names, but the duo has the litigation experience and mental firepower to profoundly after the civil rights landscape. Both have blazed the outer frontiers in their respective areas of voting law and education.

Ms. Guinier sets the standard for innovative radicalism. In a 1989 Har-

*Clint Bolick, "Clinton's Quota Queens," *Wall Street Journal* (April 30, 1993). Reprinted with permission of the Wall Street Journal © 1993, Dow Jones and Company, Inc. All rights reserved.

vard Civil Rights-Civil Liberties Law Review article, she decries "fundamental flaws in our democracy," urging that "certain social goods—health care, day care, job training, housing—must be recognized as basic entitlements." In the same article, she proclaims that anti-discrimination laws mandate "a result-oriented inquiry, in which roughly equal outcomes, not merely an apparently fair process, are the goal," and calls for racial quotas in judicial appointments.

But for this new vanguard, quotas are only a starting point. In a 1991 Virginia Law Review article entitled "No Two Seats: The Elusive Quest for Political Equality," Ms. Guinier argues that proportional legislative representation for minority groups, which the Voting Rights Act of 1965 presently is construed to guarantee, is not enough. Instead, she demands equal legislative outcomes, requiring abandonment, not only of the "one person, one vote" principle, but majority rule itself.

The current voting rights quota system, she complains, is inadequate since it only "protects the right to be 'present,' whereas the right to control government policy is reserved to those who can organize a majority." The solution, she urges, is to eliminate the "winner-take-all" features of any majoritarian electoral or legislative voting process in which the minority is identifiable, racially homogenous, insular, and permanent."

Ms. Guinier would invoke the Voting Rights Act in such circumstances to eliminate "one person, one vote" procedures and the requirement of winning electoral or legislative majorities. Instead, she would create an "aggregating device" with which "voluntary minority interest constituencies could choose to cumulate their votes to express the intensity of their distinctive groups interests."

In the election context, this means 1) eliminating single-member legislative districts, 2) giving each voter the same number of votes as open seats, 3) allowing voters to spread out their votes among candidates or "cumulate" them, and 4) eliminating the majority threshold for election. In a contest for nine legislative seats, for instance, a candidate could win with just over 9% of the votes under this complex formula.

In the legislative arena, "simple-minded notions of majority rule," Ms. Guinier asserts, "interact with racial block voting to make statutorily protected groups perennial legislative losers." Wherever this is true, she contends, the Voting Rights Act should require new procedures to ensure "a fairer distribution of political power." Though her proposals in this context are amorphous, they include cumulative voting and elimination of majority thresholds to ensure "each group has a right to have its interests satisfied a fair proportion of the time."

Whether or not these proposals have merit as public policy, Ms. Guinier clearly believes they are compelled by the Voting Rights Act, which she would be charged with enforcing as assistant attorney general. Ms. Guinier would graft onto the existing system a complex racial spoils system that would further polarize an already divided nation.

Likewise, Ms. Cantu brings to her civil rights post in the Department of Education a zeal for social engineering both old and new. In Austin, Ms.

Cantu argued (unsuccessfully) that a community that has desegregated its schools cannot phase out forced busing until residential integration is achieved. Since residential racial balance almost never occurs in most communities, the logical extension of her argument is—surprise!—busing as a permanent part of the American landscape. In the past few years, Ms. Cantu and her allies have turned their attention to "funding equity" suits in which courts are called upon to equalize spending among school districts.

The appointments of Ms. Guinier and Ms. Cantu would place the powerful federal civil rights arsenal in the hands of ideologues. It also would blur the lines between advocacy groups and government agencies, as they were in the pre-Reagan years, when the executive branch subordinated law enforcement to its ideological agenda.

If these nominations are part of Mr. Clinton's payback to extreme left-wing elements of the Democratic Party, the price may prove too high. Republicans learned in the midterm Senate elections in 1990 (but forgot two years later) that voters, white or black, don't like quotas. White voters often view quotas as a barrier to opportunity, while few blacks or other minorities view them as beneficial in their individual circumstances.

Mr. Clinton owes his election in no small part to the disappearance of the "Q" word from the political lexicon in 1992. If he persists in entrusting the civil rights law enforcement apparatus to the likes of Ms. Guinier and Ms. Cantu, the in-your-face civil rights agenda they no doubt will promote may ultimately prove the most incendiary of political miscalculations.

NO MORE DIVISION?

See text p. 590

As the text notes, the problems of gridlock have not disappeared, as many political observers had hoped, with the election of a Democratic president. David Broder and Michael Weisskopf, political writers for the Washington Post, *point out that "the capital and Congress really are [resistant] to change." Kenneth Duberstein, the top congressional lobbyist for the Reagan White House, argues in the article that "[t]he system is biased toward inaction. . . . Members of Congress do not feel beholden to any president, let alone one who trailed them in their districts. . . . Every time they vote with the President, their instinct will be to vote against him the next time—just to show their independence."*

David S. Broder and Michael Weisskopf "Return to Gridlock: Clinton Confronts a Resistant Capital"*

"This is one tough town!"

That exclamation—half complaint, half admission—from a junior staff member in the Clinton White House last week marks the transformation of a presidency that began with a pledge to "end the era of deadlock and drift" and has come to seem a punching bag for every rebellious Democratic senator, congressional caucus or interest group that wants to take a jab.

While President Clinton has been given at least his share of the blame for the lurch back to gridlock, there are those who say the larger story is how resistant the capital and Congress really are to change.

House Ways and Means Committee Chairman Dan Rostenkowski (D-Ill.), who has not been reluctant in recent weeks to second-guess White House tactics, still insists that the fault is not entirely Clinton's.

"There are too damn many people here in both parties who are a helluva lot more comfortable with the status quo," he said in an interview, angry after the House Democratic caucus declined to discipline 11 subcommittee chairmen who voted against the Clinton budget. "Clinton ran on change and the public embraced it. . . . Is Congress rejecting change? You're damned right it is. So who's at fault?"

Other veterans of the Washington scene are less willing to let Clinton off the hook, arguing that he and his staff underestimated the institutional forces in the city, bungled the job of building public support for his program and failed to understand how early concessions could embolden interest groups and unravel his congressional coalition.

If there was a turning point in Clinton's legislative fortunes, lobbyists here say, it was the president's decision March 29 to humor western senators by dropping provisions in his budget for higher grazing, timber-cutting and mining fees on millions of acres of public lands in their states.

Clinton promised separate legislation or administrative action to achieve the same goals, but his concession to the westerners so early in the process was seen as a sign of willingness to compromise on the principle of shared sacrifice that he called for in his Feb. 17 budget speech.

"The message was unmistakable to interest groups in Washington," said Kenneth Simonson, the American Trucking Associations' chief economist. "The way to get relief was to turn up the heat. If you can exert enough influence on your members of Congress and get them to transmit the pressure to the administration, you have a strong chance of not having to share as much sacrifice as some other folks."

*David S. Broder and Michael Weisskopf, "Return to Gridlock: Clinton Confronts a Resistant Capital," *Washington Post* (June 1, 1993).

The exemption game began quickly in the House. Working through rural lawmakers, farming interests got a lower levy on farm equipment fuels. Aluminum smelters, concentrated in the state of House Speaker Thomas S. Foley (D-Wash.), were partially exempted from the tax. Northeastern members helped heating oil dealers land a lower rate for fuel use by commercial establishments, and utility lobbyists were able to shift the collection point of a new tax from the plant to consumers, sparing power companies, the need for new rate hearings.

Still, the president's proposed Btu tax, based on the heat content of fuels, survived until the Senate Finance Committee got hold of it.

With Democrats holding a narrow 11 to 9 majority on that committee, the energy lobby saw an opening and, along with a Republican anti-tax group, mounted a costly campaign against the Btu tax in the oil-rich states of two Democratic committee members—Sens. David L. Boren (Okla.) and John Breaux (La.)

Boren was the first to defect, proposing May 20 to scrap the tax and replace it with deeper cuts in Social Security benefits and proposed tax credits for the working poor.

By late last week, after Clinton abandoned his controversial tax plan, the committee had turned into a scramble of special interests. Every proposal inspired a new lobbying counteroffensive, locking lawmakers into the kind of game that Clinton had pledged to end.

The senior citizens lobby, a populist juggernaut quieted by Clinton's plans for health care reform, sprang into action after Sen. Daniel Patrick Moynihan (D-N.Y.), the committee chairman, suggested further cuts in Medicare. Sen. John D. "Jay" Rockefeller IV (W.Va.) took up its cause.

When Breaux proposed increases in transportation fuel taxes, Transportation Secretary Federico Peña attacked the proposal for leaning too heavily on already ailing industries—a position echoed by trucking and airline lobbyists.

Just as the Breaux proposal emerged as a likely alternative to the Btu tax, Sen. Max Baucus (Mont.), another of the committee Democrats, announced his opposition to it because of the long distances driven by his constituents.

And from the House came expressions of anger toward Clinton by members who had reluctantly voted for his energy tax. The Congressional Black Caucus said there must be no further cuts in programs for the disadvantaged, and Hispanic members mobilized to protect tax breaks for U.S. companies operating in Puerto Rico.

"Gridlock is back," observed John Rother, chief lobbyist of the American Association of Retired Persons. "There was a rosy glow after the president's [Feb. 17] speech. It was sustainable, but not sustained."

Others say the problems plaguing the Clinton program stem primarily from his failure to build the kind of public support that President Ronald Reagan generated when he was moving his budget through an opposition-controlled House of Representatives in 1981.

Thomas E. Mann, a Brookings Institution scholar of Congress, dismissed the significance of much of the criticism Clinton has been getting from Democratic legislators, but said "the one legitimate gripe they have is that he has failed to provide the political cover for them to do the right thing. He has not made it easier; he has made it harder."

But Nelson Polsby, a University of California-Berkeley author of many books on Congress and the presidency, argues that "people who thought that partisanship was the only cause of the gridlock we had in Washington for 10 years haven't read the Constitution lately."

Polsby and others say the separation of powers virtually guarantees that a president's program will be radically altered, if not chopped to bits, as it moves through the House and Senate, where the political and economic interests of legislators and their constituents come strongly into play.

"All the potholes this thing has hit are reflective of how difficult this is," said Lawrence F. O'Brien III, a tax lobbyist. "What you're seeing is the contours of the modern legislative process. It's very reactive, very much organized interest group-oriented and sensitized."

One man who predicted the course of events was Kenneth M. Duberstein, the top congressional lobbyist in the Reagan White House. Back in February, when Clinton was looking briefly invincible on Capitol Hill, Duberstein rattled off a list of institutional factors that he said would make it difficult for Clinton to dominate the legislative scene.

"The system is biased toward inaction," he said. "There is little leadership or followership on the Hill. Members of Congress do not feel beholden to any president, let alone one who trailed them in their districts. . . . Every time they vote with the president, their instinct will be to vote against him the next time—just to show their independence."

That is what has happened to Clinton. After winning quick and relatively painless passage of the broad outlines of his economic plan, he has found each successive step more difficult. Interest groups, operating through small numbers of strategically placed legislators, have steadily raised the price for delivering their votes.

"The idea of fairness and shared sacrifice is a broadly shared value in this country," said Rother. "When you start carving out exceptions, it completely undermines the moral authority of that appeal."

That is why the first concession to Baucus and his fellow westerners looms so large. Clinton had described the measure to raise the fees that mining, grazing and timber interests pay to extract resources on federal lands as a needed environmental reform and a ready source of revenue estimated at $1 billion over five years.

But when Baucus and his group came to the White House on March 22 and asked for an easing of the economic burden on their region, where Clinton had run better than any other Democrat in a generation, the president was more conciliatory than Baucus had expected.

"We did not have a specific proposal and lo and behold, about a week later, the White House just announced it was taking those three [provisions] out of the budget, which surprised me," he said.

"All the time we were saying we were just looking for resolution, we didn't want to eliminate all those things."

CAN DEMOCRATIC POLITICS FUNCTION WITHOUT VOTERS?

See text p. 597

As the text suggests, there seems to be a crisis of leadership as members of Congress and the President seem unable to garner a sufficient base of popular support. Richard Reeves, a political writer for the Los Angeles Times, *argues that Americans do not really want leadership; Americans have a great deal of information at their fingertips, and they do not want to be told what to do. The nation has moved into a "post-leadership" era, Reeves says, in which the country is "governed by the people for themselves."*

Richard Reeves
"Where Have All the Leaders Gone? The People Have Replaced Them"*

American democracy, 1990:

- In California, the people vote to lessen the power of the men and women who represent them in the Legislature by limiting the time they can serve.
- In New Jersey, the governor answers pleas for leadership by producing laws and funding to improve the state's worst schools—and destroys himself in the process.
- In Washington, the two most recent chairmen of the Joint Chiefs of Staff warn members of Congress that the country should avoid war because the military cannot do what Americans want done.

All these events illustrate a breakdown of old-fashioned authority. That is the way democracy works in Post-Leadership America.

This seems to be what Americans have been waiting for—the chance to really try government by the people. It is not a question of initiative and referendum, California-style, although these blunt weapons are being used against politicians wherever possible. Rather, it is a question of more and more people wanting to exercise power themselves rather than delegating it to elected or anointed betters.

Gridlock in Washington? People love it. If "they" fight among themselves, maybe they'll leave "us" alone.

I have never really believed that Americans wanted "Leadership!" no matter how many demands for such mystical guidance I have heard in conversations and read in polls. It is like "family values." We talk about them so much because we don't have them. We are a nation of leavers, greatly preferring individual freedom and mobility to shared obligation since the days we left home and family in the Old World.

"Government is best that governs least" goes back at least to Thomas Jefferson. And we have lived for more than 200 years under a Constitution that deliberately divides powers into branches, even twigs. When anyone of

*Richard Reeves, "Where Have All the Leaders Gone? The People Have Replaced Them," *Los Angeles Times* (December 16, 1990). Reprinted with permission.

us says "leadership," we mean leadership by someone who agrees with us, or leadership that leads less.

Obviously, the nation has accepted leadership in war and peace, and in other things, too. But that acceptance was often grudging and usually based on the resigned assumption that "they," our leaders, knew something the rest of us did not. Now, more and more Americans no longer believe that—or are sure of it. More mobility, the communications revolution, particularly satellite television transmission, better education or, at least, more knowledge and national street-smarts, all are persuading many Americans that maybe we do know more than we thought we did. Or our leaders know less.

What the people know and when they know it is the engine that drives the politics of a democracy. And control of the flow of information has been the greatest of presidential powers this century. But now, all of us and each of us know more and know it sooner.

It is not only politicians who are finding that the half-lives of leadership seem to get shorter and shorter. That deterioration has been partly offset by a lowering of the standards by which leadership is judged. President Harry S. Truman's definition—"Leadership is the ability to get men to do what they don't want to do and like it"—has been transformed along the slippery slope of recent years to being interviewed by Ted Koppel or getting on the cover of a newsmagazine with a headline that indicates you seem to know what you're doing—at least for now.

As power and fame come together, some future Andy Warhol will be able to say that each American will be the leader for 15 minutes. Among the heroic leaders whose time passed this year were Lee Iacocca and Donald Trump. These two salesmen were defined as important, as daring and competent, in apposition to indecisive and evasive politicians. Iacocca and Trump were, in a sense, empty vessels filled by many—especially editors and other professional worriers—to make a point about the decline of political leadership.

But it seems that empty vessels are exactly what people want. What used to be called "being all things to all men" is being transformed into "being all things to me—for now." Leadership as winetasting.

As Americans in the lonely crowd struggle to define themselves by wearing a Rolex or driving a Jeep or reading Vanity Fair, they can also attach themselves to political (or cultural) symbols—Jesse Helms or Jesse Jackson, Jerry Falwell or Jerry Brown, Bill Cosby or Bart Simpson. The symbols come and they go. What they say or do, if they do anything at all of significance, is not the important thing.

It's not as if they're Milli Vanilli, and people are going to check on whether or not this is lip-synching. In Post-Leadership America, those who once were followers now have greater choice. They can define and re-define themselves just as politicians always have, in the land of the free and the home of the brave, phony résumé.

Americans are trying to lead themselves by switching symbols, styles, channels or venues.

Jim Florio, the governor of New Jersey, provided a lesson in why, given a choice, politicians prefer to let political consumers do with them what they will. Leaving aside the question of whether or not Florio deliberately misled the people about his intentions, within weeks of taking office he announced that the state was in real trouble and he was going to do something about it.

He said that the books were cooked, that phony numbers and other political accounting tricks had been used to hide billions of dollars in debt. Worse, the new governor said, schools in New Jersey's cities and poor rural areas were turning out functional illiterates, many of them dangerously anti-social.

So, he pushed through legislation raising state income taxes on families making more than $80,000 a year and shifting revenues from prosperous suburban school districts to the poor schools.

That might be called leadership. But that was not one of the words that leaped from the lips of Jersey's voting classes.

The message for more traditional contemporary politicians was summarized by the senior U.S. senator from Florio's state, Bill Bradley. Asked how he intended to deal with the Florio furor, he replied: Stay out of the state.

Getting involved with leadership was the last thing on Bradley's mind. It might be contagious. And that is how it will be.

Military matters are one area in which political leaders have had some recent success in controlling the flow of information to the people they are leading—by cutting it off totally for short periods of time. In blacking out almost all information for two or three days in the invasions of Grenada and Panama, the government developed (or stumbled into) an essentially psychological strategy that neutralized public reaction by, in effect, launching a surprise attack on the American people. In the controlled confusion at home, the government was able to substitute feelings for facts about less controlled confusion in the field.

But rising public doubt and disenchantment about the Administration's gulf policy reveals the limits of information containment over time. It also shows the wisdom of President Bush's strategy of sharing power and responsibility from the start with other countries and the United Nations. The only place Bush did not feel compelled to deal at first was in the U.S. Congress. Members made it perfectly clear that they had not the slightest intention of saying or doing anything until orders came up from the public.

Legislative bodies are like that, often inert, desperately turning leadership over to the courts when the going gets rough on issues. This time, the crudest declarations of Post-Leadership politics were Democratic senators and representatives who said they would only speak out after body bags starting coming back to their constituencies.

If the President manages to come off looking like a determined and effective leader in his confrontation with Saddam Hussein—perceived victory at costs acceptable to the American people—that will almost certainly be because he accepted the limits or the leadership conceived by these same people. If he misunderstands or violates the limits—if he is capable of exerting old-fashioned leadership—he could not only find himself in a larger version of the Florio fix, destined for electoral defeat in 1992, but for impeachment talk in 1991.

That kind of reaction is greatly speeded up now but it is not entirely new, and I don't believe it is a passing thing. Americans, individually, have always wanted to run things themselves and have been encouraged in that by the rhetoric and conviction of government governing least. Now, new mechanisms have provided more information—and with it a certain individual confidence, or arrogance—putting more of the levers of knowledge and power within the reach of most of the people, most of the time. More and more people are trying to beat the system. Or, the system, the Republic is being made new before our eyes.

Political "leaders" can deal with that. Dealing is what they do, so long as part of the deal is their own reelection. And now even that may be in question in California—and, soon enough, in the rest of Post-Leadership America, governed by the people for themselves.

Debating the Issues: Opposing Views

IS AMERICA DECLINING?

See text pp. 606–7

The text has suggested that the prospects for robust and active political participation are slim. The following two articles explore this theme. Paul Taylor, a staff writer for the Washington Post, *chronicles the growing indifference among the electorate. The "decline of civic participation," he argues, is attributable to a number of causes; some attribute it to "a long season [of] anti-government populism", some to the weakening of political parties, some to the inefficacy of governmental policy in the face of increasingly complex social problems, some to the fragmenting of the social and political community in modern (or postmodern) life, some to a loss of faith as American power ebbs, and some to simply "happy apathy." Whatever the cause, however, it is a problem. Quoting Sanford Horwitt, who studies citizen participation for People for the American Way, Taylor concludes that "a democracy that does not value citizenship is not a very healthy place."*

Robert Samuelson, a political writer for the Washington Post, *disagrees. While Americans may be distressed about current conditions, he argues, the American political system remains "basically sound." Even if the system is messy and imperfect, he contends, it is a system that has maintained its legitimacy over the long term. "Our constant complaints about politics and government obscure a deep devotion to [principles of individual liberty and opportunity]."*

Paul Taylor
"For Disconnected Americans, Citizenship Fades"*

What if they held an election and nobody came? This fall an estimated 110 million to 120 million Americans, nearly two-thirds of the electorate, will not vote—the largest group of nonvoters in U.S. history.

What if they took a census and nobody stood up to be counted? This spring, 33 million American households have not sent back their forms. The 63 percent mailback rate is a dozen points lower than government officials had expected. A preliminary review suggests that most of the problem is not in poor communities, where the Census Bureau had conducted an intensive promotional campaign, but in middle-class communities, where it had not thought promotion was necessary.

What if they sent out tax forms and nobody paid? This year, for every $5 in federal taxes owed, $1 is being evaded—mostly by sole proprietors and small businesses. The annual tax gap is expected to exceed $100 billion for the first time ever, according to the Internal Revenue Service.

The voting booth, the census form and the tax return are among the few civic venues where the federal government asks its citizens to take part in the ongoing enterprise of public life. And now, more than ever, Americans are declining the invitation. At a time when democracy is flourishing around the globe, it is losing market share here.

"I get so embarrassed when I see elections in Central America where you can get shot by either the left or the right for voting, and yet they vote at twice the rate we do in this country," said Rep. Bill Frenzel (R-Minn.). "I think that as a society we're going through a scattering of what used to be called national purpose. At one time this country had a manifest destiny. Nowadays, everyone is chasing a different butterfly."

"Clearly we have something of great interest going on here, and it sounds to me like what we've got is a collective national morale problem," said Walter Dean Burnham, a professor of government at the University of Texas.

"For a lot of Americans, there is no longer a moral distinction between those who choose to be involved and those who don't," said Geoffrey Garin, a Democratic pollster who has done extensive research on citizenship. "People don't feel any sense of ownership over the federal government. It isn't them, and it isn't theirs."

As these varied observations suggest, explanation for the decline in civic participation cut a wide swath across the realms of ideology, sociology and history. Among them:

- It is a byproduct of a long season in which anti-government populism has been the reigning political idea. This is a favorite theory of liberals, and

*Paul Taylor, "For Disconnected Americans, Citizenship Fades," *Washington Post* (May 6, 1990).

ERRATUM

Readings for American Government, Third Edition

On page 209, the following text should appear after the third paragraph:

on it." By cultivating favorable public opinion, present-day rulers hope to persuade their citizens to voluntarily obey, support, and make whatever sacrifices are needed to further the state's goals. In the twentieth century, management of public opinion has become a routine public function in the democracies as well as in the dictatorships. Typically, the censor has been supplanted, or at least joined, by the public relations officer as the governmental functionary most responsible for dealing with public opinion. . . .

Polling is the spearhead of this vast opinion-management apparatus. Opinion surveys provide governments with more or less reliable information about current popular sentiment, offer a guide to the character of the public relations efforts that might usefully be made, and serve as means of measuring the effect of "information programs" upon a target population. Though it cannot guarantee success, polling allows governments a better opportunity to anticipate, regulate, and manipulate popular attitudes. Ironically, some of its early students believed that polling would open the way for "government by opinion." Instead, polling has mainly helped to promote the governance of opinion.

it implicates former president Ronald Reagan as the villain. Sen. Edward M. Kennedy (D-Mass.) says Reagan used the Oval Office to issue a "summons to selfishness" and Garin says his message was that "you can love your country but hate your government."

Liberals also blame Reagan's laissez-faire economic policies for making the poor poorer and less tethered to the civic order. They note that the drop-off in voting over the last three decades has occurred disproportionately among these least well-off Americans. "I would think there is something to the proposition that we have had this enormous pig-out atmosphere in the past decade and it has created a morale problem for everyone not invited to the barbecue," said Burnham.

- It is the result of the long-term weakening of the political parties. In virtually every other democracy around the world, political parties still play the vital role in delivering political information and mobilizing citizen participation. "In this country, our parties can no longer punch their way out of a paper sack," said Frenzel, who will retire next year after 20 years in Congress. "When I was first elected, the most powerful political forces in my state were the Democrats and the Republicans. Now, they are the Minnesotans for Life, the AFL-CIO and the National Education Association. They have legitimate claims on the process, but all of them operate under a much smaller umbrella than the parties."
- It is the result of wholesale failures of government for the past quarter-century. The list is familiar: Vietnam, Watergate, inflation, standard-of-living stagnation, gas lines, budget and trade deficits. These setbacks have been magnified by media that are both more adversarial and, as a result of television, more pervasive than ever before. "If the message [people] get is that politics is all about tactics and corruption and hypocrisy, it should be no surprise that they are going to develop a 'voting-just-encourages 'em' sort of cynicism," said Garry Orren, a professor of public policy at Harvard's Kennedy School of Government.
- It is the result of the atomization of the popular culture—the segmenting of the population by forces of modern marketing and technology into demographic ghettos, each with its own cable channel, primetime television show, shopping mall and consumer magazine, and none with a felt need to connect up to the broader community.
- It is a result of Americans' loss of faith in the future. Nations turn inward when they lose their self-confidence Our economic position, relative to the rest of the world's, has been declining for a generation. Our political structure seems ossified, in hock to special interests and unable to balance a budget, much less confront the larger problems. Burnham calls it a "revolution of declining expectations"—the less people demand from their government, the less they get, the more they drop out.
- It is the result of happy apathy, and it is a far healthier development than the naysayers suggest. This is a favorite theory of conservatives, who note that while participation may have atrophied at the federal level, it is

> vibrant and growing at the local level, where volunteerism, charitable giving and neighborhood associations are on the rise. "It's only people inside the Beltway who think government and politics is the most important way to participate in America," said Burton Yale Pines, executive vice president of the Heritage Foundation, a conservative think tank. "I see it as an inverse indicator. When people are upset, they get involved. When they're not upset, they drop out to a degree. As a conservative, I'm much more interested in parents going to PTA meetings. That's citizenship.

None of the theories is without flaws. Just as the liberal critique fails to account for the degree to which Reagan was a creature, rather than a creator, of the anti-government era, the conservative explanation fails to account for polling data that show nonvoters are among the *least* content members of the electorate.

There is a strong—and growing—class dimension to nonvoting. People in the highest 20 percent of income are almost twice as likely to vote as people in the lowest 20 percent. Poor people tend to be most cynical about, and least connected to, "the system." Ruy Teíxeíra, a leading authority on nonvoting, cites the decline in what he calls "political efficacy" as the chief cause of the drop in voter turnout in presidential campaigns from a modern high of 63 percent in 1960 to a 64-year low of 50.2 percent in 1988. Turnout rates in off-year elections are even lower; in 1986, it was 37.6 percent, the lowest since 1942.

Garin marvels at how profound this feeling of disconnection can be. "In focus-group discussions, when we bring up the cost of the savings and loans bailout, we often hear people say, 'Why do the taxpayers have to come up with the money? Why can't the government?' "

Disconnection can easily sour into hostility. The low return rate on census forms and the high incidence of tax evasion both seem, in part, to be expressions of anger at government. "A lot of people who don't pay their taxes feel like all they are doing is getting even," Garin said. "They feel like the system is rigged—that somebody else has been getting all the breaks and that they're the victim."

There is another explanation for the growth in tax evasion: The federal government has slashed funding for the IS to the level that fewer than one percent of all returns were audited last year, a modern low. When Michael S. Dukakis tried to make an issue of this in 1988, George Bush ridiculed him for advocating "an IRS agent in every kitchen."

In general though, President Bush has paid much more attention to the idea of civic participation than did his predecessor. His inaugural address was an elegant exhortation to Americans turn away from material self-interest. "From now on in America, any definition of a successful life must include serving others," he said last year as he set up a "points of light" initiative that encourages volunteerism at the local level.

But Bush's critics think this is the equivalent of "cheap grace," in the phrase of New York Gov. Mario M. Cuomo (D).

"It creates a very peculiar dynamic when the leaders we elect to perform the public tasks that are too large for us to do by ourselves tell us that these tasks are worthy but that we should accomplish them by our own altruism," said Benjamin Barber, a professor of political science at Rutgers University. "Altruism isn't enough when the problems are structural and will only respond to structural solutions. Altruism isn't citizenship, and there is some harm when we confuse the two."

In the long run, Barber added, the danger is that as the ties that bind a big and pluralistic nation corrode, we will lack the sense of common purpose to respond to great challenges.

"One of the things we've found from our research is that young people, in particular, have an impoverished notion of citizenship," said Sanford Horwitt, director of a citizen participation project at People for the American Way. "Basically, they think it's not breaking the law, and that's all. I don't think they have been well-served by the adult world. Unless these values are passed along, they disappear. And a democracy that does not value citizenship is not a very healthy place."

Robert J. Samuelson
"The Luckiest Accident"*

If you ever wondered about the importance of politics, you should have been relieved of doubt in 1992. By politics, I do not mean whether Bill beat George or whether Boris Yeltsin survives in Russia or whether Helmut Kohl is high or low in German opinion polls. I mean something more basic: the ability of societies to build systems of popular consent that allow for effective government and the peaceful resolution of conflicts.

We take this for granted. We shouldn't. You can't find it in the former Soviet Union, Somalia, South Africa or much of Asia. Even in the developed world (Europe, Japan, Canada), political foundations that seemed sturdy only a few years ago are now a bit wobbly. Governments aren't collapsing, but they are having more trouble governing. The continuing disorder of the post-Cold War world—a good prediction for 1993—is a reflection of this.

Governments rule either by force or legitimacy. In Eastern Europe and the former Soviet Union, the downfall of government by force left a huge void into which new loyalties—religion, ethnic background, varying ideologies—have rushed. The consequences, as in the former Yugoslavia, can be tragic. All these societies face the hard task of creating political legitimacy. The alternatives are a return to force or a slide into chaos.

A subtler process assaults advanced societies. These governments have buttressed their legitimacy by guaranteeing their populaces steady eco-

*Robert J. Samuelson, "The Luckiest Accident," *Washington Post* (January 7, 1993).

nomic growth and generous welfare states. Both promises are increasingly ill-kept. In Europe, the unemployment rate is creeping toward 11 percent. Japan's worst slump since the mid-1970s is compounding disillusion with the scandal-ridden Liberal Democratic Party, which has ruled the country since 1955. And the end of the Cold War has posed special problems: Germany reels from the cost of rebuilding Eastern Germany and absorbing new refugees.

Whatever's wrong, there's no simple formula for fixing it. Every society creates its own politics, and success is at best haphazard. Political scientist Edward Banfield, a college professor of mine, once put this eloquently:

"A political system is an accident," he wrote. "It is an accumulation of habits, customs, prejudices and principles that have survived a long process of trial and error and of ceaseless response to changing circumstance. If the system works well on the whole, it is a lucky accident—the luckiest, indeed, that can befall a society, for all the institutions of a society . . . depend ultimately upon the government and the political order."

By this standard, we Americans are lucky. On the whole, our system works, and it has survived many severe tests. Sure, we have plenty of problems. Like Europe, we have an overcommitted welfare state and a slow-growing economy. But we have a consensus on basic values. In most societies, political legitimacy rests on nationality, which is ethnic or religious. Japanese, Germans and Greeks are born, not made. Our nationalism rests on a set of ideas—the commitment to individual liberty and opportunity.

Our constant complaints about politics and government obscure a deep devotion to these principles. Simply put, we are proud to be Americans, because we believe our values are unique. Consider how Americans react to the following statements, as reported by the Roper Center for Public Opinion Research. "Whatever its faults, the U.S. still has the best system of government in the world." About 85 percent of us agree. "The system [of government] is good but the people in government are not doing their jobs well enough." Nearly 70 percent of us agree. Indeed, Bill Clinton now benefits from our faith. A new leader will, we hope, make the system—basically sound—work better.

No doubt, our optimism is often naive. But the pervasive faith in American values preserves our system. Disputes involve means more than ends. Winners and losers abide by the results, because they believe the system embodies virtues more important than any specific disagreement. Whether this consensus endures is always the central question of U.S. politics. All democracies, as Banfield has argued, seem pushed by their electorates to make impossible promises and thereby bring themselves into disrepute. And there are specific strains, from budget deficits to "multiculturalism."

Still, our system works. Without this sort of political competence, societies struggle. For starters, it's hard to prosper. Commerce can't easily flourish without fixed rules, and that requires political stability. A new study released by the National Bureau of Economic Research confirms this. It examined economic growth and political stability in 75 countries. You can quibble with the study's definition of political stability, but the relationship is clear. Of the 10 fastest-growing countries, six also were among the 10 most stable politically. Economic growth in the former Soviet Union will be difficult unless there's political order.

The trouble now is an excess of political breakdown. Too much domestic strife feeds global strife. Old borders disintegrate. As governments weaken, they try to shore up support by blaming problems on outsiders. It's harder to cooperate on common interests or, without the unifying enemy of communism, even identify common interests. In Europe and Japan, insecure governments cannot take unpopular actions—on everything from trade to security matters—to bolster the global order. We, too, are turning inward. What used to be called the "Western alliance" of the United States, Europe and Japan is rapidly fraying.

So the Cold War gives way to a partial and aimless peace. The connection between local disorder and global disorder is obvious, even if inexact. The world's major nations lack self-confidence and a sense of direction. Every society strives for its own lucky accident. Those that don't achieve it (and their number is growing) begin to grasp the importance of politics. It is widely disdained everywhere, because it is so messy and imperfect. But it is not only a critical social discipline—it's the most critical.

QUESTIONS

1. Thomas Jefferson often remarked that a little rebellion now and then is a good thing. What kind of rebellion would be sufficient to breathe new life into the American political system without destroying much that is worthwhile?
2. The RIP process discussed in the text, and illustrated by the successful campaign against Lani Guinier, appears to be a permanent feature of the American political landscape. Were Guinier's supporters justified in calling "Foul!"? Was the unfairness, if any, located in the attack upon Guinier, or the way in which the outcry against her nomination allowed her opponents to short-circuit the nomination so that she was unable to defend or explain her views in the appropriate forum before the Senate Judiciary Committee?
3. David Broder and Michael Weisskopf argue that gridlock is inevitable. Why does gridlock appear to be an unavoidable aspect of contemporary politics? Do Americans secretly like gridlock, because, as Cokie Roberts has pointed out, we distrust government altogether and are particularly wary of acceding power to any party or any branch of government, or is gridlock the cause of that distrust?
4. Throughout the text, the problem of providing leadership—through either Congress or the President—has been touched upon. The piece by Richard Reeves suggests that Americans no longer desire leadership. On what basis could that argument be sustained? If that argument is not accurate, what might the profile of an effective leader look like?
5. The meaning of citizenship in today's political system is far from clear

and the articles in the "Debating the Issues" section for this chapter raise the question of the obligations of citizenship itself. Should Americans sit back in "happy apathy," secure in the notion that for all its faults the system is basically sound? Or are deeper problems lurking? What kinds of actions are the marks of a robust citizenry? Do you think America is declining?

CHAPTER 15

An Introduction to Public Policy

TECHNIQUES OF CONTROL

See text p. 620

As the text notes, many of the nation's first policies were directed at facilitating private ownership of property, the key component of a capitalist economy. During the early part of the nation's history, especially as the nation expanded westward, Congress spent a good deal of its time enacting laws that transferred property into private hands, either to individuals or corporations like the railroads, whose business Congress wanted to facilitate.

Following is an excerpt from the Homestead Act of 1862. Under that act, individuals could obtain titles to lands simply by settling and cultivating them—a task, of course, that often proved impossible. The homesteader had to file a document called an entry with the appropriate federal land office; three years later, upon proof that a residence had been built and the land had been improved, the homesteader was entitled to a deed of ownership called a patent.

Homestead Act of 1862*

§ 161. Entry of unappropriated public lands

Every person who is the head of a family, or who has arrived at the age of twenty-one years, and is a citizen of the United States, or who has filed his declaration of intention to become such, as required by the naturalization laws, shall be entitled to enter one quarter-section or a less quantity of unappropriated public lands, to be located in a body in conformity to the legal subdivisions of the public lands; but no person who is the proprietor of more than one hundred and sixty acres of land in any State or Territory, shall acquire any right under the homestead law. And every person owning and residing on land may, under the provisions of this section, enter other land lying contiguous to his land, which shall not, with the land so already owned and occupied, exceed in the aggregate one hundred and sixty acres. . . .

*The Homestead Act of 1862, Subchapter 1. R.S. § 2289; March 3, 1891, c. 561 § 5, 26 Stat. 1097.

§ 162. Application for entry; affidavit

Any person applying to enter land under section 161 of this title shall first make and subscribe before the proper officer and file in the proper land office an affidavit that he or she is the head of a family, or is over twenty-one years of age, and that such application is honestly and in good faith made for the purpose of actual settlement and cultivation, and not for the benefit of any other person, persons or corporation, and that he or she will faithfully and honestly endeavor to comply with all the requirements of law as to settlement, residence, and cultivation necessary to acquire title to the land applied for; that he or she is not acting as agent of any person, corporation, or syndicate in making such entry, nor in collusion with any person, corporation, or syndicate to give them the benefit of the land entered, or any part thereof, or the timber thereon; that he or she does not apply to enter the same for the purpose of speculation, but in good faith to obtain a home for himself, or herself, and that he or she has not directly or indirectly made, and will not make, any agreement or contract in any way or manner, with any person or persons, corporation, or syndicate whatsoever, by which the title which he or she might acquire from the Government of the United States should inure, in whole or in part, to the benefit of any person, except himself, or herself, and upon filing such affidavit with the officer designated by the Secretary of the Interior on payment of $5 when the entry is of not more than eighty acres, and on payment of $10 when the entry is for more than eighty acres, he or she shall thereupon be permitted to enter the amount of land specified. . . .

§ 164. Certificate or patent; issuance

No certificate shall be given or patent issued therefor until the expiration of three years from the date of such entry; and if at the expiration of such time, or at any time within two years thereafter, the person making such entry, or if he be dead his widow, or in case of her death his heirs or devisee, or in case of a widow making such entry her heirs or devisee, in case of her death, proves by himself and by two credible witnesses that he, she, or they have a habitable house upon the land and have actually resided upon and cultivated the same for the term of three years succeeding the time of filing the affidavit, and makes affidavit that no part of such land has been alienated, except as provided in section 174 of this title, and that he, she, or they will bear true allegiance to the Government of the United States, then in such case he, she, or they, if at that time citizens of the United States, shall be entitled to a patent, as in other cases provided by law: *Provided,* That upon filing in the local land office notice of the beginning of such absence the entryman shall be entitled to a continuous leave of absence from the land for a period not exceeding five months in each year after establishing residence, and upon the termination of such absence the entryman shall file a notice of such termination in the local land office, but in case of commutation the fourteen months' actual residence required by law must be shown, and the person commuting must be at the time a citizen of the United States: . . . *Provided further,* That the entryman shall, in order to comply with the requirements of cultivation herein provided for, cultivate not less than one-sixteenth of the area of his entry, beginning with the second year of the entry, and not less than one-eighth, beginning with the third year of the entry, . . . and that the provisions of this section relative to the homestead period shall apply to all unperfected entries as well as entries hereafter made upon which residence is required.

See text p. 624

The federal government did not engage in extensive direct regulation of private enterprise until a relatively late date. As noted in the text, the government accomplished its goals for many years with the use of subsidies, contracts, and licensing. By the end of the nineteenth century, however, it became clear that the free market was not entirely self-regulating, or at least that the ups and downs of a capitalist system could exact a large human toll. Initially, regulatory efforts were aimed at correcting aberrations in the market system that prevented its smooth functioning, as for example, government efforts to prevent the development of business monopolies. Government regulatory activities expanded dramatically in response to the economic collapse of the 1930s. Regulatory efforts expanded again thereafter in the late 1960s and early 1970s as it became clear that solutions to widespread problems like environmental pollution and workplace safety were not likely to be resolved through the normal operation of the market—at least not at a satisfactory pace.

Following is a 1978 addition to the Clean Air Act, one of the major pieces of environmental regulation of the 1970s. The act authorizes the Environmental Protection Agency to enact a variety of programs aimed at alleviating problems of air pollution, from providing technical research assistance to states to establishing national ambient air quality standards. Only a few of the provisions of the act are reproduced here—the act's declaration of purpose, the section authorizing the agency to establish ambient air quality standards, and part of the section relating to enforcement. The latter provisions are interesting because they include provisions for criminal penalties for violations of the act. Most regulatory agencies have authority to impose fines and/or close down a business whose operation offends particular regulatory provisions, but rarely do they have authority to impose a jail sentence upon the offender.

Clean Air Act of 1972*

§ 7401. Congressional findings and declaration of purpose

(a) The Congress finds—

(1) that the predominant part of the Nation's population is located in its rapidly expanding metropolitan and other urban areas, which generally cross the boundary lines of local jurisdictions and often extend into two or more States;

(2) that the growth in the amount and complexity of air pollution brought about by urbanization, industrial development, and the increasing use of motor vehicles, has resulted in mounting dangers to the public health and welfare, including injury to agricultural crops and livestock, damage to and the deterioration of property, and hazards to air and ground transportation;

(3) that the prevention and control of air pollution at its source is the primary responsibility of States and local governments; and

(4) that Federal financial assistance and leadership is essential for the development of cooperative Federal, State, regional, and local programs to prevent and control air pollution.

(b) The purposes of this subchapter are—

(1) to protect and enhance the quality of the Nation's air resources so as to promote the public health and welfare and the productive capacity of its population;

(2) to initiate and accelerate a national research and development program to achieve the prevention and control of air pollution;

(3) to provide technical and financial assistance to State and local governments in connection with the development and execution of their air pollution prevention and control programs; and

(4) to encourage and assist the development and operation of regional air pollution control programs. . . .

§ 7409. National primary and secondary ambient air quality standards

(a) Promulgation

(1) The Administrator [of the Environmental Protection Agency]—

(A) within 30 days after December 31, 1970, shall publish proposed regulations prescribing a national primary ambient air quality standard and a national secondary ambient air quality standard for each air pollutant for which air quality criteria have been issued prior to such date; and

(B) after a reasonable time for interested persons to submit written

*Clean Air Act of 1972, Subchapter 1. 1977 Amendment. Pub. L. 95-95, Title I, § 117(a), August 7, 1977, 91 Stat. 712.

comments thereon (but no later than 90 days after the initial publication of such proposed standards) shall by regulation promulgate such proposed national primary and secondary ambient air quality standards with such modifications as he deems appropriate.

(2) with respect to any air pollutant for which air quality criteria are issued after December 31, 1970, the Administrator shall publish, simultaneously with the issuance of such criteria and information, proposed national primary and secondary ambient air quality standards for any such pollutant. The procedure provided for in paragraph (1)(B) of this subsection shall apply to the promulgation of such standards.

(b) Protection of public health and welfare

(1) National primary ambient air quality standards, prescribed under subsection (a) of this section shall be ambient air quality standards the attainment and maintenance of which in the judgment of the Administrator, based on such criteria and allowing an adequate margin of safety, are requisite to protect the public health. Such primary standards may be revised in the same manner as promulgated.

(2) Any national secondary ambient air quality standard prescribed under subsection (a) of this section shall specify a level of air quality the attainment and maintenance of which in the judgment of the Administrator, based on such criteria, is requisite to protect the public welfare from any known or anticipated adverse effects associated with the presence of such air pollutant in the ambient air. Such secondary standards may be revised in the same manner as promulgated. . . .

(c) Review and revision of criteria and standards; independent scientific review committee; appointment; advisory functions

(1) Not later than December 31, 1980, and at five-year intervals thereafter, the Administrator shall complete a thorough review of the criteria published under [this Act] and the national ambient air quality standards promulgated under this section and shall make such revisions in such criteria and standards and promulgate such new standards as may be appropriate in accordance with [other provisions of this Act]. The Administrator may review and revise criteria or promulgate new standards earlier or more frequently than required under this paragraph.

(2)(A) The Administrator shall appoint an independent scientific review committee composed of seven members including at least one member of the National Academy of Sciences, one physician, and one person representing State air pollution control agencies.

(B) Not later than January 1, 1980, and at five-year intervals thereafter, the committee referred to in subparagraph (A) shall complete a review of the criteria published under [other provisions] of this title and the national primary and secondary ambient air quality standards promulgated under this section and shall recommend to the Administrator any new national ambient air quality standards and revisions of existing criteria and standards as may be appropriate under section 7408 of this title and subsection (b) of this section.

(C) Such committee shall also (i) advise the Administrator of areas in which additional knowledge is required to appraise the adequacy and basis of existing, new, or revised national ambient air quality standards, (ii) describe the research efforts necessary to provide the required information, (iii) advise the Administrator on the relative contribution to air pollution concentrations of natural as well as anthropogenic activity, and (iv) advise the Administrator of any adverse public health, welfare, social, economic, or energy effects which may result from various strategies for attainment and maintenance of such national ambient air quality standards. . . .

§ 7413. Federal enforcement procedures

(a) Finding of violation; notice; compliance order; civil action; State failure to enforce plan; construction or modification of major stationary sources

(1) Whenever, on the basis of any information available to him, the Administrator finds that any person is in violation of any requirement of an applicable implementation plan, the Administrator shall notify the person in violation of the plan and the State in which the plan applies of such finding. If such violation extends beyond the 30th day after the date of the Administrator's notification, the Administrator may issue an order requiring such person to comply with the requirements of such plan or he may bring a civil action in accordance with subsection (b) of this section.

(2) Whenever, on the basis of information available to him, the Administrator finds that violations of an applicable implementation plan are so widespread that such violations appear to result from a failure of the State in which the plan applies to enforce the plan effectively, he shall so notify the State. If the Administrator finds such failure extends beyond the 30th day after such notice, he shall give public notice of such finding. During the period beginning with such public notice and ending when such State satisfies the Administrator that it will enforce such plan (hereafter referred to in this section as "period of federally assumed enforcement"), the Administrator may enforce any requirement of such plan with respect to any person—

(A) by issuing an order to comply with such requirement, or

(B) by bringing a civil action under subsection (b) of this section.

(3) Whenever, on the basis of any information available to him, the Administrator finds that any person is in violation of section 7411(e) of this title (relating to new source performance standards), section 7412(c) of this title (relating to standards for hazardous emissions), or section 1857c-10(g) of this title (relating to energy-related authorities) is in violation of any requirement of section 7414 of this title (relating to inspections, etc.), he may issue an order requiring such person to comply with such section or requirement, or he may bring a civil action in accordance with subsection (b) of this section.

(4) An order issued under this subsection (other than an order relating to a violation of section 7412 of this title) shall not take effect until the person to whom it is issued has had an opportunity to confer with the

Administrator concerning the alleged violation. A copy of any order issued under this subsection shall be sent to the State air pollution control agency of any State in which the violation occurs. Any order issued under this subsection shall state with reasonable specificity the nature of the violation, specify a time for compliance which the Administrator determines is reasonable, taking into account the seriousness of the violation and any good faith efforts to comply with applicable requirements. In any case in which an order under this subsection (or notice to a violator under paragraph (1) is issued to a corporation, a copy of such order (or notice) shall be issued to appropriate corporate officers. . . .

(b) Violations by owners or operators of major stationary sources

The Administrator shall, in the case of any person which is the owner or operator of a major stationary source, and may, in the case of any other person, commence a civil action for a permanent or temporary injunction, or to assess and recover a civil penalty of not more than $25,000 per day of violation, or both, whenever such person—

(1) violates or fails or refuses to comply with any order issued under subsection (a) of this section; or

(2) violates any requirement of an applicable implementation plan (A) during any period of Federally assumed enforcement, or (B) more than 30 days after having been notified by the Administrator under subsection (a)(1) of this section of a finding that such person is violating such requirement; or

(3) violates section 7411(e), section 7412(c), section 1857c-10(g) of this title (as in effect before August 7, 1977), subsection (d)(5) of this section (relating to coal conversion), section 7624 of this title (relating to cost of certain vapor recovery), section 7419 of this title (relating to smelter orders), or any regulation under part B of this subchapter (relating to ozone); or

(4) fails or refuses to comply with any requirement of section 7414 of this title or subsection (d) of this section; or

(5) attempts to construct or modify a major stationary source in any area with respect to which a finding under subsection (a)(5) of this section has been made.

The Administrator may commence a civil action for recovery of any noncompliance penalty under section 7420 of this title or for recovery of any nonpayment penalty for which any person is liable under section 7420 of this title or for both. Any action under this subsection may be brought in the district court of the United States for the district in which the violation occurred or in which the defendant resides or has his principal place of business, and such court shall have jurisdiction to restrain such violation, to require compliance, to assess such civil penalty and to collect any noncompliance penalty (and nonpayment penalty) owed under section 7420 of this title. In determining the amount of any civil penalty to be assessed under this subsection, the courts shall take into consideration (in addition to other factors) the size of the business, the economic impact of the penalty on the business, and the seriousness of the violation. Notice of the commencement of such action shall be given to the appropriate State air pollution control agency. In the case of any action brought by the Administrator under this subsection, the court may award costs of litigation (including reasonable attorney and expert witness fees) to the party or parties against whom such action was brought in any case where the court finds that such action was unreasonable.

(c) Penalties

(1) Any person who knowingly—

(A) violates any requirement of an applicable implementation plan (i) during any period of Federally assumed enforcement, or (ii) more than 30 days after having been notified by the Administrator under subsection (a)(1) of this section that such person is violating such requirement, or

(B) violates or fails or refuses to comply with any order under section 7419 of this title or under subsection (a) or (d) of this section, or

(C) violates section 7411(e), section 7412(c) of this title, or

(D) violates any requirement of section 1857c-10(g) of this title (as in effect before August 7, 1977), subsection (b)(7) or (d)(5) of section 7420 of this title (relating to noncompliance penalties), or any requirement of part B of this subchapter (relating to ozone) shall be punished by a fine of not more than $25,000 per day of violation, or by imprisonment for not more than one year, or by both. If the conviction is for a violation committed after the first conviction of such person under this paragraph, punishment shall be by a fine of not more than $50,000 per day of violation, or by imprisonment for not more than two years, or by both.

(2) Any person who knowingly makes any false statement, representation, or certification in any application, record, report, plan, or other document filed or required to be maintained under this chapter or who falsifies, tampers with, or knowingly renders inaccurate any monitoring device or method required to be maintained under this chapter, shall upon conviction, be punished by a fine of not more than $10,000, or by imprisonment for not more than six months, or by both.

(3) For the purpose of this subsection, the term "person" includes, in addition to the entities referred to in section 7602(e) of this title, any responsible corporate officer.

REGULATORY POLICY AND PLURALIST POLITICS

See text p. 624

Regulatory policies have kept an army of Washington lawyers in business for the last four decades: because regulatory policies have a direct impact on the conduct of the individual or industry to whom they are directed, they are frequently the target of litigation. Cases are filed as soon as an agency adopts regulations; the industry subject to the regulation usually argues that the agency has gone too far, while citizen's groups are likely to argue that the agency has not gone far enough. The results, of course, are legal battles that often tie up agency enforcement for years.

In the following article, New York Times *reporter Matthew Wald chronicles a new trend in regulatory policy. That new approach is one of negotiation rather than confrontation. Interested parties—the agency, representatives from the regulated industry, and citizen groups who have an interest in the subject matter to be regulated—discuss options before regulations are drafted in an effort to avoid the litigation that has become a matter of course for every regulatory policy enacted.*

Matthew L. Wald "U.S. Agencies Use Negotiations to Pre-empt Lawsuits Over Rules"*

Washington, a city of lawsuits, is embracing a new way of doing business. At stake are rules that govern everything from who may sit in the exit rows on airliners to how much a power plant can pollute.

More and more, Federal agencies are collaring industries and interest groups and getting them together to decide what the new rules will say.

So far the reviews are glowing. And one of the most popular elements of these negotiations is that all parties promise not to use lawsuits to upset any settlements that they reach.

The Lawsuit System

Lawsuits to overturn regulations have become commonplace under the system that has been used for 45 years: an agency studies an issue, writes a rule, takes comments, issues a final version and then defends it in court against attacks by industry associations or citizens' groups. That system still predominates, but agencies are seeking negotiated settlements wherever they can.

The Environmental Protection Agency used the new system recently to develop rules to put into effect provisions of the Clean Air Act.

"We had people at the table who probably wouldn't have returned each other's telephone calls," said William Rosenberg, deputy administrator for air and radiation. The environmental agency cannot hope to write all the regulations needed under the new law without similar negotiations in other fields, he said.

One of those at the table was Urvan R. Sternfels, president of the National Petroleum Refiners Associations, who said he was an advocate of the new system. "It's a better situation," he said, "when people who are

*Matthew L. Wald, "U.S. Agencies Use Negotiations to Pre-empt Lawsuits Over Rules," *New York Times* (September 23, 1991).

adversaries can sit down at the table and talk about it rather than throwing bricks at each other in courtrooms and the press."

Environmental groups like the new system, too. "We'd love to see it used again and again," said Fred Krupp, president of the Environmental Defense Fund, which recently concluded a negotiation over air pollution from a power plant near the Grand Canyon. "The E.P.A. brought the environmentalists and the industry together to hammer out a creative, strong solution." . . .

. . . In coming months, the E.P.A. hopes to conclude negotiations on rules governing everything from how to dispose of lead-acid batteries, which can contaminate underground water, to how to glue down wall-to-wall carpeting, which can poison indoor air. . . . This is a major advance, Mr. Reilly said, because in recent years the main battleground has been the courts. "Four of every five decisions I make are contested in court," he said in a recent telephone interview. "We spend as much time designing our rules to withstand court attack as we do getting the rules right and out in the first place."

Mr. Reilly is not the only one who wants to keep the environmental agency out of court. In the just-concluded agreement for clean fuels, oil refiners were expecting to spend billions of dollars, and wanted assurance that they would not be racing to comply with requirements that would be overturned later by a judge. As part of that negotiation, environmental groups and the oil industry promised that neither would sue to overturn the provisions of what they had agreed to.

Discouraging Defectors

They even agreed that if a defector emerged from one side or the other—for example, an oil company that broke ranks and decided to challenge the rules, or an environmental group that took legal action to block one portion of the rules—the other oil companies or environmental groups would go to court to support the consensus.

In the negotiations over clean fuels, other participants were the states, which have the authority to issue their own rules within their borders and were believed ready to do so if they thought the Federal regulations were not strong enough. The threat that they would do so, creating a patchwork system of gasoline regulations, was another incentive for the industry to reach an agreement.

The negotiations do not set policy; that is supposed to be done by Congress. But often the law is a bare-bones structure, and the affected parties sometimes disagree over exactly what the language means.

In the agreement on clean fuels, the law set certain standards for the content of gasoline, but the petroleum industry won a provision in the regulations so that the standards had to be met on average, rather than in every case. The industry believes that this interpretation will reduce its cost.

Environmentalists gained in resolving an apparent ambiguity in the legislative language. At one point, Congress appears to set an absolute limit on a parameter of gasoline called Reid vapor pressure, which measures the tendency of the fuel to evaporate. But in another section, the law appears to require a percentage reduction in Reid vapor pressure, leaving unclear whether the percentage was to be applied to the absolute limit or to the existing level.

Grand Canyon Compromise

In [a case concerning efforts to limit emissions at a coal fired generating plant near] the Grand Canyon, industry and environmentalists compromised on how reliable the anti-pollution equipment on the power plant would have to be, settling on a rule that requires a 90 percent reduction in emissions on an annual basis, rather than the original proposal of 70 percent in any given month. The change eliminated the need for a backup unit for reducing emissions.

According to Mr. Rosenberg, the E.P.A. air and radiation official, settling for 90 percent a year instead of 70 percent each month resulted in a 40 percent greater improvement in visibility at a 20 percent lower cost.

Experts say both those settlements are "win-win" solutions, in which both parties gain from being flexible.

Finding such compromises, reducing costs and staying out of court are also goals for environmentalists, said Mr. Krupp of the Environmental Defense Fund, which had sued over the air at the Grand Canyon. If the job is done more economically, he said, that leaves more money to use elsewhere, and keeping the case out of court "can foreclose the industry from appealing the regulations and bringing the process to a stall."

While negotiations are more frequent now, they are not new. Philip J. Harter, a lawyer in Washington and professor of administrative law at American University Law School, who drafted the 1990 law, traced the origin of the technique to Washington State, where it was used in the mid-1970s to plan a route for Interstate 5 across a scenic lake near Seattle.

But negotiation is far from universally successful. Chris Kirtz, chief of the consensus and dispute resolution staff at the E.P.A., said his agency had tried over the years to steer 60 disputes into negotiation, but only 12 succeeded.

Sometimes, he said, the dispute was too politicized, or the potential participants thought they faced a backlash. For example, he said, environmental groups declined to enter negotiations on radioactive waste regulations, fearing that whatever they agreed to would anger their constituents.

The new system will also fail in cases where the decision is "bipolar," said Mr. Harter, such as, "Are we going to locate a nuclear plant in your back yard, yes or no?"

But it can settle disputes that have persisted for years. Mr. Harter cited the first Federal use of the new system, by the F.A.A., to revise 30-year-old rules on when pilots are required to take rest breaks.

The revision was needed because the industry had gone from DC-3s to 747s, he said, but "every time the F.A.A. tried to revise the rules some political group had the horsepower to knock it down." As a result, Mr. Harter said, the agency kept issuing interpretations of its rule, until they had reached a total of 1,000 pages. The negotiated settlement, he said, was two pages.

Debating the Issues: Opposing Views

REGULATION: GOVERNMENTAL SCALPEL OR BLUNT INSTRUMENT?

See text pp. 642–43

In a capitalist economic system, the legitimacy of regulation is always a subject of debate, as the text points out. Regulatory programs impose costs on businesses. Those costs affect the competitiveness of businesses differently, depending upon the ability of a particular enterprise to absorb and eventually pass those costs off to consumers. The following two pieces raise several interesting questions about the nature of regulatory programs in the context of a proposed family leave policy for the United States.

With the rise of women in the workforce, a number of interest groups during the last decade worked to persuade members of Congress that a federally mandated family leave policy, allowing workers to take unpaid leave when required to care for family members, was necessary. During the Bush administration, a family leave bill was passed by Congress and twice vetoed by President Bush, who objected to the creation of a new regulatory program.

In the piece that follows, written on the eve of Congress's second passage of a family leave bill in the fall of 1992, Charles Krauthammer, a columnist for the Washington Post*, urges Congress to defeat the proposed bill. Krauthammer argues that while family leave is an admirable idea, it should not be adopted through the enactment of a regulatory program. Regulatory programs, he contends, impose too many costs on business; a family leave policy should be mandated, but supported through tax subsidies so that the costs are properly socialized.*

Democratic representative Patricia Schroeder disagrees in a response written just days after the family leave bill was passed and subsequently vetoed by President Bush. Regulatory programs, she argues, serve a worthy purpose. "Imposing regulatory costs on employers is as legitimate as it is time-honored. Moreover, under the tax code, business [regulatory] expenses . . . can be written off against a company's income." Subsidizing a family leave policy is unwarranted, Schroeder contends; the government regulates businesses for many valid reasons, and does not pay those businesses a subsidy for complying with minimal environmental or worker safety standards. "The best way to socialize costs is to establish a broad minimum standard that every employer must adhere to. . . . If standards are not imposed, some employers will avoid their responsibilities."

The family leave bill was enacted yet a third time, and was the first piece of legislation signed into law by President Clinton.

Charles Krauthammer
"Family Leave Flimflam"*

We have to pay for the social services we want.

In the old days when government wanted to do something nice for the people, it doled out the money. Health care for the poor? Government would pay for Medicaid. In the heyday of the Great Society, expansive social feeling coincided with explosive economic growth to produce government largess on a scale unseen before or since. The reductio ad absurdum of this approach was George McGovern's 1972 campaign promise of a $1,000 "demogrant" to every breathing American, a simple presentation of cash from a bountiful government to a grateful citizenry.

Then came Reagan, tax cuts and fantastic debt. Government is broke. Giveaways are not obsolete—Congress and the president have just granted 10.5 billion borrowed dollars for hurricane relief—but except for emergencies, government has grown wary of dipping into a treasury already $4 trillion in debt.

Yet the politician's determination to continue giving is unswerving. No money? No problem. Nowadays politicians give and make someone else pay.

A perfect example is the family leave bill just passed by Congress. The bill would mandate that businesses with more than 50 employees provide up to 12 weeks per year of leave per employee (unpaid, but with health care benefits and a job guaranteed) for reasons of family or personal illness, birth or adoption.

Family leave is a good idea. It spares workers the cruel choice between a loved one and a job. A generous country should have family leave. And a generous country should pay for it. How? Not by adding yet another regulatory burden on American business already struggling to survive in a highly competitive global economy, but by socializing the cost. Have government pay for it. Indeed, among our competitors that do have family leave, the costs are heavily subsidized by the state.

The Bush administration in a late counterproposal offered tax subsidies to reimburse businesses that voluntarily offer family leave. Make it mandatory, and it's the right idea: Government mandates, government pays.

Politicians of both parties are constantly sounding off about America's growing lack of competitiveness. Yet they heap mandate upon uncompensated mandate on business, adding relentlessly to the cost of production, inevitably jeopardizing the capacity of American business to compete.

Take, for example, the "play-or-pay" health care plan proposed by Senate Democrats and endorsed by Clinton. Guess who pays. "Play-or-pay"

*Charles Krauthammer, "Family Leave Flimflam," *Washington Post* (September 18, 1992).

says to small business: You either provide health insurance for your employees, or you pay the government an additional payroll tax estimated by the OMB at 7 percent to 9 percent (and we will provide the health insurance).

Now, business already has a 6.2 percent payroll tax for Social Security and 1.5 percent for Medicare. Adding another 7 percent to 9 percent tax is only going to make it harder for American business to meet foreign competition.

Yet in the same spirit Clinton proposes another tax on business. His worker retraining proposal mandates that a business must either have its own retraining program or pay another payroll tax (1.5 percent) to finance a government training program. More play-or-pay.

Yes, we need worker retraining, particularly in a world of free trade with its inevitable social dislocations. But adding the cost to business is simply a way to kill the golden goose that generates economic growth.

Payroll taxes, which raise the cost of labor, are a particularly bad idea. They distort the employer's choice when deciding whether to hire a worker or buy a machine. Distorted economic choices in general make for inefficiency and slower economic growth. This distortion, moreover, biases the choice in a particular direction: against labor. And that has an even more baleful consequence: joblessness. The more expensive an employee is for a given amount of output, the less likely he is to be hired.

Do we want family leave, universal health insurance, worker retraining? Then let's all pay for it. Socialize the cost. First, because it is more honest. There is no free lunch. We are going to have to pay for these social goods one way or the other. Fobbing them off on business does not eliminate the cost. It only hides it.

Socializing the cost is also more rational. For example: We could, as Clinton proposes, charge all these goodies to American business. Alternatively, government could pay for them directly, financing them with, say, an energy tax or a national sales tax.

At least now we can make judgments. Doing it the first way means a decrease in international competitiveness and an increase in joblessness. Doing it the second way means a decrease in consumption spread through the general population. We can now choose our poisons.

In my view, equity argues for depressing everyone's standard of living somewhat rather than visiting extreme hardship on the unlucky jobless (while the rest of us carry on unscathed). There are, of course, other ways to weigh the trade-offs. But the only way we will see the trade-offs at all and make rational choices between them is if the costs of these social benefits are acknowledged openly.

We have some distance to go in finishing the edifice of the welfare state. Unfortunately, it will cost. The only people it suits to hide the cost are the politicians. It allows them to say to the great "forgotten" middle class: I bring you new and wondrous things. And, by the way, for you: no new taxes.

Pat Schroeder
"Affordable Family Leave"*

In a critique of the family leave bill passed by Congress—and vetoed this week by President Bush—Charles Krauthammer [op-ed, Sept. 18] takes the position that benefits such as this are a good thing, but that they should be socialized. That's a worthy goal, but does it really mean we need to give employers cash—"Do-the-Right-Thing Stamps," as it were—just because we ask them to adhere to a minimum universal standard that benefits society as a whole? I don't think so. Imposing regulatory costs on employers is as legitimate as it is time-honored. Moreover, under the tax code, business expenses—even the minimal costs associated with family and medical leave—can be written off against a company's income.

So why should employers be paid cash, or a tax credit, as Krauthammer proposes, by the taxpayers to do what is required of them by law? Do the taxpayers reimburse General Motors for overtime costs imposed by wage-and-hour laws? Do we write a check to the Marriott Corp. every time it installs a smoke detector in accordance with safety laws? Do we give Exxon a $1,000 U.S. Savings Bond every time it doesn't spill oil in Prince William Sound? Do we pay McDonald's a stipend for maintaining a clean kitchen in accordance with local health codes?

The best way to socialize costs is to establish a broad minimum standard that every employer must adhere to. Then the costs are shared equally. If standards are not imposed, some employers will avoid their responsibilities. Consider the health care mess. The employees of companies with no health insurance plan often end up in public hospitals. The taxpayers pay the bill.

In reality, these companies have access to free health care (i.e., free to them, not to the taxpayers), giving them a competitive advantage over those companies that provide health insurance. The latter company pays twice, once for health insurance for its own employees and a second time in taxes to pay for the health care of its competitors' employees who have been dumped onto the public health care system. If every company were required to offer a minimum health care plan, the costs would be shared, and every employee would have health insurance.

Krauthammer's goal of socializing costs is laudable. But the most efficient way to do that is to require a minimum standard for every employer. That is what minimum wage laws do, that is what federal safety laws do, and that is what the family and medical leave law just vetoed by the president would do.

*Pat Schroeder, "Affordable Family Leave," *Washington Post* (September 24, 1992).

QUESTIONS

1. Even when presidential and congressional elections seem to represent dramatic shifts in ideology, like the transition from President Carter to President Reagan, or President Bush to President Clinton, there is a way in which governmental agencies continue to chug along; legislation creating the agencies is not rewritten every time the administration changes. In what ways does the existence of this permanent government provide stability or simply render government inflexible?
2. Attempts to bypass expensive and time-consuming litigation and other forms of regulatory politics has led many agencies to initiate negotiations among interested parties over the content of certain rules, as the Wald article reprinted above suggests. In what ways might these kinds of negotiations be said to violate principles of representative democracy? Are they simply a pragmatic response to a serious regulatory problem?
3. Do regulatory policies impose special burdens on some sectors of the economy and not others, as Charles Krauthammer argues with respect to the Family and Medical Leave Act, or are those policies a reasonable way of allocating the costs and benefits of life in a community, as Representative Schroeder suggests?
4. Krauthammer suggests the adoption of a family and medical leave policy through redistributive rather than regulatory policies. What are the appeals of the two approaches?

CHAPTER 16

Government and the Economy

POLICIES FOR PUBLIC ORDER AND PRIVATE PROPERTY

See text p. 657

Few institutions are more fundamental to our understanding of American life than that of private property. The American economic system is built upon the assumption that property will be privately owned—in the pure capitalist vision, private entrepreneurs produce goods as demand requires, and the market will regulate itself as though guided by an invisible hand. As the text notes, however, private property ownership is not a natural phenomenon. Private property would be of little value without public policies to protect it—policies that enforce contracts or prohibit theft.

In this country, the government has long distributed its vast natural resources to encourage social stability and economic growth. From its earliest history, the United States has transferred public lands and resources into private hands using a series of distributive policies like those noted in Chapter 15. Some of those policies distributed property directly into private hands; a number of other policies granted permits and licenses for the use of the nation's resources. The aim of these policies was to encourage the development and exploitation of the nation's lands and minerals, and thereby to stimulate economic growth.

In recent years, many of these policies have been criticized. Prior to the 1970s, there were few restrictions placed upon the private use of public resources: individuals or companies holding licenses and permits could develop the properties free of any kind of regulatory control. Critics argue that these policies have allowed indiscriminate and wasteful use of public resources. In a number of cases, lands have been overgrazed or overlogged, water has been misappropriated, and mining lands are not reclaimed. Moreover, critics claim, these policies have benefitted a privileged few by subsidizing their businesses, leaving the American taxpayer footing the bill.

Beginning in the late 1970s, a number of regulatory policies were enacted to shift more of the costs of development to licensees and permitees. Those groups—ranchers and logging and timber companies—have strong lobbies, and changes have been slow to develop. The Clinton administration, however, promised to take a hard look at a variety of federal land policies. The article that follows chronicles some of the proposed changes and notes the kinds of political battles that are likely to ensue as those policies are scrutinized.

Timothy Egan
"Sweeping Reversal of U.S. Land Policy Sought by Clinton"*

Acting on orders from President Clinton to cut grazing, timber, mining and water subsidies, Interior Secretary Bruce Babbitt is trying to roll back more than a century of practices that have promoted the development of the West at Government expense.

While the plan to charge market rates for commercial use of public resources is being billed as an effort to reduce the deficit, its real importance would be to reverse the way nearly 500 million acres of Western land, equal to about one-fifth of the United States, are managed.

By encouraging ranchers to run cattle on land once thought to be essentially useless and trying to lure miners and loggers to remote high country, the Government has long treated the public lands of the West as a resource to be exploited. Under the Reagan and Bush Administrations, development was further encouraged by land managers who fought environmental restrictions.

Who Would Pay More

With the Clinton plan, the Government would no longer allow timber companies to log national forests at below-market rates. It would begin charging royalties on gold, silver and other metals now mined at no charge from Federal land, and would raise the fee that ranchers pay to graze livestock on 280 million acres of public range. In addition, farmers would pay surcharges to irrigate more than nine million acres. Fees for recreation, like hiking, hunting and camping, are also under consideration.

Much of the revenue, estimated at $1 billion over five years, would then be used to repair rivers, forests, range lands and wildlife habitats that have come under strain.

"It's a brand new era in land management," said Mr. Babbitt, who promoted the new thinking in a tour of the West last week.

Halt to Dam Building

He said the Government would no longer build dams "for dumb, stupid political reasons," and that fees for natural resources uses that now encourage poor stewardship would be raised to "give incentives for good management of the land."

*Timothy Egan, "Sweeping Reversal of U.S. Land Policy Sought by Clinton," *New York Times* (February 24, 1993).

Conservationists have long called for many of the changes, saying that the Government was selling off Western resources at 19th century prices and allowing the land to be degraded.

But some Western political leaders, as well as those directly affected by an end to the subsidies, say the changes may drive smaller ranchers off the land, threaten isolated rural communities and put a damper on a recent boom in mining claims.

Still, critics concede that the proposed changes, some of which have been sought before by Republican Administrations but never as a single, sweeping package, stand a good chance of passing this time around under the banner of deficit reduction.

The Administration says the proposals can bring in $1 billion over five years. While the figure is minuscule compared with the overall Federal deficit of nearly $300 billion, the mere act of trying to charge fair-market prices for cutting trees, grazing or mining in marginal areas is likely to have a lasting affect on how the land is used. The Government manages more than half the land in many big states in the West.

"I see us as the department of the environment," Mr. Babbitt said in a speech in Phoenix that earned him a standing ovation before a room of Federal employees. "We are about the perpetual American love affair with the land and the parks."

Reflecting the change in outlook President Clinton nominated two environmentalists today for top Administration posts: George T. Frampton, Jr., president of the Wilderness Society, as Assistant Secretary in charge of national parks and fish and wildlife, and Jim Baca, New Mexico's land commissioner and a former board member of the Wilderness Society, as head of the Bureau of Land Management, the nation's largest land manager. Both appointments are subject to Senate confirmation.

Support for New Approach

In talking up the new approach, Mr. Babbitt was well received by park rangers, biologists and other land managers who say they have suffered through years of political pressure to favor industrial uses of the land.

"Most of us are ecstatic," said Jim Walters, a veteran National Park Service employee based in New Mexico. "We all look forward to a new day. It's like a dark period is over."

But the intended changes are generating a strong reaction from groups that have banded together calling themselves the Wise Use movement, many of whom view their grazing, mining and timber-cutting permits as property rights protected by the Constitution.

"If Babbitt tries to go through with this, what you'll see happen is some resource-dependent communities turn into ghost towns," said Chuck Cushman of Battleground, Wash., who is a leader of the groups that have been fighting environmental restrictions on public land.

Representative George Miller, Democrat of California who is chairman of the House committee that has jurisdiction over most Western land issues, predicts approval for the changes. Congress may even raise the fees more than the Administration's proposal, he said.

Votes for Clinton

Most Westerners, he said, support the changes. Western states that have traditionally voted Republican, Colorado, Nevada, Montana and New Mexico among them, voted for Mr. Clinton last year.

"Reagan and Bush were just holding back the future," Mr. Miller said. "They were the last gasp of an outdated philosophy."

Senator Conrad Burns, Republican of Montana, said Mr. Clinton's plan, along with the proposal to tax energy, "is going to put Montana in a depression."

"The West is under siege right now," he said. "We've got no other way to make a living than the areas Clinton wants to tax and raise fees on. We'll be left selling 20-acre ranchettes to fancy-pants Easterners."

Most of the changes proposed by the Clinton Administration will need legislative approval, but Mr. Babbitt said he could take some action, like raising grazing fees, without Congressional consent.

'Question Is How Much'

"The question is not whether there should be an increase," he said of grazing, an issue that Congress has fought over but never resolved. "The question is how much."

About 28,000 ranchers graze livestock on 280 million acres of public land, run by the Forest Service and the Bureau of Land Management. They are charged $1.92 to graze one cow and her calf for a month, a rate that the Government has said is one-fifth of the market rate for Western states.

Some ranchers who hold permits are actually corporations like the Metropolitan Life Company that run cattle over millions of acres of public land. But most are small operations of less than 500 cattle. The Government lost about $50 million in administering the grazing program in 1990, according to the most recent report.

"I wouldn't complain if they raise it 50 cents or a dollar more, but if it goes much higher than that, a lot of people will be run off the land," said Arthur Lyman, a fifth-generation rancher who runs cattle on about 200,000 acres in Utah. "This is rough country. It's not easy to graze on. Not like private land. As far as I'm concerned, we already pay dearly for it."

Fees for Mineral Rights

In mining, President Clinton wants to begin charging royalties for hardrock minerals removed from Federal land. More than a million people hold mining claims on public land, most of them bought for prices set by the Ulysses S. Grant Administration in 1872. Critics have long considered mining one of the big areas of abuse of Western lands. But supporters say it one of the last opportunities left in the country for a "little guy" to make it big with a mining strike.

On numerous attempts, Congress has failed to change the law under which any person can establish a mining claim to Federal land for $2.50 an acre. The practice has been abused by people who have no interest in mining, but instead wanted to obtain a right to Federal property at a rock bottom price for other commercial uses, critics have said.

Charging a royalty will ultimately hurt the small mining industry, Mr. Cushman said. "You'll kill the goose that lays the golden egg because most prospecting is done by the little guy," he said. "Now he won't have any incentive."

Mr. Miller said some of the biggest users of public land were wealthy individuals who used the "cover of the little guy" to keep the Government from raising fees to a market level. "They trot out the argument of hurting the small rancher or small miner to scare politicians," he said. The Government can exempt the small users from the fee increase, he added.

Timber sales in which the Government spends more money building roads and surveying land before any logging is done than it takes in from the sales have been a continual source of criticism. In 1991, timber programs in 69 of the 120 national forests were losing money. The Forest Service, which is run by the Agriculture Department, has announced a plan to end these so-called below-cost sales as part of the President's package.

Mr. Babbitt, who as a lawyer in his home state battled the Government over water allocation policies, seems to take particular pleasure in being in charge of the Bureau of Reclamation, which manages more than half of the West's water supply.

End of Building Dams

He the said era of building dams is largely over. Now, the agency will devote more effort to protecting wildlife habitats.

"For half a century, the bureau has been the largest construction agency in the country," he said. "Those days are pretty much over. We've run out of places to dam. So, they'll have a new role, as a water manager."

The water rates for big agricultural users in 17 Western states would raised enough to generate $45 million over four years, Administration officials said.

MAKING AND MAINTAINING A NATIONAL MARKET ECONOMY

See text p. 659

While Article I, Section 8, of the Constitution grants the federal government authority to "regulate commerce . . . among the several states," the extent of that power was by no means a settled question at the nation's founding. While it seemed obvious that the creation of a national marketplace was essential if a nation was to be molded from the several states, those states were understandably reluctant to relinquish power over their own economic affairs.

By the early nineteenth century, however, it became apparent that uneven regulation of commerce by the states was a problem of national dimensions, and the Supreme Court was soon called to make a pronouncement on the scope of national authority under the "commerce clause." The Court's decision in Gibbons v. Ogden *(1824), as the text notes, emphatically established federal authority over matters affecting interstate commerce. The case had broad implications for the entire federalist structure of the American state: together with* McCulloch v. Maryland *(1819), reprinted in Chapter 3, it established the supremacy of federal law, significantly diminishing the sovereign powers of the states.*

Gibbons v. *Ogden* (1824)*

[The New York legislature passed a law granting two individuals, Robert Livingston and Robert Fulton, the exclusive right to operate steamships in New York waters, based upon their development of the steamship. The legislation also provided that no one else could operate a steamship in New York waters unless a license was first obtained from Mssrs. Livingston and Fulton. The operation of this law gave Fulton and Livingston a virtual stranglehold on traffic in and out of the New York ports—at that time, of course, one of the most significant ports in the nation.

Mr. Ogden received a license from Fulton and Livingston, and operated steamships between New York and New Jersey. Mr. Gibbons, a former partner of Mr. Ogden but now a rival, obtained a license from the United States, enabling him to engage in "coasting trade;" under the authority of that license, Mr. Gibbons began competing for business against Mr. Ogden. Ogden sued, seeking an order from the New York courts prohibiting Gibbons from operating in New York waters.

The most difficult question in the case was whether the New York law interfered with interstate *commerce, since Ogden argued that the law limited only commerce carried out* within *the boundaries of New York. Even then, he argued, the law did not prohibit all ships from operating—only steamships—so that a sailing ship could continue to operate in New York waters. Justice Marshall, writing for the Court, rejected that argument.]*

*Gibbons v. Ogden, 22 U.S. 23, 1824.

CHIEF JUSTICE MARSHALL delivered the opinion of the Court.

The appellant contends that this decree is erroneous, because the laws which purport to give the exclusive privilege it sustains, are repugnant to the constitution and laws of the United States.

The words are: "Congress shall have power to regulate commerce with foreign nations, and among the several states, and with the Indian tribes."

The subject to be regulated is commerce; and our constitution being, as was aptly said at the bar, one of enumeration and not of definition, to ascertain the extent of the power it becomes necessary to settle the meaning of the word. . . . Commerce, undoubtedly, is traffic, but it is something more; it is intercourse. It describes the commercial intercourse between nations, and parts of nations, in all its branches, and is regulated by prescribing rules for carrying on that intercourse. The mind can scarcely conceive a system for regulating commerce between nations, which shall exclude all laws concerning navigation, which shall be silent on the admission of the vessels of the one nation into the ports of the other, and be confined to prescribing rules for the conduct of individuals, in the actual employment of buying and selling, or of barter.

If commerce does not include navigation, the government of the Union has no direct power over that subject, and can make no law prescribing what shall constitute American vessels, or requiring that they shall be navigated by American seamen. Yet this power has been exercised from the commencement of the government, has been exercised with the consent of all, and has been understood by all to be a commercial regulation. All America understands, and has uniformly understood, the word "commerce" to comprehend navigation. It was so understood, and must have been so understood, when the constitution was framed. The power over commerce, including navigation, was one of the primary objects for which the people of America adopted their government, and must have been contemplated in forming it. The convention must have used the word in that sense; because all have understood it in that sense, and the attempt to restrict it comes too late.

The word used in the constitution, then, comprehends, and has been always understood to comprehend, navigation within its meaning; and a power to regulate navigation is as expressly granted as if that term had been added to the word "commerce."

The subject to which the power is applied, is to commerce "among the several states." The word "among" means intermingled with. A thing which is among others, is intermingled with them. Commerce among the states cannot stop at the external boundary line of each state, but may be introduced into the interior.

It is not intended to say that these words comprehend that commerce which is completely internal, which is carried on between man and man in a state, or between different parts of the same state, and which does not extend to or affect other states. Such a power would be inconvenient, and is certainly unnecessary. Comprehensive as the word "among" is, it may very properly be restricted to that commerce which concerns more states than one. The phrase is not one which would probably have been selected to indicate the completely interior traffic of a state, because it is not an apt phrase for that purpose; and the enumeration of the particular classes of commerce to which the power was to be extended, would not have been made had the intention been to extend the power to every description. The enumeration presupposes something not enumerated; and that something, if we regard the language or the subject of the sentence, must be the exclusively internal commerce of a state. The genius and character of the whole government seem to be, that its action is to be applied to all the external concerns of the nation, and to those internal concerns which affect the states generally; but not to those which are completely within a particular state, which do not affect other states, and with which it is not necessary to interfere, for the purpose of executing some of the general powers of the government. The completely internal commerce of a state, then, may be considered as reserved for the state itself.

But, in regulating commerce with foreign nations, the power of Congress does not stop at the jurisdictional lines of the several states. It would be a very useless power if it could not pass those lines. The commerce of the United States with foreign nations, is that of the whole United States. Every district has a right to participate in it. The deep streams which penetrate our country in every direction, pass through the interior of almost every state in the Union, and furnish the means of exercising this right. If Congress has the power to regulate it, that power must be exercised whenever the subject exists. If it exists within the states, if a foreign voyage may commence or terminate at a port within a state, then the power of Congress may be exercised within a state.

We are now arrived at the inquiry. What is this power?

It is the power to regulate; that is, to prescribe the rule by which commerce is to be governed. This power, like all others vested in Congress, is complete in itself, may be exercised to its utmost extent, and acknowledges no limitations, other than are prescribed in the constitution. These are expressed in plain terms, and do not affect the questions which arise in this case, or which have been discussed at the bar. If, as has always been understood, the sovereignty of Congress, though limited to specified objects, is plenary as to those objects, the power over commerce with foreign nations, and among the several states, is vested in Congress as absolutely as it would be in a single government, having in its constitution the same restrictions on the exercise of the power as are found in the constitution of the United States. The wisdom and the discretion of Congress, their identity with the people, and the influence which their constituents possess at elections, are, in this, as in many other instances, as that, for example, of declaring war, the sole restraints on which they have relied, to secure them from its abuse. They are the restraints on which the people most often rely solely, in all representative governments.

The power of Congress, then, comprehends navigation within the limits of every state in the Union; so far as that navigation may be, in any manner, connected with "commerce with foreign nations, or among the several states, or with the Indian tribes." It may, of consequence, pass the jurisdictional line of New York, and act upon the very waters to which the prohibition now under consideration applies.

[I]t has been urged with great earnestness that, although the power of Congress to regulate commerce with foreign nations, or among the several states, be coextensive with the subject itself, and have no other limits than are prescribed in the Constitution, yet the states may severally exercise the same power within their respective jurisdictions. In support of this argument, it is said that they possessed it as an inseparable attribute of sovereignty before the formation of the Constitution, and still retain it, except so far as they have surrendered it by that instrument; that this principle results from the nature of the government, and is secured by the Tenth Amendment; that an affirmative grant of power is not exclusive, unless in its own nature it be such that the continued exercise of it by the former possessor is inconsistent with the grant, and that this is not of that description. The appellant, conceding these postulates, except the last, contends that full power to regulate a particular subject implies the whole power, and leaves no residuum; that a grant of the whole is incompatible with the existence of a right in another to any part of it.

The grant of the power to lay and collect taxes is, like the power to regulate commerce, made in general terms, and has never been understood to interfere with the exercise of the same power by the states; and hence has been drawn an argument which has been applied to the question under consideration. But the two grants are not, it is conceived, similar in their terms or their nature. Although many of the powers formerly exercised by the states are transferred to the government of the Union, yet the state governments remain, and constitute a most important part of our system. The power of taxation is indispensable to their existence, and is a power which, in its own nature, is capable of residing in, and being exercised by, different authorities at the same time. When, then, each government exercises the power of taxation, neither is exercising the power of the other. But when a state proceeds to regulate commerce with foreign nations, or among the several states, it is exercising the very power that is granted to Congress, and is doing the very thing which Congress is authorized to do. There is no analogy, then, between the power of taxation and the power of regulating commerce. . . .

[I]f a state, in passing laws on subjects acknowledged to be within its control, and with a view to those subjects, shall adopt a measure of the same character with one which Congress may adopt, it does not derive its authority from the particular power which has been granted, but from some other which remains with the state, and may be executed by the same means. All experience shows that the same measures, or measures scarcely distinguishable from each other, may flow from distinct powers; but this does not prove that the powers themselves are identical. Although the means used in their execution may sometimes approach each other so nearly as to be confounded, there are other situations in which they are sufficiently distinct to establish their individuality.

In our complex system, presenting the rare and difficult scheme of one general government whose action extends over the whole, but which possesses only certain enumerated powers; and of numerous state governments, which retain and exercise all powers not delegated to the Union, contests respecting power must arise. Were it ever otherwise, the measures taken by the respective governments to execute their acknowledged powers would often be of the same description, and might sometimes interfere. This, however, does not prove that the one is exercising, or has a right to exercise, the powers of the other.

It has been contended by the counsel for the appellant that, as the word to "regulate" implies in its nature full power over the thing to be regulated, it excludes, necessarily, the action of all others that would perform the same operation on the same thing. That regulation is designed for the entire result, applying to those parts which remain as they were, as well as to those which are altered. It produces a uniform whole, which is as much disturbed and deranged by changing what the regulating power designs to leave untouched, as that on which it has operated. There is great force in this argument, and the court is not satisfied that it has been refuted.

Since, however, in exercising the power of regulating their own purely internal affairs, whether of trading or police, the States may sometimes enact laws, the validity of which depends on their interfering with and being contrary to, an act of Congress passed in pursuance of the Constitution, the Court will enter upon an inquiry, whether the laws of New York, as expounded by the highest tribunal of that State, have, in their application to this case, come into collision with an Act of Congress, and deprive a citizen of a right to which that act entitled him. Should this collision exist, it will be immaterial whether those laws were passed in virtue of a concurrent power "to regulate commerce with foreign nations and among the several States," or in virtue of a power to regulate their domestic trade and police. In one case and the other, the acts of New York must yield to the law of Congress; and the decision sustaining the privilege they confer, against the right given by a law of the Union, must be erroneous.

Reversed.

REGULATING THE MARKET

See text p. 661

Given this nation's commitment to a free market economy, it is not surprising that we have never had a fully articulated "industrial policy." Yet, as this chapter has emphasized, the failure to specify an industrial policy has not meant that the market has gone unregulated. Indeed, the problem is precisely that the free market as such does not exist: even in a capitalist economy, certain policies—like those supporting the institution of private property—are essential prerequisites.

More importantly, we have discovered that many factors argue against the establishment of a truly "free" market. In some cases, government has stepped in to regulate the economy to mitigate the harsher consequences of capitalism when the human costs have proven too great to bear; in other cases, we have simply been dissatisfied with the speed at which the market "corrects" itself, such as when we decide that we do not have time to wait until the market itself forces companies to clean up the environment. But the basic commitment to a free market economy has led to a piecemeal approach, and the result is a confusing and often inefficient array of regulatory policies.

The following article, written for Financial World *magazine, provides an interesting look into the paradoxes of market regulation in a capitalist economy, and should be considered in connection with both this section of the chapter and the one that follows on making and maintaining a capitalist economy. The author suggests that "Washington's adversarial stance toward business is unique among [Western] industrialized countries. . . . [M]any of our most formidable foreign competitors enjoy something approaching a commercial alliance with their governments." The author is clearly concerned about the level of governmental regulation, but a close look at the arguments reveals the extent to which the author considers governmental regulation a necessity: "[G]overnment regulation should enhance competition, not suppress it."*

This article was written prior to the election of President Clinton, who has proposed a closer alliance between government and business in order to stimulate economic growth. While it is still too early to determine the direction that the Clinton administration's regulatory policies will take, there is little likelihood that the new administration will support extensive deregulation. Despite the change from a Republican to a Democratic executive, the arguments about the nature of regulation—how much is too much, what kind of regulation is the "right" kind—remain the same.

Financial World
"Government vs. Business: The Endless Struggle"*

When President Jimmy Carter signed the Airline Deregulation Act in October 1978, it was hailed as a turning point in business-government relations—the reversal of a century-long trend toward greater government intervention in the affairs of private enterprise.

Today, that euphoria seems premature. True, in a number of industries, the heavy hand of bureaucratic control has indeed been lifted. But the results are, in many cases, highly controversial. What's more, a series of new rules—designed to clean up the environment, enhance public safety, protect workers, accommodate the handicapped and increase job opportunities for minorities—have been imposed that now affect more companies than ever before. And proposals to make new social demands on business are put forward almost daily.

Washington's adversarial stance toward business is unique among the industrialized countries in the non-Communist world. In no other nation are companies subjected to so many bureaucratic restraints by their own government. Indeed, many of our most formidable foreign competitors

*"Government vs. Business: The Endless Struggle," *Financial World* (June 25, 1991). Reprinted from *Financial World*, 1326 Broadway, New York, N.Y. 10001.

enjoy something approaching a commercial alliance with their governments.

That fact, in the context of today's intense global competition, has prompted many business leaders, economists and politicians to call for a revolutionary change in the relationship between business and government in the U.S. Some would even like to establish a formal industrial policy in this country, with Uncle Sam selecting which industries and new technologies to subsidize. . . .

Regulation began in the form of state commissions to supervise public utilities. It was clear to most people that these [utilities] were "natural monopolies"—businesses in which investment costs and economies of scale were so great that encouraging competition and duplication of facilities would be wasteful and do little to improve service. To keep such companies from gouging customers, regulation would take the place of competition.

The railroads were another obvious target. Railroads were the first really large companies in the U.S., with widely scattered operations. And because they were often the economic lifeblood of the communities they served, they represented a unique concentration of power.

By the mid-1800s, a number of states had established railroad commissions, but it quickly became apparent that companies doing business in many states could only be regulated effectively by a national agency. So, in 1887, the Interstate Commerce Commission was formed. It became the model for many federal regulatory agencies that followed. The ICC's early experience also foreshadowed the problems that have plagued most regulators since; notably the time-consuming, case-by-case determination of rates to balance the diametrically opposed interests of producers and consumers. The task proved incredibly difficult.

In 1898, the Supreme Court ruled that a railroad was entitled to a "reasonable" return on "the fair value of the property being used for the convenience of the public." That seemed sensible enough, but according to McCraw it simply opened a bottomless can of worms [because no one could decide what amounted to a fair rate of return]. . . .

As some early experts also recognized, establishing a fixed rate of return on investment (however defined) made little economic sense. Among other things, they pointed out, it destroyed any incentive to improve efficiency. In fact, regulators over the years have often used their influence over pricing to preserve competition by restricting it: They have kept weak firms in business by forbidding stronger rivals to take advantage of their efficiency and ability to cut prices.

As the ICC was getting under way, Congress also laid down the fundamental law against monopoly. The Sherman Antitrust Act of 1890 made illegal "every contact, combination of the form of trust or otherwise, or conspiracy, in restraint of trade or commerce." . . . By 1904, the law had prevented a big railroad merger, and a few years later, it was used to break up Standard Oil, American Tobacco and the Sugar Trust. In 1914, Congress toughened the rules further by passing the Clayton Act (which forbade corporations that were not holding companies to acquire the stock of other firms or to engage in price discrimination) and by establishing the Federal Trade Commission to enforce the law.

At this point, however, the early trust-busting fervor was waning. During World War I, business cooperation proved so useful in expanding production that people began to see that larger organizations could have value. What's more, according to William A. Lovett, professor of law and history at Tulane University, "prosperity and economic growth with a significant spread of new industries—automobiles, gasoline stations, airplanes, radios, movies, records and plastics—continued through World War I into the 1920s. A proliferation of new appliances and improved technology changed everyday life. In these circumstances, with a shift to more conservative faith in free enterprise, there was less populist alarm about the dangers of bigger business."

In that atmosphere, the courts drew distinctions between "good trusts" and "bad trusts." In particular, the Supreme Court held that "mere size" or the "existence of unexerted power" did not constitute violations of the law. Some actions that had been considered anticompetitive were also deemed legal—for example, granting big discounts to large distributors of manufactured products.

With the Great Depression, though, came a violent new shift in the public's attitude toward business. Not only were its leaders bitterly criticized, but there was a widespread conviction that the system itself was fatally flawed. With Roosevelt's New Deal came a proliferation of new regulatory agencies.

The Securities and Exchange Commission brought Wall Street under control. The Federal Communications Commission took over management of the airwaves. The National Labor Relations Board issued rules governing companies' treatment of their workers. The Civil Aeronautics Board took jurisdiction over the nation's airlines. In addition, existing regulators were given new powers and wider authority.

The idea, to which most New Dealers subscribed, was that because the free market was not functioning properly, government should take a hand. Expert public servants, they believed, would be more likely than business executives to make decisions that would bring the greatest benefits to society.

The late Thirties turned out to be the high-water mark of regulation. World War II rehabilitated business's reputation, and postwar prosperity boosted it even higher. There was little public interest in riding herd on the companies that were providing Americans with such a cornucopia of material blessings.

At the same time, many experts had begun to call for reform of the regulatory agencies, which had become somnolent bureaucracies, peopled by second-raters. Their performance showed it. By 1960, the Federal Power Commission had a 13-year back log of undecided cases and, according to a report written for President-elect John F. Kennedy, "with the contemplated 6,500 cases that would be filed during that 13-year period, it could not become current until 2043 A.D., even if its staff were tripled."

Critics also charged that the agencies had largely become captives of the very industries they were supposed to supervise. In particular, says McCraw, the CAB and FCC "appeared to be following policies that equated the public interest with the desires of the most powerful elements in the airline and communications industries."

When Kennedy took office, he raised the caliber of regulators significantly and tried to launch a program of reform. But Congress rejected some of his most important recommendations, and his attention quickly turned to more pressing issues: foreign affairs, civil rights, tax policy. The issue of reforming the regulatory process was largely set aside.

Meanwhile, a new generation of trustbusters in the Justice Department strove to enlarge the definition of illegal conduct. This was a logical outcome of the landmark 1945 decision of Judge Learned Hand in the Alcoa case. "Great industrial concentrations," he wrote, "are inherently undesirable regardless of their economic consequences."

In the years that followed, Lovett observes, "A tough line was laid down on larger horizontal and vertical mergers. Big companies with hefty market shares were not allowed to make mergers within their own industries or markets nor to buy up their leading competitors or suppliers. The only significant exception was the 'failing company' doctrine, under which firms in serious financial trouble with doubtful prospects of survival could be acquired."

As the economy slowed in the 1970s, a new attitude toward business was gaining adherents. In their view, economics was replacing ideology as the rationale for regulation and antitrust—with greater concern for efficiency and less worry about equity. When the "Chicago school" of economists called for more freedom of action for business during this period, they found increasing favor.

The shift toward deregulation took place, ironically, during a Democratic Administration. The Civil Aeronautics Board, formed in 1938, was one of the youngest regulatory commissions, but it shared most of the bad habits and counter-productive policies of its older models. While the CAB had stabilized what had become a chaotic business, it had essentially cartelized the industry. "The overall effect of board policies," says McCraw, "tended to freeze the industry more or less in its configuration. In fact, over the entire history of CAB, no trunk-line carrier had been permitted to join the 16 that existed in 1938." . . . Most of the CAB's flaws were glaringly obvious when Alfred E. Kahn came to Washington in 1977 after a career as a professor of economics at Cornell University and as the reformist chairman of the New York Public Service Commission. In fact, a remarkable coalition of groups from across the political and ideological spectrum had formed to urge a change in the rules that would at least permit lower fares.

Kahn set to work to revitalize the CAB—with the ultimate aim of eliminating it. In spite of the almost unanimous opposition of the airlines, he managed to decontrol fares, permit new firms to enter the industry and allow airlines to fly where they wished. Perhaps more important, he was a tireless advocate of deregulation, citing the fare cuts that permitted millions of new passengers to fly and responding to complaints about deteriorating service (which he acknowledged as the chief cost of expanding business).

In October 1978, persuaded that the airlines no longer needed government control, Congress passed the Airline Deregulation Act—calling for the disappearance of the CAB in 1985.

The CAB decision opened the floodgates of deregulation. Many rules governing the railroads, truckers, telecommunications firms and financial institutions were relaxed or jettisoned over the next few years. The rush to deregulate got an enormous boost from President Ronald Reagan and the aggressive free marketers who accompanied him to Washington. The new Administration also held a more permissive view of antitrust than any since Herbert Hoover's. It issued guidelines that virtually ended government challenges of mergers, and the 1980s saw an explosive increase in such combinations.

Many Americans, though, worried that the pendulum had swung too far. Deregulation had some unexpected and occasionally grave results: failing airlines and S&Ls, or higher prices for some telephone services. Benign neglect of antitrust facilitated a wave of takeovers that piled up corporate debt (sometimes resulting in defaults and bankruptcies) and cost thousands of workers their jobs.

Since President Bush's inauguration, there has been no official policy reversal, but enthusiasm for more mergers or further deregulation (in banking, for example) has clearly been dampened. In a few cases, calls for reregulation are being heard. And there is strong political support for laws that sometimes specify in rigid detail what companies must do to avoid polluting the air and water or to assure the rights of their workers. The costs of these mandates—often tougher than the rules laid down by the old regulatory agencies—are literally incalculable. And that has added force to a new debate over the proper relationship of business and government.

In today's global market domestic antitrust policy has inevitably become entangled with the issues of international competitiveness. As Professor Lovett puts it: "To some degree, the U.S. will have to match, respond in kind, or achieve more effective responses to foreign industrial policies."

That means that our antitrust and regulatory policies may have to be tempered lest they cripple U.S. companies in global markets. And they may have to set new goals such as encouraging research and development of new technology, enabling American companies to work together in ways that are now considered illegal, perhaps even directing resources to industries held to be vital to our national interests.

A small library of books has been published in recent years offering a plethora of prescriptions to cure what one of them labeled The American Disease. Most of them call for massive doses of government intervention. Another stage in the endless search for the proper balance between business freedom and government control may well be getting under way. What is crucial, warns Kahn, is that government intervention should enhance competition, rather than suppress it.

Debating the Issues: Opposing Views

DOES THE DEFICIT MATTER?

See text pp. 680–81

As the text notes, the deficit poses a genuine dilemma for policymakers. The American economy is enormously complex. Moreover, the aims and functions of the state are not the same as those of private business, so that managing a public debt is not entirely analogous to managing private debt. Because there are many sides to this complex issue, the four brief articles (which all appeared on the same New York Times *op-ed page on June 10, 1992) reprinted below provide a more in-depth look at this highly debated issue.*

One of the proposals that has floated around in recent years has been the suggestion that Congress approve a constitutional amendment that would prohibit it from spending more than it receives in tax revenues. The following pieces, written on the eve of Congress's 1992 consideration of a balanced budget amendment, discuss the arguments for and against such a proposal. The 1992 effort was not successful, although the idea has not been discarded by a number of policymakers.

In the first place, former President Ronald Reagan asserts that Congress is by nature profligate, and that adopting a balanced budget amendment goes one step toward restoring Americans' faith in government. He argues that balancing the budget can be achieved if "we simply limit the growth in spending per beneficiary to the rate of inflation. . . ."

Robert Heilbroner, a professor emeritus of economics at the New School for Social Research, and Peter Bernstein, an economic consultant for institutional investors, argue that a requiring Congress to balance the budget across the board is unwise. They argue that some kinds of deficit spending—spending to build up the nation's infrastructure, for example, or to improve education—increase the nation's overall wealth, because those projects have a high payoff over time. The problem, they assert, is that the government presently has no means of distinguishing between good and bad deficit spending, and requiring the reduction of all programs to balance the budget will, in the long run, "crush the prime method of financing growth."

Martin Mayer, author of Stealing the Market, *contends that a balanced budget amendment is not the right response to the nation's current economic woes. Mayer argues that Congress should adopt a ceiling on debt; balancing the budget allows numbers to be faked and does little to remedy the real problems. Pointing to the recent Savings and Loan debacle, Mayer argues that because there is no limit on public borrowing, Congress and the president routinely guarantee disastrous private borrowing programs that cost taxpayers millions and millions of dollars.*

Finally, Laurence Kotlikoff, an economics professor at Boston University and author of a book entitled Generational Accounting, *suggests that a balanced-budget effort only skims the surface of the problem. The real issue, he says, is understanding how debt accumulates over time and places a burden on forthcoming generations. These kinds of "generational" debts do not show up in current deficit figures, impoverishing our understanding of the problem. The solution, he suggests, is to "raise taxes on adult—young, middle-aged, and old—and to limit the growth of Social Security, Medicare, and other government transfer programs."*

Ronald Reagan
"Bush Leads the Way"*

Here I go again. . . .

Ten years ago, in a speech on the Capitol steps, I urged Congress to adopt a balanced-budget amendment. I reminded Congress of a warning by Thomas Jefferson: "The public debt is the greatest of dangers to be feared." Since then, Congress has refused to work with the President and pass the amendment and has shown little restraint in spending.

While pundits will want to blame the White House for deficits, the blame game won't work. Congress alone has responsibility and authority for passing budgets, and Congress alone can balance them. No finger-pointing will change that. As the debt soars toward $4 trillion, not surprisingly Congress suffers from its lowest approval ratings in decades.

But this year, Congress has a chance to restore public faith in our Government. Today it is debating a balanced-budget amendment more seriously than ever before. Several versions compete for approval but each requires these basics: The President must submit a balanced budget; Congress must pass a balanced budget; at year's end, spending cannot outrun revenues, and Congress can engage in deficit spending only if both chambers vote to do so.

The best proposals add something more: a requirement that Congress approve increases in spending and taxation by "super-majority" votes—60 percent of each house. The super-majority requirement insures that Congress treats your money with the same respect that you do.

An amendment as proposed by President Bush will do more than obliterate deficits. It also will encourage wise social and economic policies. The system does not punish members of Congress when they waste taxpayers' money. It often rewards big spenders with political action committee contributions and new terms of office.

A sound balanced-budget amendment reverses this trend by restraining spending and taxation. It's important to understand that tax increases don't balance budgets. In recent years, Congress raised taxes dozens of times. In each case, Congressional spending outpaced the tax increase, and the deficit grew.

Today, each new dollar in revenue inspires Congress to spend an additional $1.59. The way Congress loves to spend money reminds me of a T-shirt I saw that said: "How can I be out of money? I still have some checks left!" A balanced-budget amendment also ought to support growth. If we balance the budget by taking every last dime that workers earn, we haven't accomplished a thing. In the post-cold-war world, the U.S. must remain competitive, strong and vigorous. We must not heap taxes, massive Government borrowing and burdensome regulations on workers and entrepreneurs.

*Ronald Reagan, "Bush Leads the Way," *New York Times* (June 10, 1992).

The need to restrain Government gets more urgent every day. Total government spending (Federal, state and local) consumes more than one in every three dollars produced by the economy. Congress has balanced only five budgets since 1950, the last in 1969.

If present trends continue, total debt will exceed our gross domestic product within the next 20 to 25 years. In other words, the Government will owe more money than the economy generates. To put it in perspective, every child in America arrives on this earth owing $16,000 for the Government's profligacy.

Worse, mandatory spending—entitlement and other programs that grow without Congressional review or approval—consume almost two-thirds of today's Federal budget. In addition, Congress increasingly imposes new burdens on state and local government without providing the money to finance them. That's unfair and irresponsible, and President Bush wisely has vowed to veto measures that include such mandates.

We cannot possibly balance the budget unless we show the courage to bring these programs under control. It doesn't require Draconian action. If we simply limit the growth in spending per beneficiary to the rate of inflation, we save tens of billions of dollars.

But Congress has not risen to this challenge. Even though the amendment is popular with Americans, Congress has refused to pass it. Congress has also refused to give the President the line-item veto most governors have. Even when Congress adopted budget discipline under the Gramm-Rudman-Hollings law, it dropped the restraints at the first opportunity. Some in Congress also want to abandon the restraints of the 1990 Budget Act, just as they begin to take full effect.

A balanced-budget amendment provides the discipline that members of Congress say they want and need. George Washington said in his Farewell Address, "The basis of our political system is the right of the people to make and to alter their constitutions of government." Today, we have a historic opportunity to approve an amendment that restrains spending and liberates the taxpayer. We can take a bold step toward a dynamic society where government is truly the servant of the people.

Robert Heilbroner and Peter Bernstein "Create Two Budgets"*

Congress is scheduled to vote tomorrow on a constitutional amendment to prevent the Government from spending more than it receives in tax reve-

*Robert Heilbroner and Peter Bernstein, "Create Two Budgets," *New York Times* (June 10, 1992).

nues, except under special circumstances such as recession or war. Who can fault this idea, whose manifest purpose is to assure the fiscal soundness of our Government and moral integrity of our nation?

Although some people worry that the amendment goes too far, its real flaw shows up when we make the case that it does not go far enough. If balanced budgets are such a noble objective, why limit the requirement to the Government? Surely, local governments are also sinners, although to a lesser degree. And while we are at it, why should American corporations be permitted to spend each year some $100 billion more than the revenue they receive for their goods and services?

Although simple consistency mandates that the Constitution be amended to prevent all of us from ruining ourselves, a mixed reaction to this broadened proposal is also likely. Isn't borrowing a good thing when it enables a profitable business to expand or a family to buy a house or a student to finance a college education? If businesses or individuals were constitutionally prohibited from running deficits, our economic virtue might be improved, but we would assuredly wreck our capacity for economic growth.

Why is it that public deficits are so abhorrent when most private borrowing is an acceptable form of finance? Government borrowing increases the nation's wealth when we use it to build up our infrastructure, strengthen our educational system or augment the housing stock.

Yes, but there is a catch. Our Government has no method for separating "good" borrowing from "bad"—unlike other major capitalist countries, most state governments, all businesses and prudent households. All the borrowed money goes into the Treasury as a lump sum to finance anything and everything from the President's salary and emergency aid to Ethiopia to interstate highways and grants to states for capital spending. No one has any way of judging whether the means to repay new debts will be forthcoming later on or whether the money spent will just be down the drain. This is precisely the difference between good borrowing and bad borrowing, between capital creation and what is deservedly called a deficit.

Yet if we pass the balanced-budget amendment as it now stands, all kinds of Federal spending, regardless of purpose, must be financed by taxes. Rectitude will crush the prime method of financing growth.

The obvious way out of this impending mess is simple. The Government should adopt the conventional accounting system that separates operating expenses from capital spending. Under normal circumstances, borrowing should be prohibited for ordinary and continuing purposes that have nothing to do with creating growth. These include farm subsidies, Medicare, foreign aid, the administration of justice, the Securities and Exchange Commission and salaries of the armed forces.

With a capital budget also in place, to be financed by borrowing if necessary, the public will know that every penny of the "deficit" that finances that capital budget is used for the same purposes as the "deficits"—the good borrowings—of corporations and households.

This idea has been around for a long time. Opposition to it is political:

Congressmen like to slip pet spending programs in under the roof of the capital budget. The issue is so important, however, that the country should be willing to spend the time needed to develop a well-conceived set of checks and balances, including super-majority votes in Congress.

Then, by simple legislation, we can save our souls, put the nation's finances in better shape, and move on to serious things, like deciding how we can best use the power of public investment to achieve ends that private investment cannot.

Martin Mayer
"Limit the Debt"*

The balanced-budget amendment won't work, but there is a way to use the Constitution to impose discipline.

Governments run deficits because they can borrow. In the absence of legal restrictions, the Federal Government can borrow virtually without limit, because it prints the money it will use to service its debts.

We have laws that limit the national debt, and every so often Washington has a flap until Congress lifts the debt ceiling.

If a constitutional amendment set a ceiling on the debt, the executive branch and Congress would have to live with it. For the purposes of this amendment, the currency in circulation would have to be considered part of the national debt, to make sure the Government could not print money to get out of a jam.

By taking the debt as the subject of an amendment, we would avoid the fakery surrounding the Social Security surplus. Tens of billions a year pour into Social Security as interest on Treasury bonds, the fund's only asset. These payments to Social Security are treated as income in the budget, reducing the published deficit. But they add to the debt because the Government pays interest by creating new bonds that are added to the Social Security Administration's account. An amendment limiting debt would stop this flim flam.

Limiting borrowing would make Congress and the President think twice about extending the guarantees the Government spreads promiscuously around so many kinds of private borrowing. If they knew they would have to raise taxes or cut programs when depositors in failed S&Ls and banks claimed deposit insurance, they would make sure regulators in failed S&Ls and banks claimed deposit insurtors did their job.

A constitutional debt limit could not and should not be a flat dollar amount. Instead, the maximum debt should be set at some fraction—say,

*Martin Mayer, "Limit the Debt," *New York Times* (June 10, 1992).

two-thirds—of the gross national product of the year preceding the budget year. That is about where we are now, and the amendment would thus permit a growth of the debt equal to two-thirds of the growth in the G.N.P. each year.

But the debt would never grow that fast. No President or Congress would dare let a deficit push the debt near the ceiling, creating the possibility that the Government couldn't pay its bills or its employees because there was no money to cover the checks. Everybody involved in budgeting would feel a need to built a rainy-day fund—a cushion between the total borrowings the budget would require and the constitutional limits, to guard the country against the year when a shortfall in receipts or a need for extraordinary outlays might create a crisis.

In theory, any restriction of deficits reduces the Government's capacity to use fiscal policy to fight a recession. In fact, a rainy-day fund would give future governments much greater leeway than the Bush Administration has had, because large deficits of recent years have made it impossible to give the economy a jolt of budgetary stimulus.

Debt as a fraction of G.N.P. is the measurement international economic organizations use to determine a nation's fiscal health. The continued borrowing such a debt-limit amendment permits would cover most of the interest payments on existing debt, allowing the Government to use tax receipts for ongoing purposes, without having to transfer too much money yearly from taxpayers to bond holders.

If the President and Congress really wish to put the candy jar out of reach, they should write an amendment that truly limits the debt, not one that pretends to eliminate the deficit.

Laurence J. Kotlikoff
"Taxes: Future Shock"*

Set aside the debate about the balanced-budget amendment. Down deep, we know this will just end up in another round of smoke-and-mirrors bookkeeping. What we don't know, and what we need to know, is the likely size of the fiscal burden to be piled on our children's and grandchildren's shoulders. Unfortunately, we'll never learn the answer by focusing on the Federal deficit.

First, there are almost as many definitions of the deficit as there are economists. The Congressional Budget Office, an arm of Congress, is so confused as to which deficit to discuss that it has taken to reporting five figures, ranging from 2 percent to 7 percent of the gross national product.

*Laurence J. Kotlikoff, "Taxes: Future Shock," *New York Times* (June 10, 1992).

To which of the five deficit definitions, or the many other definitions, will the balanced-budget amendment apply?

Second, the deficit only tells us about our immediate cash flows. It ignores the future, including demographic changes that will, over 35 years, leave the U.S. with the same age profile as Florida has now. Will balancing the budget be sufficient to keep tax rates from soaring when baby-boomers retire?

Third, even if we could all agree on the definition, the deficit would still miss most of the Government's redistribution across generations. The colossal growth since 1950 of pay-as-you-go Social Security and Medicare is a prime example. While the taxes collected by these programs have in past years equaled benefits paid out, and thus have not increased the deficit, the programs have redistributed huge sums across generations.

The generations fortunate enough to be old during the buildup of these programs received much more in benefits than the sum of principal plus interest on their prior tax contributions. The consequence is that middle-aged and young Americans will receive substantially less in benefits than the sum of what they contributed plus interest.

"Revenue neutral" shifts in the tax structure that lower taxes paid by the elderly and raise taxes paid by the young is another example of passing the generational buck. We have done for four decades. Since 1950 Federal, state and local governments have shifted from relying on sales, excise and capital income taxes, which fall disproportionately on the elderly, to labor income taxes, which fall disproportionately on the young. In 1950 income taxes represented a third of government taxes. Today they represent almost three-fifths.

Pay-as-you-go Social Security and "revenue neutral" tax changes are only two of the many generational policies that never show up in the deficit. Rather than fret about a number—the Federal deficit—that tells us next to nothing, why not measure directly how much current and future generations are being asked and will be asked to pay? This generational accounting is not a pie-in-the-sky alternative to deficit accounting. The accounts have been calculated, indeed even published, in the President's budget for fiscal 1993. They provide a troubling picture of the burden Federal, state and local governments are imposing on our progeny.

Today's children will pay more than 40 percent of their lifetime incomes to government. Even worse, future generations, those born after the year 2000, will face a 60 percent or greater lifetime net tax rate unless current policies are changed soon. Even a 40 percent lifetime tax rate is a huge proportion when compared with the tax rates paid by older generations.

How can we reduce the tax burden on our children and future generations? The answer is to raise taxes on adults—young, middle-aged and old—and to limit the growth of Social Security, Medicare and other Government transfer payments.

And how can this be done, given that neither party is willing to take the heat? By setting up an independent board that would recommend policies to prevent the taxing of future generations at ever higher rates. Such a panel was successful in 1983 in realigning Social Security finances. The proposed agency would provide an ongoing accounting to show each generation how it is being treated and guarantee that the sacrifices we make today will benefit our children and grandchildren.

QUESTIONS

1. As the text explains, the government has long distributed its resources through a variety of programs designed to encourage private development of resources and capital. As the article on federal land policy reforms suggests, the federal government is now considering revising its subsidization of private resource development. What concerns motivate the proposed changes in policy? Has the system simply outgrown its usefulness, or will changes unfairly penalize those who have come to rely on this distribution of governmental largesse?
2. In *Gibbons v. Ogden,* the U.S. Supreme Court struck down state regulations that it found to constitute a burden on interstate commerce. What policy concerns about the development of a national market surface in the language of the opinion? Can similar policy concerns be used to justify the exercise of national power in other areas, such as civil rights?
3. In a capitalist society, as discussed above, government policies are typically aimed at both enhancing economic growth and mitigating the sometimes harsh consequences of unregulated market development. Is it time to adopt a more explicit trade policy for the United States? To what extent should the government act as a mediator in both internal issues, like those relating to labor/management relations, and external issues, like those relating to trade with other nations and among multinational corporations?
4. The enormous federal deficit poses an intractable problem. The point/counterpoint pieces concerning the balanced budget amendment point out the range of policy options available, depending upon the way in which the problem is characterized in the first place. Which of the four pieces best describes the problem? What policy responses would be appropriate to each of the four descriptions?

CHAPTER 17

Government and Society

THE WELFARE STATE

See text p. 693

Understanding the evolution of the American welfare state requires understanding the manner in which our broader perceptions of the state's obligations to its citizens has evolved. As the text notes, this country was not founded on the idea that the state had any affirmative duty to promote the welfare of its citizens. Thus, assistance for those in need was considered a private obligation, and public assistance programs were virtually non-existent during the early part of the nation's history.

By the late 1960s, however, a variety of governmental welfare programs were well established and well accepted. The extent to which an individual receiving governmental assistance had rights, however, was an open question, and a number of cases reached the courts in this country arguing that the receipt of government benefits alone did not defeat one's rights to privacy or fair treatment generally. In 1970, the Supreme Court issued a decision that dramatically illustrated a shift in at least the Court's attitude toward the rights of welfare recipients. In Goldberg v. Kelly *(1970), the Supreme Court was asked to determine the conditions under which a state could terminate a welfare recipient's benefits. At issue were a set of New York social service regulations that allowed the agency to terminate welfare benefits upon an administrator's determination that the recipient was no longer qualified to receive them; the recipient was entitled to contest the decision and seek reinstatement, but could be left without any resources during the interim. Broadly construing the concept of fair treatment under the Fourteenth Amendment's due process clause, the Court held that a welfare recipient, who might have a "brutal need" for the benefits, was entitled to a hearing on whether he or she could continue receiving benefits prior to their termination. In reaching that decision, the Court characterized welfare benefits as "entitlements" (legal rights) rather than mere privileges.*

Justice Brennan, who authored the Goldberg *case, considered it the most important decision he wrote during his long career on the Court. The case had far reaching implications for the kinds of procedures that the government must observe in its treatment of individuals who receive government benefits. More importantly, it raised the status of government benefits: while benefits, recharacterized as "entitlements," are not exactly rights, they are more carefully protected than mere privileges conferred by the state.*

Goldberg v. *Kelly* (1970)*

Justice Brennan delivered the opinion of the Court.

The constitutional issue to be decided is the narrow one whether the Due Process Clause requires that the recipient be afforded an evidentiary hearing before the termination of benefits.

[Welfare] benefits are a matter of statutory entitlement for persons qualified to receive them. Their termination involves state action that adjudicates important rights. The constitutional challenge cannot be answered by an argument that public assistance benefits are "a 'privilege' and not a 'right' ". Relevant constitutional restraints apply as much to the withdrawal of public assistance benefits as to disqualification for unemployment compensation or to denial of a tax exemption or to discharge from public employment. The extent to which procedural due process must be afforded the recipient is influenced by the extent to which he may be "condemned to suffer grievous loss," and depends upon whether the recipient's interest in avoiding the loss outweighs the governmental interest in summary adjudication.

[W]hen welfare is discontinued, only a pre-termination evidentiary hearing provides the recipient with procedural due process. For qualified recipients, welfare provides the means to obtain essential food, clothing, housing, and medical care. Thus the crucial factor in this context is that termination of aid pending resolution of a controversy over eligibility may deprive an eligible recipient of the very means by which to live while he waits. Since he lacks independent resources, his situation becomes immediately desperate. His need to concentrate upon finding the means for daily subsistence, in turn, adversely affects his ability to seek redress from the welfare bureaucracy.

Moreover, important governmental interests are promoted by affording recipients a pre-termination evidentiary hearing. From its founding the Nation's basic commitment has been to foster the dignity and well-being of all persons within its borders. We have come to recognize that forces not within the control of the poor contribute to their poverty. This perception, against the background of our traditions, has significantly influenced the development of the contemporary public assistance system. Welfare, by meeting the basic demands of subsistence, can help bring them within the reach of the poor the same opportunities that are available to others to participate meaningfully in the life of the community. At the same time, welfare guards against the societal malaise that may flow from a widespread sense of unjustified frustration and insecurity. Public assistance, then, is not mere charity, but a means to "promote the general Welfare, and secure the Blessings of Liberty to ourselves and our Posterity." The same governmental

*Goldberg v. Kelly, 397 U.S. 254, 1970.

interests that counsel the provision of welfare, counsel as well its uninterrupted provision to those eligible to receive it; pre-termination evidentiary hearings are indispensable to that end. . . .

The city's procedures presently do not permit recipients to appear personally with or without counsel before the official who finally determines continued eligibility. Thus a recipient is not permitted to present evidence to that official orally, or to confront or cross-examine adverse witnesses. These omissions are fatal to the constitutional adequacy of the procedures.

It may be realistic today to regard welfare entitlements as more like "property" than a "gratuity." Much of the existing wealth in this country takes the form of rights that do not fall within traditional common-law concepts of property. It has been aptly noted that "[society] today is built around entitlement. The automobile dealer has his franchise, the doctor and lawyer their professional licenses, the worker his union membership, contract, and pension rights, the executive his contract and stock options; all are devices to aid security and independence. Many of the most important of these entitlements now flow from government: subsidies to farmers and businessmen, routes for airlines and channels for television stations; long term contracts for defense, space, and education; social security pensions for individuals. Such sources of security, whether private or public, are no longer regarded as luxuries or gratuities; to the recipients they are essentials, fully deserved, and in no sense a form of charity. It is only the poor whose entitlements, although recognized by public policy, have not been effectively enforced."

Justice Black, dissenting.

In the last half century the United States, along with many, perhaps most, other nations of the world, has moved far toward becoming a welfare state, that is, a nation that for one reason or another taxes its most affluent people to help support, feed, clothe, and shelter its less fortunate citizens. The result is that today more than nine million men, women, and children in the United States receive some kind of state or federally financed public assistance in the form of allowances or gratuities, generally paid them periodically, usually by the week, month, or quarter. Since these gratuities are paid on the basis of need, the list of recipients is not static, and some people go off the lists and others are added from time to time. These ever-changing lists put a constant administrative burden on government and it certainly could not have reasonably anticipated that this burden would include the additional procedural expense imposed by the Court today.

The dilemma of the ever-increasing poor in the midst of constantly growing affluence presses upon us and must inevitably be met within the framework of our democratic constitutional government, if our system is to survive as such.

The more than a million names on the relief rolls in New York, and the more than nine million names on the rolls of all the 50 States were not put there at random. The names are there because state welfare officials believed that those people were eligible for assistance. Probably in the officials' haste to make out the lists many names were put there erroneously in order to alleviate immediate suffering, and undoubtedly some people are drawing relief who are not entitled under the law to do so. Doubtless some draw relief checks from time to time who know they are not eligible, either because they are not actually in need or for some other reason. Many of those who thus draw undeserved gratuities are without sufficient property to enable the government to collect back from them any money they wrongfully receive. But the Court today holds that it would violate the Due Process Clause of the Fourteenth Amendment to stop paying those people weekly or monthly allowances unless the government first affords them a full "evidentiary hearing" even though welfare officials are persuaded that the recipients are not rightfully entitled to receive a penny under the law. In other words, although some recipients might be on the lists for payment wholly because of deliberate fraud on their part, the Court holds that the government is helpless and must continue, until after an evidentiary hearing, to pay money that it does not owe, never has owed, and never could owe. I do not believe there is any provision in our Constitution that should thus paralyze the government's efforts to protect itself against making payments to people who are not entitled to them. . . . Once the verbiage is pared away it is obvious that this Court today adopts the views of the District Court "that to cut off a welfare recipient in the face of . . . 'brutal need' without a prior hearing of some sort is unconscionable," and therefore, says the Court, unconstitutional. [I]t is obvious that today's result does not depend on the language of the Constitution itself or the principles of other decisions, but solely on the collective judgment of the majority as to what would be a fair and humane procedure in this case.

The Court apparently feels that this decision will benefit the poor and needy. In my judgment the eventual result will be just the opposite. While today's decision requires only an administrative, evidentiary hearing, the inevitable logic of the approach taken will lead to constitutionally imposed, time-consuming delays of a full adversary process of administrative and judicial review.

The operation of a welfare state is a new experiment for our Nation. For this reason, among others, I feel that new experiments in carrying out a welfare program should not be frozen into our constitutional structure.

FOUNDATIONS OF THE WELFARE STATE

See text p. 695

As the text notes, in 1935 the Social Security Act represented the first step toward a national welfare program. In recent years, the program has been subject to criticism: many of those who receive the greatest benefits already have substantial resources.

Suggestions that Social Security benefits be reduced, however, has proved to be a political hot potato: retirees, whatever their income level, rally quickly to retain what they consider to be their full share of entitlements.

In the following article, written just a few days before the 1992 presidential election, Mickey Kaus, a senior editor of the New Republic *and author of* The End of Equality *argues that benefits should be subject to "means-testing" to limit the receipt of benefits by individuals who have sufficient alternative resources to care for themselves.*

Mickey Kaus
"Telling the Truth About Social Security"*

"The agenda I published today contains specific proposals to cut the fat . . . without touching Social Security. . . ."

—George Bush, September 10 speech before the Detroit Economic Club

"I do think that the people are concerned about—they are right to be concerned about—the entitlements [that] are driving the deficit. But most people have the wrong prescription for it. That is, most people think that the thing that would fix the entitlements is to subject more Social Security income to taxation and raise the cost of Medicare to upper-income people . . ."

—Bill Clinton, June 28 interview with the *New York Times*

Okay, there's been a campaign going on. Nobody expected honesty. After the election, whoever wins will have to face the budget deficit no matter what he's said during the campaign, right? Plenty of time then to figure out how to wriggle out of any promises not to touch Social Security benefits.

Unfortunately, there's a good chance that the next president will actually keep these particular promises, in the process ruling out the single most obvious fix for the nation's budget problem. Cutting the benefits of the affluent—"means-testing," in policyspeak—has worked in other countries. But here in the United States our candidates seem to have convinced themselves that it's not only politically dangerous, it's somehow impossible. Clinton has at times even suggested that shaving the Social Security and Medicare benefits of the well-off wouldn't save that much money—"When we ran every conceivable set of numbers on that, [it] is very modest revenues." Only "modest revenues," from a program whose costs are approaching $450 billion a year?

Worse, respectable Washington opinion appears to agree with this pessimistic assessment. It was only a few years ago that the mainstream press was heaping praise on former Arizona governor Bruce Babbitt for having the

*Mickey Kaus, "Telling the Truth About Social Security," *Washington Post* (November 1, 1992).

courage to propose means-testing. Yet last month, when the pretentiously high-minded "Strengthening of America Commission" released its "tough" budget recommendations, it listed means-testing as a mere "option" to be considered—and even then not for Social Security! When Ross Perot had the temerity to claim, earlier this year, that he might save $20–$100 billion a year through means-testing, he was ridiculed by NBC's Tim Russert in a now-legendary confrontation on "Meet the Press." Didn't Perot know that saving even $20 billion would require ending benefits for "anyone making over $40,000"? The idea seemed to be that only an ignorant rube would even suggest means-testing.

In fact, of course, Perot had been right. The government could *easily* save $25 to $30 billion immediately by taking away only some of the Social Security benefits now received by the richest 25 percent of recipients. A more vigorous means test could easily bring in $60 billion a year. Applying the same principle to Medicare would save still more.

By now, even Perot seems to have been effectively mau-maued by the experts. "United We Stand," Perot's deficit-cutting manifesto, calls only for "*taxing* an additional 35 percent of the benefits" [emphasis added] for the affluent. Taxing benefits is the respectable, watered-down version of means-testing—more acceptable, in theory, because it preserves the fictional analogy of Social Security with private insurance benefits (which are already taxed). Taxing is undoubtedly what Clinton meant when he suggested in the final debate that "upper-income people" could "pay more for Social Security." The problem, of course, is that merely taxing the benefits of the rich doesn't do nearly as much for the deficit as actually taking those benefits away.

It's especially ironic that Democrats, who argue vehemently for "progressivity" in virtually every other context, oppose making the Social Security program more progressive by directing its benefits to the non-affluent. Before such a conspicuous, progressive fiscal solution is dismissed as a "non-starter" by those who will staff the next administration, let's examine the most common arguments against it:

- "It is very modest revenues." When Clinton suggests there are only marginal savings to be had from Social Security, he's being a bit disingenuous. If all you are willing to do is *tax* Social Security, then, yes, there are only modest revenues to be had. The top marginal tax rate is only 31 percent, and even the rich don't pay those rates on all their income. Currently, half of Social Security benefits are taxed above an income threshold ($32,000 for a couple)—yet even recipients with incomes over $100,000 lose only 15 percent of their benefits to this tax. That's why Perot's plan to tax an additional, smaller chunk of benefits raises merely $6 billion annually. Clinton's number-crunching probably produced an even lower figure, because (according to aides) he adopted $100,000-and-up as his definition of "upper-income"—meaning his tax would apply to only the richest 3 percent of beneficiaries. No wonder the revenues were modest!

  But if taxing benefits doesn't raise enough money, that's a good reason to go beyond taxing to full-fledged *cutting*. The most affluent 30 percent of Social Security beneficiaries currently receive $98 billion in payments, according to the Congressional Budget Office. Take away even half of those benefits and you're talking real money.

- "Those people aren't rich." Assume Perot's original means test would, as the Bush administration charged, have required taking away benefits from retirees with over $60,000 in income. Is that crazy? *New York Times* columnist William Safire seemed to think so: "These people do not deserve to be penalized." But we're talking about people who make $60,000 a year *in retirement*, not people who make $60,000 during their prime working years. Retirees who get $60,000 in interest income (in the current era of 5 percent returns) have a nest egg of more than a million dollars. They're not middle class. They're rich. Even if a means test kicked in at the current $32,000-a-year tax threshold, it would only affect the richest 22 percent of recipients. Keep in mind that the vast majority of these retirees own their homes and consequently have lower living expenses.
- "Means-testing will turn Social Security into welfare." No it won't. Welfare programs such as food stamps and Aid to Families with Dependent Children are stigmatized because they give economic aid to able-bodied people, whether or not they are working. Social Security, in sharp contrast, only goes to *workers*. You can't qualify for Social Security unless you've worked (and therefore contributed payroll taxes) for 40 quarter-years. Means-testing won't remove this requirement; hence it won't turn Social Security into welfare. It will, rather, turn Social Security into insurance against poverty in retirement—insurance that is earned through work. (Those elderly Americans who haven't worked would be relegated, as they are now, to the less generous Supplemental Security Income program.)
- "It's unfair to take benefits away from those who have been expecting them." This is an elastic principle. Extended to its logical conclusion it says you can never cut the benefits of anyone, at least anyone who has already been born (and who might therefore have expectations). In practice, we must make some judgment as to which expectations are reasonable and which aren't. And today's elderly have pressured Congress into cutting them a far cushier deal than they had any right to expect. Congress raised benefits rapidly between 1965 (when the basic monthly check for an average earner was $178.50) and 1985 (by which year the average earner's benefit had risen to $825). Benefits were double-indexed for inflation in 1972, a mistake that wasn't corrected until 1977.

  All these benefit hikes were financed by increasing the payroll taxes on the non-retired population. As a result, the generation that is now receiving Social Security checks is getting back far, far more than it has put in—more than its contributions *plus* the interest those contributions would have earned had they actually been invested. It's hardly unfair to take away this bonanza from retirees rich enough not to need it.
- "Means-testing will discourage savings." If those who build up a retirement nest egg are penalized by having their Social Security slashed, the

argument goes, people might save less. But this disincentive would only apply to workers who knew they weren't going to be rich enough to lose *all* their benefits. If benefits were cut off completely for couples making $50,000, for example, those who expected to be in this fortunate group would have every reason to save, since they couldn't count on Social Security to supplement their incomes after they'd retired. Indeed, for these people, means-testing would counteract the much-discussed potential of Social Security benefits to substitute for investment income in retirement and therefore to discourage savings.

- "It can't be done politically." This is the familiar claim that only a "universal" benefit program, mailing out checks to rich and poor alike, will have sufficient political support. The Australian left, like the American left, once bought this argument. But then the Australians discovered that their country was going bankrupt and they changed their minds. It was the Labor government of Prime Minister Robert Hawke that restored Australia's means-test without, apparently, prompting a middle-class rebellion. The Australian means test is politically palatable in part because the income limits are set high enough so that most people qualify for some benefits. About half of Australia's aged get full pensions; another 25 percent get reduced benefits. Only a quarter of the aged get nothing because they have too much money. This is just the sort of common sense set-up American policy experts fiercely resist. But if Australia can do it, why can't we?

Keep in mind, I'm arguing for a Social Security means test only on practical, not ideological grounds. It would be *nice* to live in a country with enough money to finance a universal pension system that paid full benefits to the rich as well as the poor. We just don't happen to live in such a country.

It would also be nice to live in a country in which issues like means-testing could be honestly discussed even in the heat of an election campaign. We don't seem to live in that country either. Until Tuesday, anyone who wants to have a shot at election—even poor old Perot—will have to pretend that the means-testing option is simply unthinkable. But just between us, it isn't.

Debating the Issues: Opposing Views

THE WAR ON POVERTY: SUCCESS OR FAILURE?

See text pp. 704–5

As the text points out, the American welfare state is composed of a number of programs ranging from Social Security, Medicare, and Veteran's benefits to Medicaid and Aid to Families with Dependent Children. Those programs in the first category are often seen as programs geared to helping the "worthy" poor, while those in the latter category assist the undeserving poor. Therefore, most critics of the welfare system take aim at the latter programs.

The following two articles look at the issue of welfare reform. The first, written by Irving Kristol, a fellow at the American Enterprise Institute and publisher of The National Interest, *argues that the system should be reformed to eliminate benefits to people whose poverty results from their own behavior. He draws a line between "mothers on welfare"—those who have been divorced, widowed, or abandoned by their husbands—and "welfare mothers"—young girls who, he argues, permit themselves to get pregnant. In addition, he would also eliminate benefits for any able-bodied or mentally healthy men whose problems are traced to alcoholism or drug addiction.*

Mimi Abramovitz, a professor of social welfare policy at Hunter College School of Social Work, and Martha Davis, a staff attorney for the NOW Legal Defense and Education Fund, argue that these solutions are not solutions at all. These reforms, they say, are based upon unfounded assumptions about the extent to which women and young girls take welfare eligibility into account in making decisions about childbirth and marriage. "[T]he popular perception of a conniving female welfare recipient spurning marriage proposals in order to continue receiving benefits . . . is a myth, pure and simple." These reforms, aimed primarily at linking women and children to men and reducing birth rates among the poor, have significant racial undertones and "reflect . . . a deep-seated societal distrust of the capacity of poor unmarried mothers to properly socialize their children, especially poor women of color."

Irving Kristol
"A Conservative Welfare State"*

I had it coming. In my last article in this newspaper, I challenged conservatives in general, and the Republican Party in particular, to come up with their ideas for a reformed welfare state. Inevitably, my challenge redounded upon me. "Well," my friends, associates and many correspondents replied, "where are *your* ideas? Stop sermonizing and get down to specifics." I now rise to that challenge, though with apprehension, since my ideas happen to

*Irving Kristol, "A Conservative Welfare State," *Wall Street Journal* (June 14, 1993).

be rather controversial, and I fear many conservatives will be unappreciative of their merits.

Let me lay down the basic principles—the basic deficiency, some will say—of my approach. I shall, to begin with, assume that the welfare state is with us, for better or worse, and that conservatives should try to make it better rather than worse. And I shall pay no attention to the economics of the welfare state, which I regard as a secondary issue. What conservatives ought to seek, first of all, is a welfare state consistent with the basic moral principles of our civilization and the basic political principles of our nation. The essential purpose of politics, after all, is to transmit to our children a civilization and a nation that they can be proud of. This means we should figure out what we want before we calculate what we can afford, not the reverse, which is the normal conservative predisposition. In this respect, public finance differs fundamentally from household economics.

Fiscal Monomania

It has long been my opinion that the conservative hostility to Social Security, derived from a traditional conservative fiscal monomania, leads to political impotence and a bankrupt social policy. Our Social Security system is enormously popular. If the American people want to be generous to their elderly, even to the point of some extravagance, I think it is very nice of them. After all, the elderly are such wonderful, unproblematic citizens. They are patriotic, they do not have illegitimate children, they do not commit crimes, they do not riot in the streets, their popular entertainments are decent rather than degrading, and if they find themselves a bit flush with funds, they happily distribute the money to their grandchildren.

So, in my welfare state, we leave Social Security alone—except for being a bit more generous, perhaps. Certainly, all restrictions on the earnings of the elderly should be abolished, as a matter of fairness. As for Medicare—well, conservatives believe in honoring thy father and mother, and the Good Book does not say that such honor should be limited only to parents (or grandparents) who are in good health and do not live too long. Medicare's cost is not a conservative problem, except for those conservatives whose Good Book is the annual budget.

As with the elderly, so with children. Ever since World War II, weak-minded and budget-conscious Republican administrations have conspired with liberals to cheat the children of middle-class and working-class households. The income tax deduction for children, now $2,500, would now be $7,500 had it been indexed for inflation. The next Republican administration should address this scandal, giving it the highest priority. The budget consequences are considerable, so perhaps we would want to phase in the indexed increase over a five-year period. But nothing less than that, I would say.

The charms of this reform would, from the conservative point of view, be significant and various. It would be enormously popular, which is no small thing. But it would also be much more than that. These households represent the conservative ideal of the normal household—the household that exemplifies "family values"—and we wish to encourage such households instead of adding to their financial difficulties, as we have been doing. One could also contemplate unanticipated benefits, instead of the unanticipated ills that are so characteristic of liberal reform. After all, one of the things these parents could do is use the money for the children's education, thereby making "school choice" an actuality, not merely an advocated possibility.

Now for the more contentious part. It is easy and attractive to discriminate in favor of large sections of the population. It is far less attractive, and makes us all uneasy, to discriminate against any section of the population. Yet such discrimination is absolutely necessary if we are to change the welfare state into something more deserving of that name.

This issue, of "discriminating against," is most sharply posed when we consider the reform of welfare itself. The problem with our current welfare programs is not that they are costly—which they are—but that they have such perverse consequences for the people they are supposed to benefit. The emergence of a growing and self-perpetuating "under-class" that makes our cities close to uninhabitable is a demonstrable consequence of the present, liberal-inspired welfare system. The system breeds social pathologies—crime, juvenile delinquency, illegitimacy, drug addiction and alcoholism, along with the destruction of a once functioning public school system.

The neo-liberal response, advocated by Mr. Clinton during his campaign, which calls for "two years and out" for all able-bodied welfare recipients, is a fantasy. It will not happen. We are not going to see state legislatures and the huge welfare establishment ruthlessly dumping welfare families onto the streets. Public opinion will not stand for it, liberal politicians will not be able to stomach it. It is merely a rhetorical diversionary tactic, and conservatives who are now attracted to it will end up distancing themselves from it as fast as they can.

The key to a conservative reform would be (a) to discourage young women from having an illegitimate child in the first place and (b) to discriminate between "welfare mothers" and "mothers on welfare." Such discrimination must have a clear moral basis.

"Mothers on welfare" includes married women with children who have been divorced or widowed or abandoned by their husbands. Most such women have little connection with any kind of underclass. For the most part, they have middle-class aspirations, subscribe to "family values," and create no intergenerational class of welfare dependents. Their stay on welfare is usually less than two years—they don't like being on welfare. They exit from the welfare population by reason of remarriage or getting a job (sometimes after diligently taking vocational training). They are not a problem population, and deserve our generous assistance as well as our sympathy.

"Welfare mothers," on the other hand, usually end up on welfare as a result of their own actions. Young girls permit themselves to get pregnant, and to bear a child, because the prospect of going on welfare does not frighten them. Welfare permits them to leave homes that are often squalid or worse. It provides them with support, in cash and kind (food stamps, housing allowances, Medicaid), that is in many ways superior to what they could earn working at the minimum wage.

These girls should be made to look upon welfare not as an opportunity, but as a frightening possibility. It follows that they should receive no housing allowance—this is probably the most important change of all. Having your own apartment, in which you can raise your child, can be seen as "fun." Living with your child in your parents' home is a lot less alluring. This would especially be the case if the mother received no food stamps and was ineligible for Medicaid. (She would have to rely on the hospital clinic.) The child, on the other hand, would be eligible for food stamps and Medicaid, as well as a children's cash allowance. But the net effect of such reforms would be to reduce the mother's income by 30% to 50%—at which point there is little to be said in favor of welfare, from her point of view. There is, of course, the danger that she won't spend the money on the child. But that is true of the present system as well.

In addition, able-bodied men and mentally healthy men would have no entitlement whatever to welfare. If they are alcoholics or drug addicts or just allergic to responsibilities, they can rely on private charities. (Remember the Salvation Army.) The general rule has to be: If it is your own behavior that could land you on welfare, then you don't get it, or you get very little of it.

'Phasing Out' Needed

Such a reform of welfare as I am proposing will surely be denounced as cruel and "judgmental." It would indeed be cruel—and unfair, too—if all those currently on welfare, their situations and characters formed by the current system, were summarily incorporated in the new system. A "phasing out" procedure would have to be invented. But I would argue that it is crueler to entice people into the blind alley of welfare, where their very humanity is dissipated and degraded, than to sternly warn them off. In social policy, consequences ought always to trump intentions, however benign.

The "judgmental" issue, however, does get to the heart of the matter. A conservative welfare state should express conservative moral values, just as a liberal welfare state tries to impose liberal moral values upon us. It should discriminate in favor of satisfactory human results, not humane intentions. In the end, the American people will have ample political opportunity to decide what kind of society they wish to live in, what kind of welfare state they wish to live with. But they will never have such a choice if conservatives fail to offer them a conservative vision.

Mimi Abramovitz and Martha Davis
" 'Wedfare'—Or Welfare?"*

A recent spate of legislative proposals in states across the country seeks to use welfare programs to control the behavior and family structure of poor women.

Proposed legislation in New Jersey would deny custodial parents, 95 percent of whom are women, minimal need-based benefits increases—$64 per child—if they have additional children while on welfare, and attempts to encourage marriage by allowing certain married-couple households to retain more of their earnings than single-parent families. An initiative by the governor of California, scheduled for statewide referendum in November, would also eliminate incremental benefit increases for welfare families, while requiring that single teen mothers live with their parents or guardians in order to receive benefits. And earlier this year, Wisconsin's governor proposed "wedfare," a plan to eliminate need-based increases to teen mothers with additional children while offering a "marriage bonus" of $73 a month to AFDC families headed by a married couple.

The dual purpose of each of these proposals is to (1) limit births by women on welfare and (2) encourage welfare mothers to marry as a way out of poverty. But both the assumptions underlying these proposals and the strategies they employ are misguided, falling heavily on women of color, and thus promising to fuel the politics of race.

First, the popular perception of a conniving female welfare recipient spurning marriage proposals in order to continue receiving benefits and surrounded by a half-dozen children is a myth, pure and simple. Although by restricting and to all but a limited group of two-parent families, AFDC forces many couples in need to live apart, solid empirical evidence has demonstrated again and again that the configuration of welfare benefits does not shape childbirth and marriage decisions.

Single-parent families on welfare average only 1.8 children—considerably less than the average national family size. The decisions of poor women to marry and have children are shaped by more potent social and psychological forces than income, just as those of middle class women are.

The "new paternalism" implicit in conditioning public assistance on conformity to traditional wife and mother roles is part of a predictable, if unsuccessful cycle. As in the late 1940s and 1950s, when jobs for women became scarce and welfare rolls swelled, the government today resorts to making value-laden distinctions between "deserving" and "undeserving" poor women. These behavior-based distinctions were recognized as illegal during the 1960s, when states' attempts to deny welfare benefits to "illegitimate" children and to restrict unmarried women on welfare from having romantic attachments were squarely disallowed by the federal courts.

*Mimi Abramovitz and Martha Davis, " 'Wedfare'—Or Welfare?" *Washington Post* (February 4, 1992).

If the new welfare proposals will not affect family composition and have failed past legal tests, what will they do? They will deepen the already debilitating poverty of the average AFDC family. No state pays enough AFDC and Food Stamps to keep such a family out of poverty.

By offering higher benefits to married women than single, the new plans imply that marriage is an effective antipoverty strategy for poor women. Yet not only is the institution of marriage changing dramatically in the general population, but despite the presence of two earners, the number of married couples in poverty is on the rise. The "marriage bonus" also suggests that poor women should accept a marriage regardless of its safety and security just to survive.

In addition to creating invidious distinctions between married and unmarried women, these latest welfare "reforms" violate a woman's constitutional rights to equal protection and to make decisions concerning the timing of marriage and childbirth free of governmental interference. All three plans are specifically intended to punish or reward marriage and childbirth decisions of single AFDC parents, more than 95 percent of whom are women. Fathers will be largely exempt from these paternalistic programs.

The "new paternalism" in fact reflects a deep-seated societal distrust of the capacity of poor unmarried mothers to properly socialize their children, especially poor women of color who, while far from a majority, are overrepresented on the welfare rolls.

The popular view that social welfare programs do not work increases support for these new punitive welfare proposals. This view is not supported by studies of how effective less value-laden entitlement programs can be in cushioning poverty.

Recent research shows that based on market income alone, the United States, Canada, Australia, Great Britain, Germany, the Netherlands, France and Sweden have similar overall poverty rates. But the antipoverty impact of income maintenance programs is different. Because of weaker programs in the United States, the poverty rate in this country fell only 6.6 percent in the mid-1980s, compared with a 16.5 percent drop in the other nations mentioned. Among children of single parents in the United States, poverty dropped less than 4 percent, while it plummeted nearly 30 percent in the other countries.

The "new paternalism" promises to deepen these international differences, while continuing to blame poverty on poor women rather the adverse economic policies of business and the state.

INEQUALITY: WHO SHALL BE POOR?

See text p. 711

As the text notes, the adequacy of the nation's health care system has come under close scrutiny in the last few years, and President Bill Clinton has pledged to make health care reform one of his top priorities while in office. When considering the health care crisis, however, it is important to understand the links between personal health and personal income. The following article explores these connections in detail. "The poor are likelier to be sick, and the sick are likelier to be poor," according to one expert in the article, "and without intervention, the poor grow sicker and the sick grow poorer."

Don Colburn
"A Vicious Cycle of Risk"*

Any nurse, doctor or social worker practicing in a poor neighborhood or a general hospital sees the tell-tale proof every day: Poverty is a stacked deck.

"Poverty is definitely a risk factor for ill health and premature death," said Marsha Lillie-Blanton, assistant professor of health policy and management at Johns Hopkins University in Baltimore. "People don't even question that anymore."

The poverty-health connection cuts in both directions. Being poor heightens health risk. But illness also impoverishes people by raising their expenses and limiting their capacity to work.

"The poor are likelier to be sick, and the sick are likelier to be poor," said H. Jack Geiger, chairman of the department of community health and social medicine at City University of New York Medical School. "And without intervention, the poor grow sicker and the sick grow poorer."

Poverty erodes health first by the physical and emotional damage it inflicts: the cumulative effect of malnourishment, unsanitary housing, lack of education, joblessness and exposure to pollutants and crime. Strike two is the lack of access to health care that comes of being uninsured or underinsured and living in neighborhoods where few doctors practice.

"If I had just one magic wand to wave and I wanted to cut the infant mortality rate in half in Bolivar County [Mississippi], I would wave the wand and double the per capita income," Geiger said.

Survey after survey and study after study show that illness and chronic conditions take a higher toll on the daily lives of poor people as on the affluent.

- Poor people go to the hospital more often, and stay longer. For families with incomes under $14,000, the hospitalization rate in 1989 was 131 per 1,000; for families with incomes over $50,000, the rate was 72, according to the National Center for Health Statistics. The poorest group spent more than twice as many days in the hospital as the affluent group.

*Don Colburn, "A Vicious Cycle of Risk," *Washington Post* (July 8, 1992).

- The average number of days a person is bedridden or has to cut down on usual activity because of illness goes sharply up as income goes down, according to the National Health Interview Survey.
- Work-related injuries are most common among workers earning less than $10,000 per year and the risk declines steadily with rising income, according to the National Center for Health Statistics.
- The unemployed are more likely to report dissatisfaction, tension in family life and insomnia. Low-paying jobs tend to be noisier and more boring, dangerous and physically taxing.
- Poor people die younger, on average. At age 25, affluent white men (with family incomes above $50,000) can expect to live 10 years longer than those with the lowest incomes (below $5,000), according to a study in the current Public Health Reports. For white women, the difference in life expectancy between rich and poor at age 25 is four years.

"The big changes that have occurred in longevity and improved health have affected mainly the middle class, not the poor," said Massimo A. Righini, chairman of surgery at Greater Southeast Community Hospital. For example, the biggest beneficiary of the dramatic drop in death rates from heart disease over the past two decades if "the 40-year-old middle-class male." . . .

Class, Race and the 'Prism of Culture'

The overlapping effects of income, race, education and lifestyle on health are hard to disentangle. For example, ever since cancer statistics have been kept, it has been known that cancer rates are higher in blacks than in whites, especially for tumors of the lung, prostate and cervix.

But the question is: Why?

A National Cancer Institute study published last year found that the main reason for the black-white cancer gap was not race but socioeconomics. Indeed, if differences in income, education and living conditions could be eliminated, the study found, the cancer pattern would be reversed and blacks would have a lower overall cancer rate than whites. . . .

. . . The effects of poverty are so pervasive and devastating that simply granting poor people medical insurance and access to doctors and hospitals will not solve their problem, said Freeman, who is director of surgery at Harlem Hospital Center in New York and former president of the American Cancer Society.

"I work at Harlem Hospital," he said. "I think we ought to try to make this the best hospital we can and get the best doctors. But to tell you the truth, if we don't do something beyond that to make sure people don't come in here in the condition they do—then, no matter if we're miracle workers, it won't matter."

Black men in Harlem are less likely to reach age 65 than men in

Bangladesh, a study reported in the New England Journal of Medicine in 1990.

It is misleading and "artificial," Freeman said, to look at health care access as though it were separate from all the other circumstances people live in. "Suppose patients have had poor nutrition for 20 years. Suppose they're unemployed. Suppose they're not educated. Suppose they have no social support. Suppose they live in substandard housing.

"To just give them a Medicaid card isn't enough."

All those aspects of being poor—from low income to high stress, from dangerous work to dangerous neighborhoods, from bad housing to bad schools—do not work in isolation. As medical sociologists Diana B. Dutton and Sol Levine have emphasized, "It is not so much any single aspect of being poor that undermines health as the entire experience of being at the bottom of the socioeconomic ladder."

Income, the quickest measure of who is poor, is only "a snapshot," Freeman cautioned. It doesn't tell the difference between someone who just earned $20,000 for the first time and someone who has had a modest but steady income for 10 years. It doesn't show how poverty strikes "through the prism of culture"—the overlapping patterns of racism, education, housing, joblessness, crime, family structure and lifestyle that can worsen or ease a person's plight.

Income alone doesn't account for the ecology—and pathology—of poverty.

"There is something about poverty that smells like death," wrote Zora Neale Hurston in her autobiographical novel. "Dust Tracks on a Road," published in 1942. "Dead dreams dropping off the heart like leaves in a dry season and rotting around the feet; impulses smothered too long in the fetid air of underground caves. The soul lives in a sickly air. People can be slave-ships in shoes."

Poverty itself can be measured in numerous ways. Social scientists use the more general term socioeconomic status—or class—whose main yardsticks are income, education and occupation.

Unlike Britain, where class differences are accepted as a social given, the United States likes to think of itself as a classless country. The United States is the only Western developed nation whose government does not collect data on death rates by class, said Vicente Navarro, professor of health policy management and international health at the Johns Hopkins School of Public Health. The United States tends to compile mortality statistics by age, sex and race—but not by class indicators such as income, education and occupation.

Too often, Navarro said, race is seen by American statisticians and politicians alike as a surrogate, or mask, for class.

But when Navarro analyzed death rates from heart disease according to both race and occupation, he found that class mattered more than race. The death rate was more than twice as high for manual laborers as it was for the managerial and professional groups, for example. The black-white disparity was less. Navarro reported in the British medical journal, *The Lancet.*

Americans cling to the myth that "we are a middle-class society,"

Navarro said. People who see themselves as middle class tend to dismiss the poor as "others," he added.

Medical Coverage and Access to Care

Lack of insurance is a key barrier to decent health care, and coverage in the United States depends strikingly on income.

Americans in families making $50,000 or more a year are almost sure to have private health insurance: 96 percent do. But the poorest families, with incomes below $14,000, fall into three roughly equal-sized groups: 35 percent have private health insurance, 27 percent have Medicaid and 37 percent have no coverage at all.

Not only are the poor more likely to get sick, but uninsured people—who are disproportionately poor—are also less likely to receive the best available treatment.

Uninsured patients in the hospital are more likely to die than privately insured patients and less likely to receive state-of-the-art care, a study reported last year in the Journal of the American Medical Association. The study, by health policy experts at Georgetown and Johns Hopkins universities, looked at nearly 600,000 cases in a national sample of hospitals. Uninsured patients had death rates 44 percent to 124 percent higher than privately insured patients. The uninsured were also much less likely to undergo high-cost procedures usually performed at the discretion of the physician, such as total hip replacement or heart bypass surgery.

For a single parent trying to support a family on an hourly wage as a short-order cook or a housekeeper or a day care center worker, health insurance is not a priority, said Celia Maxwell, assistant professor of medicine at Howard University Medical Center. "It can't be."

The priority is getting by: paying the rent and buying food and clothes for the kids. For the poor and near-poor, including those with marginal jobs, Maxwell said, "their health insurance policy is the hope that nothing will happen."

Unfortunately, in terms of illness, these are precisely the people to whom things tend to happen.

"Just being poor sets you up to die early," Maxwell said. "If you don't get it from violence, you're going to get it from disease." . . .

. . . Largely because of Medicaid, poor people see a doctor about as often as affluent people: an average of six physician contacts per year. The difference is in the locale. Poor patients are more likely to enter the health care system by way of a hospital outpatient clinic or emergency room; and less likely to visit a doctor's office.

About one third of the uninsured patients admitted to District hospitals had medical conditions that could have been treated or prevented with timely care in a clinic or doctor's office, the D.C. Hospital Association reported in 1988. A majority of the uninsured patients treated were poor, and 8 percent were homeless.

Many poor people use a hospital emergency room as a substitute for a regular family physician or other source of primary health care—a practice that experts agree is a wasteful use of expensive medical resources. Hospital emergency rooms are not designed to provide preventive or primary care such as prenatal care or immunizations or blood pressure monitoring. They are better able to deal with stab wounds, cardiac arrest or broken bones than with earaches, stomach flu or yeast infections.

But a person who has no insurance, no personal physician and no regular source of health care has every incentive to delay treatment until the crisis point—and then to seek help in the nearest hospital emergency room.

"When a woman comes in to the emergency room at 4 in the morning with a vaginal infection," Howard's Maxwell said, "that is not an emergency to the doctor treating gunshot wounds and car accident victims." So she waits for hours and finally gets frustrated and stomps out—"and then you've lost her."

That woman may not re-enter the health care system until her next medical crisis takes her again to the emergency room.

Poor people go to emergency rooms for routine care "because that's the only place open to many of them," said Tom Ricketts, director of the rural health research program at the University of North Carolina in Chapel Hill.

Use of the emergency room is just one example of how poor people think of doctors and health care "in a very different way than rich people do," Ricketts said. They don't sit down and worry about which federal health plan they're going to join. They don't wonder whether they should call their doctor in the middle of the night—because they don't have a doctor. They don't have the luxury of avoiding the lines at the free clinic. They don't think of the emergency room as a place to go only by ambulance.

Because they rarely get regular checkups or good preventive care, poor people often don't realize they are sick until it's too late for easy treatment. And even if they do realize it, they may have trouble getting off work, finding someone to take care of the kids, getting transportation to a clinic.

"It's a whole series of things that middle-class patients don't have to worry about," said health policy consultant John Billings, who has studied use of medical care by the poor and uninsured. "For low-income people, it's the center of what they have to worry about."

Even patients covered by Medicaid, the main government health insurance plan for the poor, often have trouble finding medical care in their neighborhood, Billings noted. Many doctors refuse to accept Medicaid patients, because Medicaid does not reimburse them as fully as they can charge private patients. The basic Medicaid payment for a routine doctor's office visit by an adult in New York ranges from $7 to $25. At that rate, few doctors seek Medicaid business, and those who do are not going to spend more than a few minutes with each patient.

Universal health coverage would help bring poor people better access to health care but would not eliminate the health gap between rich and poor, experts say. They point to the experience in Britain, which introduced universal coverage under the National Health Service in 1948. Thirty years later, the gap in death rates between rich and poor Britons actually had widened, according to a 1980 report headed by Sir Douglas Black and commissioned by the Labour Party.

"Better insurance coverage would certainly help," said Jack Hadley, co-director of the Center for Health Policy Studies in the department of community and family medicine at Georgetown University Medical Center. "But most people agree that if we did have universal health insurance, the differences in health by income would not disappear. They would become smaller."

Poor people get less care "even after they come to the attention of the medical system," said Arnold M. Epstein, associate professor of medicine at Harvard Medical School and chief of the section on health services and policy research at Brigham and Women's Hospital in Boston.

What's more, when poor patients get the same amount of acute medical care as more affluent patients for the same illness, they still tend to do worse, he said. "So there's something else going on there."

The "something else" is probably all the other roadblocks—besides lack of insurance and inability to pay—that poverty throws up in the way of a patient trying to recover from a given disease or condition.

Epstein and his colleagues are currently studying differences in the follow-up care of people hospitalized for asthma attacks. The assumption of the study was that admission to the hospital is a signal that these patients—rich or poor—are seriously ill and need close attention. But preliminary findings suggest that poor patients often still get lost in the follow-up shuffle.

Three months after leaving the hospital, the more affluent patients "were feeling better and had higher levels of activity and better lung function," Epstein said. They were more likely than poor patients to see a specialist, receive close monitoring and get good outpatient treatment.

"In every respect, rich patients did better."

QUESTIONS

1. In what ways did *Goldberg v. Kelly* change the understanding of the relationship between citizens and the government? How did changing the designation of welfare monies from benefits to entitlements change the character of those funds? Was the Court correct to view welfare payments as more than simply benefits?
2. Suggestions for altering the Social Security system invariably excite a great deal of public concern. What kinds of redistributive functions are served by the Social Security system? Does the system operate fairly, or do you agree with Mickey Kaus that some kind of "means-testing" would be an appropriate alteration in the system?
3. Reforms of the welfare system are often premised, as noted above, upon distinctions between the worthy and the unworthy poor. Are those adjec-

tives appropriate when talking about the problem of poverty in this nation? How does the use of those adjectives affect the policies that are developed?

4. The intersections of race, class, and gender are important for understanding who is poor and who stays poor in this nation. The article on the relationship between health and poverty provides one example of the connection. What factors should an adequate national health care policy or national poverty policy take into consideration?

CHAPTER 18

Foreign Policy and World Politics

THE SETTING: A WORLD OF NATION-STATES

See text p. 729

As the text explains, foreign policy for the last several centuries has operated from assumptions about the relations between nation-states in an anarchic world order. The global order has changed dramatically since 1988. Americans must not only seek new answers to the questions that have dominated foreign policy concerns for decades; they must rethink the questions themselves. In a world order marked by growing economic interdependence and increasing instances of internal or cross-regional political and military conflicts, the utility of nation-states must be examined.

The following article asks the question, "Is the nation-state obsolete?" The writer, Tomaz Mastnak, a Senior Fellow at the Institute of Philosophy of the Slovene Academy of Sciences and Arts in Ljubljana, examines the effect of the war in the former state of Yugoslavia on the concept of "the nation." Mastnak argues that Western nations' reluctance to recognize the newly formed nations of Eastern Europe can be traced to misunderstandings about the objects of recent developments in Eastern Europe. The new states were seeking, first, to establish a legitimate internal order, which they did by ousting Soviet rule, and second, to gain recognition in the international community. The reluctance of the Western powers to grant such recognition "frustrated any 'normal' development of the political communities . . . [and n]ationalism degenerated into a politicized and armed ethnocentrism."

Tomaz Mastnak
"Is the Nation-State Really Obsolete?"*

The war on the territory of the former Yugoslavia cuts deeper into Europe than one cares to think. It is not so much the fear of the war spilling over the boundaries of the defunct state (which may happen when the bulk of Serbian soldiery moves from Bosnia-Herzegovina to Kosova and starts slaying Albanians) that I have in mind. It is what it does to the idea of Europe and to the idea of the nation. No wonder that Westerners deny their responsibility for what is happening and relegate the blame to "Balkan tribalism." The situation calls for urgent and effective action before it is too late. Yet it also requires reflection—which, by definition, always comes too late.

*Tomaz Mastnak, "Is the Nation-State Really Obsolete?" *Times Literary Supplement* (August 7, 1992). Reprinted with permission.

There are two interrelated questions here, national sovereignty and anti-nationalism. Western observers have, as a rule, condemned the formation of new nation-states in Eastern Europe as nationalism, and Western governments have been extremely reluctant to recognize the newly formed nations. Such negative attitudes have contributed to the negative developments in the countries concerned. How are they to be understood?

Anti-nationalism feeds predominantly on the blind spots of liberalism, which have, in the course of time, hardened into liberal prejudices, and on Marxist insights inherited as articles of blind faith. This is why anti-nationalists cannot see anything good in the nation-state and customarily understand nationalism as ethnic hatred, xenophobia, anti-Semitism and other equally abominable phenomena. Because progress is part of their credo, it gives them particular satisfaction to present nationalism as something obsolete. The nation-state supposedly belongs to the past, and nation-state building is simply nineteenth-century nationalism: retrogressive and atavistic. If this argument was consistent, it would have to discard more or less the whole political language we speak today, the key terms of which are more than a century old. Yet it is not; it is just meant to dismiss. If we were, for the sake of argument, to accept the terms of discussion, the first thing to be said would be that the nationalism we are talking about is of the eighteenth, not the nineteenth, century. (And the history of the nation-state would take us even further back in time.) Vattel, in the first modern book on international law, uses the term nation interchangeably with state. "A nation," he says, is "a sovereign state, an independent political society." This was precisely the aim of East Central European nationalism in general, and of North Yugoslav nationalism in particular: to constitute a political community which would have control over its destiny; an independent and sovereign state in which citizens, and not an external power, would have a say in determining what is happening to their lives.

From this point of view, it is obvious that the image of nationalism cultivated by anti-nationalists ill fits the object to which it is applied. For them, this is a minor problem. The righteous work hard to fulfil their prophecies, regardless of how catastrophic they are. The world may perish but they have to be right. Their "nationalism" reminds me of those ideas of which Heine spoke in his remarks on Rousseau. It is a bodyless soul which, after it had been invented, haunted its inventors relentlessly, demanding that it be given a body, and it would not stop chasing them until they had helped it come into bodily existence. Western anti-nationalists were willingly helping their worst ideas of nationalism come true, while their governments, for their own reasons, assisted them.

There are two aspects to the national sovereignty striven for in East Central Europe. As seen against communist rule, sovereignty meant, internally, a legitimate power, and externally, independence. The latter was perceived as the necessary condition of the former. What nations, as political communities, could do for themselves was to create legitimate power, of a democratic character, and that is what they did accomplish. External sovereignty, the recognition by the international community, the acceptance into those systemic relations of nation-states in which alone a nation-state can exist, was not within their power.

The unwillingness of Western powers to grant recognition frustrated any "normal" development of the political communities I am discussing here. Being unable to act as political communities, they turned to inner resources and became more and more ethnocentric. Political community imploded into a *Gemeinschaft,* an imaginary community. Nationalism degenerated into a politicized and armed ethnocentrism. The international isolation was also psychologically and economically devastating. It created a fertile breeding ground for chauvinism and xenophobia. The reforms of a ruined economy, under these conditions, brought about social anomie, desperation and poverty rather than relief and prosperity. Add to this the war with horrors unseen since the worst mischiefs of Hitlerism, and we get the nationalism of the anti-nationalists. The missing ingredient was, for all too long, what the indigenous nationalists actually strove for: national sovereignty. Had they got it at the right time, had their internal sovereignty been recognized when it was established, we would not have heaven on earth, yet we might have been spared this hell.

I do not wish to imply that this was the intended consequence of Western anti-nationalism and diplomacy, yet it was an easily predictable one. As to the anti-nationalists, I know that they have been trying to do good and that they will continue to do so. They will carry on their crusade against national sovereignty in order not to have to grapple with fascism, xenophobia, chauvinism, racism, anti-Semitism, politicized ethnocentrism, *Blut und Boden* movements. They will keep on translating real dangers into one great imaginary danger—to fight them more effectively. They will tie up the phenomena they do not approve of into a bundle, "nationalism"—to break them more easily. They will not only make this *fascio* but send it off to the East, in order to confront it as something alien and not to have to look at monsters and monstrosities in their own homes. In a word, they will continue to do good that evil may come. The other question is how to explain the reluctance of Western governments to recognize new nation-states.

The background against which the formation of nation-states is seen as retrogressive is European integration. Time and again one hears: "while Europe is integrating, you are fragmenting"; "we are abolishing borders, you are drawing up new ones": "for us, nation-state and sovereignty is becoming a thing of the past, you are setting them up as the future." It has been argued convincingly that the idea of the sovereign state is challenged by the nature of the pattern of global interconnections. This is certainly true, and there is much evidence to support this argument. What I find questionable is that a value judgment is made on the basis of this evidence. If the evidence becomes the standard, the only thing to appear problematic would be the insistence on national sovereignty, while any questioning of the basic tendency would be ruled out. And if the basic tendency is the withering away of the nation-state, what does this mean?

John Pocock has recently challenged what he called the "mystique of 'Europe' " because this "mystique seemed to proclaim the subjection of national sovereignty to international market forces without making more than sporadic progress toward the creation of any new kind of political community governed by its citizens, to replace those whose obsolescence it so readily proclaimed." Indeed, what appears to be getting lost with the withering away of the nation-state is the political framework of citizenship, the condition of the possibility of individuals having, as citizens, a voice in the production of the social. "European citizenship" can hardly be conceived of as an alternative to political community or to citizenship itself. If it is anything more than an appealing catchword for the complacent well-off of the centre and the desperados of the periphery, it is to be understood as a phenomenon of an other, non-political, order. It may consist in the right to move freely through a continent ruled by corporations and some kind of *Polizei* (a kind of *jus peregrinandi* and, one hopes, *jus predicandi)*. It may mean adherence to the idea of a universal European civil society, the dream of stateless totalitarianism come true, civil society becoming what in Hegel's philosophy the state was meant to be—the embodiment of the ethical idea. I find these developments as disturbing as the light-mindedness with which they are praised. I can understand the mind to which the practice of *anti-étatisme* and the spirit of anti-politics appeal. But I really do not understand what there is to rejoice at in seeing Europe get out of the grip of the Leviathan only to fall into the clutches of the Behemoth.

If one reason for the West's reluctance to recognize the new nation-states is that it is not willing, or able, to grant what it itself is losing, national sovereignty, then another reason lies, paradoxically, in its clinging to the existing systemic relations of those very same nation-states which have been declared obsolete. This is a system that emerged in the eighteenth century, the balance of power being its regulative principle. The emergence of a new state disrupts the balance, not only by its coming into existence and undoing an older framework, but also by making it necessary for the existing states to define their relations to it. This implies the unsettling of their mutual relations which have appeared to be well defined and stable but turn out to be fragile and loaded with unresolved questions and uneasiness. Even more important: this system has become excessively fragile because its bearers, sovereign states, are fading away and the slightest crack could cause the empty shell to fall into pieces. European states, unwilling or unable to address the real cause of the vulnerability of their international system, would rather prevent anyone from exposing it.

The recognition of Slovenia and Croatia, because it came so late, is a good case in point. Disagreements between EC member states and mutual jealousies blocked any decisive action. One group of states was more concerned with the rising power of Germany than with the war on their continent. The most curious argument to be heard was that Germany was pressing for recognition because this was in her interest; as if pursuing one's interest was not what international politics is about. The problem was that Germany, whose "Yugoslav" policy appears to have been the least disastrous in Europe, happened to know what was in its interest better than others did. In giving Germanophobia priority over polemophobia, European states acted in the spirit of the balance of power. Rather than trying to stop the war effectively, they chased the "exorbitant power." This was how Defoe imagined European union at the time when the present European system began to emerge: as a pack of hounds chasing "exorbitant power."

To understand how deeply disturbing this story is, one has to be clear about what kind of war is being waged in the former Yugoslavia. A general and abstract condemnation of war is just a more complete hypocrisy than pretending it is not happening. This is a war in which one party, Serbia and the Yugoslav army, has used such (in Kant's words) "dishonourable stratagems" that the other sides cannot have any confidence in the disposition of the enemy. Serbia has not behaved differently in relation to the international community: "They only lie," a UN official in the occupied Croatian territory was recently heard to say bitterly. This has made the conclusion of peace impossible and turned the hostilities into a war of extermination. The genocide being carried out by the Serbian military is not an excess of this war, it is its very nature. And the disturbing thing is that the EC seems to have so far found it easier to deal (that is, not to deal) with the undeclared war which is tearing away the most basic principles of international law than with the emergence of a few new states. What is one to think about the European order which has for more than three years now tolerated genocide (which started in Kosova in 1989) and was shaken by the assertion of self-determination?

Debating the Issues: Opposing Views

AMERICAN FOREIGN POLICY: SELF-INTEREST OR IDEALISM?

See text pp. 734–35

The startling changes in the global order have raised fundamental questions about the place of the United States in that order. Understanding what direction American foreign policy ought to take requires examining American aims and values.

Early in 1992 the Pentagon released a report outlining a strategy designed to position the United States as the predominant world power. The following two articles discuss that Pentagon report.

In the first piece Charles Krauthammer, a commentator for the Washington Post, *defends the Pentagon position. He argues that American predominance should be maintained: the world is not a safe place, and only dreamers place their faith in ideas like "collective internationalism," which envisions multilateral cooperation through organizations like the United Nations.*

David Scheffer, an international lawyer who is a senior associate of the Carnegie Endowment for International Peace, disagrees. Scheffer argues that the real dangers facing the world today come from conflicts within the established nation-states, and legitimate intervention into those affairs—in the forms of mediation, peacekeeping and enforcement—can only be achieved through multilateral cooperation.

Charles Krauthammer
"What's Wrong with the Pentagon Paper?"*

When an administration meets the legal definition for brain death, one should be grateful if some part of the government still manages a thoughtful articulation of American purpose. Indeed, a "vision thing" document addressing America's role in the post-Cold War world has emerged. It comes not from the White House, not from the State Department (its Policy Planning staff is too busy studying aerial photographs of garden apartment construction in the West Bank settlement of Maale Adumim), but from the Pentagon.

Naturally enough, the document has come under anonymous attack from the White House and the State Department and open attack from the more usual suspects: Democratic senators and the *New York Times,* which leaked this newest "Pentagon Paper."

With enemies like these, one can assume that the Pentagon Paper is doing something right. In fact, it is. It starts with the fact that this is a one-superpower world. It proceeds on the assumption that for us, for our friends and for our values, this is a good thing. It then offers a program for keeping things that way.

The program is not terribly new. Secretary of Defense Dick Cheney has publicly testified as to how he intends to maintain American predominance. He proposes a radical reduction in U.S. defense spending to 3.4 percent of GNP by 1997—lower than before Pearl Harbor, less than half what JFK spent. But Cheney is not prepared to cut beyond that, because that would jeopardize the core force necessary to maintain American predominance.

Why maintain American predominance? To deter hostile powers (an Iran or a post-Yeltsin anti-Western Russia, for example) and—here is where the Pentagon Paper gets provocative—to prevent currently friendly powers from presenting new threats in the future.

The logic is simple. If America's allies believe that they can rely on American power, they will have no reason to turn themselves into military superpowers. If, on the other hand, the United States gives up its worldwide predominance, Germany and Japan, military midgets today, will quite reasonably seek to ensure their own security by turning themselves into military giants.

The critics are deeply troubled by the Pentagon Paper's idea of "deterring potential competitors from even aspiring to a larger regional or global

*Charles Krauthammer, "What's Wrong with the Pentagon Paper?" *Washington Post* (March 15, 1992).

role." Sen. Robert Byrd mocks the paper as saying, "We love being the sole remaining superpower in the world."

What's love got to do with it? It is a matter of necessity. What is the alternative? The alternative is Japanese carriers patrolling the Strait of Malacca and a nuclear Germany dominating Europe. We have had 40 years of competition with one heavily armed nuclear superpower. Do we really want to devote the next 40 years to competition with two, three, many such countries—countries such as Germany and Japan that have historically displayed far less prudence in their drive for hegemony than even Stalin's Russia?

Bipolarity was scary, but superpower multipolarity is a nightmare. The critics either ignore the awful dangers of military multipolarity or pretend that it will not come about. They dream that if the United States abdicates its world leadership, today's military midgets will be content to stay that way. Why? Because, like our dreamers, the world will place its faith in the "collective internationalism" of the United Nations.

Indeed, notes the *New York Times* pointedly, "the Pentagon document articulates the clearest rejection to date of collective internationalism, the strategy that emerged from World War II when the five victorious powers sought to form a United Nations that could mediate disputes and police outbreaks of violence."

Now, the idea of placing our security in the hands of "collective internationalism" is dangerous nonsense. The "five victorious powers" includes, one should note, China. What possible reason—moral, prudential, strategic—can we have for assigning responsibility for ultimate questions of security to a committee on which sits the last great communist dictatorship?

It is true that in return for some post-Tiananmen bootlicking on our part, Deng deigned to allow us to go and fight Saddam. But it was a close call. Next time he might not be so broad-minded.

More important, who needs him? We have the power, we have the friends, we have the real alliances with real democracies to enable us to act in concert with them to defend our common interests. To entrust our security instead to the "collective internationalism" of the U.N., which requires us to get the approval of all kinds of despots in countries that do not share our interests let alone our values, is not Utopian. It is merely stupid. What other country having finally achieved the kind of strategic security that we now have would rush to reduce its autonomy and defensive self-reliance for such a will-o'-the-wisp as "collective internationalism"?

The Pentagon Paper asks a simple question: To whom shall we entrust the security of our children? Boutros Boutros-Ghali? The chancelleries of Boon and Tokyo? The correct answer is: the president of the United States. If the cost of that choice is 3.4 percent of GNP, it's the bargain of the century.

David J. Scheffer
"Not the World's Policeman"*

Pentagon staffers replayed old tunes recently with their leaked musings about cross-border threats from rogue states and America's dominance as the global policeman. Likewise, Charles Krauthammer remains stuck on two misconceptions: that the United States must prevent its allies from achieving "superpower multipolarity" by using its own predominance to police the world and that "collective internationalism" is a fatal abdication of power ["What's Wrong With the 'Pentagon Paper'?" copied, March 13].

The real and proliferating dangers of the post-Cold War era are the scores of conflicts within nations that kill tens of thousands of civilians, push millions of refugees across borders, and cause massive property and environmental damage. The only plausible interventions to manage these dangers are those being organized through collective decision-making—namely, collective internationalism.

In fact, America already risks becoming the isolationist superpower. On the one hand, there is neither the political will nor the legal authority for the United States to intervene unilaterally in nations where conflicts now rage or threaten to explode. On the other hand, congressmen go ballistic over comparatively small peacekeeping costs. Though some U.S. soldiers are U.N. observers, none is assigned to U.N. peacekeeping forces that are increasingly being relied upon—in Yugoslavia, Cambodia, El Salvador and perhaps soon in Haiti, Somalia and Nagorno-Karabakh—to cope with internal conflicts and shaky cease-fires. While the Pentagon speculates about future Iraqs, Russian troops wearing U.N. armbands patrol Croatia.

Nor is there much U.S. enthusiasm to build up the military capabilities of regional bodies—such as the Organization of American States and the Conference on Security and Cooperation in Europe—that will become more engaged, with or without U.S. participation.

The action today is with collective internationalism and its missions of mediation, peacekeeping and enforcement. The Pentagon and Krauthammer unwittingly isolate U.S. forces from the real enemies—internal aggression and human rights atrocities—that collective internationalism is confronting.

The United States must fundamentally reorient its global military role—from creeping isolationism to collective internationalism, including collective interventionism. The world desperately needs collective interventions for worthy causes. There is a growing consensus that internal conflicts can be threats to international peace and security and that human rights are not "internal affairs."

The United States will exercise far more flexibility in responding to these internal conflicts if it focuses its military planning on them and en-

*David J. Scheffer, "Not the World's Policeman," *Washington Post* (April 7, 1992).

gages more directly in multilateral peace-keeping and enforcement actions. Otherwise, historians will call America's single-mindedness the isolationism of the 1990s.

Krauthammer's fears about such powers as China blocking America's freedom of action overlook the trends and sophisticated politics of the post-Cold War era. China has not cast a single veto against strong U.N. Security Council actions in recent years, and would do so now as its political and economic peril. Even if China blocks future U.N. action, collective internationalism will evolve in new directions to uphold the principles of international law that in the end Krauthammer wants defended. The United States likely will not do it alone.

Nor is there much chance of Germany and Japan rushing to achieve military predominance. They see power quite differently—as a function of the global economy. We can avoid "superpower multipolarity" by bringing these two giants into the Security Council on a permanent basis, where they can flex their muscles diplomatically rather than build up forces simply to match America's daily grab for dominance.

The era before us will be one of humanitarian imperatives from which the United States must not shrink:

- The Pentagon should reassess the real threats and train forces for multilateral action in internal conflicts—particularly for humanitarian purposes—and for collective responses to interstate aggression.
- The U.S. share of U.N. peace-keeping expenses should be shifted from the strapped State Department budget to the defense budget and adequately funded. U.S. political and military leaders need to give priority to U.N. and other collective operations in order to galvanize entrenched Cold War bureaucrats.
- The gulf war and its messy aftermath show the need to build a U.N. capability to deter potential aggressors with rapid deployment forces that (1) can intercede in time to prevent cross-border assaults and (2) can protect peoples within national borders from internal aggression. Washington should take the lead to create a U.N. rapid deployment force as envisaged by the U.N. Charter and ultimately make available "on call" to the Security Council a set number of U.S. forces—remaining under American command—for deterrence, enforcement and humanitarian missions.

The new reality—however difficult it may be to swallow—cautions that old-style military predominance is a straitjacket, not a liberator.

THE INSTRUMENTS OF AMERICAN FOREIGN POLICY

See text p. 737

The text discusses a number of instruments through which foreign policy objectives are realized. As noted, American presidents have typically balked at developing and enforcing foreign policy through a professional diplomatic corps. Nonetheless, as the world order evolves, and the issues become more complex and intertwined, the need for professionalism increases: diplomacy in the future will be increasingly concerned with negotiation of complex transnational trade and human rights issues.

In the face of these changes, the need for an overhaul of the American Foreign Service has become apparent. The following news article from the Washington Post *reports on a number of proposed changes in the operation of the Foreign Service, analyzing those changes in light of the new functions demanded by rapidly changing conditions in global economics and politics.*

John M. Goshko
"Post Cold War Overhaul of Foreign Service Is Urged"*

The U.S. Foreign Service corps must reinvent itself and produce a new generation of diplomats trained to look beyond traditional, country-to-country relations and view foreign policy in terms of transnational issues like economics and the environment.

That is the conclusion of a report, "The Foreign Service in 2001," prepared by Georgetown University's Institute for the Study of Diplomacy and diplomats, members of Congress, academics and businessmen.

"For the past 60 years, U.S. foreign policy has been characterized primarily by resistance first to fascist and then to communist expansionism," the report said. "These two battles have been largely won. There is no historic precedent for the present period in which an activist, engaged United States is the dominant player in a [relatively] peaceful world."

Other federal agencies that fought the Cold War, notably the Defense Department and the Central Intelligence Agency, have begun to redefine their roles, noted the report released today. It characterized the Foreign Service's slow reaction to change as "less a crisis than a disappointment."

To overcome that problem, the report continued, the State Department and other agencies where the Foreign Service has a presence—the Agency for International Development, the U.S. Information Agency and the Commerce and Agriculture departments—must start thinking in terms that go beyond traditional duties such as stamping passports, negotiating treaties and keeping Washington abreast of political developments.

"Multilateral diplomacy will increasingly eclipse bilateral diplomacy," the report said, noting that the most prominent items on the U.S. foreign

*John M. Goshko, "Post Cold War Overhaul of Foreign Service is Urged," *Washington Post* (August 4, 1992).

policy agenda increasingly are given to matters of trade and international monetary policy, control of narcotics-trafficking and terrorism and ecological cooperation.

Increasingly, the report continued, the arenas for dealing with these issues most effectively are proving to be not the capitals of individual states but joint actions through a "reinvigorated United Nations Security Council" or such regional groupings as the European Community, the Association of Southeast Asian Nations and the Organization of American States.

Even the old-fashioned diplomatic practice of dealing with countries on a one-on-one basis needs new emphasis, as was made clear when the United States opened about 20 new embassies within two years to deal with the breakup of the former Soviet Union.

"Most Foreign Service officers will spend most of their careers at posts other than the 'Top Twenty,' such as Paris, London, Ottawa and Tokyo." Instead they will be in more small, "storefront" embassies with skeleton staffs, the report predicted. However, because business, the media and other branches of the government will rely heavily on expertise in these outposts, the report added, "where the service's greatest contributions are more likely to be made."

To carry out this new diplomacy, the report said, the Foreign Service must recruit officers with academic training different from what was valued in the past. It also must have people, who while possessing the requisite language and area expertise, are generalists able to handle the diverse demands of a "lean and mean" Foreign Service.

The report stressed that the Foreign Service must change its recruitment and personnel management practices and search for talent in areas previously considered off-limits.

Asserting that the Foreign Service must reflect American society, the report says that the service not only must do far more to recruit women and minorities but also "must address the needs of two-career families, single parents, alternate lifestyles, those with disabilities and others to allow the service the luxury of choosing the most-talented candidates from the widest possible range."

It says that the Foreign Service can no longer rely exclusively for personnel on the "closed, bottom-entry system," borrowed from the military, where new members begin as junior officers and rise rung-by-rung through the ranks toward ambassador level over a 20- to 30-year career.

It added that the Foreign Service should open doors at all levels to individuals who have worked in business or universities. Such "lateral entries" might last for a short time or mark a permanent career change.

The report recommends eliminating regulations and pension differences that hamper shifts between the Foreign and Civil services. Foreign Service officers who resign to follow other career paths but who might later want to return could then do so, and use the skills they have acquired elsewhere.

The report also called for the service to find ways to offer "meaningful employment" in overseas posts to spouses of Foreign Service officers.

Finally, the report pinpointed a need to streamline the top-heavy executive structure of the State Department. It offered several ways to do that: by eliminating layers of authority and consolidating bureaus with overlapping functions, for example, merging human rights with refugee affairs and narcotics matters with counter-terrorism.

"We believe the Foreign Service can meet the new challenges," the report concluded. "Precisely because of the difficulties of the work, the Foreign Service should continue to attract top-notch Americans looking for challenging and rewarding careers.

"Conditions are ideal for the service to enjoy its finest hour, if it is willing to perform at the new state of the art."

THE ROLES NATIONS PLAY

See text p. 759

The questions raised earlier in the chapter about American foreign policy values govern many of the issues raised in this section of the text. No one can be sure yet what role the United States ought to play. The following article, written shortly after President Clinton took office in 1993, notes that American diplomacy is requiring an entirely new and different approach. The United States has had to redefine what constitutes success in foreign policy, reorienting its actions to the problems posed by an increasingly fragmented political world and increasingly integrated economic one.

Thomas L. Friedman
"Friends Like Russia Make Diplomacy a Mess"*

As President Clinton struggles to have an impact on events in Bosnia, Haiti and Russia, it is clear how much American foreign policy has changed in just the past two years. While Mr. Clinton's predecessors usually had the luxury of dealing with clearly defined conflicts between states. Mr. Clinton has the burden of trying to deal with the international spillover of conflicts within states. This has created the paradoxical situation in which the United States has never been more powerful, in standing astride the world without another superpower competitor, and has never seemed more powerless in trying to influence internal events inside countries, with a Treasury short of cash, a Pentagon short of will and a public that can't sort out the good guys from the bad guys without a scorecard.

No wonder that American foreign policy under Mr. Clinton has so far been largely symbolic gestures in places like Haiti, Bosnia and the Middle East. The President is at least trying in all of these places, but his efforts so far only underscore how many foreign problems today are beyond diplo-

*Thomas L. Friedman, "Friends Like Russia Make Diplomacy a Mess," *New York Times* (March 28, 1993).

macy, or at least the conventional practice of it. Many days it seems that the unfolding dramas in Bosnia, Russia, Haiti and Somalia are better raw material for a poet's lament than a diplomat's labor, the stuff for a Keats, not a Kissinger.

Stanley Hoffmann, a European affairs expert at Harvard University, says that one of the main problems in teaching international relations these days is that all the classical textbooks begin with the mantra that what happens inside states is largely irrelevant to explaining the international system; what really counts is the balance of power between states, and how to manage that. "This wisdom calls itself 'realism,' but it is utter nonsense today," said Mr. Hoffmann.

Which is why Mr. Clinton is being forced to adapt to managing the game within nations, more than among nations. This is demanding some very different approaches to American diplomacy.

The first is redefining what constitutes success in foreign policy. During the cold war, success was easy to define. When the Berlin Wall was dismantled, that was success. When Washington and Moscow signed an arms control treaty, that was success. But what is success in American policy toward Russia today?

Tempering Expectations

What Mr. Clinton is trying to do, aides say, is define success in American foreign policy toward Russia as maintaining Russia on a generally upward trend-line toward greater democracy and free-market characteristics, knowing that there will be many bumps and back-steps along the way. Mr. Clinton seems to understand that if the yardstick for success in Russia is a perfect transplant of Jeffersonian democracy there, then he is doomed to fail. If it is simply keeping Russia moving in the right direction, he has a chance to succeed. To temper expectations about Russia, Mr. Clinton could remind Americans of their own turbulent history: while our own revolution happened in 1776, we did not have our first President until 1789, and in between there was a constant power struggle over the Articles of Confederation, between federalists and state's rights advocates.

Micro-Diplomacy

In an effort to keep Russia on a general path toward reform, Mr. Clinton also has had to learn Dale Carnegie diplomacy. His policy toward Russia is increasingly focused on practical, micro forms of assistance that will promote privatization, pluralism and entreprenuerial skills on the ground there, no matter what happens inside the Kremlin. These will include everything from American farmers teaching Russians about grain distribution to American accountants teaching kiosk entrepreneurs about capitalist bookkeeping—not the usual stuff of high diplomacy.

Yet another new role for American diplomacy will be as divorce counselor. Mediating between warring states is something American presidents have often been called upon to do, but now Mr. Clinton finds himself refereeing the property settlement between Ukraine and Russia. All recent arms control agreements signed between the United States and Russia depend on Ukraine turning over its warheads to Russia, which it will not do without American security guarantees. So Mr. Clinton quietly spent Thursday afternoon in the Oval Office trying to persuade Ukraine's Foreign Minister to give up his nukes to his historical enemy. Good luck.

Still another role Mr. Clinton must prepare Americans for is that of peacemaker. The United States has long been ready to send its sons and daughters to be peacekeepers in places like the Sinai Desert, where they are separating nations that have signed a treaty. But in Bosnia, the United States has committed itself in principle to separate combatants in a civil war who most likely will not have buried the hatchet. American soldiers will be called upon to disarm them; dodge their crossfire and make a paper peace into a real peace. Any volunteers?

The last new role called for by this new world is that of existentialist diplomat, learning to accept the irrationality in many of these internal conflicts as one would a chronic illness. This is very un-American. But consider the situation in the West Bank. Last week a Palestinian woman stabbed an Israeli policeman. When she was asked why, besides the usual antipathy to Israelis, she said it was because she woke up with a headache; a few days later two Israeli Arabs stabbed an Israeli soldier, after they failed their high school matriculation exams.

"Diplomats look at the world in terms of linear progressions moving from war to peace, but many conflicts today are simply cyclical, with no clear war or peace, no clear boundaries between the parties and no rules," said Meron Benvenisti, an Israeli ethnographer. "These conflicts are endemic, fed by internally generated friction between people who share the same sidewalks. Diplomats trying to deal with them often resemble peacocks in three-piece suits strutting through the ruins."

QUESTIONS

1. What are the characteristics of a nation-state? Who should have authority to decide whether a nation-state exists, and what kind of evidence should go into that analysis?
2. In a new global order, is stability best assured by the continued existence of at least one superpower, or is it better assured by a system of multilateralism? If the former is preferable, how should the United States retain its status? If the latter, on what fronts should the United States agree to cooperate with other nations in a set of multilaterally?
3. What is the function of a diplomatic service in the contemporary world

order? Do the reforms suggested in the Goshko article comport with those aims, or do they simply create another set of bureaucratic rules?

4. In the future, as the article by Thomas L. Friedman points out, the United States will have to play a number of different roles in its interactions with other nations. What factors should affect the roles it plays in different areas of policy concern?

CHAPTER 19

The State of the Union

CONCLUDING THOUGHTS

See text p. 784

Once again, Alexis de Tocqueville's insightful analysis of the American democratic system is worthy of consideration. The problem of balancing freedom and order has been at the center of this book: it is the central problem of the American political system. Democracy is not a panacea; as de Tocqueville notes, the tyranny of a democratic system may lie in the extent to which it anesthetizes its citizens to the realities of how power over them is exercised.

Alexis de Tocqueville
"What Sort of Despotism Democratic Nations Have to Fear"*

I noticed during my stay in the United States that a democratic state of society similar to that found there could lay itself peculiarly open to the establishment of a depotism. . . .

In past ages there had never been a sovereign so absolute and so powerful that he could by himself alone, without the aid of secondary powers, undertake to administer every part of a great empire. No one had ever tried to subject all his people indiscriminately to the details of a uniform code, nor personally to prompt and lead every single one of his subjects. It had never occurred to the mind of man to embark on such an undertaking, and had it done so, inadequate education, imperfect administrative machinery, and above all the natural obstacles raised by unequal conditions would soon have put a stop to so grandoise a design. . . . But if a despotism should be established among the democratic nations of our day, it would probably have a different character. It would be more widespread and milder; it would degrade men rather than torment them.

Doubtless, in such an age of education and equality as our own, rulers could more easily bring all public powers into their own hands alone, and

*Alexis de Tocqueville, "What Sort of Despotism Democratic Nations Have to Fear," in *Democracy in America,* ed. J.P. Mayer and Max Lerner, tr. George Lawrence.

they could impinge deeper and more habitually into the sphere of private interests than was ever possible in antiquity. But that same equality which makes despotism easy tempers it. We have seen how, as men become more alike and more nearly equal, public mores become more humane and gentle. When there is no citizen with great power or wealth, tyranny in some degree lacks both target and stage. When all fortunes are middling, passions are naturally restrained, imagination limited, and pleasures simple. Such universal moderation tempers the sovereign's own spirit and keeps within certain limits the disorderly urges of desire. . . .

Democratic governments might become violent and cruel at times of great excitement and danger, but such crises will be rare and brief.

Taking into consideration the trivial nature of men's passions now, the softness of their mores, the extent of their education, the purity of their religion, their steady habits of patient work, and the restraint which they all show in the indulgence of both their vices and their virtues, I do not expect their leaders to be tyrants, but rather schoolmasters.

Thus I think that the type of oppression which threatens democracies is different from anything there has ever been in the world before. . . .

I am trying to imagine under what novel features despotism may appear in the world. In the first place, I see an innumerable multitude of men, alike and equal, constantly circling around in pursuit of the petty and banal pleasures with which they glut their souls. Each one of them, withdrawn into himself, is almost unaware of the fate of the rest. Mankind, for him, consists in his children and his personal friends. As for the rest of his fellow citizens, they are near enough, but he does not notice them. He touches them but feels nothing. He exists in and for himself, and though he still may have a family, one can at least say that he has not got a fatherland.

Over this kind of men stands an immense, protective power which is alone responsible for securing their enjoyment and watching over their fate. That power is absolute, thoughtful of detail, orderly, provident, and gentle. It would resemble parental authority if, fatherlike, it tried to prepare its charges for a man's life, but on the contrary, it only tries to keep them in perpetual childhood. It likes to see the citizens enjoy themselves, provided that they think of nothing but enjoyment. It gladly works for their happiness but wants to be sole agent and judge of it. It provides for their security, foresees and supplies their necessities, facilitates their pleasures, manages their principal concerns, directs their industry, makes rules for their testaments, and divides their inheritances. Why should it not entirely relieve them from the trouble of thinking and all the cares of living?

Thus it daily makes the exercise of free choice less useful and rarer, restricts the activity of free will within a narrower compass, and little by little robs each citizen of the proper use of his own faculties. Equality has prepared men for all this, predisposing them to endure it and often even regard it as beneficial.

Having thus taken each citizen in turn in its powerful grasp and shaped him to its will, government then extends its embrace to include the whole of society. It covers the whole of social life with a network of petty, complicated rules that are both minute and uniform, through which even men of the greatest originality and the most vigorous temperament cannot force their heads above the crowd. It does not break men's will, but softens, bends, and guides it; it seldom enjoins, but often inhibits, action; it does not destroy anything, but prevents much being born; it is not at all tyrannical, but it hinders, restrains, enervates, stifles, and stultifies so much that in the end each nation is no more than a flock of timid and hardworking animals with the government as its shepherd.

I have always thought that this brand of orderly, gentle, peaceful slavery which I have just described could be combined, more easily than is generally supposed, with some of the external forms of freedom, and that there is a possibility of its getting itself established even under the shadow of the sovereignty of the people.

Our contemporaries are ever a prey to two conflicting passions: they feel the need of guidance, and they long to stay free. Unable to wipe out these two contradictory instincts, they try to satisfy them both together. Their imagination conceives a government which is unitary, protective, and all-powerful, but elected by the people. Centralization is combined with the sovereignty of the people. That gives them a chance to relax. They console themselves for being under schoolmasters by thinking that they have chosen them themselves. Each individual lets them put the collar on, for he sees that it is not a person, or a class of persons, but society itself which holds the end of the chain.

Under this system the citizens quit their state of dependence just long enough to choose their masters and then fall back into it.

A great many people nowadays very easily fall in with this brand of compromise between administrative despotism and the sovereignty of the people. They think they have done enough to guarantee personal freedom when it is to the government of the state that they have handed it over. That is not good enough for me. I am much less interested in the question who my master is than in the fact of obedience. . . . Subjection in petty affairs, is manifest daily and touches all citizens indiscriminately. It never drives men to despair, but continually thwarts them and leads them to give up using their free will. It slowly stifles their spirits and enervates their souls, whereas obedience demanded only occasionally in matters of great moment brings servitude into play only from time to time, and its weight falls only on certain people. It does little good to summon those very citizens who have been made so dependent on the central power to choose the representatives of that power from time to time. However important, this brief and occasional exercise of free will will not prevent them from gradually losing the faculty of thinking, feeling, and acting for themselves, so that they will slowly fall below the level of humanity.

I must add that they will soon become incapable of using the one great privilege left to them. Those democratic peoples which have introduced freedom into the sphere of politics, while allowing despotism to grow in the administrative sphere, have been led into the strangest paradoxes. For the conduct of small affairs, where plain common sense is enough, they hold that the citizens are not up to the job. But they give these citizens immense prerogatives where the government of the whole state is concerned. They are turned alternatively into the playthings of the sovereign and into his masters, being either greater than kings or less than men. When they have tried all the different systems of election without finding one to suit them, they look surprised and go on seeking for another, as if the ills they see did not belong much more to the constitution of the country itself than to that of the electoral body.

It really is difficult to imagine how people who have entirely given up managing their own affairs could make a wise choice of those who are to do that for them. One should never expect a liberal, energetic, and wise government to originate in the votes of a people of servants.